STUDY OF IMPACT OF FTAs SIGNED WITH THAILAND, SINGAPORE AND SRILANKA

STUDY OF IMPACT OF FTAs SIGNED WITH THAILAND, SINGAPORE AND SRILANKA

CA. ATAL BIHARI BHANJA, F.C.A., DITL (ICAI)

PUBLICATIONS

KALPAZ PUBLICATIONS

DELHI-110052

Study of Impact of FTAs Signed with Thailand, Singapore and Srilanka

Rs. 750

ISBN: 81-7835-684-8

Published in 2008 in India by
Kalpaz Publications
C-30, Satyawati Nagar,
Delhi-110052
E-mail: kalpaz@hotmail.com
Phone : 9212729499

Lasser Type Setting by: Quick Media, Delhi
Printed at : G. Print Process, Delhi

My Sincere thanks and respect to the guides for this Dissertation, without whose active participation, I would have reduced to a direction less person being thrown into an ocean and searching for the shore. They are the backbone of this study and deserve all credits.

PROF. INDRA NATH MUKHERJI
South Asian Studies Division, School of International Studies, J.N.U., New Delhi

and

MR. A.K. GUPTA
Managing Director, TPM Consultants Pvt. Ltd., New Delhi

Contents

I am indebted and thankful to the following dignitaries for their valuable guidance, help and inspiration for preparation of this Dissertation.

1	Mr. S.N.Sahu	Director, Prime Minister's Office, GOI
2	Mr. Kedar C. Rout	Director, Department of Commerce, GOI
3	Mr. Rajan Sudesh Ratna	Director, Department of Commerce, GOI
4	Mr. Rajiv Arora, Ph.D	Director, Ministry of Non-Conventional Energy Sources, GOI
5	Dr. Ram Upendra Das	Fellow, Research and Information System for Developing Countries (RIS)
6	Dr. Jaya Prakash Pradhan	Asst. Professor, Institute for Studies in Industrial Development (ISID)
7	Mr. Manish Mohan	Sr. Asst. Director, FICCI
8	Mr. Chetan Bijesure	Asst. Director, FICCI
9	Mr. Umesh Adhikary	Asst. Vice President, Corporate Strategy and Business Development, Aditya Birla Management Corporation Ltd.
10	Mr. Rajiv Budhraja	Sec. General, Automotive Tyre Manufacturers' Association (ATMA)
11	Mr. Sanjay Karn	AGM (Market Development), Sterlite Industries (I) Ltd.
12	MR. N.K. Ramachandran	General Manager (Exports), Hindalco Industries Limited
13	Mr. Suresh Khanna	Secretary General, Consumer Electronics and TV Manufacturers' Association
14	Mr. D.V. Malhan	Executive Secretary, All India Food Processors Association of India

15	Mr. S.C. Kapur	Secretary General, Association of Synthetic Fibre Industry
16	Mr. Shyam Sujan	Secretary General, Electric Lamp and Component Manufacturers Association of India
17	Mr. S.K. Khanna	Advisor, Telecom Equipment Manufacturers Association of India
18	Mr. Vinnie Mehta	Executive Director, Manufacturers Association for Information Technology
19	Mr. Narayan Moorthy	Secretary General, Indian Paper Manufacturers Association
20	Mr. S. Gurumoorthi	Executive Secretary, The Vanaspati Manufacturers Association of India
21	Mr. Sugato Sen	Director, Society of Indian Automobile Manufacturers
22	Mr. Abhigyan Sengupta	Executive Officer, Automotive Component Manufacturers Association of India
23	Dr. Y.R. Singh	Executive Director, Alkali Manufacturers' Association of India
24	Mr. Kiran B. Kakatkar	Chief Executive Officer, Process Plant and Machinery Association of India
25	Mr. T.S. Sundaresan	Secretary General, The Indian Ferro Alloy Producers' Association
26	Mr. R.R. Gokhale	Secretary General, Indian Chemical Council
27	Mr. B.V. Mehta	Executive Director, The Solvent Extractors' Association of India
28	Mr. M.P. Joseph	Secretary General, Association of Man-Made Fibre Industry of India
29	Mr. M.K. Panthaki	Director, The Clothing Manufacturers Association of India

30	Mr. Bhaskar Kanchan	Sr. Deputy Director, Tool and Gauge Manufacturers Association
31	Mr. P.N. Surendranath	Technology Advisor, Tool and Gauge Manufacturers Association
32	Mr. Jagannathan	Regional Director, Apparel Export Promotion Council
33	Mr. P. A. Narayanan	Joint Director, Apparel Export Promotion Council
34	Mr. S. Chakrabarty	Secretary, Textile Machinery Manufacturers' Association (India)
35	Mr. V. Gujral	Secretary, Ball and Roller Bearing Manufacturers Association Of India
36	Mr. Deepak Lawale	Secretary General, Organization of Plastics Processors of India

REFERENCES

Sl. No.	Sources	Authors
1	**INDO- SRI LANKA FREE TRADE AGREEMENT: AN ASSESSMENT OF POTENTIAL AND IMPACT**	Indra Nath Mukherji, Tilani Jayawardhana & Saman Kelegama
2	WORKING PAPER NO. 165 ON NON-TARIFF BARRIERS AND INDIA'S EXPORTS: THE CASE OF ASEAN AND SRI LANKA JULY 2005 INDIAN COUNCIL FOR RESEARCH ON INTERNATIONAL ECONOMIC RELATIONS **(ICRIER)**	Mohammed Saqib Nisha Taneja
3	WORKING PAPER NO. 145 INDO-SRI LANKA TRADE IN SERVICES: FTA II AND BEYOND NOVEMBER 2004 INDIAN COUNCIL FOR RESEARCH ON INTERNATIONAL ECONOMIC RELATIONS **(ICRIER)**	Nisha Taneja Arpita Mukherjee Sanath Jayanetti Tilani Jayawardane
4	**COMPENDIUM OF ISSUES RELATED TO REGIONAL TRADE AGREEMENTS** Background Note by the Secretariat (**Negotiating Group on Rules**)	TN/RL/W/8/Rev.1 1 August 2002 **WORLD TRADE ORGANIZATION**
5	RIS-DP # 91/2005 India-East Asia Integration: A Win-Win for Asia **Research and Information System for the Non-Aligned and Other Developing Countries** (RIS)	**Mukul G. Asher** Rahul Sen
6	RIS-DP # 96/2005 Advancing the ASEAN-India Partnership in the New Millennium Research and Information System for the Non-Aligned and Other Developing Countries **(RIS)**	Ong Keng Yong

Sl. No.	Sources	Authors
7	**WTO: 2006 NEWS ITEMS & OTHER ARTICLES**	www.wto.org
8	**RTAs and WTO** (A power point presentation given in the oral classes of Part-I of PQC in "International Trade Laws & WTO" of ICAI)	Vijaya Katti Professor and Chairperson (MDPs), IIFT, New Delhi
9	**Box 6.6 : India and Regional Cooperation in Asia** Economic Survey 2005-2006	http:/ indiabudget.nic.in
10	**Regional Trade Agreements in South Asia** Discussion Paper No.8,2005: 1 South Asian Year Book of Trade and Development 2005 **(CENTAD)**	Indra Nath Mukherji
11	JSG Report on **INDIA-SRILANKA COMPREHENSIVE ECONOMIC PARTNERSHIP AGREEMENT**	Joint Study Group set up by India & Srilanka OCT'2003
12	**Notification on South Asian Free Trade Area (SAFTA)** DT. 22.03.2006	http://www.saarc-sec.org/main.php?t=5 (SAARC WEBSITE)
13	**STATUS PAPER on INDIA SRILANKA ECONOMIC RELATIONS** Federation of Indian Chambers of Commerce and Industry **(FICCI)**	Manish Mohan Asstt. Director, FICCI
14	**FICCI SURVEY on INDIA THAILAND FTA – EMERGING ISSUES, JUNE 2005** Federation of Indian Chambers of Commerce and Industry **(FICCI)**	FICCI ECONOMIC AFFAIRS & RESEARCH DIVISION
15	**REGIONAL TRADE AGREEMENTS (RTAs), May 2006 and** www.atmaindia.org	AUTOMOTIVE TYRE MANUFACTURERS' ASSOCIATION (ATMA), New Delhi
16	**Research Paper on INDIA'S APPROACH TO FTAs**	Vijaya Katti Professor and Chairperson

Sl. No.	Sources	Authors
.	(Draft Report)	(MDPs), IIFT, New Delhi
17	**TEXTS OF THE FTAs with Srilanka, Thailand and CECA with Singapore**	Department of Commerce website, GOI www.commerce.nic.in
18	**EXPORT IMPORT DATA BANK maintained by DGFT, GOI**	www.dgft.delhi.nic.in
19	**R.K.JAIN's CUSTOMS TARIFF OF INDIA** 41st Edition 2006-2007	CENTAX PUBLICATIONS PVT. LTD., New Delhi
20	**Texts of the FTAs signed by Singapore with EFTA, USA, Japan, Korea, Newzeland and Australia**	www.wto.org

SECTION - I

(Executive Summary & Objectives of The Study)

Contents

1

EXECUTIVE SUMMARY

BACKGROUND

The recent surge in signing Free Trade Agreements (a form of Regional Trade Agreement) is a global phenomenon. Except Mongolia as on date, all other WTO members are already part of at least one Free Trade Agreement existing in any part of the globe. These agreements are required to be notified under Article XXIV of the GATT 1947 with the World Trade Organization (WTO), Geneva. As on date, 197 notified RTA s are in force globally.

The objective of signing FTAs is to open up the markets among a limited number of partner countries and increase trade among themselves in a free and fair atmosphere. Reduction in Customs Tariff to zero level is an attached objective to the FTAs. Of course, the tariff reduction takes place in gradual process rather than with immediate effect. Based upon the circumstances, there may be either Trade Creation or Trade Diversion happening in case the trade among the partner countries increases.

The Government of India has also started signing a number of FTAs with the neighbouring countries, the objective being to further develop the trade and social relations among the countries in vicinity. Among them, three significant FTAs signed are FTA with Srilanka (ISLFTA), FTA with Thailand and CECA with Singapore.

OBJECTIVES OF THE IMPACT STUDY

There has been a lot of uproars listened currently, especially against the misuse of FTAs with Srilanka and Thailand. Our impact study aims at arriving broad based conclusions about the real impact of these FTAs/ CECA on the Indian industrial economy and suggesting measures so that the anomalies can be removed and the real benefit of trade growth can be derived from implementation of these Free Trade Agreements.

METHODOLOGY

Data of imports and exports from/to the concerned countries have been analysed from the financial year 1998-99 to 2004-05 in case of Srilanka and 2001-02 to 2004-05 in case of Thailand. Data for imports have been studied and limited analysis done incase of imports from Singapore for the period 2003-04 to 2005-06.

Along with the data analysis, it is much important and the study cannot be completed comprehensively without holding dialogues with the industries, government machinery and other interested parties. Real interactions and survey by way of questionnaires are integral part of this impact study.

Our study is a much comprehensive one containing live interviews held with 22 industry associations, 2 big copper industries and one export promotion council based at Mumbai and New Delhi. The real interactions, apart from analyzing trade data from 1998-99 till 2004-05 and *2005-06(for imports from Singapore only)* have made this dissertation a conclusive one. Of course, steps should be regularly followed in future to update them with real happenings in the coming years.

SUMMARY OF DEMANDS FROM INDUSTRY ASSOCIATIONS

Based upon our real interviews with the industry associations representing the major product sectors covered under these FTAs/ CECA, we have summarized the problems faced by the Indian industry and their demands with & expectations from the Government of India in a brief manner. These are:

- Stricter implementation of Rules of Origins (ROOs).
- Addition of CTH (Change in Tariff Heading) with VA (Value Addition) clauses in the ROOs.
- Appointment of professional accountants for verifying the ROO Certification procedures in the partner country.
- Abolition of State level VAT/ Octroi check posts.
- Implementation of Nation wide Goods & Services Tax Act in replacement to Central Excise and VAT acts.
- Improvement in the public infrastructure like roads, cheap electricity etc. to remain cost competitive in comparison to the industries in the partner country.
- The government should take the industries into confidence before finalizing the list of items to be put under the preferential duty list/early harvest schemes.
- Import from the partner country should not be given any preferential treatment where actually no manufacturing facilities exist.
- Category of products on which any anti-dumping/anti-subsidy duty is being already levied, should not be given any preferential treatment again under the FTAs.

- ➢ Incase of raw material intensive industry, if the raw material is on the negative list, then the finished products should not be allowed to be imported on preferential basis.
- ➢ The Government should not allow the partner countries to put our export competitive products in their negative lists.

CONCLUSIONS

- ❑ It has been found that the surge in imports from these partner countries have actually affected selected sectors of the Indian economy badly.
- ❑ Increase in exports has not caused any material benefits to the Indian industry. The reason may be the geographical size and the consumer bases in these countries are very small.
- ❑ **It is interesting to note that even the affected industries do not specifically want the FTAs to be stopped**. But every one wants them to be consulted first, improvement in the general infrastructure facilities & rationalization of taxation laws etc. which are strategically linked to the overall state policies.
- ❑ *It is felt that*; the Government should initiate the advocacy functions in better manner and prior consultation with interested industries should be taken place frequently.
- ❑ ***It is suggested further*** *that*;
    - Rules of Origin factors should be brought in the Customs Act of India itself. Enforceability of the ROO clauses in any FTA can come after that only.
    - Monitoring systems should be found out and implemented properly.
    - Where as the safeguard actions are prospective based only, but no remedy exists for past injuries caused on industries because of cheap imports. Steps should be there fore taken to remove these anomalies.
    - On the services sectors; mutual recognition of the professional qualifications at par with the other country (ies) should be done immediately.
    - The industries should try to upgrade their skills and create facilities to remain competitive in the *free trade regime*.
    - Under the FTAs, a win-win situation for the Indian as well as the partner country's industries should be always welcomed.

Summary of trade statistics between Singapore, Thailand and Srilanka (revised data downloaded from DGFT website on 10.09.2006) have been given in the next page.

SUMMARY OF TRADE STATISTICS BETWEEN SINGAPORE, THAILAND AND SRILANKA (DATA DOWNLOADED FROM DGFT WEBSITE ON 10.09.2006)

Values in Rs. Lacs

	Singapore					Thailand					Sri Lanka DSR				
Particulars\ Year	2001-02	2002-03	2003-04	2004-05	2005-06	2001-02	2002-03	2003-04	2004-05	2005-06	2001-02	2002-03	2003-04	2004-05	2005-06
1 EXPORT	463713	687978	976393	1797535	2401965	301954	344186	382172	405008	476076	300885	445712	606191	634965	896391
2 %Growth		48.36	41.92	84.1	33.63		13.99	11.04	5.98	17.55		48.13	36.01	4.75	41.17
3 India's Total Export	20901798	25513728	29336674	37533952	45641788	20901798	25513728	29336674	37533952	45641788	20901798	25513728	29336674	37533952	45641788
4 %Growth		22.06	14.98	27.94	21.6		22.06	14.98	27.94	21.6		22.06	14.98	27.94	21.6
5 %Share	2.22	2.7	3.33	4.79	5.26	1.44	1.35	1.3	1.08	1.04	1.44	1.75	2.07	1.69	1.96
6 IMPORT	621945	694381	958260	1191312	1484833	201779	183419	279869	389051	536410	32134	43955	89485	170019	255768
7 %Growth		11.65	38	24.32	24.64		-9.1	52.58	39.01	37.88		36.79	103.58	90	50.43
8 India's Total Import	24519972	29720586	35910764	50106456	66040888	24519972	29720586	35910764	50106456	66040888	24519972	29720586	35910764	50106456	66040888
9 %Growth		21.21	20.83	39.53	31.8		21.21	20.83	39.53	31.8		21.21	20.83	39.53	31.8
10 %Share	2.54	2.34	2.67	2.38	2.25	0.82	0.62	0.78	0.78	0.81	0.13	0.15	0.25	0.34	0.39
11 Total Trade	1085658	1382359	1934653	2988847	3886799	503733	527604	662041	794059	1012486	333019	489667	695676	804984	1152159
12 %Growth		27.33	39.95	54.49	30.04		4.74	25.48	19.94	27.51		47.04	42.07	15.71	43.13
13 India's Total Trade	45421770	55234314	65247438	87640408	111682676	45421770	55234314	65247438	87640408	111682676	45421770	55234314	65247438	87640408	111682676
14 %Growth		21.6	18.13	34.32	27.43		21.6	18.13	34.32	27.43		21.6	18.13	34.32	27.43
15 %Share	2.39	2.5	2.97	3.41	3.48	1.11	0.96	1.01	0.91	0.91	0.73	0.89	1.07	0.92	1.03
16 Trade Balance			18133	606223	917132	100175	160767	102303	15957		268750	401756	516706	464946	640623
17 India's Trade Balance	-3618174	-4206858	-6574090	-12572504	-20399100	-3618174	-4206858	-6574090	-12572504	-20399100	-3618174	-4206858	-6574090	-12572504	-20399100

Note: The country's total imports since 2000-2001 does not include import of Petroleum Products (27100093) and Crude Oil (27090000)

2

Objectives of the Study

The Government of India has given emphasis on signing the Free Trade Agreements (FTAs) with the South East Asian nations. These countries constitute one of the major trading blocks with whom Indians are doing trading since thousand of years before. Some of the significant agreements signed are:

1. FTA between India and Srilanka
2. Frame Work Agreement for establishing FTA between India and Thailand
3. CECA Between India and Singapore

An impact study constitutes study of these agreements, analysis of the import/export data covering a majority of products, creating a database for comparison purposes of pre and post implementation situations, assessment of the current and the future adverse impact on Indian industry and need for safeguard actions in appropriate cases.

This dissertation covers the FTAs signed with Thailand, Singapore and Srilanka. Analysis is done for approximately 250 major products (exports and imports) traded preferentially under each FTA in the past years over 1998-99 to 2004-05 in case of Srilanka and 2001-02 to 2004-05 incase of Thailand. Analysis is done for 155 products from 2003-04 to 2005-06 in case of imports from Singapore. The data used are as per the figures available in the EXPORT IMPORT DATA BANK maintained in the official website of the *Director General of Foreign Trade* and downloaded by us during Apl'06 and May'06. In case of data for imports from Singapore during 2005-06, these were downloaded on 10.09.2006. The minor revision in trade data for the earlier years appearing during Sep'06 in the website of DGFT were not considered. The analysis is done at eight digit HS Classification. The study focuses on the following:

Major products imported from the countries/exported to the countries under study

The sampled products analysed in each case were selected on the basis of value of imports being more than 0.1% of the total value of imports from the specific countries for the financial year 2004-05. The samples were taken in a judicious and scientific manner and in the descending order of value of imports in 2004-05. Similarly, studies of the samples were done for exports to these countries also.

Trend Analysis, CAGR calculation and Correlation Analysis

The above analyses were done for all the products both individually, group wise and chapter wise under different list of concessions.

% Share of country wise imports/exports

Share of these countries in India's imports/ exports for the selected sample is observed.

Comparison of import/ export prices between the specific country with all India import/ export prices

The Import/ export prices for these products related to these countries are analysed year wise and compared with all India import/export prices.

Real Interaction with the Industry Associations

Correspondences had been made with the leading Indian Producers, Exporters and Importers to get their real feedback. At a later stage, personal interactions were made with two leading industries in the Copper Industry, 22 Industry Associations and One Export Promotion Council. Due recognition are given to the inputs received from them. A *case study* is also given in case of the Automotive Tyre Industries.

The objective is to establish broad based conclusion regarding impact of these FTAs on the total industrial economy of India and hence sector specific impacts are out of purview. Also, the impact on the direct agriculture sector is not studied, as the scope is restricted and the time allotted to submit the dissertation is very much limited.

The concluding remarks are separately given under SECTION-VI of the report.

SECTION - II

(Background Notes)

Contents

3

HISTORY AND DEVELOPMENT OF REGIONAL TRADE AGREEMENT (RTAs)

RTAs AND DEVELOPMENT[10]

Theoretically, a free trade regime extending globally is the first best choice for achieving maximum global welfare from trade. However, if for various reasons examined earlier, trade liberalisation is initiated or accelerated at the regional level, this is often considered to be the second best option. Regional trade liberalisation would result in increased competition, efficiency and acquisition of new technology through widening of the market and increased specialisation. The net welfare implications would however, depend on the initial conditions and the nature of regional trade liberalisation.

The classical trade theory framework was provided by Jacob Viner (1950). Viner introduced the concept of 'trade creation' and 'trade diversion'. According to him **Trade Creation** takes place when there is movement of factors of production from high domestic cost to a low cost domestic source of one or more partner countries. **Trade diversion** takes place when there is a movement of factors of production from low cost extra-regional producers to high cost regional producers.

Kemal (2005) has pointed out that change in welfare due to preferences granted to members would depend upon whether the most efficient producer in the world is part of the group or is outside the group. If it is part of the group, the economic integration would be welfare promoting. However, even if the most efficient producer is outside the group, then forming of regional blocks could result in trade diversion or trade creation depending on the initial conditions. Prior to the formation of a regional block, let us say that the tariff was prohibitive and the country met the entire demand of the product from domestic supplies. However, when the tariff rates are reduced preferentially, some participating regional member State may become competitive enough to enter the regional market, thereby replacing the erstwhile high cost domestic producers. This will be trade creating and welfare enhancing.

Thus, in any preferential trading arrangement, trade creating (welfare augmenting) and trade diverting (welfare diminishing) influences will be at work simultaneously and the net outcome on welfare will depend on the strength of the two influences.

Viner made restrictive assumptions of inelastic supply and demand. Subsequently, Meade (1955) relaxed the assumption of zero price elasticity of demand. Lipsey (1957) relaxed the assumption of zero supply elasticity as well. Consumers get the goods cheaper than before PTA was introduced so that they realise pecuniary gains. The domestic firms also realise producer's surplus. However, the importing country loses tariff revenue by shifting to an intra-PTA source. In the case of trade diversion the member country's import price increases, even though domestic consumer prices are lower on account of the tariff reductions. It is not clear a priori whether the direct gain for consumers and producers is larger or smaller than the revenue and terms of trade loss sustained by the importing country. The empirical studies give conflicting results to the desirability or otherwise of PTAs. The analysis presented by Viner, Meade and Lipsey has been static and it has been argued that the dynamic advantages may be even stronger. Traditional trade theory is typically based on perfect competition, constant returns to scale and abstracts from innovations and economies of scale. PTAs increase the market size for producers and allow them to move down the average cost curve by exploiting the economies of scale.

The theoretical literature on regional trade integration covers every side of the argument. Models based on traditional trade theory tend to find PTAs being potentially welfare reducing. However, models based on new trade theories find PTAs to provide avenues for welfare improvements that arise from the dynamic context.

A PTA can trigger increase in both domestic and foreign direct investment because of increased market size. In such a context even small countries offering a congenial investment climate can attract large inflows of foreign direct investment in order to cater to the enlarged regional market. Besides gains from specialisation can, be realised by breaking up the value added chain, including for commodities that will eventually be exported from the PTA.

MAIN TRENDS AND CHARACTERISTICS OF REGIONAL TRADE AGREEMENTS[10]

Regional Trade Agreements (RTAs) are a major and perhaps irreversible feature of today's multilateral trading system. The number of preferential arrangements as well as the world share of preferential trade has been steadily increasing over the last decade. The growing number of RTAs has resulted in a **'spaghetti bowl'** of criss-crossing RTAs with overlapping membership and a complex myriad of trade rules.

Before the WTO come into operation in 1995, the world witnessed two waves of regionalism. Modern regionalism began with the signing of the Treaty of Rome in 1957 which established a common market of six European countries: the Federal Republic of Germany, France, the Netherlands, Belgium, Italy and Luxembourg. This triggered an upsurge of regionalism all over the world, particularly in Africa and Latin America.

By the early 1970s, most of these regional groupings failed or survived on paper only except the EU, EFTA and ASEAN. The main reasons for their failure to meet external shocks were their excessively inward looking policies, inability to implement deeper integration measures, low level of infrastructure links and similar production structures. In many cases political and security objectives dominated the formation of most of the groupings.

A **second wave** of regionalism started sweeping the economies of the world from the end of the 1980s and the beginning of the 1990s. This saw the unprecedented deepening of the European integration in the form of a single market, the establishment of such mega groupings such as the North American Free Trade Area (NAFTA) and the Asia and Pacific Economic Cooperation (APEC) and the revival and deepening of the existing regional integration schemes in new forms, with a new agenda and sometimes under new names such like the MERCOSUR (South American Common Market), ASEAN free trade area (AFTA), East Asian Economic Caucus (EAEC), African Economic Community (AEC), etc.

The second wave of integration differed markedly from the first wave in several respects. During the second wave we notice the participation of the United States, a country that was earlier the staunchest advocate of multilateralism. Secondly, this phase coincided with globalisation that supported multilateral trade liberalisation as well. Thirdly, these groupings brought together both developed and developing countries as well as economies in transition transcending geographical continuity (eg. Asia Pacific Economic Community).

Fourthly, these groupings are multi-dimensional providing not only for trade preferences, but also co-operation in security, as well as in the social and cultural fields. Finally, almost all of them involve a process of deeper integration incorporating liberalisation in services, movement of capital, evolving or harmonizing common standards and competition policies and protection of intellectual property rights. Some of these policies are WTO-plus, implying that they even go beyond the baseline requirements set under WTO.

The recent upsurge of Bilateral Free Trade Agreements (BFTAs) manifests the **third wave** of RTAs. For example, Singapore has signed Free Trade Agreements (FTAs) with New Zealand, Japan, Australia, the US, EFTA and Jordan. Thailand has signed or is contemplating FTAs with the US, New Zealand, Australia, China and Japan.

The increasing numbers of RTAs that include large industrial countries as well take the shape of a ***'hub-and-spoke'*** structure in world trade. In a hub-and-spoke system, the largest countries sign bilateral agreements with many small countries. Such a system could marginalise the spokes where market access conditions are much less advantageous than in the hub, which offers improved access to all of the spokes.

Thus, RTAs are being embraced by most WTO members as trade policy instruments where economic considerations are only one facet of the complex RTA strategies being pursued by WTO Members which often include broader foreign policy aims such as political and security considerations. Besides, the sluggish progress in multilateral trade negotiations under the Doha Development Round appears to have accelerated further the urge to forge RTAs. The emergence of NAFTA is an illustration of this.

Under RTA with limited Members, decisions can be taken faster in contrast to the multilateral process under WTO in which decision-making has to be arrived at by consensus among a large group of heterogeneous members. Countries participating in RTAs seek to secure access to large markets. Access to large markets permits opportunities to even smaller countries to attract more domestic and foreign investment. A regional agreement can also help with region specific issues such as environment, border controls, transit, migration or movement of labour or development of trans-boundary infrastructure. Some RTAs have also included dispute resolution mechanisms.

DISTINCTIONS BETWEEN VARIOUS FORMS OF RTAS[8]

Preferential Trading Areas

- This is the first tier of integration.
- Trading partners grant partial non-discriminatory tariff reductions to each others, but leave their other tariffs, non-tariff barriers and quantitative restrictions unchanged.

Free Trade Areas

- To eliminate completely quantitative trade restrictions and customs tariffs against each other's goods
- Member countries retain the sovereign power to decide the trade policies to be imposed on non-members

Customs Union

- Similar to free trade area
- Adopt uniform import tariffs and common quota restrictions to non-members
- Weakened the ability of member countries to determine national trade policies independently

Common Markets

- Similar to customs union
- Plus free movement of factors of production
- A significant reduction of national sovereignty

An example of a common market is the EEC, which is composed of Belgium, Denmark, France, Germany, Ireland, Italy, Luxemburg, Netherlands and the UK.

Economic Unions

- Similar to common markets
- Harmonization of monetary, fiscal and social policies
- A single common policy as an essential prerequisite for the effective functioning of the union

- An example of an economic union is the Benelux which is the economic union formed by Belgium, the Netherlands and Luxembourg.
- In fact Belgium, Netherlands and Luxemburg formed a customs union in as early as 1948 and they became an economic union in 1960.

MOTIVATIONS FOR RTAS[8]

Market factors:

1. To maintain market access and to open new markets
2. To attract foreign direct investments (FDI)
3. To benefit from economies of scale

Political factors:

1. To act as a counterbalance to other RTAs
2. To act as a commitment to internal reform
3. Inspired by previous successful examples
4. To increase bargaining power and to maintain interregional security

SCOPE OF RTAS[7]

Regionalism is described in the Dictionary of Trade Policy Terms, as "actions by governments to liberalize or facilitate trade on a regional basis, sometimes through free-trade areas or customs unions". In the WTO context, regional trade agreements (RTAs) have both a more general and a more specific meaning: more general, because RTAs may be agreements concluded between countries not necessarily belonging to the same geographical region; more specific, because the WTO provisions which relate specifically to conditions of preferential trade liberalization with RTAs.

The coverage and depth of preferential treatment varies from one RTA to another. Modern RTAs, and not exclusively those linking the most developed economies, tend to go far beyond tariff-cutting exercises. They provide for increasingly complex regulations governing intra-trade (e.g. with respect to standards, safeguard provisions, customs administration, etc.) and they often also provide for a preferential regulatory framework for mutual services trade. A unique feature of the post-Uruguay Round agreements or the

"New Age FTAs" is that they go beyond just merchandise trade liberalisation to encompass liberalisation of services trade focusing on high growth services sectors such as the transport, finance, and information and communication technology. The most sophisticated RTAs go beyond traditional trade policy mechanisms, to include regional rules on investment, competition, environment and labour.

A note of Caution:

RTAs can complement the multilateral trading system, help to build and strengthen it. But by their very nature RTAs are discriminatory: they are a departure from the MFN principle, a cornerstone of the multilateral trading system. Their effects on global trade liberalization and economic growth are not clear given that the regional economic impact of RTAs is ex- ante inherently ambiguous. Though RTAs are designed to the advantage of signatory countries, expected benefits may be undercut if distortions in resource allocation, as well as trade and investment diversion, potentially present in any RTA process, are not minimized, if not eliminated altogether. An RTA's net economic impact will certainly depend on its own architecture and the choice of its major internal parameters (in particular, the depth of trade liberalization and sectoral coverage). Concurrent MFN trade liberalization by RTA parties, either unilaterally or in the context of multilateral trade negotiations, can play an important role in defusing potential distortions, both at the regional and at the global level.

The increase in RTAs, coupled with the preference shown for concluding bilateral free-trade agreements, has produced the phenomenon of overlapping membership. Because each RTA will tend to develop its own mini-trade regime, the coexistence in a single country of differing trade rules applying to different RTA partners has become a frequent feature. This can hamper trade flows merely by the costs involved for traders in meeting multiple sets of trade rules. The proliferation of RTAs, especially as their scope broadens to include policy areas not regulated multilaterally, increases the risks of inconsistencies in the rules and procedures among RTAs themselves, and between RTAs and the multilateral framework. This is likely to give rise to regulatory confusion, distortion of regional markets, and severe implementation problems, especially where there are overlapping RTAs.

INTERACTION BETWEEN REGIONAL TRADE AGREEMENTS AND THE MULTILATERAL TRADING SYSTEM[4]

In the traditional, conceptual debate on "regionalism vs. multilateralism", it has been argued that RTAs, by moving generally at a faster pace than the MTS and sharing its goals, represent a way of strengthening the latter. The positive effects of RTAs on the integration of developing countries in the world economy are also usually noted.

These views have been contested on the grounds of the fundamental changes observed in the geographical scale and trade-policy scope of the RTA process. It has been argued that the impact of these changes, coupled with the lack of flexible accession provisions in many RTAs hampers their effectiveness in contributing to the growth of world trade and the traditional synergies between the RTA and multilateral processes.

OVERLAPPING AND NETWORKS OF RTAS[4]

It has been observed that overlapping RTA membership impacts on trade and investment patterns; increases the complexity of RTAs, and magnifies negative effects on trade of complex and varying methods of determining regional content through preferential rules of origin. In addition, it has been argued that when diagonal cumulation is applied within a RTA network, the preferential nature of any individual RTA is extended to parties to other RTAs, without any legal basis; furthermore, such treatment is discriminatory, since some third parties to the original RTA – those participating in the diagonal cumulation scheme – benefit from preferential treatment, while other third parties – those not participating in the scheme – are not eligible.

Conversely, it has been argued that the constitution of RTA networks acts as a positive force for the multilateral system. Parties to individual RTAs within a network move toward the harmonization of rules of origin with the view to greater integration. Diagonal cumulation schemes under preferential rules of origin regimes reduce barriers and facilitate trade among participating economies, by simplifying and harmonizing customs procedures.

RULES OF ORIGIN (ROO): AN IMPORTANT PART OF ANY RTA

Rules of Origin (ROO) are the criteria to determine the nationality (origin) of goods being imported. ROO are an essential adjunct to the RTAs. Unless provided for, RTAs could serve as merely conduits for trade deflection for products imported by member states with low external tariffs to preferential markets of other Member states with high external tariffs. Unless devised properly, ROO could itself take the form of either trade deflection from third countries (when ROO are too liberal) or that of NTBs (when the required discipline is too exacting). The main objectives of ROO have to be developmental. This can be promoted by preventing trade deflection, facilitating value addition through backward linkages, and promoting balanced regional trade.

In the **Kyoto Convention** held in 1974, twenty countries made the first attempt to harmonize the ROOs. The **WTO Agreement on Rules of Origins** now provides the useful definition for the Harmonized Rules of Origins. On the basis of application of the ROO criterias, the classification of a product can be made as;

a. Whether the products have been wholly obtained or produced in the exporting country,

b. Whether the products have not been wholly obtained or produced in the exporting country and

c. Whether the products have been obtained through regional cumulation.

The methods to assess substantial product transformation for eligibility of a product for preferences are as follows:

Percentage test (Value Addition) criterion:

When the value of domestic inputs to total FOB export value meets the prescribed minimum, the products qualify the ROO criteria. The percentage criterion can be applied in the form of *maximum import content stipulation* or *minimum domestic content requirement* or *the requirement of originating parts reaching a certain percentage of the total value of parts*. The value addition is calculated either following the *cost based method* or the *transaction value-based method*.

Change in tariff heading (CTH):

This criterion is generally applied at the HS 4-digit level. This happens when the exported product undergoes such transformation as to be classified differently from the used imported material inputs.

Exceptions to CTH:

Exceptional cases to CTH are described.

Cumulation:

If the raw materials are sourced from within Regional Cumulation, then CTH is not applicable if provided under the RTA.

Specific Manufacturing Process (SMP) test criterion:

Under this criterion certain products need to perform the required processing so as to qualify as eligible products.

Normally, in the maximum number of RTAs, at least two tests are prescribed to determine the ROO.

NOT THE END OF OBSERVATIONS

While an active debate on whether bilateralism/regionalism is a stepping stone towards multilateralism or whether such arrangements detract from liberalisation and fragment the global trading system continues to persist, the point to recognise is that regionalism is here to stay and grow.[3]

RTAs are a major and perhaps an irreversible feature of today's multilateral trading system. It is often simpler to negotiate or strike deals among a smaller group of compact members (whether contiguous or not), rather than with a diverse and heterogeneous group of 151 members in a global multilateral framework such as that of the WTO.[10]

4

WTO COMPATIBILITY OF RTAs

By August 2006, only one WTO members — Mongolia,— was not party to any regional trade agreement. The surge in these agreements has continued unabated since the early 1990s. 197 RTAs are currently in force as on 15.06.2006, where as several others are believed to be operational although not yet notified. It is estimated that more than half of world trade is now conducted under RTAs.[7]

RTAs in force by date of entry into force as on 15.06.06

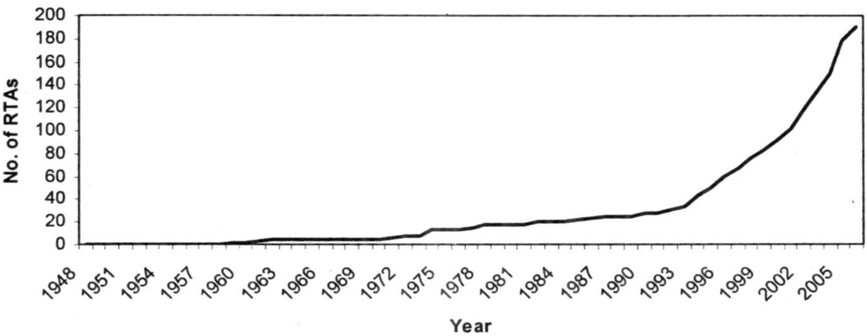

NOTIFICATIONS OF RTAS IN FORCE TO GATT/ WTO AS OF 15 JUNE 2006

	Accessions	New RTAs	Total
GATT Art. XXIV (FTA)	4	122	**126**
GATT Art. XXIV (CU)	5	6	**11**
Enabling Clause	1	21	**22**
GATS Art. V	2	36	**38**
Total	**12**	**185**	**197**

EXAMINATION PROCESS AS ON 15 JUNE 2006

	WTO provision			
Status	Enabling Clause	GATS Art. V	GATS Art. XXIV	Grand
Examination not requested	19	1	1	**21**
Factual examination not started	0	12	51	**63**
Under factual examination	0	6	17	**23**
Factual examination concluded	1	16	46	**63**
Consultations on draft report	0	3	4	**7**
Report adopted	2	0	18	**20**
Grand Total	**22**	**38**	**137**	**197**

(Details status of all the RTAs notified to WTO as on 15th June 2006 are given in the Annexures) (Source: www.wto.org)

Dealing with non-notified RTAs

A number of RTAs currently in force have not been notified to the WTO, in particular preferential arrangements between developing countries. This is often cited as hindering any comprehensive and precise evaluation of the RTA phenomenon *vis-à-vis* the multilateral trading system.

Multilateral surveillance

RTAs notified to the WTO are subject to surveillance in various Bodies, at various levels of depth and complexity, depending upon which provision the notifying Member avails itself of.

Work of the Committee on Regional Trade Agreements (CRTA)[7]

In 6 February 1996, the WTO General Council established the **Committee on Regional Trade Agreements**. Its duties are to;

- Examine individual regional agreements;
- Consider the systemic implications of the agreements for the multilateral trading system and the relationship between them.

- Consider how the required reporting on the operation of agreements should be carried out
- Develop procedures to facilitate and improve the examination process.

A new WTO Agreement on RTAs?

Director-General Pascal Lamy, on 10 July 2006, welcomed the Negotiating Group on Rules' formal approval of a *new WTO transparency mechanism* for all regional trade agreements (RTAs).

"This decision will help break the current logjam in the WTO on regional trade agreements. This is an important step towards ensuring that regional trade agreements become building blocks, not stumbling blocks to world trade. It is important to note as well that this breakthrough comes at a critical juncture in our broader Doha round negotiations. Hopefully this decision is a good omen for much needed progress in other areas of the talks, such as agriculture and industrial goods trade, where agreement is urgently needed."[7]

Current RTA examination procedures[4]

- The notification of an agreement (together with its text) is considered by the CTG (if notified under GATT Article XXIV), the CTS (if notified under GATS Article V) or the Committee on Trade and Development, if notified under the Enabling Clause). If examination of the agreement is needed, the relevant body adopts the terms of reference for the examination and transfers the examination task to the CRTA.
- The parties to the RTA are invited to submit preliminary information on the agreement in the form of a Standard Format, which is published as a formal document. This is the initial step of what is called the "factual" examination.
- During (at least one or two) CRTA regular sessions, there is an exchange of oral questions and replies on the examined RTA, as well as more general statements by the parties and other Members. Detailed minutes are produced on each meeting devoted to the RTA examination, and published as formal documents.
- Between each of those meetings, usually a round of additional written questions and replies takes place. These are also published as a formal document.

- Once the CRTA feels that the factual part of the examination has concluded, the Secretariat is requested to draft a report on the examination, as the basis for consultations among Members (in open-ended informal CRTA meetings.
- The consensual CRTA report on a given agreement would then be sent to the WTO body that had mandated the examination, for adoption.

RTA examination procedures under the GATT[4]

For RTAs seeking legal cover under Article XXIV of the GATT 1947, the process consisted of the following steps:

- The notification of an agreement (of which the text was also made available) was considered by the Council, which mandated the examination to a working party and invited contracting parties to ask written questions to the parties and these to reply to them, also in writing.
- Once a formal document was produced with all these questions and replies, the working party began its work.
- Working party meetings (usually with the participation of parties' experts from capitals) comprised a further exchange of questions and replies, political statements and legal comments. Sometimes, the parties submitted further information in writing (usually, statistics). This information was in some cases reproduced in a formal document.
- The working party's report on the examination, once agreed, was transmitted to the Council, for adoption.

Dispute settlement[4]

Another area of growing concern refers to the effects of the dispute settlement provisions contained in "new generation" RTAs, which could build jurisprudence conflicting with that of the WTO. This issue has been raised in particular with respect to RTA clauses providing that, in the event of inconsistency, RTA rules prevail over WTO rules. It has been argued that this could result in a diminution of the rights that the parties had under the WTO in relation to their trade with one another. It has however been noted that such situation was not contemplated in the language calling for RTA rules to prevail in the event of inconsistency; that language was geared toward situations in which the RTA provisions went beyond WTO disciplines. Also, the argument that parallel dispute settlement procedures could nullify or impair WTO rights of third parties has been contested on the grounds that such procedures concerned trade between the parties and not trade with third parties.

Panel's jurisdiction to assess compatibility of RTAs[4]

While WTO rules provide for a multilateral assessment of the consistency of an RTA with the rules, the possibility of recourse to dispute settlement is explicitly referred to in paragraph 12 of the Understanding:

> ***Dispute Settlement.*** *The provisions of Articles XXII and XXIII of GATT 1994 as elaborated and applied by the Dispute Settlement Understanding may be invoked with respect to any matters arising from the application of those provisions of Article XXIV relating to customs unions, free-trade areas or interim agreements leading to the formation of a customs union or free-trade area.* »

However, while inconclusive on the issue of the imposition or maintenance of safeguard measures between the constituent territories of a customs union or of a free-trade area in relation to Article XXIV, Panel and Appellate Body findings have stressed the need for a parallelism between the scope of a safeguard investigation and the scope of the application of safeguard measures.

A Brief Account of GATT/WTO Rules and Procedures on RTAs[4]

WTO provisions governing Members' participation in customs unions, free-trade areas (FTAs), and interim agreements are contained in paragraphs 4-11 of *GATT Article* XXIV. During the Uruguay Round, a number of provisions contained in the original Article XXIV, drafted in 1947, were clarified or interpreted, as contained in paragraphs 1-12 of the 1994 Understanding.

Rules with respect to reciprocal (tariff and non-tariff) preferential arrangements on trade in goods among developing countries are found in paragraphs 1, 2(c), 3(a & b) and 4 of the *Enabling Clause*.

GATS Article V lays down the rules governing economic integration agreements in the area of trade in services, including those implemented in stages.

The WTO's rules[7]

When a WTO member enters into a regional integration arrangement through which it grants more favourable conditions to its trade with other parties to that arrangement than to other WTO members' trade, it departs from the guiding principle of non-discrimination defined in Article I (MFN clause) of GATT, Article II of GATS, and elsewhere. WTO Members are however permitted to enter into such arrangements under specific conditions, which are spelled out in three sets of rules:

- *Paragraphs 4 to 10 of Article XXIV of GATT* (as clarified in the Understanding on the Interpretation of Article XXIV of the GATT 1994) provide for the formation and operation of customs unions and free-trade areas covering trade in goods;
- The so-called *Enabling Clause* (i.e., the 1979 Decision on Differential and More Favorable Treatment, Reciprocity and Fuller Participation of Developing Countries) refers to preferential trade arrangements in trade in goods between developing country Members; and
- *Article V of GATS* governs the conclusion of RTAs in the area of trade in services, for both developed and developing countries.

Other non-generalized preferential schemes, for example non-reciprocal preferential agreements involving developing and developed countries, require Members to seek a waiver from WTO rules. Such waivers require the approval of three quarters of WTO Members. Examples of such agreements, which are currently in force, include the US — Caribbean Basin Economic Recovery Act (CBERA), the CARIBCAN agreement whereby Canada offers duty-free non-reciprocal access to most Caribbean countries, Turkey-Preferential treatment for Bosnia-Herzegovina and the EC-ACP Partnership Agreement.

TRADE REGULATORY PROCESS

It has been argued that the current trend towards the creation of self-contained regional legal frameworks within RTAs is likely to lead to a progressive erosion of the multilateral legal framework. While the impact of regional trade policy disciplines differing from those under the WTO Agreements is practically impossible to gauge, it has been observed that their development could lead to Members forgoing some of their WTO rights when becoming parties to an RTA. An example cited in this context is the fact that some RTAs provide for the use of competition or anti-trust policy measures in intra-trade, in cases where anti-dumping measures would apply to third parties. It has been argued that the maintenance of a dual system (of anti-dumping duties for third parties and competition policy among RTA parties) can create distortions where different criteria and conditions apply to the invocation of such measures.[4]

Conversely, the potential benefits to be gathered from the development and application of trade disciplines in individual RTAs or RTA networks have been highlighted, in particular their potential contribution to further multilateral liberalization. There is wide recognition, however, that there is a need to find ways to coordinate different approaches to particular problem areas or trade disciplines developed regionally, so that they interact positively with the progress of multilateral disciplines in those areas. Contingency protection instruments, technical barriers to trade and sanitary and phytosanitary measures have been identified as areas to be considered in this respect, given the potential impact of such measures on third-party trade.[4]

The practical reason for permitting free trade areas or customs unions was that many countries would not have joined GATT if it totally prohibited RTAs with neighbours or between countries having a special relationship historically. At the theoretical level, genuine FTAs or customs unions were viewed as compatible with the principle of non-discrimination when the move was in the direction of freeing trade among members rather than raising fresh barriers with non-members.[10]

5

RTAs in ASIA – AN INDIAN PERSPECTIVE

In Asia, there have been several efforts towards sub-regional, cross-regional, and bilateral regional trading arrangements. While bilateral initiatives largely involve ASEAN economies, viz. Singapore and Thailand, some of the notable sub-regional economic cooperation efforts are the BIMSTEC (Bay of Bengal Initiative among Member States for Multi-Sectoral Technical and Economic Cooperation) comprising Bangladesh, India, Myanmar, Nepal, Bhutan, Sri Lanka, and Thailand; the Mekong-Ganga Cooperation Group, involving India, Cambodia, Laos, Myanmar, Vietnam and Thailand. All the major Asian economies, and some of the subregional organizations such as ASEAN (Association of Southeast Asian Nations) have been pursuing bilateral regional trading agreements.[5]

Proliferation of Free Trade Agreements (FTAs) is the clearest evidence of Asian countries' desire to forge closer economic relationships. The growing importance of CECA's indicates that such agreements are becoming deeper, extending to areas beyond just tariff reduction. Intra-regional trade and investment require building up of shared infrastructure. Many Asian countries have joined together to develop cross-border infrastructure to lay the foundations for closer trading relationships and increased connectivity among countries.[9]

The Greater Mekong Sub-region is quite advanced in this endeavor. Similar initiatives are underway in South Asia and in Central Asia, with exciting prospects for future development. The spirit of enhanced monetary cooperation in Asia is evident from initiatives like the Chiang Mai Initiative and the Asian Bond Fund having major potential for financing regional investments.[9]

Asia remains one of the least integrated regions lacking a continent-wide regicnal organization. Forging closer links among Asian nations through appropriate institutional mechanisms can lead to substantial enhancement of national, regional and global productivity and output. In the past, India had adopted a very cautious approach to regionalism, and was engaged in only a few bilateral/regional initiatives, mainly through Preferential Trade Agreements (PTAs). Recognising that RTAs would continue to feature in world trade for a long time, and with the intention of expanding its export market, India began concluding in principle agreements as a possible step towards CECAs, which cover FTA in goods (zero customs duty regime within a fixed time frame on items covering substantial trade, and a relatively small negative list of sensitive items with no or limited duty concessions), services, investment and identified areas of economic cooperation. The recently concluded CECA with Singapore was implemented from 1st August, 2005. The Agreement on South Asia Free Trade Area (SAFTA) was signed by member countries of South Asian Association for Regional Cooperation (SAARC) in January 2004. Negotiation on all aspects of SAFTA was concluded recently and the tariff liberalization programme was implemented from July 1, 2006. Framework Agreement on Comprehensive Economic Cooperation between ASEAN and India, Framework Agreement for Bangladesh, India, Myanmar, Srilanka and Thailand Economic Cooperation (BIMSTEC) FTA, and India-Thailand Framework Agreement have also been signed, and FTA on Goods, Services and Investment with BIMSTEC are under negotiation. India-China, India-Japan, and India-South Korea joint study groups have also been set up.[9]

China emerged as the second major trading partner of India in 2005-06 and the share of combined China- Hong Kong at 9.4 per cent was close to that of USA. The impressive growth in trade with China was contributed by ores, slag, ash, iron and steel and organic chemicals on the export side, and by electrical machinery, other machinery and organic chemicals on the import side. While UAE is the next major trading partner, and is important both in terms of imports and exports, another important country, whose share has been increasing steadily, is Singapore, with which India has recently signed a Comprehensive Economic Cooperation Agreement (CECA). In the case of India Singapore trade, precious stones, metals, mineral fuel, oil, ships and boats and other machinery were the major contributors in exports, and other machinery, electrical machinery, organic chemicals, books, newspapers and manuscript, and aircraft & spacecraft in imports.[9]

Region-wise, in 2004-05, India's exports to Asia and Oceania, (with a share of 47.4 per cent) registered a robust growth of 27 per cent. This was powered by the high growth of exports to China, Singapore, UAE and the Republic of Korea. The other two major regions — EU-25 and America (with shares of 21.7 per cent and 20.4 per cent respectively) registered growth of around 20 per cent. Exports to Africa and Latin American countries were also impressive. In April-October, 2005, while performance was similar to that in 2004-05, growth of exports to EU 25 accelerated, and exports to China-Hong Kong, Singapore and Korea continued to be impressive. Significant growth was also seen in trade with Sri Lanka and Thailand, with which India has a Free Trade Agreement (FTA). The growing importance of Asia in India's exports indicates that the regional trading arrangements (RTAs) strategy is bearing fruit. Framework Agreements on economic cooperation have also been entered into with MERCOSUR and Chile. India is also engaged with Gulf Cooperation Council and Mauritius for FTA/ Comprehensive Economic Cooperation Partnership Agreement. India-Israel and India, Brazil, South Africa (IBSA) joint Study Groups have also been set up. In 2004-05, India's imports from Asia and Oceania, accounting for 35.4 per cent of total imports, was buoyant with growth of 40 per cent. Import growth from EU 25 (with a share of 16.9 per cent) at 20 per cent and that from America (with a share of 8.4 per cent) at 29 per cent were also impressive.[9]

In April- October 2005, there was an acceleration of growth in imports from EU 25, and growth in imports from Asia and Oceania, and from America continued to be impressive, despite moderation. While the country-wise performance was almost similar to that in 2004-05, within SAARC, besides Sri Lanka and Pakistan, imports from Bangladesh witnessed an impressive rebound in growth in the first seven months of 2005-06, after a decline in 2004-05.[9]

6

RTAs IN SOUTH ASIA – AN INDIAN PERSPECTIVE

An important dimension of RTAs in South Asia would be to address the NTBs that stand in the way of free flow of goods trade in the region. Another dimension is the need to open up the services trade and to promote a common investment area so that the nexus between trade, services and investment is established.

While Free Trade Agreements would certainly imply a reduction in tariffs, the gains from such trade would be limited in the presence of non-tariff barriers. The incidence of non-tariff measures on India's exports to ASEAN and Sri Lanka has increased. The incidence is higher for India's exports to Indonesia, Philippines, Malaysia and Thailand than for exports to Singapore, Vietnam and Sri Lanka. At the firm level, most of the barriers were related to the application of measures on Technical Barriers to Trade and Sanitary and Phytosanitary Measures. For example; for some products (e.g., peanuts) standards amongst the ASEAN countries vary significantly making it difficult for Indian exporters to target the ASEAN market as a region. There are barriers related to certification, registration and testing. There is need for Mutual Recognition Agreements between India and the ASEAN countries, which would reduce transaction costs through duplication of testing and certification. Domestic measures should also be implemented to meet standards related to the application of TBT and SPS measures.[2]

MULTILATERAL/INTER-REGIONAL AGREEMENTS RTAS IN SOUTH ASIA

ASEAN (Association of South East Asian Nations)

- ASEAN includes Indonesia, Malaysia, Philippines, Singapore, Brunei Darussalam, Cambodia, Laos, Myanmar, Thailand and Vietnam. Among them Malaysia, Singapore, Thailand and Indonesia are all emerging as strong trading partners of India.

- ASEAN and India are natural partners. Geographically, India shares maritime borders with Indonesia & Thailand and a land border of 1,600 kilometers with Myanmar. History-wise, Indian legacy exists in ASEAN.

South Asian Preferential Trading Agreement (SAPTA)[10]

- A regional trade block among seven countries, namely, Bangladesh, Bhutan, India, Maldives, Nepal, Pakistan and Sri Lanka members was formed when SAARC Preferential Trading Arrangement (SAPTA) was signed in April, 1993 for giving preferential market access to the exports of the member countries in a limited way. The operationali-sation of SAPTA happened in December 1995.
- A modest beginning was made in the First Round when 226 products were conceded at the HS 6- digit level. The number of products offered concessions accelerated to 1868 and 3456 items during the Second and Third Rounds, making a total of 5550 items of which 3449 items were exclusively for LDCs, viz. Bangladesh, Bhutan, Maldives and Nepal.
- The largest number of concessions was offered by India, being 2927 products of which as many as 2450 products were in favour of LDCs. Bilaterally, the largest number of non-reciprocal concessions were offered in favour of Bangladesh (later multilatera-lised in favour of all LDCs). Exchange of concessions with Sri Lanka and Pakistan was limited to a few items.
- Four rounds of negotiations have been completed and no further round is now contemplated following the signing of the Agreement on SAFTA.

Agreement on South Asian Free Trade Area (SAFTA)[12]

- The Agreement was signed during the 12th SAARC Summit held in Islamabad on 4-6 January 2004.
- The SAFTA agreement has been enter into force on 1 January 2006 and the customs rules were notified w.e.f. 1 July 2006. **This Agreement superseded the Agreement on SAARC Preferential Trading Arrangement (SAPTA).**
- The entry into force of the Agreement thus launches the South Asian Free Trade Area which would be completed by

1st January 2016. The first round of customs duty reduction would take place, as agreed by the Member States, in July/ August 2006.

- It may be recalled that the Twelfth Meeting of the Committee of Experts (COE) on SAFTA held at the SAARC Secretariat, Kathmandu on 29 November – 1 December 2005 successfully concluded the negotiations on the following issues which now form an integral part of the Agreement:
  1. Sensitive Lists – of products that would be temporarily exempt from reduction in customs tariffs to be applied across the board for all other products;
  2. Rules of Origin – specifying the conditions that would have to be met by products to qualify for application of reduced customs tariffs on export to another SAARC Member State;
  3. Mechanism for Compensation of Revenue Loss for LDC Member States (Bangladesh, Bhutan, Maldives and Nepal) in the event of revenue loss resulting from lowering of customs tariffs in terms of the Agreement; and
  4. Technical Assistance to the LDC Member States.
- Under Article 7 - Trade Liberalisation Programme (TLP) – in the first phase, India, Pakistan and Sri Lanka will bring down their customs tariff to 20% by 1st January 2008. As far as the LDC Member States i.e. Bangladesh, Bhutan, Maldives and Nepal are concerned, they would reduce their customs tariff to 30%. It has also been agreed by the COE that the first tariff reduction would be effected on 1st July 2006 by all Member States with the exception of Nepal, which will, do so on 1st August 2006.
- It may also be noted that India, Pakistan and Sri Lanka would bring their customs tariff down to the level of 0-5% for the export products of Bangladesh, Bhutan, Maldives and Nepal by 1st January 2009. However, Bangladesh, Bhutan, Maldives and Nepal are required to do so by 1st January 2016.
- With the coming into force of the Agreement, the SAFTA Ministerial Council (SMC) and the SAFTA Committee of

Experts (COE) have also been established under Article 10 of the Agreement. The SMC is the highest decision-making body and is responsible for implementation of the Agreement. It consists of Commerce/Trade Ministers of the Member States and is required to meet at least once annually or more often as and when considered necessary. The COE, consisting of one nominee from each Member State at the level of senior economic official, is to support the SMC and monitor, review and facilitate implementation of the Agreement. The COE is to meet once every six months or more often as necessary.

ASIA PACIFIC TRADE AGREEMENT (BANGKOK AGREEMENT)

- The Agreement was signed in 31st July 1975 for contributing to expansion in trade through exchange of tariff concessions among developing country members of the *Economic and Social Commission for Asia and the Pacific(* ESCAP) region.
- The Agreement is currently operational between Bangladesh, India, Republic of Korea, China and Sri Lanka.
- China's accession to this agreement was finalised in April 2000.

BIMST- EC

- The Initiative was taken by Thailand in 1994 and with the admission of Myanmar in December 1997 it was named as "Bangladesh, India, Myanmar, Sri Lanka, Thailand Economic Cooperation" (BIMST-EC) to serve as a bridge linking ASEAN and SAARC. It may be noted that the initiative involves three members of SAARC (India, Bangladesh & Sri Lanka) ana two members of ASEAN (Thailand, Myanmar).
- Six areas of Trade and Investment, Technology, Transportation and Communication, Energy, Tourism and Fisheries were identified for cooperation.
- The Second Economic/ Trade Ministers meeting in April 2000 decided to constitute an Inter Governmental Group (IGG) to prepare a Concept Paper on possible approaches towards a PTA leading to an FTA.

- IGG's recommendation was considered by the Ministers in their third meeting held in Yangon in 2001 and a Group of Experts was constituted to examine in detail the two approaches.
- GOE has recommended to go for a 'negative list approach' for FTA in BIMST-EC.
- The Framework Agreement on the BIMST-EC FTA was signed on 8 February 2004 by Bhutan, India, Myanmar, Nepal, Sri Lanka and Thailand during the Fifth BIMST-EC Economic Ministers' Meeting. Bhutan and Nepal had joined BIMST-EC as new members formally, only the day prior to the signing of the Framework Agreement. Bangladesh had participated in the GoE all along for drafting the Framework Agreement, but did not sign it.

GENERALISED SYSTEM OF PREFERENCES[8]

- Unilateral and generalised tariff concessions given by the developed countries to the developing countries under the GSP Scheme.
- Important to India are GSP given by USA, EU, Japan etc.
- Rules of Origin to be fulfilled.
- Graduation process defined for no concessions.

INDIAN OCEAN RIM - ASSOCIATION FOR REGIONAL COOPERATION (IOR - ARC)[8]

- IOR - ARC was founded in 1995 with the first meeting on Working Group held in Mauritius.
- The focus for economic cooperation is in the areas of Trade Facilitation, Promotion and Liberalization, Promotion of Foreign Investment, Promotion of Scientific and Technological exchanges, Promotion of Tourism, Promotion of Movement of Natural persons and Service providers, Development of Infrastruc-ture and Human Resources.

7

INDIA's POLICIES TOWARDS RTAs

On the economic front, India is an emerging economy of the world with a Gross Domestic Product of more than US$500 billion and a consumer market of more than 1.2 billion people. India will grow steadily by 6 percent in the next few years. It has persistently and purposefully pursued **Look East Policy** initiated in 1991. India and Bhutan have BFTA since fifties. It has implemented bilateral trade agreements with Sri Lanka, Thailand and Singapore, and is at an advanced stage of negotiation with and ASEAN. BFTA between India and Sri Lanka became operational in March 2000. India is currently contemplating similar BFTA with Bangladesh and Maldives. India is actively pursuing bilateral /regional free trade arrangements as part of its trade policy. India has signed a FTA with Thailand in 2003 and CECA with Singapore in 2005. It has also simultaneously signed a Free Trade Agreement with ASEAN.

India has decided to upgrade all current FTAs to FTA plus, covering non-merchandise trade areas as well. This policy is to be followed in all current and future such negotiations. The bilateral agreements with China and Korea have been proposed and joint study groups have been established. An India-Japan study group to examine the feasibility for a similar agreement has also been established. It is hoped that this group will enable the two countries to evolve a strategic partnership. India is also deepening its linkages with the EU and the US as a part of its continuing efforts to seek constructive and mutually beneficial partnerships with key entities around the world. The bilateral trade between India and the EU was Euro 27.5 billion in 2003-04. The EU was the single largest investor in India. At the fifth summit in Hague in November 2004, India and the EU announced the launch of a strategic partnership covering both economic and security issues.[5]

The bilateral trade between India and the US was US $ 18 billion in 2003, and is growing rapidly. The two countries have been deepening their engagement and the prospects for robust bilateral economic dialogue are encouraging (Mansingh, 2004). As India's Prime Minister has stated in November 2004, India-US strategic partnership is "..an idea whose time has come". Indeed, there is a preliminary thinking about an FTA between the two countries (Bery, 2004). India, Brazil and South Africa have also established an informal yet substantive dialogue covering a wide range of economic and security issues.[5]

It is observed that with the exception of Japan, India's trade with other East Asian countries has increased rapidly since the crisis of 1997-98. Thus, barring few exceptions, the growth rate of India's exports to and imports from East Asian economies (viz. China, Japan, Korea and the ASEAN-6) was in general higher than that of India's exports and imports to the world. [5]

India's overall merchandise trade with East Asia more than doubled from about US$ 13 billion in 1997-98 to about US $ 27 billion in 2003-04 registering a compound annual growth rate of 13 per cent. The bulk of this increase was contributed by the rapid increase in bilateral merchandise trade between India and China, which expanded more than four-fold from about US.[5]

India has averaged a real annual growth rate of 6 per cent during the 1992-93 to 2003-04 period, and is expected to grow at a slightly higher rate over the next decade. In PPP (Purchasing Power Parity) terms, India's 2002 GNI at US $2.8 trillion makes it the 4th largest economy in the world. Even on conservative estimates, India's GDP is set to exceed US $1 trillion by the end of this decade (Sen *et al.*, 2004). India has now achieved a high degree of consensus on the need to vigorously pursue economic reforms. This is indicated by the continuity in broad economic policies and strategies by the successive governments representing different political parties. As an example, this is reflected in India's announcement of the first ever National Foreign Trade Policy 2004-09, which integrates foreign trade with broader economic growth and employment generation strategies just as East Asian countries have done so successfully for several decades. India aims to double its share of global merchandise trade from 0.8 per cent to between 1.5-2 per cent by 2009. India also aims to substantially increase its current 1.4 per cent share in global trade in commercial services, particularly in the Information and Communication Technology (ICT) related services.[5]

India is also interested in plugging itself to the East Asia economy due to its latent potential. The Indian economy is increasingly integrated with East Asian economies. The East Asian countries account for nearly 25% of India's total trade. India has a web of cooperation with East Asian countries, especially ASEAN through the ASEAN-India dialogue process, the bilateral free trade agreements with Singapore and Thailand and sub-regional initiatives such as the Mekong-Ganga Cooperation and the Bangladesh-India-Myanmar-Sri Lanka-Thailand Economic Cooperation (BIMST-EC). [6]

BILATERAL RTAS

India has signed the following Bilateral treaties;

Indo-Nepal Treaty

- On 2nd March 2002, the validity of India-Nepal Treaty of Trade and Protocol was extended for a period of 5 years w.e.f. 6.3.2002.
- Rules of Origin along with local content and substantial manufacturing clauses introduced.
- TRQ for Vanaspati, acrylic yarn, copper products and zinc oxide introduced.

Indo-Bhutan Treaty

- Agreement on Trade and Commerce between India and Bhutan signed on 28th February, 1995
- Preferential market access allowed for products originating from respective countries
- All exports and imports of Bhutan to and from countries other than India will be free from and not subject to customs duties and trade restrictions of the Government of India.

India Srilanka Free Trade Agreement

Specific History and Detailed Analysis is given under SECTION-III.

Frame Work Agreement for FTA with Thailand

Specific History and Detailed Analysis is given under SECTION-III.

CECA Between India and Singapore

Specific History and Detailed Analysis is given under SECTION-III.

Apart from the above, India has also signed bilateral pacts with ASEAN, BIMST-EC and the MERCOSUR group. However, due to various operational difficulties, these agreements have not yet been effected into.

SECTION - III

(Textual Analysis of FTAs)

Contents

8

FREE TRADE AGREEMENT BETWEEN THE REPUBLIC OF INDIA AND THE DEMOCRATIC SOCIALIST REPUBLIC OF SRI LANKA

A Bilateral Free Trade Agreement was signed between India and Sri Lanka in New Delhi on 28 December 1998 and has been in operation since March 2000. (The agreement can be accessed at: http://www.commerce.nic.in/agree.htm). The Tariff Rate Quota Mechanisms for the import of Tea and Garments were finalised in April 2000 in New Delhi. The agreement was renegotiated at various authority levels during June to July 2002.

STRUCTURE OF CONCESSION IN TARIFFS

Tariff Concessions offered by India

1 Duty concession of 100 percent is granted on 1351 products. **(Zero Duty)**

2. 50% tariff preference on five tea items, subject to a quota of 15 million Kg. per year. India offered two more ports Mumbai and Vishakhapatnam in addition to existing Cochin and Kolkata as entry points for tea with immediate effect. **(Tea)**

3. 50% tariff concessions on 233 garment products was given on a fixed basis, subject to an annual restriction of eight million pieces, of which six million shall be extended the concession only if made of Indian fabric. On utilization of the unrestricted quota, an additional quota of 2 million pieces out of 8 million pieces is permitted. The quota level per category is increased from 1.5 million to 2 million pieces per category per year. India agreed to provide Kolkata and JNPT (Mumbai) as additional port entry points for garments. **(Garments)**

4 50% margin of preference on (2799 products) all items, except for those on the negative list. To be phased out to zero duty in two stages within three years. *100% concession in duty comes into effect from 18.03.2003 on these products.* **(Phased Residual List: IR)**

5. Concessions on 528 Textile items restricted to 25% on Chapters 51-56, 58-60, & 63. **(Textiles)**
6. Four Chapters under the Textile sector retained in the negative list (Chapters 50,57,61 and 62).
7. Negative List of items to be retained on 429 products. **D (I)**

Tariff Concessions offered by Srilanka

1. **Zero duty** on about 319 items upon entering into force of the Agreement. **(F I)**
2. 50% margin of preference on 889 products upon coming into force of the Agreement, with up to 70% at the end of the 1st year, up to 90% at the end of the 2nd year and 100% at the end of 3rd year. *100% concession in duty comes into effect from 05.03.2003 on these products.* **(F II)**
3. For the remaining items of 2724 products, (except for those on the negative list), which is the Residual List, preference would be not less than 35% before the expiry of three years, 70% before the expiry of six years and 100% before the expiry of eighth year. **(Phased Residual List: SLR)**
4. A Negative List (**D II**): 1180 products.

A comparable analysis for overview of the different levels of duty reduction based on number of tariff lines at HS Code Six digit level is given in next page:

Level of Duty Reduction	Offer of Sri Lanka	Offer of India
Nil (Negative List)	1180	429
100% (zero duty)	319	1351
25% (fixed) – Textile Items	-	528
50% (fixed) – Tea quota	-	5
50% (fixed)- Garment Quota	-	233
50% (phased out to 100% in 3 years)	889	2799
Up to 100% in 8 years	2724	-
Total No. of Items	5112	5345

SAFEGUARD MEASURES

The provisions are contained in **Article VIII** of the agreement:

1. The importing country may with prior consultations (except in critical circumstances) with the exporting country,

suspend provisionally without discrimination the preferential treatment given to some product, if such product is imported in such a manner or in such quantities as to cause or threaten to cause serious injury to the corresponding industries in the importing country.

2. Immediately on applying the safeguard measures, the importing country shall simultaneously notify the exporting country and the Joint Committee established in terms of Article XI.
3. The Committee shall enter into consultations with the both the countries and endeavor to reach mutually acceptable agreement to remedy the situation.
4. In case, the Committee fails to resolve the issue within sixty days, the country affected by such action shall have the right to withdraw the preferential treatment.

JOINT COMMITTEE

The provisions are contained in **Article XI** of the Agreement:

a) A Joint Committee shall be established at Ministerial level.

b) The Committee shall meet at least once a year to review the progress in implementation status of this Agreement and to ensure that benefits of trade expansion emanating from this Agreement accrue to both the countries equitably.

c) The Committee may set up Sub-Committees and/or Working Groups as considered necessary.

d) In order to facilitate cooperation in customs matters, both the countries agreed to establish a Working Group on customs related issues including harmonization of tariff headings.

e) The Working Group shall meet as often as required and shall report to the Committee on its deliberations.

f) The Committee shall accord adequate opportunities for consultation on representations made by any country with respect to any matter affecting the implementation of the Agreement.

g) The Committee shall adopt appropriate measures for settling any matter arising from such representa-tions within six months of the representation being made. Each country shall implement such measures immediately.

h) The Committee shall nominate one apex chamber of trade and industry in each country as the nodal chamber to represent the views of the trade and industry on matters relating to this Agreement.

SETTLEMENT OF DISPUTES

The provisions are contained in **Article XIII** of the Agreement:

1. Any dispute that may arise between commercial entities of these two countries shall be referred for amicable settlement to the nodal apex chambers. The Chambers shall as far as possible, settle such references through mutual consultations.
2. In the event of an amicable solution not being found, the matter shall be referred to an Arbitral Tribunal for a binding decision. The Tribunal shall be constituted by the Joint Committee in consultation with the relevant Arbitration Bodies in the two countries.
3. Any dispute between the countries regarding the interpretation and application of the provisions of this Agreement or any instrument adopted within its framework shall be amicably settled through negotiations, failing which a notification may be made to the Committee by any one of the aggrieved country.

RULES OF ORIGIN

1. The provisions are contained in **Article VII** and **Annexure – 'C'** of the Agreement. The preferential trade under the FTA is governed by the Rules of Origin which specify three criteria namely:
   a. The domestic value addition should be 35 percent
   b. Inputs to undergo substantial transformation at the four digit level of customs harmonized code, and
   c. Lists of operations like simple packing, labeling, cutting and assembly, etc. have been defined which would not qualify for duty free market access.
2. If the other contracting party sources the raw material/ inputs from one country, the value addition is reduced to 25 percent of the Free On Board (FOB) value of the product under export subject to the condition that the aggregate value addition in the territories of the contracting parties is not less than 35 percent of the FOB value of the product under export.

3. Sri Lanka's exports with a domestic value addition content of 25% will also qualify for entry to the Indian market if they have a minimum 10% Indian content.
4. *Wholly produced or obtained* products are also eligible under the ROO criterias. These include;
   a. Raw or mineral products extracted from soil, water or seabed of either of the countries
   b. Vegetable products harvested there
   c. Animals born and raised there
   d. Products obtained from animals referred to in clause (c) above
   e. Products obtained by hunting or fishing conducted there
   f. Products of sea fishing and other marine products from the high seas by its vessels
   g. Products processed and/or made on board its factory ships exclusively from products referred to in clause (f) above
   h. Used articles collected there, fit only for the recovery of raw materials
   i. Waste and scrap resulting from manufacturing operations conducted there
   j. Products extracted from the seabed or below seabed which is situated outside its territorial waters, provided that it has exclusive exploitation rights
   k. Goods produced there exclusively from the products referred to in clauses (a) to (j) above.

From FTA to Comprehensive Economic Partnership Agreement (CEPA):

A Joint Study Group (JSG) was set up to explore ways and means of deepening and widening economic cooperation through a Comprehensive Economic Partnership Agreement (CEPA). The JSG completed its study and had submitted its report in October 2003 at New Delhi.

Summary of Recommendations of the JSG[11]:

- Enter into a Comprehensive Economic Partnership Agreement AND to establish institutional mechanisms to monitor the progress.

- Build upon the ILFTA by deepening and widening the coverage of trade in goods.
- Enter into broad negotiations covering all service sectors and modes of supply under the GATS framework.
- Facilitate greater investment flows by addressing identified regulatory and operational constraints.
- Implement measures to enhance economic co-operation to complement trade and investment liberalisation.
- To commence negotiations for Mutual Recognition Agreements (MRAs) and recognition of Product Standards.
- Additional flexibility in ROO criteria by abolition of the HS 4 digit level conversion requirement where DVA (domestic value addition) is more than 40%of the FOB of the finished products, dispensing the conversion requirement where CIF value of non domestic input is less than 7% of the FOB value of the finished products, adoption of 6digit HS conversion for identified tariff lines and encouragement of exporters of both countries to source inputs of each others.
- A verification procedure for ROO is to be institutionalized for further refine the process of issuance of Certificate of Origins.
- Customs departments of both countries to adopt risk management procedures on high-risk goods and clear low risk goods through the green channels.
- Institutionalise the paperless trading system and on priority basis at the major ports of Mumbai, Chennai, Nhava Sheva and Colombo.
- Identification and elimination of Non Tariff Barriers and adoption of full transparent mechanisms.

POTENTIAL AREAS FOR INDIANS TO INVEST IN SRILANKA

A list of illustrative but not exhaustive areas, as suggested by a study[13] conducted by FICCI, where Indian investors could exploit their comparative advantages are;

Port Development, Information & Communication Technology Projects, Rail Transportation, Petroleum Exploration, Power Generation & Transmission, Film & Entertainment, Tourism, Infrastructure Development, Research and Development in Biotechnology & Agriculture, Land Bridge connecting India with Srilanka, Health and Education etc.

9

FRAMEWORK AGREEMENT FOR ESTABLISHING FREE TRADE AREA BETWEEN THE REPUBLIC OF INDIA AND THE KINGDOM OF THAILAND

India and Thailand have agreed upon a Frame Work Agreement for establishing an India-Thailand FTA (the agreement can be accessed at: http://www.commerce.nic.in/india_thailand_fta.htm) with a view to strengthening and enhancing liberalization of trade through the following:

- Progressive elimination of tariffs and non-tariff barriers substantially in all trade in goods. (**Article3**)
- Progressive liberalization of trade in services between the countries with substantial sectoral coverage by progressive elimination of substantially all discrimination, prohibition of new or more discriminatory measures [except for measures permitted under Article V (1)(b) of the General Agreement on Trade in Services (GATS)], expansion in the depth and scope of liberalisation of trade in services and enhanced co-operation in services to improve efficiency and competitiveness. (**Article 4**)
- Establishment of an open and competitive investment regime that facilitates, protect and promotes bi-lateral investment. The provisions of the Agreement for the Promotion and Protection of Investments signed on 10 July 2000 by both the countries shall also be referred in applicable cases. (**Article 5**)
- Establishment of effective trade & investment facilitation measures and expansion of economic co-operation. (**Article 6**)
- Any Country may take action and adopt measures for the protection of its national security or the protection of articles of artistic, historic and archaeological value, or such other

measures which it deems necessary for the protection of public morals or for the protection of human, animal or plant life, health and conservation of exhaustible natural resources. However, these actions or measures should not be taken in an arbitrary or unjustifiable discrimination manner. **(Article 9)**

- Any dispute arising between the Parties regarding interpretation, application or implementation of this Agreement shall be settled amicably through consultations. **(Article 10)**

The Agreement was signed on 9th October 2003 at Bangkok among the Minister of Commerce of both the countries. A **PROTOCOL to amend the said agreement** was signed on 30th August 2004 at New Delhi.

TRADE IN GOODS (ARTICLE 3)

1. Duties and other restrictive commercial regulations shall be eliminated on substantially all trade in goods, with exceptions to those permitted under Article XXIV (8)(b) of the WTO General Agreement on Tariffs and Trade (GATT) 1994.
2. The tariff reduction or elimination program of the Countries shall require tariffs on listed products to be gradually reduced and where applicable, eliminated, in accordance with this Article.
3. Under the tariff reduction or elimination program under this Article, products shall be categorised into two tracks, namely, the **Normal Track** and the **Sensitive Track** and they should not have been included *by the Early Harvest Scheme under Article 7 of this Agreement.*
4. The commitments undertaken by the Countries under this Article and Article 7 of this Agreement shall fulfill the WTO requirements to eliminate tariffs on substantially all the trade between the Countries.
5. Any Country may accelerate its tariff reduction or elimination programme than the limits agreed, if it so desires.
6. Application of GATT/ WTO principles shall be made incase of Safeguard Actions, Subsidies & Countervailing Measures, Anti-Dumping Measures, Dispute Settlement Mechanism

and protection of intellectual property rights based on existing WTO Agreements, World Intellectual Property Organisation (WIPO) and other relevant disciplines.

AREAS OF ECONOMIC COOPERATION (ARTICLE 6)

A. The countries agree to strengthen their cooperation, but not limited to, in the following areas:

- ✓ Trade Facilitation: Mutual Recognition Arrangements (MRAs), conformity assessment, accreditation procedures, and standards and technical regulations, Removal of non-tariff barriers (NTBs), Customs cooperation, Trade finance, Business visa and travel facilitation.
- ✓ Sectors of Cooperation: Fisheries and Aquaculture, Information & Communications Technology, Space Technology, Biotechnology, Finance and Banking, Tourism, Infrastructure Development, Health Care, Construction, Education and Government Procurement.
- ✓ Trade and Investment Promotion: trade and investment fairs and exhibitions, India-Thailand portal and business sector dialogues.

B. Co-operation shall be extended to other areas, including, but not limited to; industrial cooperation, intellectual property rights, small and medium enterprises (SMEs), civil aviation, environment, forestry and forestry products, mining, energy and sub-regional development.

C. Measures to strengthen co-operation shall include, but not be limited to; promotion & facilitation of trade in goods, services and investment, increasing the competitiveness of SMEs, promotion of electronic commerce, capacity building & technology transfer.

TIMEFRAMES (ARTICLE 8)

1. For trade in goods; the negotiations for tariff reductions or elimination and other matters as set out in Article 3 of this Agreement shall commence in January 2004 and be concluded by March 2005 in order to establish the India-Thailand FTA covering trade in goods by 2010.
2. For trade in services and investments; the negotiations on the respective agreements shall commence in January 2004 and be concluded by January 2006. The identification and

liberalisation of the sectors of services and investment shall be finalised for implementation subsequently in accordance with the timeframes to be mutually agreed, taking into account the sensitive sectors of the Countries.

3. For other areas of economic cooperation under Article 6; the Countries shall continue to build upon existing or agreed programmes set out in that Article, develop new economic cooperation programmes, and conclude agreements on other areas of economic cooperation.

INSTITUTIONAL ARRANGEMENTS FOR THE NEGOTIATIONS (ARTICLE 11)

1. The India-Thailand Trade Negotiating Committee (TNC) shall be established to carry out the program of negotiations.
2. The India-Thailand TNC may co-opt other members/experts and/or set up working groups as may be necessary to assist the negotiations from time to time.
3. The countries can establish other mechanisms, which may be necessary to coordinate and implement any economic cooperation activities undertaken pursuant to the Agreement.

EARLY HARVEST SCHEME (ARTICLE 7)

An Early Harvest Scheme (EHS) has been adopted by both the countries covering 82 products for duty free imports. Initially, when the Framework Agreement was signed, 84 products were included in the EHS. However, later on products under HS Code 390210 (Polypropylene, In Primary Forms) and 390760 (Polyethylene Terephthalate In Primary Forms) were excluded from the list of EHS under the PROTOCOL to amend the Agreement signed on 30.08.2004. Application of non-tariff measures adversely affecting trade on early harvest products is discouraged. The products covered under the EHS are mentioned in the **ANNEXURE-IV**.

Application of WTO provisions

The WTO provisions governing modification of commitments, safeguard actions and other trade remedies, including anti-dumping and subsidies and countervailing measures, are in the interim, applicable to the products covered under the Early Harvest Scheme and may be superseded and replaced by the relevant disciplines negotiated and agreed to by the Parties under Article 3(6) of the Agreement at a later stage.

Tariff Reduction and Elimination:

a. The products covered under the EHS are subjected to the following tariff reduction and elimination:

Original Period	Amended Period as per the PROTOCOL to amend the Frame Work Agreement	Tariff reduction on applied MFN tariff rates as of 1st January 2004
1.3.2004-28.2.2005	1.9.2004- 31.8.2005	50%
1.3.2005-28.2.2006	1.9.2005- 31.8.2006	75%
1.3.2006	1.9.2006	100%

b. All products where the applied MFN tariff rates are 0% shall remain at 0%.

c. Where the implemented tariff rates are reduced to 0%, they shall remain at 0%.

Trade Remedies and Emergency Measures:

Provisional suspension in giving preferential treatment to any product being covered under EHS is possible, if it is proved that; the manner and increased quantity of import of such product into the importing Country has either caused or threatened to cause serious injury to the domestic producers of such product in the importing Country. However there should be prior consultations with the other country, which need to be concluded within 90 days or on any mutually agreed timeframe from the date of notification.

INTERIM RULES OF ORIGIN (IRO):

The Interim Rules of Origin applicable to the products covered under the Early Harvest Scheme for products originating from either of the countries and shall be further negotiated by the Sub-group of Expert on Rules of Origin. The Interim Rules of Origin shall be superseded and replaced by the Rules of Origin to be negotiated and implemented by the Parties under Article 3(6)(ii) of the Agreement. **To qualify under the EHS, the ROO criteria stipulate for minimum value addition of 40%. Both change in tariff heading and product specific rules have been prescribed.**

A. Products which are wholly obtained or produced (IRO 5) and Products not wholly produced or obtained but eligible under IRO 6 or 7, and 8 are defined as products originated in the exporting country. (**IRO 4**)

B. Products *wholly produced or obtained* in a country shall include; Plant and plant products harvested or grown, Live animals born & raised there and products obtained from them, Products obtained by hunting, trapping, fishing or aquaculture conducted there, Minerals and other naturally occurring substances extracted or taken from its soil, waters, seabed or beneath their seabed, Products taken from the water, seabed or beneath the seabed outside the territorial waters of a country, provided that the country has the rights to exploit such places in accordance with the United Nations Convention on the Law of the sea, Products of sea fishing and other marine products taken from outside its territory by its vessels and Products processed and/or made on board its factory ships exclusively from these items, Articles collected there and fit only for disposal or recovery of parts of raw materials or for recycling purposes and Products obtained or produced in a country solely from products referred to the previous cases. (**IRO 5**)

C. Provided that the final process of the manufacture is performed within the territory of the exporting Country and subject to Rule 8, For products *not-wholly produced or obtained* (**IRO 6**);

- *Local value added content criterion* and change *in tariff classification criterion* between the export product and all non-originating materials used in its production should be applied.
- Products specified in **PSR** which fulfill one or a combination of the above criteria shall be considered as originating from the exporting Country
- For the products not specified in **PSR** , the following criteria shall be applied: local value added content of 40% of the FOB value of the product so produced or obtained and change in tariff heading at the 4 digit level of Harmonised System where the final export product is classified differently from all the non-originating materials used in its production.
- The formula for calculation of local value added content is as follows:

% of Local Value Added Content (LVAC)=
{(FOB value of the export product - Value of non originating materials)/ FOB value of the export product}*100

> ➢ The value of the non-originating materials shall be; either the CIF value at the time of importation of the materials or the earliest ascertained price paid for the materials of undetermined origin in the territory of the Country where the processing takes place.

D. Products complying with origin requirements provided for in IRO 4 and used as inputs for a finished product eligible for preferential treatment shall be considered as products originating in the exporting country (***Cumulation***) subject to fulfillment of conditions of IRO 8 and that the aggregate India-Thailand value added content on the final product is not less than 40% or the local value added content specified for products in product specific rules. **(IRO 7)**

E. The *minimal operations or processes* considered to be insufficient to confer the status of originating products, whether or not there is a change in tariff classification have been defined as; operations to ensure the preservation during transport and storage, simple operations consisting of removal of dust, sifting, sorting, washing, painting, cutting etc., changes of packing and breaking up and assembly of consignments, Simple slicing, and repacking, affixing of marks, labels or other like distinguishing signs, simple mixing of products, simple assembly of parts of products, disassembly, slaughter of animals, mere dilution with water or another substance not materially altering the characteristics of the goods, simple cleaning, including removal of oxide, oil, paint or other coverings, oil application and a combination of any of these two operations. **(IRO 8)**

F. The packages and packing materials shall not be taken into account for considering whether all non-originating materials used in the manufacture of a product fulfill the criterion corresponding to a *CTH* of the said product, but shall be taken into account in its origin assessment in case of ad *valor percentage criterion*, if they are treated as being one for customs purposes with the products in question. The containers and packing materials exclusively used for the transport of a product shall not be taken into account for determining the origin of any product. (**IRO 10**)

G. Accessories, spare parts and tools delivered with a product that form part of the product's standard accessories, spare parts and tools (to be billed combine with the original product) as per standard trade practice prevailing in the exporting country, shall be treated as originating products if the product is an originating product and shall be disregarded in determining change in tariff classification for non-originating materials, provided that the local value added content criterion shall also be calculated accordingly in applicable cases.(**IRO 11)**

H. An indirect material shall be treated as an originating material without regard to where it is produced and its value shall be the cost registered in the accounting records of the producer of the export product. **(IRO 12)**

I. Generally accepted accounting principles of stock control applicable in the exporting country shall be used for the purposes of determining origin of identical and interchangeable originating and non-originating materials. **(IRO 13)**

J. Products sent from an exporting country for exhibition in another country and sold during or after the exhibition for importation into the importing country shall benefit from the preferential tariff treatment. These provisions shall apply to any exhibitions, fairs or similar shows or displays where the products remain under Customs control during these events. (**IRO 19)**

10

COMPREHENSIVE ECONOMIC COOPERATION AGREEMENT (CECA) BETWEEN THE REPUBLIC OF INDIA AND THE REPUBLIC OF SINGAPORE

SALIENT FEATURES OF THE CECA

(The agreement can be accessed at: http://www.commerce.nic.in/ceca/toc.htm)

- The Declaration of Intent was signed on 8th April 2003 at New Delhi.
- The final Agreement was signed by the Prime Minister of both the countries at New Delhi on 29th June 2005 and it became effective from 1st August 2005.
- Comprehensive enough to cover major sectors and areas of trade.
- Each Country shall designate a *contact point* to facilitate communications between the Countries.
- The countries may adopt mutual consultations for settlement of any matter affecting the implementation, interpretation or application of CECA. They have also the option for referring the matter to an Arbitral Tribunal. The detailed procedure for constitution, style of functioning, proceedings and method of issuing award in regard to the arbitral tribunal have been provided in the CHAPTER 15 on Dispute Settlement.
- The Countries have undertaken to develop and promote mutually beneficial co-operation between themselves in the area of intellectual property rights and rights in plant varieties.

Structure of the Agreement and Annexes

The original agreement contains 17 chapters and 24 annexes (including 9 Exchange of Letters as annexes).

Chapter 0	Preamble
Chapter 1	Objectives and General Definitions
Chapter 2	Trade in Goods
Chapter 3	Rules of Origin
Chapter 4	Customs
Chapter 5	Standards
Chapter 6	Investment
Chapter 7	Services
Chapter 8	Air services
Chapter 9	Movement of Natural Persons
Chapter 10	E-Commerce
Chapter 11	Intellectual Property Cooperation
Chapter 12	Science and Technology
Chapter 13	Education
Chapter 14	Media
Chapter 15	Dispute Settlement
Chapter 16	General and Final Provisions
Annex 2A	India's Tariff Concession
Annex 2B	Singapore's Tariff Concession
Annex 3A	Product Specific Rule
Annex 3B	Operational Certification Procedure
Annex 5A	Sectoral Annex of Telecommunications Equipments
Annex 5B	Sectoral Annex on Food Products
Annex 5C	Sectoral Annex on Electronics and Electronic Equipments
Annex 6A	India's Schedule of Commitments for Investment
Annex 6B	Singapore's Reservations on Investment
Annex 7A	India's Schedule of Commitment for Services
Annex 7B	Singapore's Schedule of Commitment for Services
Annex 7C	Financial Services
Annex 7D	Telecommunications Services
Annex 9A	List of Professionals
Annex 14A	Framework for Media Cooperation

Exchange of Letter with Annexes

a. De Minimis and Outward Processing (Annex 1)

b. Standards and Technical Regulations, Sanitary and Phytosanitary Measures (Annex 2)

c. Expropriation (Annex 3)

d. Security Exceptions for Investment (Annex 4)

e. Non-justiciability of Security Exceptions (Annex 5)

f. Compulsory Investor-to-State-Dispute In Relation to Pre-establishment (Annex 6)

g. Aggregation of Shares (Annex 7)

h. Security Exceptions for Services (Annex 8)

i. Cooperation on Financial Services (Annex 9)

ANALYSIS OF THE AGREEMENT AND ANNEXES RELATED WITH TRADE IN GOODS

Trade in Goods

- Each Country shall reduce and/or eliminate its customs duties on imports from the other Country in accordance with Annex 2A and Annex 2B and their respective head notes.
- Both the countries may adopt steps to accelerate the programme for reduction and/or elimination of customs duties before the period specified in these annexes.
- Non Tariff Measures are not to be imposed by any of the country on imports or exports effected by the other country, unless it become necessary and the WTO rules along with the other provisions of this agreement allow a country to do so.
- Determination of customs value of the goods traded shall be done in accordance with the provisions of Article VII of the GATT 1994 and the WTO Agreement on Implementation of Article VII of the GATT 1994.
- Anti-Dumping actions on applicable products is possible by giving 7 working days advance notice to the other country (notice may be communicated to the contact point of the other country) about the investigation. Provision of the WTO Anti-Dumping Agreement along with CECA shall be applicable in such cases.

- Provisions of the WTO Agreement on Subsidies and Countervailing Measures is also applicable in cases where substantial import of any such product availing subsidies causes serious injury or threat of serious injury to domestic industry producing a like or directly competitive product in any country.
- In such cases; either reduction in preferential treatment for customs duty or increase of customs duty up to the level of MFN rate is possible. In the case of a customs duty applied to a good on a seasonal basis, increase is possible up to the level of the MFN applied rate of customs duty that was in effect on the good for the corresponding season immediately preceding the date of the start of the period of investigation.
- The investigation shall be promptly terminated and no measure taken if imports of the subject good represent less than 2 per cent of market share in terms of domestic sales or less than 3 per cent of total imports. The investigation shall in all cases be completed within one year following its date of initiation.
- The safeguard measures shall be taken maximum up to two years from the date of first imposition of the measure and up to three years in exceptional circumstances.
- No bilateral safeguard measure shall be taken against a particular good while a global safeguard measure in respect of that good is in place. When a global safeguard measure is taken in respect of a particular good, any existing bilateral safeguard measure against that good shall be terminated.
- Within 5 years after entry into force of this Agreement, the Countries shall meet to review the need to maintain any bilateral safeguard mechanism at all.
- The Country proposing to apply a safeguard measure shall provide to the other Country mutually agreed adequate means of trade liberalizing compensation in the form of concessions having substantially equivalent trade effects or equivalent to the value of the additional duties expected to result from the measure.
- If the Countries are unable to agree on compensation within 30 days in the consultations, the exporting country may take action having trade effects substantially equivalent to the

measure applied by the importing country. This action shall be applied only for the minimum period necessary to achieve the substantially equivalent effects.

- Such compensation shall not be provided if the measure is applied for either up to two years *or* up to three years and in the later case, the country imposing the measures provides evidence to the other Country that the industry concerned is adjusting during the period up to the end of the second year respectively.
- Each country retains its rights and obligations under Article XIX of GATT 1994 and the WTO Agreement on Safeguards. A country taking a safeguard measure under Article XIX and the Agreement on Safeguards may, to the extent consistent with the obligations under the WTO Agreements, exclude imports of an originating good from the other country if such imports are not a substantial cause of serious injury or threat thereof.
- Article XII of the GATT 1994 and the Understanding on the Balance-of-Payments Provisions of the GATT 1994 shall be incorporated into and made a part of this Agreement, for measures taken for balance of payments purposes for trade in goods.
- A Country is not prevented from maintaining or establishing a state trading enterprise in accordance with Article XVII of the GATT 1994.
- Each Country shall accept ATA carnets valid for its territory and issued & used in accordance with the conditions laid down in the ATA Carnet Convention in lieu of its national customs documents and due security, for temporary admission of professional equipment necessary for representatives of the press or of broadcasting or television organizations for purposes of reporting or to transmit or record material for specified programs, cinematographic equipment necessary in order to make a specified film or films or other professional equipment necessary in this regard.

RULES OF ORIGIN

- The ROOs conform to the origin requirement for both Products *wholly produced or obtained* and *Products not wholly produced or obtained* in the exporting country.

- Detailed list of goods considered as being *wholly obtained or produced* in a country are mentioned under Article 3.3. The list normally represents the minerals, animals, goods extracted from soil, waters, seabed or beneath the seabed of a country.
- Subject to the provisions of Article 3.6 (insufficient operations), 3.9 (accumulation) and that the final process of manufacturing is performed within the territory of the exporting Country, products which are *not wholly obtained or produced* would be considered as originating if the Local Value Added Content is more than 40% of the FOB value of the product, the product has undergone change of classification at the 4 digit HS Code level than its non-originating constituents and the product satisfies the Product Specific Rules (PSR) specified in Annex 3B.
- For the purposes of calculating the local value added content; either of the following methods can be applied: (a) Direct Method: *{(Value of Originating materials +Direct Labour Cost+ Direct Overhead Cost+ Profit)/ FOB Price} x 100 % is greater or equal to 40%}* or (b) Indirect Method: *{(Value of Non-originating materials /FOB Price) x 100 % is less or equal to 60%.*
- In order to determine whether a product originates in the territory of a Country, any indirect material used to obtain such products shall be treated as originating whether such material originates in third countries or not, and its value shall be the cost registered in the accounting records of the producer of the good.
- The operations or processes which shall not be considered as sufficient transformation provided for in Article 3.4 are; operations to ensure the preservation of products in good condition during transport and storage, simple operations consisting of removal of dust, sifting or screening, sorting, classifying, matching, washing, painting, cutting, changes of packing and breaking up and assembly of consignments, simple cutting, slicing and repacking or placing in bottles, flasks, bags, boxes, fixing on cards or boards, and all other simple packing operations, affixing of marks, labels or other like distinguishing signs, simple mixing of products, simple

assembly of parts, disassembly, slaughter of animals, mere dilution with water or another substance that does not materially alter the characteristics of the goods and a combination of two or more of these operations.

- The value of a non-originating material used in the production of a good shall be; the CIF value at the time of importation for imported materials and/or the earliest price as ascertained by the certifying authority to have been paid for in the exporting Country for materials of undetermined origin.
- A product manufactured in one Country and used in the territory of the other Country as a material for the finished product shall be considered as a product originating in the territory of the latter Country provided that it complies with the origin requirements provided for in Articles 3.3 or 3.4 and 3.6 (ACCUMULATION)
- Accessories, spare parts and tools delivered with a product that form part of the product's standard accessories, spare parts and tools (to be billed combine with the original product) as per standard trade practice prevailing in the exporting country, shall be treated as originating products if the product is an originating product and shall be disregarded in determining change in tariff classification for non-originating materials, provided that the local value added content criterion shall also be calculated accordingly in applicable cases.
- The packages and packing materials shall not be taken into account for considering whether all non-originating materials used in the manufacture of a product fulfill the criterion corresponding to a *CTH* of the said product, but shall be taken into account in its origin assessment in case of *ad valorem percentage criterion*, if they are treated as being one for customs purposes with the products in question. The containers and packing materials exclusively used for the transport of a product shall not be taken into account for determining the origin of any product
- Where identical and interchangeable originating and non-originating materials including materials of undetermined origin are used in the manufacture of a product; those

materials shall be physically segregated according to their origin, during storage. In case of real difficulties in segregation; "accounting segregation" method for managing stocks may be followed by the producer.

- The accounting method shall be recorded, applied and maintained in accordance with generally accepted accounting principles applicable in the Country in which the product is manufactured. The method chosen must permit a clear distinction to be made between originating & non-originating materials including materials of undetermined origin acquired and/or kept in stock and guarantee the status of segregation.
- Detailed provisions regarding **Advance Rulings** have been provided in Article 3.13.

CUSTOMS

- A Country shall adopt, apply, further develop and exchange information on the risk management techniques in its customs activities based on its identified risk of goods in order to facilitate the clearance of low risk consignments, while focusing its inspection activities on high-risk goods. Accordingly, each Country undertakes that customs compliance activities at the time of entry shall not normally exceed 5 per cent of total customs transactions.
- The Countries shall co-operate AND exchange views and information on realizing, promoting and developments in paperless trading.
- The Countries shall apply *Advance Rulings* in accordance with the provisions of Article 3.13.

STANDARDS AND TECHNICAL REGULATIONS, SANITARY AND PHYTOSANITARY MEASURES

- Each Country shall implement the principles of reciprocal mutual recognition that provide the most appropriate or cost-efficient approach to the removal or reduction of technical, sanitary and phyto sanitary barriers to the trade in goods between the countries for products and/or conformity assessments of manufacturers/manufacturing processes of products specified in the Sectoral Annexes to Chapter 5.

- Each Country shall accept the test reports and/or results of conformity assessment activities stipulated by the mandatory requirements of that Country specified in the relevant Sectoral Annex, including certificates and marks of conformity that are conducted by the registered conformity assessment bodies of the other Country.
- Countries are encouraged to harmonise their respective mandatory requirements taking into account relevant international standards, recommendations and guidelines in accordance with their international rights and obligations.
- Article 2.4 of the WTO Agreement on Technical Barriers to Trade shall be applicable where adoption of international standards and technical regulation is required.
- A Country shall accept the test reports and/or the results of conformity assessment activities undertaken by registered conformity assessment bodies of the other Country.
- The Countries shall give favourable consideration to accepting the equivalence of each other's mandatory
- Requirements consistent with the purpose of Chapter 5 and the WTO Agreement on the Application of Sanitary and Phytosanitary Measures.
- A Joint Committee on Mutual Recognition ("Mutual Recognition Joint Committee") led by co-chairs from both Countries and comprising an equal number of senior representatives from both countries shall be
- Established. The Joint Committee shall be responsible for administering, facilitating and enlarging the effective functioning of this Chapter 5 and the Sectoral Annexes. Apart from acting as a consultative body, it shall also undertake the administration procedures. Both the countries shall seek an amicable solution through the Mutual Recognition Joint Committee before making a request for an arbitral tribunal being appointed.
- Annex 5A, Annex 5B and Annex 5C are the sectoral annexes, which provide the detailed implementing arrangements in respect of the product sectors specified therein.

INVESTMENT

- Investment has been described broadly to mean every kind of asset and includes; movable & immovable property, other property rights, shares, stocks, debentures & similar interests in companies, rights to money or to any performance under contract having a financial value, intellectual property rights, goodwill, technical processes, know-how as conferred by law or under contract, business concessions conferred by law or under contract including concessions to search, extract or exploit oil, minerals and other natural resources.
- Each Country shall accord national treatment to investors and their investments of the other Country in relation to the establishment, acquisition or expansion of investments in the sectors listed at Annex 6A and Annex 6B. This treatment shall be extended to the management, conduct, operation, liquidation, sale and transfer (or other disposition) of investments.
- Investors of one country whose investments in the other country suffer losses owing to war or other armed conflict, a state of emergency or civil disturbances in the territory of the later Country, shall be accorded national treatment by that country as regards restitution, indemnification, compensation or other settlement, if any. Any payments in this regard shall be freely transferable.
- Each Country shall ensure to investors of the other Country the free transfer of their capital and the returns from any investments. The transfers shall be permitted in a freely useable currency at the market rate prevailing in the date of transfer without undue delay. A Country may adopt or maintain restrictions on payments or transfers related to investments only in the event of serious balance of payments and external financial difficulties or threat thereof.
- A country or any designated authority may exercise its rights of subrogation to indemnify its own investors. But such subrogated rights or claims shall not be greater than the original rights or claims of the said investor.
- The Schedule of Specific Commitments that India undertakes are set out in Annex 6A, which specifies the

terms, limitations, conditions and qualifications on national treatment in relation to paragraph 1 of Article 6.3.

- In the case of Singapore, the exceptions and measures specified by Singapore with respect to sectors, sub sectors or activities are set out in its Schedule of Reservations at Annex 6B.
- Each country shall provide national treatment to the investors of the other country with respect to access to its courts of justice, administrative tribunals and agencies in all degrees of jurisdiction both in pursuit and in defence of such investors' rights.
- India shall consider on a case-by-case basis requests from Singapore investors for exemptions from custom duties for import of capital goods (excluding consumables) for the purposes of infrastructure projects in India. Such projects may include but not limited to the sectors like; roads & highways, ports, other sea port related infrastructure like logistics, airports, other aviation related infrastructure, power (generation, transmission & distribution), water resource management, waste management, other urban infrastructure such as pollution control and management, housing including townships and telecommunications. **No reciprocal commitment is given by singapore. Is it that; singapore does not need any more improvement in existing infrastructure or they just do not want indian investment in the infrastructure sector in their country?**
- If the disputes related to investment issues can not be resolved within six months from the date of request for consultations and negotiations, the investor may submit the dispute to either the courts or administrative tribunals of the disputing Country OR The International Centre for Settlement of Investment Disputes (ICSID) for conciliation or arbitration OR hold arbitration under the rules of the United Nations Commission on International Trade Law (UNCITRAL).
- Provisions of the WTO Agreement on Trade-Related Investment Measures ("TRIMs") are applicable.

- In case the Agreement is terminated, the provisions of Chapter 6 related to Investments, the provisions in Chapter 15 and other provisions in the Agreement necessary for or consequential to the application of Chapter 6 shall continue in effect with respect to investments made or acquired before the date of termination of this Agreement for a further period of fifteen years after the date of termination and without prejudice to the application thereafter of the rules of general international law.

TRADE IN SERVICES

- Market access treatment under different modes of supply of services and service suppliers of the other Country to be no less favourable than Schedule of specific commitments.
- Unless otherwise specified in its Schedule of specific commitments in sectors where market access commitments are undertaken, a country shall not maintain or adopt measures either on the basis of a regional subdivision or on the basis of its entire territory about; limitations on the number of service suppliers, the total value of service transactions or assets, the total number of service operations or on the total quantity of service output, the total number of natural persons that may be employed in a particular service sector or that a service supplier may employ persons necessary for & directly related to the supply of a specific service, measures which restrict or require specific types of legal entity or joint venture through which a service supplier may supply a service and limitations on the quantum of foreign capital investment.
- Each Country shall accord national treatment to services and service suppliers of the other country.
- Any subsequent establishment, acquisition and expansion of investments by a service supplier of the other country shall be regarded as an investment of the other country, for the purpose of determining the applicable national treatment.
- Review of schedules of specific commitments of each country shall be done at least once in every three years.
- Recognition of education or experience obtained, requirements met and licenses or certifications of the service provider granted in the other country.

- Monopolistic suppliers of a service are to be monitored in the relevant market for their action in a manner inconsistent with their country's Schedule of specific commitments. Abusing the monopoly position by such service providers inconsistent with such commitments to be regulated by the country concerned.
- Neither Country shall take safeguard action against nor initiate or continue any safeguard investigations in respect of services and service suppliers of the other Country. Review of the issue of safeguard measures to be done in the context of developments in international foray of which both countries are members.
- A Country shall not apply restrictions on international transfers and payments for current transactions relating to its specific commitments unless serious balance of payments and external financial difficulties or threat thereof arises. Prompt notification & consultations should be made to the other country in this regard.
- Linkage between investments and services sector provided.

AIR SERVICES

The Countries recognise the strategic partnership in civil aviation and the importance of air connectivity to support the expansion of tourism, trade and investments between the Countries. To facilitate the implementation, as well as to fully harness the benefits of this Agreement, the Countries shall review and enhance their bilateral ASA and explore further areas of mutually beneficial co-operation. **Article 8.8**

MOVEMENT OF NATURAL PERSONS

- Neither Country shall require labour market testing, economic needs testing or other procedures of similar effects as a condition for temporary entry in respect of natural persons. No contributions to social security funds required and denial of social security benefits in the host country in case of temporary entry.
- Five-year multiple journey visa to be granted to eligible business visitors with easy procedures.
- Maximum 180 days immigration visa allowed to eligible short-term service suppliers.

- Grant of long term temporary entry to eligible intra-corporate transferees up to an extended period of stay of three years at a time and a total term up to eight years.
- Grant of temporary entry and stay for up to one year to professionals to perform training functions related to a particular profession including conducting seminars.
- Grant of entry and working visas to spouses or dependants of persons who have been granted the long-term temporary entry.
- Transparency and maintenance of authorized contact points to help the persons eligible for temporary entry.

E-COMMERCE

- No customs duties in connection with the importation or exportation of digital products by electronic transmission.
- The customs value of imported carrier media bearing digital products to be determined according to the cost or value of the carrier medium alone without regard to the cost or value of the digital products stored on the carrier medium.
- Equal treatment irrespective of nationality of the author (to be from either India or Singapore) shall be accorded to the digital products of the other Country in respect of all measures affecting the contracting for, commissioning, creation, publication, production, storage, distribution, marketing, sale, purchase, delivery or use of such digital products as given to the products of home front. No disguised restriction shall be maintained.
- Provisions do not apply to Government Procurement and the broadcasting sector.
- Transparency shall be maintained in respect of laws, regulations and measures of general application pertaining to electronic commerce.

SCIENCE AND TECHNOLOGY

- The Countries shall develop and promote co-operative activities between themselves for peaceful purposes in the field of science and technology on the basis of equality and mutual benefit.

- The areas of the co-operation may include research, design and development in marine biotechnology, agricultural biotechnology, space research, advanced materials, information technology and other areas.
- The forms of the co-operation may include exchange of information and data, joint seminars, workshops & meetings, visits and exchange of scientists, technical personnel or other experts including through participation in science and technology conferences and seminars, implementation of joint projects & programmes and commercialisation of technologies in both countries or any third country including participation in joint ventures.
- Scientific and technological information of a non-proprietary nature arising from Co-operative Activities may be made available to the public by the government of either Country. The Countries shall ensure the adequate and effective protection of intellectual property rights or other rights of a proprietary nature resulting from the Cooperative activities.

EDUCATION

- The Countries shall encourage close co-operation between their educational institutions.
- Both countries shall facilitate collaborations between the IITs, IISc, and the universities in Singapore to offer post-graduate research and education with industrial linkages to multinational and local companies based in India and Singapore.
- The degrees specified by the University Grants Commission of India & awarded by an approved university or deemed university or an Institution of National Importance of India and similarly degrees awarded by the universities in Singapore shall be recognised for the purposes of qualifying the holder to be considered for admission to the universities of both countries. However, complying with other admission conditions or requirements as may be imposed by the educational institutes in India or Singapore respectively shall still remain applicable.
- A *Joint Committee on Education* shall be established within 12 months from the effective date of this Agreement and its

functions shall be; overseeing & reviewing the co-operation and implementation of Chapter 13, identification & recommendation of areas of co-operation and encouragement of their implementation.

MEDIA

The Countries have agreed to exchange views and information on issues relating to the media sector which may include policy & regulatory framework for emerging media services, other issues concerning the media industry, approach to regulation of content, mechanism for promoting private sector activities and encouraging co-operation between their respective industries. A detailed framework for media co-operation is annexed to the agreement as Annex 14A.

ANNEX 2A: INDIA'S TARIFF CONCESSION (http://www.commerce.nic.in/ceca/anx2a.pdf)

The provisions of this schedule are expressed at the HS Code 8 digit level. The following modality shall apply for the elimination / reduction of basic customs duties by India:

List of Products for Early Harvest Programme:

On 506 products originating from Singapore, customs duties shall be eliminated entirely from 1st August 2005.

List of Products for Phased Elimination in Duty:

On 2202 products originating from Singapore, the duties shall be removed in five stages beginning from 1st August 2005 and such goods shall receive duty free entry into India from Singapore, effective 1st April 2009. The margin of preference offered by India has been indicated in the List.

1.8.2005	1.4.2006	1.4.2007	1.4.2008	1.4.2009
10%	25%	50%	75%	100%

List of Products for Phased Reduction in Duty:

On 2407 products originating from Singapore, the duties shall be reduced in five stages beginning 1st August 2005 and such goods shall receive entry into India at concessional duties. The margin of preference offered by India has been indicated in the List.

1.8.2005	1.4.2006	1.4.2007	1.4.2008	1.4.2009
5%	10%	20%	35%	50%

List of Products excluded from any concession in Duty:

No concessions in duties shall be offered on 6551 products goods provided in this List. Such goods whether originating or otherwise, shall enter into India from Singapore on the applied MFN duties.

Calculation of Margin of Preference: Margin of Preference (MOP) offered by India to Singapore on specific products, shall be calculated on the Most Favoured Nation (MFN) import duty applicable on the date of import. For example, if the MFN duty on a particular product is 20%, and India offers a MOP of 10% to Singapore, the duty reduction for import from Singapore will become 20% - 10% of 20% = 2%. Hence, the applicable rate of duty for that particular originating product coming from Singapore will be 20-2 = 18%. If the MOP of 100% is offered to Singapore, then such originating goods shall receive duty free entry into India from Singapore.

ANNEX 2B: SINGAPORE'S TARIFF CONCESSION

With effect from 1st August 2005, Singapore has eliminated customs duties on all originating goods from India.

ANNEX 3A: PRODUCT SPECIFIC RULES

Product Specific Rules have been provided in this annex for various products at HS Code 6 digit level.

ANNEX 3B: OPERATIONAL CERTIFICATION PROCEDURES

21 Rules containing provisions for operational procedures on the issuance & verification of the Certificate of Origin and other related administrative matters for implementation of the Rules of Origin have been provided.

ANNEX 1 : EXCHANGE OF LETTER DEFINING "DE MINIMIS" AND "OUTWARD PROCESSING"

1. *De Minimis* is understood to mean that a good would be considered as originating even if non-originating materials used in its manufacture do not undergo change in tariff heading as required in Article 3.4 of the Agreement, provided that the value of such non-originating materials does not exceed a certain percentage of the value of such a good.

2. *Outward Processing* is understood to mean that a good can be taken out of the territory of the exporting country to a third country for some processing and then brought back to the exporting country for the manufacture of the final product for exports. The concept accumulates only the value addition, which takes place in the territory of the exporting country at different stages, while disregarding the value addition, which takes place in the territory of the third country.

SECTION - IV

(Data Analysis & Comparisons)

Contents

SECTION – IV

(Data Analysis – Comparison)

Contents

BACKGROUND FOR DATA ANALYSIS [illegible]

[illegible] and CECA [illegible]

[illegible]

[illegible]

DETAILED DATA ANALYSIS FOR THE [illegible] FTA [illegible]

[illegible]

DETAILED DATA ANALYSIS FOR THE [illegible] WITH THAILAND [illegible]

[illegible]

DETAILED DATA ANALYSIS FOR THE CECA WITH SINGAPORE [illegible]

[illegible]

BACKGROUND FOR DATA ANALYSIS

The trade data for both imports from and exports to these three countries have been analysed at 8 digit HS Code level to visualize the impact caused by the FTAs. Data for these analysis have been sourced from the EXPORT IMPORT DATA BANK available online in the website of Director General of Foreign Trade, Govt. of India. The trade data for financial years 1998-99 to 2004-05 had been downloaded during April 2006. Cutoff date taken for sourcing of online data for full year of 2005-06 have been summarized below:

FTA	Cutoff Date taken for sourcing of Online Data for full year of 2005-06	Financial Years Analysed
INDO-SRILANKA FTA	31.08.2006	1998-99 to 2004-05
FTA WITH THAILAND	31.08.2006	1998-99 to 2004-05
CECA WITH SINGAPORE	07.09.2006	2003-04 to 2005-06 (value for imports only)

Since online data for full year of 2005-06 was made available in the first week of September 2006, the analysis has been restricted to period upto 2004-05 in cases of FTA with Srilanka and Thailand.

The following analysis have been done for these three FTAs:

INDO-SRILANKA FTA:

Data have been analysed from 1998-99 till 2004-05 (2004-05 being the latest full financial year for which trade data was available in the website of DGFT as on 31.08.06) in case of SRILANKA. The agreement was signed between India and Sri Lanka on 28 December 1998 and has been in operation since March 2000. The Tariff Rate Quota Mechanisms for the import of Tea and Garments were finalised in April 2000 in New Delhi.

IMPORTS FROM SRILANKA

- Trend Analysis for volume of goods imported from Srilanka for the sample products.
- Trend Analysis for volume of goods imported from World by India for the same sample products.
- Market Share (both volume-wise and value-wise) of sampled products imported from Srilanka over India's world import figures.
- Comparison of Unit Price of imports of sampled products imported from Srilanka over Unit Price of India's world import figures.
- Compounded Average Growth Rate (both volume-wise and value-wise) comparison among CAGR applicable incase of Srilanka with India's world imports.
- Correlation Analysis (using the MS-EXCEL spread sheet functions) among various data series like Correlation between trend of volume / value of imports from Srilanka.
  - Correlation between trend of volume / value of imports for all India.
  - Correlation between trend of volume of imports from Srilanka / total volume for all India.
  - Correlation between trend of value of imports from Srilanka / total value for all India.
  - Correlation between unit price of imports from Srilanka / unit price for all India.
- Trend Analysis of value of imports chapter wise under various categories of concession level for imports from Srilanka as well as India's world imports.
- Market Share of value of imports chapter wise under various categories of concession level for imports from Srilanka over India's world imports.
- CAGR of value of imports chapter wise under various categories of concession level for imports from Srilanka as well as India's world imports.
- Correlation of trend of value of imports chapter wise among imports from Srilanka with India's world imports.

EXPORTS TO SRILANKA

All such variety of analysis as done incase of imports from Srilanka have also been done incase of exports to Srilanka along with India's world exports.

FTA WITH THAILAND:

Data have been analysed from 2001-02 till 2004-05 (2004-05 being the latest full financial year for which trade data was available in the website of DGFT as on 31.08.06) in case of THAILAND. The Agreement was signed on 9th October 2003 at Bangkok between the Minister of Commerce of both the countries. A **PROTOCOL to amend the said agreement** was signed on 30th August 2004 at New Delhi. The relevant customs notifications have been effective from 01.09.2004. Variety of analysis done in case of Thailand for imports from / exports to Thailand are similar with the variety of analysis done in case of imports from / exports to Srilanka.

CECA WITH SINGAPORE:

The final Agreement was signed by both the countries on 29th June 2005 and it became effective from 1st August 2005. Online data for the full year of 2005-06 was made available in the DGFT website after 31.08.2006. Since, the cut off date for submission of the dissertation with ICAI was **already** extended up to 30.09.2006, it was not possible to do full fledged analysis like Thailand and Srilanka.

The following analysis have been done in case of imports from Singapore:

- Data for value of imports from Singapore have been analysed from 2003-04 to 2005-06.
- The sample drawn was on the basis of high value products at 8 digit HS Code level imported from Singapore during 2004-05. Products having value of imports more than 0.1% of the total value of imports during 2004-05 have been taken as the sample.
- Trend Analysis of Value of Imports from Singapore for the sampled products.
- CAGR calculation of the Sampled products.
- Reporting of cases where Indian Industry needs to be alerted because of increase in imports of the sampled products (Chapter wise and products wise) at various concession levels.

Since Singapore has offered duty free access to all goods originating from India, it is a good cause for the Indian industry to cheers up. I feel it will be very early to study the impact of opening of the exports market and considering the time constraint of submitting the dissertation latest by 30.09.2006, the analysis portion have been postponed at this moment. I feel that; it is time for our industries to increase their capacity, quality and visibility of their products so that, exports trade with Singapore can zoom in near future.

BASIS OF SAMPLING

The basis of sampling is similar in case of all three countries. The analysis has been done at 8 digit HS Code level. Products of High Value of imports / exports during the year 2004-05 have been sampled out of the total population. Products whose value of imports / exports are more than 0.1 % of total value of imports / exports during 2004-05 were taken in the samples applicable to a particular country. Details have been given under the country wise analysis, which follow below.

YARD STICKS FOR MEASURING THE GROWTH OF A GROUP OF PRODUCTS / CHAPTERS

Weighted Average CAGR of the sampled products /chapters

The Weighted Average CAGR of the sampled products have been taken as the yardstick for measuring the growth rate for the total sample of products under consideration. The Weighted Average CAGR has been derived by dividing the Sum of CAGR FACTORS (CAGR FACTOR was derived by multiplying the CAGR of a product with value of imports from / exports to a country in 2004-05 of that product) with the sum of values of imports from / exports to that country in 2004-05 of the sample products under consideration. Similar method is adopted to derive the Weighted Average CAGR for a category of products and chapters under different category.

Movement of Sum Factors of the Sampled Products /chapters

Sum of the yearly factors derived by dividing the sum of values of imports / exports from / to a country with sum of values of imports / exports from / to the world for a group of products / chapters have been plotted in graphs. The factors signify the market share of total value wise imports / exports from / to a country with total value wise imports / exports from / to the world. A rising curve indicates the growth in trade as the % share moves up. A declining curve indicates the decline in trade the % share moves down.

$$\text{Sum Factor of a year} = \frac{\text{(sum of value of imports / exports from/ to the specific country)}}{\text{(Sum of value of imports / exports from/ to the world)}}$$

12

SUMMARIES OF DATA ANALYSIS

SUMMARY OF DATA ANALYSIS IN CASE OF INDO-SRILANKA FTA

Imports

- The FTA has caused significant growth in imports.
- The varieties of parameters of the high value items have shown positive growth rate after the FTA is implemented. The growth under the FTA has exceeded the growth of world imports of India under different parameters also.
- The surge in imports observed in selected cases have shown that; in a selected cases like products of Copper, Spices & Vanaspati / edible oils etc., there is total trade diversion to Srilanka. However the over all growth pattern shows trade creation in imports as value wise India's imports from the world have also been risen a number of times. Even imports of some of the products covered under the Negative list also have grown fast.
- The correlation factors in most of the products are closure to +1 suggesting that the trend patterns are positively correlative in nature.

Exports

- The FTA alone has not caused significant growth in exports; the rise in exports to Srilanka can be attributed to other factors like competitiveness of the Indian products, general trend in growth in world exports and geographical proximity to Srilanka etc. also.
- The variety of parameters of the high value items have shown moderate growth rate. A lot of products showing high growth are covered under either the Negative List or Other Items at MFN Rate.
- The correlations among different trend series are positive.

- It can be the significance of the fact that, exports to Srilanka has risen along with India's total exports to the world. The export policy along with the competitiveness of the Indian products may be the reason that has added momentum to the FTA.
- The FTA has not benefited much to Indian exporters in comparison to their surge in exports to the whole world.

Overall

- The FTA has helped boosting export trade of Srilanka rather than boosting the exports from India. The growth in exports to Srilanka has been synonymous with increase in India's world exports. The value addition because of concessional duty offered by Srilanka is not of much significance, as most of the items of exports interest to India have remained outside the concession list provided by Srilanka.
- The opposite thing has happened in case of imports from Srilanka. The rise in imports trade has been due to the FTA narrating the acceptances by India to the concessions seek by Srilanka for their products of interest. Also the surge in imports in Copper, Edible Oil and Spices etc. are quite abnormal which raise the eyebrow to inquire about what is happening under the FTA VEIL. The FTA has affected some specified industries in badly manner.
- It is suggested to re-negotiate the list of concessions offered by both the countries, so that, real trade creation occurs and the producers in both the countries find a win-win situation for all.

SUMMARY OF DATA ANALYSIS IN CASE OF FTA WITH THAILAND

Imports

- The FTA has affected one or two particular industries badly although overall surge in imports are there. Thailand producers have benefited by surge in imports from them in comparison to India's world imports. The surge may be caused in anticipation of enlargement of the EHS list at a later stage.
- It is observed that the varieties of parameters of the high

value items have shown positive growth rate after the FTA is implemented. The growth patterns of the EHS products are relatively higher (excluding the exceptional case of HSC 84151010) with cheaper imports of basically Chapter 85 products. The correlations among different trend series are mostly positive excluding low number of cases of exceptions.

- The surge in imports observed in most of the cases signifies the diversion of trade to Thailand for products covered under EHS. The market shares of these products have also increased.
- The growth in the imports of the NON EHS items also signifies the fact that there are more opportunities available to the Thailand producers to tap the vast Indian market. It also alerts that, our domestic producers need to produce more competitive products.
- Most of the chapters covered under EHS have shown positive growth along with the implementation of the EHS of the FTA. The correlation among trend in value of imports from Thailand and World imports has been closely related in positive manner.
- Most of the chapters not covered under EHS have shown positive growth along with the implementation of the EHS of the FTA. The correlation among trend in value of imports from Thailand and World imports has been closely related in positive manner. This signifies that; people have anticipated enlargement of the EHS list in near future and the trade relation between both of the countries have developed significantly.
- The surges in import have been observed in the Furniture, Aluminium, Audio Visual Equipments and Television products.

Exports

- Although the FTA has cause increase in exports of EHS products, the list of products covered under EHS are not comprehensive enough to cover products which are of export interest / competitive for Indian producers. It signifies for extensive Government consultation with industries before the concession lists are finalized.

- It can be observed that the varieties of parameters of the high value items have shown positive growth rate after the FTA is implemented. The growth patterns of the EHS products are relatively higher, but only two EHS products have come under the top 20 high value items exported. The correlations among different trend series are mostly positive excluding small number of cases of exceptions.
- The surge in exports observed in most of the cases signifies the diversion of trade to Thailand for products covered under EHS. The market shares of these products have also increased.
- The growth in the exports of the NON EHS items also signifies the fact that there are more opportunities available to the Indian producers to tap the Thailand market. The Government should note the potential items of exports for our country and try to include them in the EHS list in the next round of negotiations.
- Most of the chapters covered under EHS have shown positive growth along with the implementation of the EHS of the FTA. The correlation among trend in value of exports to Thailand and World exports has been closely related in positive manner. The highest growth has been observed in the case of CHAPTER 87 products (Vehicles and Accessories) commanding 42% market share of India's world exports in 2004-05. Over all basis, these sampled EHS products constitute only 3.58% of India's total value of exports. Recommendation is for Broad Basing of the EHS list at the earliest.
- Most of the chapters not covered under EHS have shown positive growth along with the implementation of the EHS of the FTA. The correlation among trend in value of exports to Thailand and World exports has been closely related in positive manner. This signifies that; people have anticipated enlargement of the EHS list in near future and the trade relation between both of the countries have developed significantly.
- Where as the NON EHS products are moving in tandem with world exports, there is need to push further the export competitive products into the EHS list.

- The surge in exports has been observed in the Vehicles and Accessories products.

Overall

A transparent observation can be that the Thailand producers have benefited much than the Indian counterparts. The reason is that the EHS list is very small and the constituents are more or less favourable for the Thailand producers. It is therefore urgent to broad base the EHS list by incorporating more products into the list where the Indian producers have also export competitiveness. The over all situations should be win-win for every body and trade creation because of the FTA should become realistic. Also it is necessary to remove the inherent bottlenecks prevailing in our domestic scenario to create a level playing field.

SUMMARY OF DATA ANALYSIS IN CASE OF CECA WITH SINGAPORE

Imports

- The true Impact is not that much substantial and the impact effect are for a selected sector of industries. It remained limited to a small lot only.
- A lot of products under chapter 84 and 85 being already made duty free because of the WTO Agreement on IT Products (*Import duty on 217 IT Products is already zero under the WTO IT Agreement signed under the Singapore Declaration*), the true impact are minimized.
- But threat exists, in case the third countries route their products through Singapore to manipulate the benefits under CECA. The apprehension is to be positively considered, as Singapore is a global trading hub and not a base for manufacturing activities.
- Stricter implementation of *Rules of Origin clauses is* therefore needed to do justice to the Indian industry.

Exports

- As per latest trade data available in the DGFT website on 10.09.2006, total exports to Singapore has grown by 33.63% from Rs. 1,797,534.88 lakhs in 2004-05 to Rs. 2,401,965.25 lakhs in 2005-06.

- No comment can be given at this stage, as no data analysis have been done because of non availability of online data in due course of time before finalizing this dissertation.
- Comprehensive analysis of trade data can be done at a later stage.

Overall

- The data analysis has been done in a limited manner for imports from and no analysis has been done for exports to Singapore because of time constraint and non-availability of trade data for full year of 2005-06 till 31.08.2006.
- From the limited analysis of imports data, it has been found that the impact of CECA has remained confined to a small number of sectors, if we exclude the figures of IT related products which are already coming duty free because of WTO IT Agreement signed under the Singapore Declaration.
- In case of imports, Rules of Origins clauses need to be followed strictly, so that goods of Singapore origin can only take benefit under the CECA.
- Since under CECA with Singapore, all the products originating from India enjoys duty free treatment, it can be a testing point for our manufacturers to prove their global competitiveness under the free trade regime prevailing in that country.

DETAILED DATA ANALYSIS FOR THE INDO-SRILANKA FTA

Imports

Out of total variety of 1102 products (at 8 digit level) imported from Srilanka during 2004-05, only 111 products (10.07% in nos. and 91.057% in value) were more than value of 0.1% of total value of imports of Rs. 163725.65 lakhs during 2004-05 from Srilanka. Out of these sampled products, 18 products (1.63% in nos. and 11.874% in value) pertains to ZERO DUTY category, 75 products (6.81% in nos. and 73.043% in value) pertains to PHASED RESIDUAL LIST: IR category, 4 products (0.36% in nos. and 0.464% in value) pertains to PREFERENTIAL DUTY-TEXTILES category and 14 products (1.27% in nos. and 5.676% in value) pertains to NEGATIVE LIST category. 8 tables and 16 graphs have been attached as Annexure containing the detailed analysis of impact of the Indo-Srilanka FTA on the import segment.

Table - 1	Details of sampling (import products from Srilanka)
Table - 2	Key factors for top 20 high value imported items (based on 2004-05 value of imports) from Srilanka
Table - 3	Key factors for top 20% of sampled products covered under each category (sorted on the basis of value of imports in 2004-05)
Table - 4	Key factors for top 10% of sampled products covered under each category (sorted on the basis of cagr-value of imports from Srilanka)
Table - 5	Key factors for all sampled products covered under various categories- chapterwise
Table - 6	Movement of Sum Factors (Value of imports from Srilanka / Value of India's world imports) for all the sampled products and category of concession levels. Graph- 1: Movement of sum factors of sample products imported from Srilanka.
Table - 7	Movement of sampled products covered under different category- chapter wise (Important Chapters selected on the basis of highest CAGR and Value of Imports in 2004-05 basis). Graph- 2: Movement of sum factors of imported sample products (chapter wise) from srilanka.
Table - 8	Movement of selected 7 sampled products (High CAGR & Value of Imports from Srilanka in 2004-05 basis) {14 graphs attached showing Market Share movement (volume-wise and value wise) and Movement of Unit Price of Imports (from Srilanka and World)}.

Interpretation of Table – 1

- Apart from the details of sampling, value of imports from Srilanka as well as India's world imports have been given at total figure as well as different level of concessions.
- From Rs. 8026.85 lakhs of imports in 1998-99 from Srilanka, the figure has reached upto Rs. 149083.85 lakhs in 2004-05 (18.57 times) against India's world imports rising from Rs. 470811.07 lakhs to Rs. 3,318,220.98 lakhs (7.05 times) for the sampled products.

The Weighted **Average CAGR** for various samples have been given under:

	Nature of Sample	Imports From Srilanka (A)	India's World Import (B)	Relative Fast-ness (A/B)
1	All the sampled products	166.04%	61.97%	2.68
2	All the sampled products (covered under ZERO DUTY)	122.28%	30.84%	3.96
3	All the sampled products (covered under PHASED RESIDUAL LIST: IR)	174.27%	68.26%	2.55
4	All the sampled products (covered under PREFERENTIAL DUTY)	224.82%	81.38%	2.76
5	All the sampled products (covered under NEGATIVE LIST)	146.85%	69.42%	2.12
6	All the sampled products (covered under ZERO DUTY)-CHAPTER WISE	179.91%	22.19%	8.11
7	All the sampled products (covered under PHASED RESIDUAL LIST: IR)-CHAPTER WISE	403.11%	57.97%	6.95
8	All the sampled products (covered under PREFERENTIAL DUTY)-CHAPTER WISE	62.18%	78.76%	0 79
9	All the sampled products (covered under NEGATIVE LIST)-CHAPTER WISE	152.34%	86.26%	1.77

It can be seen that, the relative fastness of weighted average CAGR in all cases (excluding the case at sl. no. 8) are far higher in case of imports from Srilanka. **The conclusion can therefore be derived that the FTA has caused significant growth in imports.**

Interpretation of Table – 2

This table contains various key parameters of the top 20 high value imported items (based on 2004-05 value of imports) from

Srilanka like incremental trend of volume & value of imports from Srilanka as well as India's total imports from the world, market share % in volume & value, unit prices, CAGR of the items (volume and value both) of imports from Srilanka and the world and correlation factors of various trend series.

In most of the sampled items covered under this table, it can be observed that the varieties of parameters of the high value items have shown positive growth rate after the FTA is implemented. The growth under the FTA, have exceeded the growth of world trade of India under different parameters also.

Interpretation of Table – 3 & 4

Table-3 contains various key parameters (as specified in Table-2) of the top 20% of sampled products covered under each category (sorted on the basis of **value of imports** in 2004-05) being imported from Srilanka.

Table-4 contains various key parameters (as specified in Table-2) of the top 10% of sampled products covered under each category (sorted on the basis of **CAGR**-value of imports from srilanka)

The surge in imports observed in selected cases have shown that; in a selected cases like products of Copper, Spices & Vanaspati / edible oils etc., there is total trade diversion to Srilanka. However the over all growth pattern shows trade creation in imports as value wise India's imports from the world have also been risen a number of times. Even imports of some of the products covered under the Negative list also have grown fast. The correlation factors in most of the products are closure to +1 suggesting that the trend patterns are highly correlative in nature.

Interpretation of Table – 5

A further attempt is made to analyse the movement of the different chapters (individual products groupified in same chapters) under different categories.

This table contains key parameters applicable to the chapters like incremental trend of value of imports from Srilanka as well as India's total imports from the world, market share % in value, CAGR of the chapters (value only) and correlation factor among trend of value of imports among imports from Srilanka and India's world imports.

The results are similar. The chapter-wise growth under different concession levels also reflects mostly the same result as visualized in the case of individual products. Interesting to note that; a lot of negative list items are also showing high growth. It may be that; people are expecting future diversification of the concession list. However, Government should analyse the situation properly and take decisions after consulting the concerned industries.

Interpretation of Table – 6

In this table, movement of Sum Factors of the sampled products have been calculated for different concession levels as well as all of the sample products. Graphs have been plotted to analyse the movement of the sum factors for different years.

It can be observed from the graph that;

a. Products of zero duty and phased residual list have been moved decently and since maximum of the sampled products (75 out of total 111) pertains to the phased residual list category, the movement of the all sampled products curve also followed the same pattern.

b. Products of Negative list have moved up and down and later on stabilized at slightly higher level than the base year of 1998-99.

c. The maximum distortion in the curve is observed in case of Preferential Duty-Textiles category, where the factors have risen significantly up as soon as the concession notification came, but fallen down heavily almost to the base year level there after. This shows that, imports from Srilanka in textiles are either unable to compete with India's imports from the world or the domestic manufacturers of textile products are at an advantageous position in producing quality items.

Interpretation of Table – 7

In this table, sum factors of important chapters of sample products imported from Srilanka have been calculated for different concession levels. The chapters were selected on the basis of top 10% (total chapters are 37) picked up showing the *Highest CAGR* and *Highest Value of Imports in 2004-05*. The common chapters coming under these two criteria are considered once only. Graphs have been plotted to analyse the movement of the sum factors for different years for the finally selected six chapters.

It can be observed from **Graph** that;

a) The highest positive movement has been shown for CHAPTER-74 (Phased Residual List). As the concessional duty level goes on increasing, the trend of imports for the COPPER PRODUCTS kept on increasing and capturing the markets of India's world imports. Trade diversion is clearly established from this fact as far as copper industry is concerned.

b) Incase of CHAPTER 9 products (Coffee, Tea and Spices), the growth can be said to be decent, as the curve has managed to grow and sustained its trend after falling in 2003-04.

c) For Chapter 28 (Inorganic Chemicals) & Chapter 85 (Audio Visual goods and electrical machinery), even though there are rising curves, in absence of manufacturing base of such industries in Srilanka, it is to be seen whether the surge has been caused by using the FTA route to avail concessional duty access to Indian Markets by the manufacturers of other countries.

d) The growth of sum factors for Chapter 73 (Articles of Iron or Steel) and Chapter 84 (Machinery and Appliances) have been modest. However, it is to be seen whether genuine Srilankan manufacturers are deriving the benefits of FTA or manufacturers from other countries are using the FTA to gain illegally.

Interpretation of Table – 8

Seven sampled products have been selected using the criteria of High CAGR & Value of Imports from Srilanka in 2004-05 basis and then the movement of their Market Share (Volume wise & Value wise) and Unit Price of Imports (from Srilanka as well as World) have been observed by plotting graphs. The graphs have been attached to the Table itself and the comments are given in next page:

EXPORTS

Out of total variety of 5203 products (at 8 digit level) exported to Srilanka during 2004-05, only 130 products (2.499% in nos. and 68.77% in value) were more than value of 0.1% of total value of exports of Rs. 608923.17lakhs during 2004-05 to Srilanka. Out of these sampled products, 1 products (0.019% in nos. and 0.195% in value) pertains to F I : ZERO DUTY category, 12 products (0.231% in nos. and 4.102% in value) pertains to F II : 50% TO 100% Concessional duty in 3 YRS category, 57 products (1.096% in nos. and 18.056% in value) pertains to SLR: ZERO DUTY IN 8 YEARS category , 48 products (0.923% in nos. and 23.073% in value) pertains to D (ii) : NEGATIVE LIST category and 12 products

HS Code	Particulars	Concession List	Comment on Market Share	Comment on Unit Price of Imports
1. 28241010	Litharge (28241001)	Zero duty	Both quantity and value wise market share followed the same pattern. Incresed slightly in 2002-03 than 2001-02 level, rise rapidly during 2003-04 and there after stabilized in 2004-05.	Surge in imports is from 2002-03 from Srilanka. Unit prices are comparable with world import price for India there after.
2. 15162091	Othr veg fats & oils & thr frctns of edblegrade (15162009)	Phased residual list: IR	From very negligible market share both value and volume wise, suddenly the share rise to almost 70% in 2004-05.	Unit price for Srilanka after moves ups and downs, remained at approximately same level with the world import price for India in 2004-05.
3. 74031900	Other refined, copper, unwrought	Phased residual list: IR	Market Share moved up from 2000-01 and captured the majority of imports of Copper during 2004-05.	Unit price remained at same level in both the cases from 2001-02.
4. 9070020	Clove, not extracted (other than stem) (9070002)	Phased residual list: IR	After heavy increase in market share in 1999-00, the shares have fallen and then rise and finally on the rising trend during 2004-05. Both Value and Volume shares followed same pattern, with Value curve commanding more share than the volume curve.	Unit prices for imports from Srilanka remained at higher level than World imports throughout the period of seven years. Both curves followed the same pattern suggesting that, increased value realization for Srilankan products.
5. 74031200	Wire-bars of refined copper	Phased residual list: IR	Sharp increase in both types of market share observed from 2001-02 and risen steadily up to capture the whole market in 2004-05.	From initial cheaper price of imports from 2001-02 in case of imports from Srilanka, the prices have moved up and caught the world import price level.
6. 52082990	Others	Preferential duty-textiles	The imports were up from 2003-04, but still captured very less share of total Indian imports from the world.	Prices are similar among imports from Srilanka and world imports.
7. 8011100	Coconut desiccated	Negative list	Share risen to capture the whole market in 1999-00, fallen to zero level in 2001-02 and again risen to capture the whole market from 2003-04.	Import price from Srilanka fallen from 2000-01 to 2002-03 than the world import prices, but again matched with the world import prices during 2003-04 and 2004-05.

(0.231% in nos. and 23.349% in value) pertains to NOT covered under any category (MFN DUTY) of concession. 8 tables and 19 graphs have been attached as Annexure containing the detailed analysis of impact of the Indo-Srilanka FTA on the export segment.

Table - 9	Details of sampling (export products to Srilanka)
Table - 10	Key factors for top 25 high value exported items (based on 2004-05 value of exports) to Srilanka
Table - 11	Key factors for top 20% of sampled products covered under each category (sorted on the basis of value of exports in 2004-05)
Table - 12	Key factors for top 10% of sampled products covered under each category (sorted on the basis of cagr-value of exports to Srilanka)
Table - 13	Key factors for all sampled products covered under various categories- chapter wise
Table - 14	Movement of sum factors of sampled products covered under different categories. Graph- 1: Movement of sum factors of sample products exported to Silence.
Table - 15	Movement of sum factors of sampled products covered under different category- chapter wise (Important Chapters selected on the basis of highest CAGR and Value of Exports in 2004-05 basis). Graph- 2 & 3: Movement of sum factors of imported sample products (chapter wise) from srilanka.
Table - 16	Movement of selected 8 sampled products (High CAGR & Value of Exports to Srilanka in 2004-05 basis) {16 graphs attached showing Market Share movement (volume-wise and value wise) and Movement of Unit Price of Exports (to Srilanka and World) }.

Interpretation of Table – 9

- Apart from the details of sampling, value of exports to Srilanka as well as India's world exports have been given at total figure as well as different level of concessions.
- From Rs. 34631.27 lakhs of exports in 1998-99 to Srilanka, the figure has reached upto Rs. 418790.58 lakhs in 2004-05 (12.09 times) against India's world exports rising from Rs. 3091827.93 lakhs to Rs.12364459.51 lakhs (3.99 times) for the sampled products.

- Interesting to note is that products that are neither covered under any concession list offered by Srilanka nor the negative list stipulated have shown tremendous increase in turnover in 2003-04 and 2004-05. Value wise, the products under this category (other items at MFN rate) constitute 23.349% of the total value of exports to Srilanka in 2004-05.

The **Weighted Average CAGR** for various samples have been given under:

	Nature of Sample	Export to Srilanka (A)	India's World Export (B)	Relative Fastness (A/B)
1	All the sampled products	59.39%	44.92%	1.32
2	All the sampled products (covered under F I : ZERO DUTY)	115.78%	23.66%	4.89
3	All the sampled products (covered under F II : 50% TO 100% IN 3 YRS)	91.66%	109.01%	0.84
4	All the sampled products (covered under SLR: ZERO DUTY IN 8 YEARS)	75.67%	21.46%	3.53
5	All the sampled products (covered under D (ii) : NEGATIVE LIST)	80.36%	42.38%	1.90
6	All the sampled products (not covered under any category- OTHER ITEMS AT MFN RATE)	19.93%	112.43%	0.18
7	All the sampled products (covered under F I : ZERO DUTY)-CHAPTER WISE	115.78%	23.66%	4.89
8	All the sampled products (covered under F II : 50% TO 100% IN 3 YRS)-CHAPTER WISE	80.92%	95.41%	0.85
9	All the sampled products (covered under SLR: ZERO DUTY IN 8 YEARS)-CHAPTER WISE	81.85%	34.63%	2.36
10	All the sampled products (covered under D (ii) : NEGATIVE LIST)-CHAPTER WISE	68.15%	44.54%	1.53
11	All the sampled products (not covered under any category- OTHER ITEMS AT MFN RATE)-CHAPTER WISE	25.78%	82.34%	0.31

It can be seen that; where as the weighted average CAGR in cases of Zero Duty, SLR & Negative list are more for exports to Srilanka in comparison to India's world exports, it is less in cases of exports of products covered under F II and Other items at MFN Rate. The results are similar when the products are considered individually or being groupified under chapters. The majority of products sampled pertain to either the Negative list (23.073% value wise of total exports in 2004-05) or Other Items at MFN Rate (23.349% of the total value of exports to Srilanka in 2004-05). From the total sample size of 68.776% of total value of exports in 2004-05, these two category alone accounts for 46.422%. There is only one sampled product falling under the zero duty category. Products under F II category have shown lower growth rate in comparison to the world exports. The only concessional items showing high growth of exports to Srilanka in comparison to world exports are those falling under the SLR category only. **The conclusion can therefore be derived that the FTA has not caused significant growth in exports; the rise in exports to Srilanka can be attributed to other factors like competitiveness of the Indian products, general trend in growth in world exports and geographical proximity to Srilanka etc.**

Interpretation of Table – 10

This table contains various key parameters of the top 25 high value exported items (based on 2004-05 value of exports) to Srilanka like incremental trend of volume & value of exports to Srilanka as well as India's total exports to the world, market share % in volume & value, unit prices, CAGR of the items (volume and value both) of exports to Srilanka and the world and correlation factors of various trend series.

In most of the sampled items covered under this table, it can be observed that the variety of parameters of the high value items have shown moderate growth rate. A lot of products showing high growth are covered under either the Negative List or Other Items at MFN Rate. The correlations among different trend series are positively correlated.

Interpretation of Table – 11 & 12

Table-3 contains various key parameters (as specified in Table-10) of the top 20% of sampled products covered under each category (sorted on the basis of **value of exports** in 2004-05) being exported to Srilanka.

Table-4 contains various key parameters (as specified in Table-10) of the top 10% of sampled products covered under each category (sorted on the basis of **CAGR**-value of exports to srilanka)

The results are almost similar to Table-2 suggesting that the surge in exports is accounted by other factors along with the concessions offered by Srilanka under the FTA.

Interpretation of Table – 13

A further attempt is made to analyse the movement of the different chapters (individual products grouped in same chapters) under different categories.

This table contains key parameters applicable to the chapters like incremental trend of value of exports to Srilanka as well as India's total exports to the world, market share % in value, CAGR of the chapters (value only) and correlation factor among trend of value of exports among exports to Srilanka and India's world imports.

The chapter-wise growth under different concession levels also reflecting mostly the similar results as visualized in the case of individual products.

Interpretation of Table – 14

In this table, movements of Sum Factors of the sampled products have been calculated for different concession levels as well as all of the sample products. Graphs have been plotted to analyse the movement of the sum factors for different years.

It can be observed that;

a. Factors for Products of zero duty and SLR have been moved up very slow.

b. Products of F II have moved up in 1999-00, fall there after in the yr. 2000-01 and show negligible growth by the year 2004-05. This is the category showing maximum distortion in market share of sum of value of exports to Srilanka with India's world exports.

c. Sum factor for products under the Negative List has moved up in 1999-00 and there after shown growth till 2004-05 with little downside slide in 2002-03.

d. Sum factor for Other Items at MFN Rate have shown sudden value in 2003-04 and fall down moderately in 2004-05.

e. The over all sum factors for all the sampled products have shown steady but moderate growth rate.

f. It can be the significance of the fact that, exports to Srilanka has risen along with India's total exports to the world. The export policy along with the competitiveness of the Indian products may be the reason, which has added momentum to the FTA.

Interpretation of Table – 15

In this table, sum factors of important chapters of sample products exported to Srilanka have been calculated for different concession levels. The chapters were selected on the basis of top 10% (total chapters are 41) picked up showing the *Highest CAGR* and *Highest Value of Exports in 2004-05*. Separate Graphs have been plotted to analyse the movement of the sum factors for different years for these chapters selected on the basis of High CAGR and High Value basis.

It can be observed from Graph *for Value wise top 4 chapters* that;

a) The highest positive movement has been shown for CHAPTER-87 (SLR: ZERO DUTY IN 8 YEARS). As the concessional duty level goes on increasing, the trend of exports for the Vehicles and accessories kept on increasing with 1999-00 and 2000-01 being the years of exception.

b) Products of CHAPTER 87 coming under the Negative list also shown the rising trend signifying that the growth in trade is more worldly rather than being dependent on the impact of the FTA.

c) The Cereal products of CHAPTER 10 (NEGATIVE LIST) have also shown moderate rising trend in sum factors.

d) Fuels and oil products of CHAPTER 27 have shown sudden surge in market share in 2003-04 and later on slightly fallen in 2004-05. Chapter wise, the sample products covered under this chapter accounts for 22.67% of total value of exports to Srilanka in 2004-05.

It can be observed from *Graph for CAGR- Value wise top 4 chapters* that;

a) The highest growth is accounted by CHAPTER 60 (SLR: ZERO DUTY IN 8 YEARS) products consisting of Knitted and crocheted fabrics materials.

b) The Residues and waste of Food industry products under CHAPTER 23 (SLR: ZERO DUTY IN 8 YEARS).have also shown rise in the sum factors except the exceptional year of 2001-02. Both the market share of Chapter 60 and 23 products have moved up along with the increasing trend of concessions under the FTA.

c) Sum factors of CHAPTER 40 (Negative List) comprising of Rubber and related articles have moved down in 1999-00, moved up there after till 2001-02, again fall down till 2003-04 and there after stabilized in 2004-05.

d) Audio Visual goods and electrical machinery products under CHAPTER 85 (Negative List) have suddenly commanded high exports in 2003-04 and the sum factor rise two times more in 2004-05.

Out of the two criteria applied for selecting top 10% chapters, it is observed that products under the Negative List and products not covered under any list (MFN Rate) have risen more both CAGR and Value of Exports wise. **Significantly the conclusion is that the FTA has not benefited much to Indian exporters in comparison to their surge in exports to the whole world.**

Interpretation of Table – 16

Eight sampled products have been selected using the criteria of High CAGR & Value of Exports to Srilanka in 2004-05 basis and then the movement of their Market Share (Volume wise & Value wise) and Unit Price of Exports (to Srilanka as well as World) have been observed by plotting graphs. The graphs have been attached to the Table itself and the comments are given below:

HS Code	Particulars	Concession List	Comment on Market Share	Comment on Unit Price of Imports
1. 87113090	OTHR VHCL WTH CYLNDR CPCTY >250 BT<=500 CC	SLR: ZERO DUTY IN 8 YEARS	Both volume and value wise market share moved from zero in 2002-03 to approximately 50% in 2004-05.	The export price to Srilanka was cheaper than world export price for India in 2003-04. But the prices equalized in 2004-05 with decline in world export price from the 2003-04 level.
2. 85281212	COLOUR TV SET OF SCRN SIZE BETN 36 & 54 CM	D (ii) : NEGATIVE LIST	Both the market share curves followed the same rising pattern from zero level in 2002-03.	Unit price of exports followed the same trend in case of exports to Srilanka and India's world exports.
3. 85469090	OTHR ELCTRL INSLTRS OF OTHR MATRLS	D (ii) : NEGATIVE LIST	Both the market share curves followed the same rising pattern from zero level in 2002-03.	Unit price of exports followed the same trend in case of exports to Srilanka and India's world exports. The later being higher in the year 2003-04.

HS Code	Particulars	Concession List	Comment on Market Share	Comment on Unit Price of Imports
4. 87019010	OTHER TRACTORS OF ENGN CAPACITY <= 1800CC	SLR: ZERO DUTY IN 8 YEARS	Both the market share curves followed the same rising pattern from zero level in 2002-03.	Unit price of exports followed the same trend in case of exports to Srilanka and India's world exports. The later being higher in the year 2003-04 & 2004-05.
5. 27101930	HIGH SPEED DIESEL (HSD)	OTHER ITEMS AT MFN RATE	Both the market share curves followed the same rising pattern from zero level in 2002-03.	Unit price of exports followed the same trend in case of exports to Srilanka and India's world exports. Both the unit price were equal for 2003-04 and 2004-05.
6. 10063010	RICE PARBOILED (10063001)	D (ii) : NEGATIVE LIST	Both the market shares move up in 1999-00, fallen next yr. , move up till 02-03, fallen to zero level in 03-04 and there after rise to approximately 8% in 2004-05.	From the same level of Unit price of exports in 1998-99, the world export price remain at higher side till 2001-02 and there after remained in the lower side than the export price to Srilanka till both the unit prices become almost equal in 2004-05.
7. 87112029	MOTR CYCLWTH CYLNDR CPCTY >75 BT<=250 CC	SLR: ZERO DUTY IN 8 YEARS	Both the market share curves followed the same rising pattern from zero level in 2002-03 to approx. 35% in 2004-05.	Unit prices of exports remained at far lower level in case of exports to Srilanka in comparison with the India's world exports during 03-04 and 04-05.
8. 87032120	THREE-WHEELED VEHICLES WTH CYLNDR CPCTY<=1000 WTH SPRK-IGNTN	D (ii) : NEGATIVE LIST	Both the market share curves followed the same rising pattern from zero level in 2002-03 and reach upto 59% in 2004-05.	Unit price of exports followed the same trend in case of exports to Srilanka and India's world exports. Prices in 2004-05 slightly decreased from the level of 2003-04.

13

DETAILED DATA ANALYSIS FOR THE FTA WITH THAILAND

Effectively both the country have agreed to put 82 product category at Six digit HS Code level under the Early Harvest Scheme (**EHS**). The products covered under the EHS are subjected to the following tariff reduction and elimination:

Original Period	Amended Period as per the PROTOCOL to amend the Frame Work Agreement	Tariff reduction on applied MFN tariff rates as of 1st January 2004
1.3.2004-28.2.2005	1.9.2004- 31.8.2005	50%
1.3.2005-28.2.2006	1.9.2005- 31.8.2006	75%
1.3.2006	1.9.2006	100%

(Note: All products where the applied MFN tariff rates are 0%, shall remain at 0%.)

All other products other than these 82 items fall under the **NON EHS** category for which duty at the level of MFN shall be applicable, i.e., the normal duty. Detailed analysis of goods imported / exported from / to Thailand follows below.

Imports

Out of total variety of 2920 products (at 8 digit level) imported from Thailand during 2004-05, only 180 products (6.16% in nos. and 77.93% in value) were more than value of 0.1% of total value of imports of Rs. 374556.75 lakhs during 2004-05 from Thailand. Out of these sampled products, 33 products (1.13% in nos. and 16.08% in value) pertain to **EHS** category AND 147 products (5.03% in nos. and 61.85% in value) pertain to **NON EHS** category. 11 tables and 12 graphs have been attached as Annexure containing the detailed analysis of impact of the **FTA WITH THAILAND** on the import segment.

Table – 17	Details of sampling (import products from Thailand)
Table – 18	Key factors for top 30 high value imported items (based on 2004-05 value of imports) from Thailand)
Table – 19	Key factors for all sampled products covered under early harvest scheme
Table – 20	Key factors for top 20 sampled products (CAGR WISE - value of imports in 2004-05) not covered under early harvest scheme
Table – 21	Key factors for all sampled products covered under early harvest scheme- chapter wise
Table – 22	Key factors for all sampled products not covered under early harvest scheme- chapter wise
Table – 23	Key factors for top 10 chapters (sorted on cagr-value-imports from Thailand basis) (Containing Sampled Products of NON EHS category only)
Table – 24	Key factors for top 10 chapters (sorted on value of imports from Thailand in 2004-05 basis) (Containing Sampled Products of NON EHS category only)
Table – 25	Movement of sum factors of sampled products Graph 1: Movement of Sum Factors of all EHS / Non EHS Products
Table – 26	Movement of sum factors of sampled products covered under EHS- chapter wise
Table – 27	Movement of market share & unit price of imports top 3 sampled products covered under EHS (Value of Imports from Thailand in 2004-05 basis) & top 3 sampled products covered under EHS (CAGR-VALUE-Imports from Thailand basis)

Interpretation of Table – 17

- Apart from the details of sampling, value of imports from Thailand as well as India's world imports have been given at total figure as well as EHS / NON EHS categories.
- From Rs. 105668.99 lakhs of imports in 2001-02 from Thailand, the figure has reached upto Rs. 291889.83 lakhs in 2004-05 (2.76 times) against India's world imports rising from Rs. 1961469.89 lakhs to Rs. 5707305.52 lakhs (2.91 times) for the sampled products.

The **Weighted Average CAGR** for various samples have been given under:

	Nature of Sample	Imports From Thailand (A)	India's World Import (B)	Relative Fast-ness (A/B)
1	All the sampled products	115.62%	55.32%	2.09
2	All the sampled products (covered under EHS)	90.32%	64.00%	1.41
3	All the sampled products (not covered under EHS)	122.20%	54.29%	2.25
4	All the sampled products (covered under EHS)- CHAPTER WISE	200.73%	54.80%	3.66
5	All the sampled products (not covered under EHS)- CHAPTER WISE	90.73%	59.39%	1.53

It can be seen that, the relative fastness of weighted average CAGR in all cases are higher in case of imports from Thailand. Since, a number of items have shown import turnover only in the year 2004-05, the weighted average CAGR in cases of sample products (mostly CHAPTER 85 PRODUCTS) covered under EHS is showing low fastness in growth. However, the same EHS products when grouped under chapters, the position becomes better and the relative fastness increased more than 150%. The opposite trend observed in case of sample products not covered under EHS, when grouped under different chapters with relative fastness declining from 2.25 to 1.53. **The conclusion can therefore that, the FTA has affected one or two particular industries badly although overall surge in imports are there. Thailand producers have benefited by surge in imports from them in comparison to India's world imports. The surge may be caused in anticipation of enlargement of the EHS list at a later stage.**

Interpretation of Table – 18

This table contains various key parameters of the top 30 high value imported items (based on 2004-05 value of imports) from Thailand like incremental trend of volume & value of imports from Thailand as well as India's total imports from the world, market share % in volume & value, unit prices, CAGR of the items (volume and value both) of imports from Thailand and the world and correlation factors of various trend series.

In most of the sampled items covered under this table, it can be observed that the varieties of parameters of the high value items have shown positive growth rate after the FTA is implemented. The growth patterns of the EHS products are relatively higher (excluding the exceptional case of HSC 84151010) with cheaper imports of basically Chapter 85 products. The correlations among different trend series are mostly positive excluding low number of cases of exceptions.

Interpretation of Table – 19

Table-19 contains various key parameters (as specified in Table-18) of the all 33 sampled products covered under EHS.

The surges in imports observed in most of the cases signify the diversion of trade to Thailand for products covered under EHS. The market shares of these products have also increased.

Interpretation of Table – 20

Table-20 contains various key parameters (as specified in Table-18) of the top 20 sampled products (CAGR wise - value of imports in 2004-05) not covered under early harvest scheme.

The growth in the imports of the NON EHS items also signifies the fact that there are more opportunities available to the Thailand producers to tap the vast Indian market. It also alerts that, our domestic producers need to produce more competitive products.

Interpretation of Table – 21

A further attempt is made to analyse the movement of the different chapters (individual products grouped in same chapters) for products covered under EHS. All the sampled EHS products have been accommodated in 7 chapters.

This table contains key parameters applicable to the chapters like incremental trend of value of imports from Thailand as well as India's total imports from the world, market share % in value, CAGR of the chapters (value only) and correlation factor among trend of value of imports among imports from Thailand and India's world imports.

Most of the chapters covered under EHS have shown positive growth along with the implementation of the EHS of the FTA. The correlations among trend in value of imports from Thailand and World imports have been closely related in positive manner.

Interpretation of Table – 22

A further attempt is made to analyse the movement of the different chapters (individual products grouped in same chapters) for products not covered under EHS. All the sampled NON EHS products have been accommodated in 40 chapters.

This table contains key parameters applicable to the chapters and specified already under Interpretation of **Table – 21.**

Most of the chapters not covered under EHS have shown positive growth along with the implementation of the EHS of the FTA. The correlation among trend in value of imports from Thailand and World imports has been closely related in positive manner. This signifies that; people have anticipated enlargement of the EHS list in near future and the trade relation between both of the countries have developed significantly.

Interpretation of Table – 23 & 24

Table-23 contains key parameters (specified already under Interpretation of **Table – 21**) for top 10 chapters (sorted on CAGR-value-imports from Thailand basis) (containing sampled products of NON EHS category only).

Table-24 contains key parameters (specified already under Interpretation of **Table – 21**) for top 10 chapters (sorted on value of imports from Thailand in 2004-05 basis) (containing sampled products of NON EHS category only).

Results are similar to the comments given under Interpretation of **Table – 22.**

Interpretation of Table – 25

In this table, Sum Factors of the sampled products have been calculated for products coming under EHS and NON EHS basis. Graphs have been plotted to analyse the movement of the sum factors for different years.

It can be observed from the Graph that;

The factors of market share of the products coming under EHS category have rise sharply in the year 2004-05. Where as for products not covered under EHS, the movement is not significant. The result being the EHS under the FTA has caused surge in imports of the sampled products, where as the non-EHS products move in tandem with general trend of world imports combined with future anticipation of the enlargement of the EHS list.

Interpretation of Table – 26

In this table, sum factors of 7 chapters of sample products covered under the EHS of the FTA have been calculated. Graphs have been plotted to analyse the movement of the sum factors of different chapters for different years. It can be observed from Graph that;

Products of Chapter 94 (Furniture Items) have shown heavy rise followed by Chapter 76 (Aluminium and Articles thereof) and Chapter 85 (Audio Visual Equipments incl. TV). Moderate growth found in case of Chapter 71 (Natural stones, metals and imitation jewellery) products. Stability observed for Chapter 39 (Plastics and Articles thereof) and slight decline in share observed for Chapter 73 (Articles of Iron or Steel) and Chapter 84(Machinery and Mechanical appliances) products. Increase in the curve signifies increase in value of imports from Thailand over value of India's world imports. **So, the surges in import have been observed in the Furniture, Aluminium, Audio Visual Equipments and Television products.**

Interpretation of Table – 27

Six sampled products covered under **EHS** have been selected using the criteria of High CAGR (3 products) & Value of Imports (3 products) from Thailand in 2004-05 basis and then the movement of their Market Share (Volume wise & Value wise) and Unit Price of Imports (from Thailand as well as World) have been observed by plotting graphs. The graphs have been attached to the Table itself and the comments are given below:

HS Code	Particulars	Comment on Market Share	Comment on Unit Price of Imports
1. 73269099	All other articles of iron/steel nes other steering or rudder equipment for ships and boats, n.e.s. (73269019)	Both volume and value wise market share have fallen in 2004-05 than the level of 2003-04 which were earlier showing rising trend. Patterns are same for both curves.	World import price, which was lower than the Thai-imports changed trend and become higher from 2003-04. Although both unit price curves show rising trend, imports under the FTA remain cheaper than the world price.
2. 85281212	Colour TV set of scrn size betn 36 & 54 cm	From zero level in 2003-04, both the market shares captured around than 90% of total imports.	World import price remain at same level for 2003-04 and 2004-05, where as, the new entrant Thai-import prices is lower than the world prices for 2004-05.
3. 39074000 (Common product for CAGR as well as Value basis)	POLYCARBONATES	Trends are mostly same for both the curves of volume and value wise market shares. Value realizations have been little more in 2004-05. The rising curves from 01-02 to 03-04 have shown moderate growth in the latest year.	Trends are mostly same with Thai import prices remaining on higher side than the world import prices. The declining prices have increased in 04-05 than the 03-04 level. The fact that, inspite of higher prices than the world level, the Thai goods are increasingly imported signifies better quality being attached with such goods.
4.94019000	Other seats of heading 9401	Surge in imports observed, with quantitative share rising from 4.13% to 19.12% and value wise share rising from 8.26% to 29.51% for the years 03-04 and 04-05.	Except 2002-03, the import price from Thailand remained at much higher level than the world level. Where as because FTA, import prices fallen for Thai imports, prices of world imports remained at same level.
5.76012010	Aluminium ingots -alloyed (76012001)	From market share of approximately 1.6% in 2002-03, share have fallen to 0.02% in 2003-04 and there after increased to touch the level of 10% for both volume and value of imports from Thailand.	Although small rise in prices observed from 2003-04 to 2004-05 in both the case, the Thai import price remain at lower level than world level since 2002-03.

EXPORTS

Out of total variety of 3106 products (at 8 digit level) exported to Thailand during 2004-05, only 103 products (3.32% in nos. and 78.205% in value) were more than value of 0.1% of total value of exports of Rs. 395199.59 lakhs during 2004-05 to Thailand. Out of these sampled products, 11 products (0.35 % in nos. and 3.58 % in value) pertain to **EHS** category AND 92 products (2.96% in nos. and 74.63% in value) pertains to **NON EHS** category. 11 tables and 8 graphs have been attached as Annexure containing the detailed analysis of impact of the **FTA WITH THAILAND** on the export segment.

Table – 28	Details of sampling (export products to Thailand)
Table – 29	Key factors for top 20 high value exported items (based on 2004-05 value of exports) to Thailand
Table – 30	Key factors for all sampled products covered under early harvest scheme
Table – 31	Key factors for top 10 sampled products (CAGR WISE - value of exports in 2004-05) not covered under early harvest scheme
Table – 32	Key factors for all sampled products covered under early harvest scheme- chapter wise
Table – 33	Key factors for all sampled products not covered under early harvest scheme- chapter wise
Table – 34	Key factors for top 10 chapters (sorted on CAGR-value-exports to Thailand basis) (Containing Sampled Products of NON EHS category only)
Table – 35	Key factors for top 10 chapters (sorted on value of exports to Thailand in 2004-05 basis) (Containing Sampled Products of NON EHS category only)
Table – 36	Movement of sum factors of sampled products
	Graph 1:
	Movement of Sum Factors of all EHS / Non EHS Products
Table – 37	Movement of sum factors of sampled products covered under EHS- chapter wise
Table – 38	Movement of market share & unit price of exports of top 3 sampled products covered under EHS (Value of Exports to Thailand in 2004-05 basis) & (CAGR-VALUE-Exports to Thailand basis)

Interpretation of Table – 28

- ✓ Apart from the details of sampling, value of exports to Thailand as well as India's world exports have been given at total figure as well as EHS / NON EHS categories.
- ✓ From Rs. 166751.93 lakhs of exports in 2001-02 to Thailand, the figure has reached upto Rs. 309065.65lakhs in 2004-05 (1.85 times) against India's world exports rising from Rs. 5,026,480.20 lakhs to Rs. 10,759,419.76 lakhs (2.14 times)

for the sampled products.

The Weighted **Average CAGR** for various samples have been given under:

	Nature of Sample	Exports to Thailand (A)	India's World Export (B)	Relative Fast-ness (A/B)
1	All the sampled products	82.05%	45.70%	1.80
2	All the sampled products (covered under EHS)	261.46%	42.94%	6.09
3	All the sampled products (not covered under EHS)	73.45%	46.15%	1.59
4	All the sampled products (covered under EHS)-CHAPTER WISE	260.50%	41.21%	6.32
5	All the sampled products (not covered under EHS)-CHAPTER WISE	51.77%	37.99%	1.36

It can be seen that, the relative fastness of weighted average CAGR in all cases are higher in case of exports to Thailand. The fastness of weighted average CAGR for sampled products covered under EHS is much higher than the NON EHS products. However, the value wise rise is not much significant in case of EHS products and also lesser number of EHS products are covered under the sample. **This signifies that; although the FTA has cause increase in exports of EHS products, the list of products covered under EHS are not comprehensive enough to cover products which are of export interest / competitive for Indian producers. It signifies for extensive Government consultation with industries before the concession lists are finalized.**

Interpretation of Table – 29

This table contains various key parameters of the top 20 high value exported items (based on 2004-05 value of exports to Thailand) like incremental trend of volume & value of exports to Thailand as well as India's total exports to the world, market share % in volume & value, unit prices, CAGR of the items (volume and value both) of exports to Thailand and the world and correlation factors of various trend series.

In most of the sampled items covered under this table, it can be observed that the varieties of parameters of the high value items have shown positive growth rate after the FTA is implemented. The growth patterns of the EHS products are relatively higher, but only two EHS products have come under the top 20 high value items exported. The correlations among different trend series are mostly positive excluding small number of cases of exceptions.

Interpretation of Table – 30

Table-30 contains various key parameters (as specified in Table-29) of all 11 sampled products covered under EHS.

The surge in exports observed in most of the cases signifies the diversion of trade to Thailand for products covered under EHS. The market shares of these products have also increased.

Interpretation of Table – 31

Table-31 contains various key parameters (as specified in Table-29) of the top 10 sampled products (CAGR wise - value of exports in 2004-05) not covered under early harvest scheme.

The growth in the exports of the NON EHS items also signifies the fact that there are more opportunities available to the Indian producers to tap the Thailand market. The Government should note the potential items of exports for our country and try to include them in the EHS list in the next round of negotiations.

Interpretation of Table – 32

A further attempt is made to analyse the movement of the different chapters (individual products grouped in same chapters) for products covered under EHS. All the sampled EHS products have been accommodated in 8 chapters.

This table contains key parameters applicable to the chapters like incremental trend of value of exports to Thailand as well as India's total exports to the world, market share % in value, CAGR of the chapters (value only) and correlation factor among trend of value of exports among exports to Thailand and India's world exports.

Most of the chapters covered under EHS have shown positive growth along with the implementation of the EHS of the FTA. The correlations among trend in value of exports to Thailand and World exports have been closely related in positive manner. The highest growths have been observed in the case of CHAPTER 87 products (Vehicles and Accessories) commanding 42% market share of India's world exports in 2004-05. Over all basis, these sampled EHS products constitute only 3.58% of India's total value of exports. Recommendation is for Broad Basing of the EHS list at the earliest.

Interpretation of Table – 33

A further attempt is made to analyse the movement of the different chapters (individual products grouped in same chapters) for products not covered under EHS. All the sampled NON EHS products have been accommodated in 25 chapters.

This table contains key parameters applicable to the chapters and specified already under Interpretation of **Table – 32.**

Most of the chapters not covered under EHS have shown positive growth along with the implementation of the EHS of the FTA. The correlation among trend in value of exports to Thailand and World exports has been closely related in positive manner. This signifies that; people have anticipated enlargement of the EHS list in near future and the trade relation between both of the countries have developed significantly.

Interpretation of Table – 34 & 35

Table-34 contains key parameters (specified already under Interpretation of **Table – 32)** for top 10 chapters (sorted on CAGR-value-exports to Thailand basis) (containing sampled products of NON EHS category only).

Table-35 contains key parameters (specified already under Interpretation of **Table – 32)** for top 10 chapters (sorted on value of exports to Thailand in 2004-05 basis) (containing sampled products of NON EHS category only).

Results are similar to the comments given under Interpretation of **Table – 33.**

Interpretation of Table – 36

In this table, Sum Factors of the sampled products have been calculated for products coming under EHS and NON EHS basis. Graphs have been plotted to analyse the movement of the sum factors for different years.

It can be observed from the graph that;

The sum factors (value wise market share of the all the sampled products) coming under EHS category have declined during the year 2004-05 than the year 2003-04, although these were on rising trend from 2001-02 to 2004-05. Where as for products not covered under EHS, the movement is not significant, although the declining trend till 2003-04 has reversed in 2004-05. The results signifies that, where as the NON EHS products are moving in tandem with world exports, there is need to push further the export competitive products into the EHS list.

Interpretation of Table – 37

In this table, sum factors of 8 chapters of sample products covered under the EHS of the FTA have been calculated. Graphs have been plotted to analyse the movement of the sum factors of different chapters for different years. It can be observed from the Graph that;

Products of Chapter 87 (Vehicles and Accessories) have shown heavy rise and products of Chapter 72 (Iron and Steel) have shown heavy fall in market share. Moderate growth found in case of Chapter 73 (Articles of Iron or Steel) products & Chapter 85 (Audio Visual Equipments incl. TV) products. Stability observed for Chapter 28 (Inorganic Chemicals and Metallic Compounds) and Chapter 71 (Natural stones, metals and imitation jewellery) products. Slight decline in share observed for Chapter 76 (Aluminium and articles thereof). Products of Chapter 84(Machinery and Mechanical appliances) stabilized at the 2001-02 level. Increase in the curve signifies increase in value of exports to Thailand over value of India's world exports. The opposite happens in the case of declining curves. **So, the surge in exports has been observed in the Vehicles and Accessories products.**

Interpretation of Table – 38

Three sampled products covered under **EHS** have been selected using the criteria of High CAGR & Value of Exports to Thailand in 2004-05 basis and then the movement of their Market Share (Volume wise & Value wise) and Unit Price of Exports (to Thailand as well as World) have been observed by plotting graphs. The graphs have been attached to the Table itself and the comments are given below:

HS Code	Particulars	Comment on Market Share	Comment on Unit Price of Imports
1. 87084000	GEAR BOXES	After declining in 2003-04, both the market share curves rise sharply with share of volume rising to 32.82% & share of value rising to 42.57% in 2004-05 from 3.59% & 5.47% respectively in 2003-04.	Both the price curve followed same pattern. Prices fallen down in 2002-03 and there after crossed the original level of 2001-02 in 2004-05.
2. 76011010	ALUMINIUM INGOTS-NOT ALLOYED	Both the curves followed same pattern of increasing sharply from 01-02 to 03-04 and then fallen down less than the 02-03 level in 2004-05.	With low variations of up and down from 2001-02, the prices for exports to Thailand and world exports remained at almost the same level in 2004-05
3. 28182010	ALUMINA CALCINED	Market share in both cases fallen down in 2002-03, increased slightly in 2003-04 and thereafter modestly in 2004-05.	Unit price of exports to Thailand declined in 2002-03 and increased there after till 2004-05. In the case of price for world exports, the rise is slow till 2003-04 and there after modest in 2004-05. The Thai export prices remain higher than the world export prices.

DETAILED DATA ANALYSIS FOR THE CECA WITH SINGAPORE

IMPORTS

India has offered concessional duty access to products originating from Singapore under four categories.

Early Harvest Programme (EHP):

On 506 products originating from Singapore, customs duties shall be eliminated entirely from 1st August 2005.

Phased Elimination in Duty (PE):

On 2202 products originating from Singapore, the duties shall be removed in five stages beginning from 1st August 2005 and such goods shall receive duty free entry into India from Singapore, effective 1st April 2009. The margin of preference offered by India has been indicated in the List.

1.8.2005	1.4.2006	1.4.2007	1.4.2008	1.4.2009
10%	25%	50%	75%	100%

Phased Reduction in Duty (PR):

On 2407 products originating from Singapore, the duties shall be reduced in five stages beginning 1st August 2005 and such goods shall receive entry into India at concessional duties. The margin of preference offered by India has been indicated in the List.

1.8.2005	1.4.2006	1.4.2007	1.4.2008	1.4.2009
5%	10%	20%	35%	50%

Negative List (NL):

No concessions in duties shall be offered on 6551 products goods provided in this List. Such goods whether originating or otherwise, shall enter into India from Singapore on the applied MFN duties.

Objective of the Limited Analysis of Data in case of imports from Singapore

Online data for imports for full financial year 2005-06 was not available till 31.08.2006. The objective set therefore was to sample out the high value imported products at 8 digit HS Code level (each product constituting value of imports more than 0.1% of total value of imports from Singapore) based on the value of imports data available for 2004-05 and then comparison of the trend in value and CAGR calculation for value of imports from Singapore alone if the 2005-06 data will be available before 10.09.2006.

However, luckily data for full year of 2005-06 were made available around 07.09.2006 in the DGFT website. Since the time was short; I have tried to show an apparent impact, which is expected to be closely to the real impact of the CECA.

The following steps were followed:

A. Data for Value of imports from Singapore in case of sampled products had been downloaded for the full year of 2005-06. The same data had been put along with data downloaded during Apl'06 for the year 2003-04 and 2004-05.

B. Trend Analysis in value and CAGR calculation for value of imports from Singapore from 2003-04 to 2005-06 was done both product wise and chapter wise (sampled products grouped under same chapters) under various categories of concession / negative list.

C. Products / Chapters where surge in imports have been observed were marked as **ALERT**. The ALERT marks indicates that; the ***Indian producers producing such products should analyse the inherent facts and assess the situations, so that they can adopt precautionary measures before the increase in imports cause material injuries to their industries***. Apart from the ALERT mark, products/ chapters coming under the Negative List where **HIGH GROWTH** has been observed also reported. **ALERT** cases under **Concessional Duties** and **HIGH GROWTH** chapters under **Negative List** were selected on the basis of simultaneous satisfaction of the following criterias:

   (a) Incremental Trend in value of imports in comparison to the base year 2003-04 is more than 50%,

   (b) Incremental Trend in value of imports in comparison to the base year 2004-05 is more than 20% and (c) CAGR of value of imports from Singapore (over the years 2003-04 to 2005-06) is more than 20%.

FACTS AND TABLES

The 155 sampled products based on high value imported items of 2004-05 constituted 77.96% of total value of imports from Singapore in 2004-05. The same basket of 155 products constituted 70.82% of total value of imports of Rs. 1,484,833 lakhs in 2005-06. It can be therefore said that the apparent analysis done because of delay in availability of data actually expected to be close to the real impact of CECA with Singapore.

Based on the steps mentioned above, two tables of conclusion have been made. The tables are given as the Annexures.

Table 39	Key factors for chapters under different categories (imports from Singapore) & scrutiny of cases where Indian industry needs to be alerted
Table 40	Key factors for products under different categories (imports from Singapore) for which Indian industry needs to be alerted

Interpretation of Table – 39

This table contains Key factors for all Chapters covered under different categories of concession list and the Chapter wise values are the summary of the import value of various sampled products grouped under the applicable chapters under different category.

Key parameters like % of total value of imports from Singapore in 2004-05, % of total value of imports from Singapore in 2005-06, Incremental Trend of imports from Singapore (Value) in % in comparison to 2003-04, Incremental Trend of imports from Singapore (Value) in % in comparison to 2004-05 and CAGR-VALUE-Singapore (in %) based on value of imports data from the financial year 2003-04 to 2005-06.

Based on the criteria taken for deriving ALERT cases as mentioned above, a summary of products of Chapters for which Indian industry should do further analysis to assess and adopt precautionary measures to protect from the material injury which may cause to them in future is given in next page:

Chapter No.	Products	List of Concession
29	Organic Chemicals	EHP
84	Machinery and Mechanical appliances including Data Processing Machines & Computors	EHP, PE
85	Audio Visual Equipments incl. TV	EHP, PR
90	Optical, Photographic, Medical and Surgical instruments	EHP, PR
49	Printed materials	PE

Apart from above, sampled products grouped under Chapter 29 (Organic Chemicals), 73(Articles of Iron or Steel) & 76(Aluminium and articles) have shown high growth although the respective products were covered under the NEGATIVE LIST.

Out of 36 chapters covering 155 sampled products, it can be observed that only 11 chapters (common chapters under different list were counted separately) have shown real growth both trend and CAGR wise.

Hence, it can be concluded that the **true Impact is not that much substantial and the impact effect is for a selected sector of industries.** Also, a lot of products under chapter 84 and 85 are already made duty free because of the WTO Agreement on IT Products (*Import duty on 217 IT Products is already zero under the WTO IT Agreement signed under the Singapore Declaration*), the true impact is minimized. But threat exists, in case the third countries route their products through Singapore to manipulate the benefits under CECA. The apprehension is to be positively considered as Singapore is a global trading hub and not a base for manufacturing base. **Stricter implementations of Rules of Origin clauses are therefore needed to do justice to Indian industry.**

Interpretation of Table – 40

This table contains Key factors for sampled imported products covered under different categories of concession list for which Indian industry needs to be ALERTED. The selection of the products have been done based on the criterias as mentioned above for ALERT cases. Apart from that, High Growth items under the Negative List are also sorted out on following the same criteria.

It is found that 24 out of 67 sampled products under the *Early Harvest Programme*, 10 out of 35 sampled products under the *Phased Elimination in Duty* and 6 out of 21 sampled products under the *Phased Reduction in Duty* satisfied the criteria for selecting the cases where Indian industry needs to be alerted. Also it is found that; 7 out of 32 sampled products under the *Negative List* satisfy the requirement of qualifying for HIGH GROWTH items. In totality, the year wise total value of imports for these 47 ALERT/ HIGH GROWTH products constitutes 33.25% & 42.74% of total value of imports made during the financial years 2004-05 & 2005-06 respectively from Singapore.

A majority of the total 24 alerted cases under the *Early Harvest Programme* found to be related to the IT products which are required to be imported at nil duty from the whole world. **So, the impacts of CECA remain limited to a small lot only.**

It further adds strength to the conclusions already established in the Interpretation of **Table – 39** above.

EXPORTS

No analysis of data for exports to Singapore have been done as online data for full year of 2005-06 have been made available after 31.08.2006 only.

SECTION - V

(Questionaires Real Interactions and Case Study)

Contents

15

QUESTIONNAIRES, REAL INTERACTIONS AND CASE STUDY

OBJECTIVES

Since the Impact Study is basically aimed to assess the injury caused by growth imports and benefits derived by growth in exports under these FTAs, it was felt important to get personal views of the interested parties. Trade has grown undoubtedly under these FTAs. However, the questions raised are:

- Whether this growth is achieved at the cost of the closing down our own industries?
- If any case, damage has been done, whether it is restricted to some particular segments of the economy or it has covered the majority of the industries?
- What the industries expect from the Government before and after implementation of the Bi-lateral pacts?
- How, the bottlenecks in the dilemma created recently against signing more FTAs can be positively solved?

The answers to these questions could be given by the industries only. Hence, the circulation of questionnaire and survey system was followed to have real interactions from the stakeholders.

Format for the questionnaires

The questionnaires were modeled in the user-friendly manner giving three options, viz., Yes / No / Not Applicable. The respondents were requested to tick the appropriate answers only. In some applicable cases, requests were made to provide some more details / comments/ suggestions briefly. A number of issues related to ROO, Trade Diversion, Trade Creation etc. were made part of the questionnaires. Blank Questionnaires sent to the Industries in the Ist Stage and to the Industry Associations in the IInd & IIIrd stage are kept as Annexure to the Dissertation for ready references.

Ist Stage. I had sent emails to 538 Associate Members of FICCI representing a broad spectrum of industries, exporters, importers and other interested parties. The questionnaire set devised for the

Sl. No.	Name of the Industry	Short Name	Person contacted	Designation	Dt. of meeting	Time	Place
1.	Sterlite Industries (I) Ltd.	Vedanta	Mr. Sanjay Karn	AGM (Market Development)	19.06.2006	11.30a.m.	Mumbai
2.	Hindalco Industries Limited	Birla Copper	MR. N.K. Ramachandran	General Manager (Exports)	23.06.2006	3.30p.m.	Mumbai

Sl. No.	Name of the Industry	Short Name	Person contacted	Designation	Dt. of meeting	Time	Place
1.	Consumer Electronics & TV Manufacturers' Association	CETMA	Mr. Suresh Khanna	Secretary General	01.07.2006	3.30p.m.	New Delhi
2.	All India Food Processors Association of India	AIFPA	Mr. D.V. Malhan	Executive Secretary	01.07.2006 05.07.2006	5.00p.m. 4.00p.m.	New Delhi
3.	Association of Synthetic Fibre Industry	ASFI	Mr. S.C. Kapur	Secretary General	03.07.2006	10.15a.m.	New Delhi
4.	Electric Lamp and Component Manufacturers Association of India	ELCOMA	Mr. Shyam Sujan	Secretary General	03.07.2006	11.30a.m.	New Delhi
5.	Automotive Tyre Manufacturers Association	ATMA	Mr. Rajiv Budhraja	Secretary General	03.07.2006	2.30p.m.	New Delhi
6.	Telecom Equipment Manufacturers Association of India	TEMA	Mr. S.K. Khanna	Advisor	03.07.2006	3.15p.m.	New Delhi
7.	Manufacturers Association for Information Technology	MAIT	Mr. Vinnie Mehta	Executive Director	03.07.2006	4.00p.m.	New Delhi
8.	Indian Paper Manufacturers Association	IPMA	Mr. Narayan Moorthy	Secretary General	03.07.2006	4.30p.m.	New Delhi
9.	The Vanaspati Manufacturers Association of India	VMA	Mr. S. Gurumoorthi	Executive Secretary	04.07.2006	12.30p.m.	New Delhi
10.	Society of Indian Automobile Manufacturers	SIAM	Mr. Sugato Sen	Director	04.07.2006	2.00p.m.	New Delhi

Sl. No.	Name of the Industry	Short Name	Person contacted	Designation	Dt. of meeting	Time	Place
11.	Automotive Component Manufacturers Association of India	ACMA	Mr. Abhigyan Sengupta	Executive Officer	04.07.2006	3.30p.m.	New Delhi
12.	Alkali Manufacturers' Association of India	AMAI	Dr. Y.R. Singh	Executive Director	05.07.2006	2.30p.m.	New Delhi
13.	Process Plant and Machinery Association of India	PPMA	Mr. Kiran B. Kakatkar	Chief Executive Officer	17.07.2006	12.30noon	Mumbai
14.	The Indian Ferro Alloy Producers' Association	IFAPA	Mr. T.S. Sundaresan	Secretary General	17.07.2006	3.15p.m.	Mumbai
15.	Indian Chemical Council	ICC	Mr. R.R. Gokhale	Secretary General	19.07.2006	12.00 noon	Mumbai
16.	The Solvent Extractors' Association of India	SEAI	Mr. B.V. Mehta	Executive Director	20.07.2006	12.15 noon	Mumbai
17.	Association of Man-Made Fibre Industry of India	AMFII	Mr. M.P. Joseph	Secretary General	20.07.2006	1.15p.m.	Mumbai
18.	The Clothing Manufacturers Association of India	CMAI	Mr. M.K. Panthaki	Director	24.07.2006	3.00p.m.	Mumbai
19.	Tool and Gauge Manufacturers Association	TAGMA	A. Mr. Bhaskar Kanchan B. Mr. P.N. Surendranath	Sr. Deputy Director Technology Advisor	26.07.2006	1.00p.m.	Mumbai
20.	Apparel Export Promotion Council	AEPC	A. Mr. P. A. Narayanan B. Mr. Jagannathan	Joint Director Regional Director	31.07.2006	2.30p.m.	Mumbai
21.	Textile Machinery Manufacturers' Association (India)	TMMAI	Mr. S. Chakrabarty	Secretary	Correspondences made by Emails (29/30th Jun'06)		Mumbai
22.	Ball & Roller Bearing Manufacturers Association Of India	BRBMAI	Mr. V. Gujral	Secretary	Correspondences made by Emails (28/29th Jun'06)		New Delhi
23.	Organization of Plastics Processors of India	OPP	Mr. Deepak Lawale	Secretary General	05.08.06	11.30a.m.	Mumbai

Industries were sent to them. However, I have received so far just one reply from such huge list of respondents. This single respondent had expressed their inadequate exposure to the FTAs. Perhaps, the non response to the questionnaires suggest that; either the industries are not interested at all in this kind of debate or they are not aware about the bi-lateral trade pacts and hence preferred to remain silent.

IInd Stage. The questionnaire set for the industries is revised, so as to suite to the requirements of the Industry Associations. The list of Industry Associations have been sourced from the website of **CII** and other personal sources (as in many cases, the email addresses and other details displayed in the CII website are not updated at all). The new questionnaire was then sent through email to more than 90 industry associations. Out of them only two associations had only responded. **This signifies that; even the majority of the industry associations have no update knowledge about the trade pacts and there is need of conducting massive awareness programs in this regard. Along with the Government authorities, professionals and academicians have great role to play here.**

IIInd Stage. The list of Industry Associations representing the high value items of imports during 2004 - 05 have been prepared and then I have started visiting personally to two leading industries in the Copper Industry, 22 Industry Associations and One Export Promotion Council. The associations represented varied segments of the Indian Industrial Economy. Out of them, meeting with 12 industry associations were done at New Delhi. The feedback received from the IIIrd Stage of interaction becomes therefore the basis for our research conclusions.

ASSESSMENT OF THE IMPACT ON INDUSTRIES BASED ON FEED BACKS FROM THE INDUSTRY ASSOCIATIONS

Based on my interaction with the industry associations, I have summarized their overall responses in a tabular form. The following codes have been given;

A : Affected

N : Neutral

B : Benefited

PT : Potential threat may cause in future

PB : Potential benefit may cause in future

Vedanta and Birla Copper have been grouped under single cell, as both these companies represent the same Copper Industry.

Short Name		Industry	Srilanka FTA	Thailand FTA	Singapore CECA
1	Vedanta/ Birla Copper	Copper	A	N	N
2	CETMA	TV & Consumer Electronics	N	A	N
3	AIFPA	Food Processing	N	N	N
4	ASFI	Synthetic Fibre	A	A	PT
5	ELCOMA	Electric Lighting	N	N	N
6	ATMA	Automotive Tyre	A	N	PT
7	TEMA	Telecom Eqpmt.	N	N	N
8	MAIT	Information Technology	N	N	N
9	IPMA	Paper	B	PB	PB
10	VMA	Vanaspati	A	N	N
11	SIAM	Automobiles	PB	PT	N
12	ACMA	Automobile Components	PB	PT	N
13	AMAI	Alkali Chemicals	N	N	N
14	PPMA	Process Plant & Machineries	N	N	N
15	IFAPA	Ferro Alloys	A	N	N
16	ICC	Chemicals	N	N	PT
17	SEAI	Edible Oil	A	PT	N
18	AMFII	Man-Made Fibre	N	N	N
19	CMAI	Clothing	N	N	N
20	TAGMA	Tools & Gauges	N	N	N
21	AEPC	Apparel Exports	N	N	N
22	TMMAI	Textile Machineries	PB	PB	PB
23	BRBMAI	Ball & Roller Bearings	N	N	N
24	OPP	Plastics	N	N	N

Summary of these assessment factors and no. of cases under each of these FTAs are tabulated below:

(no. of cases)

Assessment Factors	FTA with Srilanka	Thailand	FTA with CECA with Singapore
Affected (A)	6	2	0
Neutral (N)	14	17	19
Benefited (B)	1	0	0
Potential threat may cause in future (PT)	0	3	3
Potential benefit may cause in future (PB)	3	2	2
Total	**24**	**24**	**24**

A graphical presentation is given below:

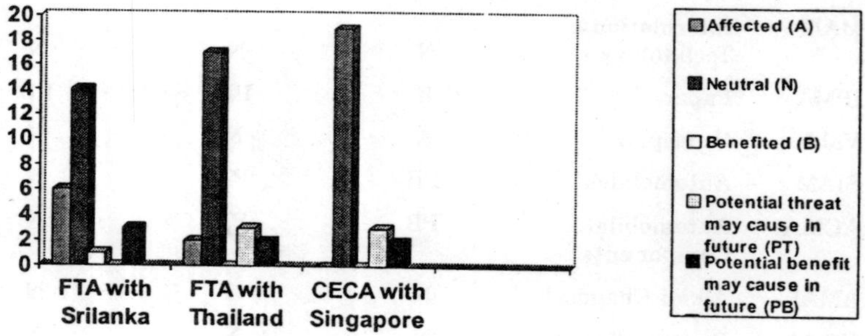

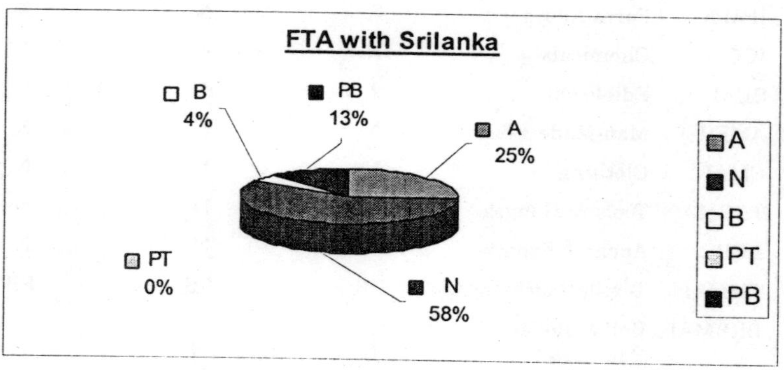

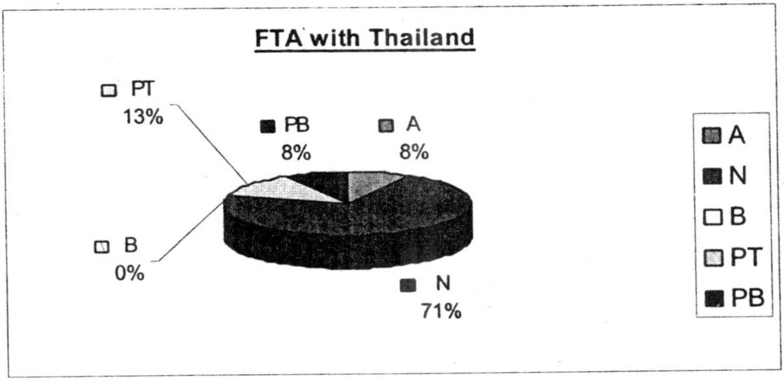
FTA with Thailand
PT
13%
PB
8%
A
8%
B
0%
N
71%
A
N
B
PT
PB

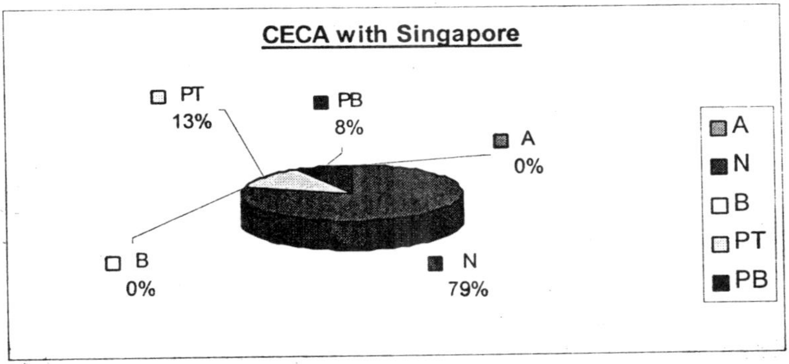
CECA with Singapore
PT
13%
PB
8%
A
0%
B
0%
N
79%
A
N
B
PT
PB

16

DIRECT RESPONSES FROM THE INDUSTRY ASSOCIATIONS

STERLITE INDUSTRIES (I) LTD. (VEDANTA)

1. The Products dealt with by them is Copper Cathode/ Copper Rod (Chapter-74 products).
2. Normal Duty is 7.5% as on date, but imports from Srilanka is coming at 0% duty.
3. From Pre-FTA imports of 10000MT the figure has risen to 65000MT imports Post-FTA from Srilanka.
4. No Non- Tariff Barrier exists while exporting these products to Srilanka.
5. There has been significant expansion in the production capacity of the leading Indian Producers from the period to 1998-99 to 2004-05. But this increase is meant to meet the over all global demand and nothing to be related with the ISALFTA.
6. The Indian production is approximately 9 lakh tons. The details are:
   a. Hindustan Copper Ltd. : 50000 mt
   b. Sterlite Industries : 300000 mt
   c. Birla Copper : 500000 mt
   d. SWIL (Jagadia Copper) :50000 mt
7. The Indian demand is approximately 4 lakh MTs out of which 2.5lakh MT is sold by the domestic producers and the balance 1.5 lakh MTs are being cheap imports coming into India, mostly from Srilanka. The balance of Indian production is exported to other countries.
8. Since the Indian production is in far excess than the total domestic demand, there is no point in encouraging imports either at preferential or nil duty.

9. The FTA is creating Inverted Duty Structure.
10. There has been increase in employment of manpower because of Global Expansion plans and not related to the FTAs.
11. A number of companies have opened up manufact-uring base in Srilanka after the FTA is implemented. However, the majority of them are not Srilankan.
12. The company has no plan to shift manufacturing base to Srilanka.
13. The Srilanka FTA has created negative volume, price & economic effect in the market. The producers in Srilanka are merely melting scraps and selling ingots to India at reduced price. This process cannot be called as REFINING PROCESS and hence do not at all qualify for the Rules of Origin Certification. The Srilankan exporters are simply over invoicing their FOB Export Prices to qualify for ROO certificates.
14. There is no harm in continuance of the FTA, provided, the mis-utilisation is totally blocked. The mis-utilisation is going in both the ways of change of product form / description and change of country.
15. The company has filed application with the concerned government authorities for invoking safeguard measures under the Srilanka FTA, but since last three years, no action have been taken by the said authorities.
16. The company believes that the Srilanka FTA has not caused increase in any genuine trade and therefore not in the interest of the economy.
17. The Rules of Origin are weekly defined in the Srilankan FTA and misapplications are rampant in nature.
18. The Government should take proactive and friendly steps towards the industry.
19. Indian producers are interested in having FTAs with countries, which can supply copper concentrate (basic raw material for the copper industry) at reduced prices.

HINDALCO INDUSTRIES LIMITED (BIRLA COPPER)

1. The Products dealt with by them is Copper Cathode/ Copper Rod (Chapter-74 products). The application are;

a. Electrolytic Refined Copper which find uses in the Telecom sector, Electrical wirings, power cables & transformers and mint, copper strips etc.

b. Copper Scrap, which find uses in brass, handicrafts, plumbing tubes & fittings.

c. Over 90% Indian market is for 99.99% pure refined copper, the essential component of energy efficient motors, transformers and telecom requiring high conductivity and purity.

2. There is no Non Tariff barrier existing for these products.
3. A number of companies have opened up manufac-turing base in Srilanka after the FTA is implemented. Examples are: Lanka Cables & Mothersons Lanka.
4. The company has no plan to shift manufacturing base to Srilanka.
5. The quantities of goods sold in the domestic market have been increased and significant exports growth has been achieved.
6. Value realization has also increased in the domestic market.
7. Manpower increase is not much significant.
8. The Srilanka FTA has created negative volume, price & economic effect in the market.
9. The mis-utilisation is going in both the ways of change of product form / description and change of country. The persons involved are Indians and not srilankans. However, they got help from the srilankan government officials in doing these mis-utilisations.
10. Indian copper producers have brought up the issue of huge surge in the imports of copper products under ISLFTA in July 2002 and the serious injury it was causing to the domestic producers. The manipulation of value addition and surge was acknowledged by the Srilankan authorities to the Indian Copper Producers during their visit in June 2003. Over invoicing of Exports is resorted by the manipulators to justify the value addition of 35% for Certificates of Origin (COO). However the Indian authorities not taken any action so far.

11. Copper and copper items under Chapter 74 and 85.44 should be placed in the negative list of India under ISLFTA, since techno-economic facts simply rule out the possibility of minimum value addition in Srilanka under the stipulated Rules of Origin.
12. Although the Srilankan FTA has not caused increase in genuine trade, the FTAs should continue to be signed with proper and adequate safeguard mechanisms.
13. The Rules of Origin are weekly defined in the Srilankan FTA and misapplications are rampant in nature.
14. Apart from Value Addition clause already mentioned in the ISLFTA, change of tariff heading (CTH) should be part of ROO.
15. Already the rate of customs duty is at 7.5% for the current financial year. As the normal tariff is already reducing, the negative effect caused by mis-utilisation of the ISLFTA shall be blocked automatically in the future years.

ASSOCIATION OF SYNTHETIC FIBRE INDUSTRY

1. All FTA s are lacking in defining the clause on Rules of Origin.
2. Substantial changes and minimum value addition of more than 40% should take place in the country of origin.
3. Changes should take place at six digit level, so that, Change in Tariff Heading (CTH) will take place.
4. The manufacturers in Srilanka and Thailand are under invoicing the cost of raw materials to become qualify for COO.
5. Because of cross subsidization, the power cost is almost half in Srilanka and Thailand in comparison to India.
6. Singapore is not producing synthetic fibres but seeking these products under the EHS. Since, there is no production base existing in Singapore currently, these products should be kept in the Negative List.
7. The industries should be consulted before finalizing the negative list.

8. FTAs should be signed but simultaneously, adequate measures should be taken for avoiding the mis-utilisation cases happening.

ELECTRIC LAMP AND COMPONENT MANUFACTURERS ASSOCIATION OF INDIA

1. Around 35% of CFL is imported and the balances are manufactured in India.
2. Phillips alone imports 35% of total imports and genuinely importing from China and they are not adopting any unfair trade practices. Hence, anti dumping duties are not applicable. These are of good quality.
3. Other companies like GE and WIPRO are importing from Thailand. But these products are actually china made only.
4. India's total consumption market is 70 million CFL, out of which 42 million pieces are manufactured locally. The leading Indian manufacturers are; Osram India, Indo Asian Fuse Gear, Havells India, Phoenix Lamps, Asian Electronics, Angelo Brothers, Bajaj Lighting and Surya Roshni etc. Crompton Greaves is both manufacturing as well as importing. All these companies produce high quality CFL.
5. A number of small importers are also importing cheap products of lower quality. However, since the BIS mark will become compulsory w.e.f. February' 2007, these small time importers shall vanish from the market place.
6. China is the largest manufacturer base having more than 1000 CFL producers. Some of our domestic companies like Havells, Indo Asian and Phoenix are exporting to Europe. The other countries are importing from China.
7. Indian exporters are facing little problems in the south East Asian markets, as Singapore has imposed higher quality standards.
8. On an over all basis, FTAs are good and in the benefit of the trade. As far as CFL industry is concerned, both imports and exports are well balanced.
9. The FTAs signed with Srilanka, Thailand and Singapore have not affected the Indian industry in significant manner.

TELECOM EQUIPMENT MANUFACTURERS ASSOCIATION OF INDIA

1. With effect from 01.04.2005, 217 items under the information technology, telecom, computer and consumer elctronics sectors have become NIL duty items among all the WTO members.
2. The industry is facing problems to compete with the outsider because of low labour & power cost prevailing in these foreign countries.
3. The taxation systems are also impeding the growth process. VAT/ CST system is a big problem. Either CST should go or VAT should be applicable on imports also.
4. Other comments are similar to CETMA.
5. The infrastructure problems are the main issue for the member industries of the association.
6. Indian standards for importing the telecom products are lower in comparison to the government stipulations imposed on the local manufacturers. Standards should be similar for both the importers and the domestic producers.
7. Level playing fields should be created before signing the FTAs.
8. Physical inspection / customs procedure for exports should be simple and transparent. These government clearance procedures should be done online.
9. When the finished goods of certain variety are put under the preferential or nil duty, then similar treatment should also be given to the raw materials used in the production process of those goods.
10. Earlier, cheap imports from Korea were killing the Indian market. The government listened to the demands rose by the association and put all the raw materials under the list of freely importable.
11. But still the local manufacturers are still suffering because of labour laws and infrastructure problems and unable to increase their production capacity.
12. Siemens is planning to shift its production base to China. There are also a number of companies thinking similarly.

13. The Rules of Origin clauses in the FTAs should have at least 35% value addition clause and adequate mechanism should be there for stricter implementation.
14. The value addition clause in case of Singapore shall be more and the ROOs clauses should be strictly followed.
15. No specific comments regarding the FTAs signed with Srilanka, Thailand and Singapore.

TEXTILE MACHINERY MANUFACTURERS' ASSOCIATION (INDIA)

1. The Association dealt with products from HS Code 8444 to 8451 covering the list of all types of machines required by the textile manufacturers, like; spinning, weaving, texturing, cutting, knitting, stitching, preparation of textile fibres, finishing, washing machines etc. and their accessories.
2. All the products under these HS Codes are covered for preferential duty of imports under all the three FTAs (Srilanka, Thailand and Singapore).
3. The interesting fact is that; none of these countries Sri Lanka, Thailand and Singapore are manufacturing textile machineries. So, there has been no injury caused by the FTAs / CECA signed with these countries.
4. The association believes that; these FTAs may improve their export performance in respect of textile machinery, spares and accessories to these countries.

BALL & ROLLER BEARING MANUFACTURERS ASSOCIATION OF INDIA

1. The association dealt with products under HS Code 8482.
2. These products under HS Code 8482 are covered for preferential duty of imports under all the three FTAs (Srilanka, Thailand and Singapore).
3. However, the association has not yet done any survey on impact of the FTAs on their member industries. They have also not received any complain from their members so far. It can be assumed therefore that; the FTAs have not caused any injury on their industries.

MANUFACTURERS ASSOCIATION FOR INFORMATION TECHNOLOGY

Import duty on 217 IT Products is zero under the WTO IT Agreement signed under the Singapore Declaration.

1. Central Excise Duty of 16% was levied on the local manufacturers. Government of India had initially assured that by 2005, the duty on all types of finished products, parts and components should be gradually reduced to zero. But, where as the duty on finished goods were reduced every year, the duty on the parts and components were started reducing since the last year. *Inverted Duty structure* was therefore created, several local units being closed down.
2. The association has represented the fact of imbalanced duty structure over the years. Finally, in the current year budget, the problem is solved by imposing 12% duty on the assembled computers. The strain created in the last two years on the local industry has therefore been removed in the current year.
3. The zero import duty is same on for products coming from all the foreign countries. Therefore, as far as this industry is concerned, these FTAs have not done any over in balancing of trade. However, the local manufacturers should be taken into confidence first, before the Government finalise any FTA. Once the industry is injured / closed down, severe loss of human skill sets does happen.

INDIAN PAPER MANUFACTURERS ASSOCIATION

1. The association did not share any industry specific information.
2. Rather, they told that; there is potential export benefits expected under these FTAs.
3. Already their members are exporting to Srilanka.

THE VANASPATI MANUFACTURERS ASSOCIATION OF INDIA

1. The Industry has faced a lot of problem due to the ISLFTA.
2. Crude Palm oil, the basic raw material for production of Vanaspati attracts very high customs duty of 88%. The local production is very less and costly. The Government is

protecting the interest of the Indian farmers and therefore not in a position to reduce duty on crude palm oil.

3. Price Parity does not exist for crude palm oil. Manufacturers at Nepal and Srilanka are importing Crude Palm Oil at Nil rate of duty and re-exporting Vanaspati at preferential duty. Where as, the cost of manufacturing Vanaspati in India is much higher.
4. No limit has been placed on imports from Srilanka, where as in case of Nepal, it is 1lakh to per year. The total Indian demand is around 12 lakh ton per year out of which 4 lakh ton are imported directly from Nepal and Srilanka constituting 25% of the total Indian demand. Out of these imports, One lakh ton comes from Nepal, 2 lakh ton (official figure is 1.7 lakh ton) comes from Srilanka and 1lakh ton is smuggled from these two countries.
5. The minimum local content requirement is not specified under the ROOs in the FTA with Srilanka. Since the ROOs are based on VALUE ADDITION rather than LOCAL MATERIAL CONTENT REQUIREMENT, these are violated arbitrarily exposing the loopholes in the treaty.
6. Investments in these two countries have been made by the Indians instead of the local persons from Srilanka and Nepal. Already 16 such units have been set up in Srilanka. However, the present licensing requirement is blocking more Indians to shift their base of manufacturing to these countries.
7. The verification of the ROO stipulations is of utmost importance for smooth conducting trade under these FTAs.
8. **There should be provisions in the FTAs for Indian Accounting Professionals to visit abroad to verify the value addition matters under the ROOs and they should be given the authority to investigate & ask for information in those exporting countries. The Government authorities concerned should recognize legal opinions offered by such accountants. The Government may send the committees for review of those findings at a later stage.**

SOCIETY OF INDIAN AUTOMOBILE MANUFACTURERS

1. The products covered are HS Code 8702-8708 and 8711.

2. More than 1000cc vehicles and three wheelers have not been included in the list of concessional duty.
3. Cost competitiveness is not there. The duties are < 20%. So, surge in imports of auto components is happening (HS Code 8708 items).
4. Gear Boxes have seen high growth of exports (Toyota Kirloskar), as duty on Thai industries is 30%, which is more than the duties paid by the Indian manufacturers.
5. Thailand adopt differential tax treatment favouring the products peculiar to the their country, e.g. 1 ton pickup vehicles (both technical and dimensional preferences given).
6. Thai industries are now expanding their production capacity. These are Japanese dominated industries. The entire Thai Automobile industry is the proxy of the Japanese companies. Because of low cost of taxation, efficient labour management in Thailand, imports from this country will surge in future. The Thai manufacturers are 20% more cost competitive than their Indian counterparts. They are now targeting to the Indian markets.
7. Several Indian companies are looking opportunities for investing there and sell in those markets.
8. Unless cost competitiveness happens, Indian markets should not be opened up.
9. The association is positive about exports to the Srilankan markets. But most of the automobile items have been put under their negative list. The association has made representation to the Government for putting these items under preferential duty list of Srilanka in the Srilankan FTA and SAFTA.
10. Since, Singapore do not have manufacturers of automobile sector, these products have been kept under the negative list.
11. A number of members of the association have seen significant growth in their exports and domestic sales. They are increasing the production capacities to cater to meet increased Indian demand and exports to other markets, not necessarily been to Thailand, Srilanka & Singapore.
12. However the industries are going for more and more automation and increase in manpower employed by them is not proportionately significant.

13. Member industries are setting up additional facilities in the ASEAN countries to cater to the entire region.
14. These FTAs have not directly benefited to the industry. Completely Built-up Units (CBUs) should be kept in the negative list of the FTAs.
15. The FTAs are not causing any genuine increase in trade and not in the overall interests of the Indian economy.
16. The FTA with Thailand may bring distortion in the domestic markets by favouring only a few members but denying the fruits to the majority.
17. SIAM wants the ROOs to include the following;
    a) Minimum Value Addition of 50%
    b) CTH at 4 digit level and
    c) Definition should be given to the Non-Inclusive Processes, viz., clearing, packing etc.

AUTOMOTIVE COMPONENT MANUFACTURERS ASSOCIATION OF INDIA

1. Six products dealt by the associations have been under the EHS of the FTA signed with Thailand. Other products have been kept under the Negative List.
2. Petroleum Engine Parts (HS Code 840991) and Gear Boxes (HS Code 870840) under the EHS of both India and Thailand are generally traded in bulk quantities under the FTA. Other products (HS Codes 732020, 841381, 848210 & 851220) under the EHS of the FTA are not traded significantly.
3. Singapore is not a manufacturing base. It may be used as a trading route for other countries. Therefore following the ROOs strictly is what is being required. As long as the ROOs are followed strictly, the Auto Component industries will not be affected in absence of any domestic industry in Singapore. The present ROO calls for 40% value addition and CTH (change in tariff heading) and the perfect one. There should not be any dilution in the present ROOs defined under the CECA.
4. Most of the Auto component items are in the negative list under the ISLFTA. Infact, the Indian industry has the opportunities to exports to Srilanka.

5. If the ASEAN FTA is signed, it will create problems, as the negative list has very small base and the ROOs are less stringent. Thailand being a participant in the ASEAN FTA, the effect of Indo-Thai FTA will be nullified in future. Since, the ASEAN market is the same, investments may flow to the low cost manufacturing base at Thailand. Therefore, ASEAN FTA is a bigger threat for the auto component industry.
6. As of now, no major threats have been received from the FTAs signed with Srilanka, Thailand and Singapore. The situation is more or less trade neutral.
7. Indian manufacturers are at 20% cost disadvantage position in comparison to their counterparts at Thailand. The implementation of the FTAs should be differed till the internal reforms are done fully.

CONSUMER ELECTRONICS & TV MANUFACTURERS' ASSOCIATION

1. The Thailand and Indian economies are not compatible.
2. Consumer Electronics and Durable industries are already very strong in Thailand. Out of 15million TVs manufactured during 2004, Thailand had exported 13million sets.
3. But the total Indian production was only 9.5 million sets of televisions. Only ICs are imported, but all other components are locally produced in India.
4. Duties have been reduced to Nil for the Thailand products.
5. Labour cost is cheaper in India. But all other indirect costs like power, capital and infrastructure is quite lower in Thailand.
6. Internal taxes are very high and of complex nature in India. The tax administration system is being deadly combined with the inefficient governance and rampant corruption. Whereas in India the effective taxation comes to 35%, the composite VAT levied at Thailand is only 7.50%.
7. The supply chain of inputs is also distributed over vast geographical area of India. So logistics (transportation of goods) is a big problem.
8. Customs duty on inputs should come down and indirect taxes imposed on the domestic producers should reduce substantially.

9. Good Infrastructure should be provided and non-official transaction costs need to be reduced in case of both imports & exports.
10. The Government machinery needs to be more cooperative and transparent.
11. There should be 40% value addition and conversion at 4-digit level.
12. The Indian industry has been under protection regime for more than 45 years and it has been opened up to the competitive environment for last 12 / 13 years only. Market forces are now playing. The manufacturers have to explore export opportunities and change their attitude to conduct trade.
13. The Government needs to bring changes in the taxation systems urgently. Low taxes, single VAT and simple rules should help the industries to compete with the cheaper imported products.

ALL INDIA FOOD PROCESSORS ASSOCIATION OF INDIA

The Government of India does not create Mass awareness before the FTAs are implemented.

ALKALI MANUFACTURERS' ASSOCIATION OF INDIA

1. Products are all types of inorganic chemicals.
2. Trade with these three countries is not much.
3. Birlas have setup factory at Thailand. There have been exports of Caustic Soda and Soda Ash. No major imports from Thailand.
4. Very small quantities of Caustic Soda were imported from Singapore during 2003-04. The quantity for the same is NIL for 2004-05 and 2005-06.
5. There is no production base for inorganic chemicals in Srilanka.
6. No significant trade between these three countries has happened.
7. ROOs are very important and should be strictly applied. Taxation rates should be lower and emphasis should be on increasing the volume of manufacturing, so that there will be more taxes and employment being generated.

PROCESS PLANT AND MACHINERY ASSOCIATION OF INDIA

1. There are 130 corporate members of the association and they produce process machineries and instruments for the petroleum and chemical industries.
2. Neither the members are worried much about the FTAs, nor the association has gathered information about the impact of the FTAs.
3. FTAs open up good opportunities for exports. Manufacturing infrastructure is better in India. The manufacturing methodology and skill set of manpower are better here. So, the Indian manufacturers enjoy price advantage over their counterparts. Even some of the foreign companies are outsourcing the process of manufacturing to Indian producers.
4. One or two foreign companies have chosen to invest in Srilanka and established manufacturing set up there. They are only exporting to India, primarily supplying to the petroleum sector. They have supplied around Rs. 75 crore worth equipment over the past three years. But despite that, they are at cost disadvantage, as they need to purchase small quantity of raw materials from outside Srilanka. Also, trained manpower is not available in Srilanka. Now they are planning to invest in India to cater to the other exports markets.
5. There are no non- tariff barriers prevailing.
6. The inverted duty structure created by the ISLFTA has done small injuries to the members. However, the association has not sought any remedial actions from the authorities.
7. Once the anomalies in the taxation structure are removed, FTAs will help in boosting trade.
8. The FTAs should continue, but value addition should be 50% in the ROOs.

THE INDIAN FERRO ALLOY PRODUCERS' ASSOCIATION

1. The association covers the whole lot of products under HS Code 7202.
2. The international tariff is not considered for this industry in India. Due to the globalisation, government has reduced

customs duty on these products every year from 105% in 1992-93 to 7.5% in the current year budget. Imports of Ferro Alloys are growing at plus 100% (year-on-year basis) for last two years.

3. Power crisis is prevalent. It is 40-70% more costly than the international prices to produce in India. Since, level playing field is not prevailing India, the Government should not put these products under preferential or nil duty level. The association had already made representations with the Ministry of Steel in this regard.
4. Typical example is Bhutan. The industrial facilities including the Hydro Power projects there are being developed by India itself. But the power cost is 50paise to 1 rupee per unit there against the prevailing rate of 3 – 4 rupees per unit in India. Even the silico-manganese products / ores are procured by Bhutan from India on duty free basis. Irrespective of these facts, the Government has allowed the final products of ferro alloys being imported from Bhutan at concessional rates. This is killing the local industry.
5. There are no manufacturers actually present in Srilanka. Producers from other countries like South Africa and Malaysia etc. are using the Srilanka route for exporting into India. ROOs are not strictly followed at all. Similar tactics are played by the scrupulous exporters of other countries in case of Thailand and Singapore and using these three countries as the bi-pass route, which is killing the Indian industry, even though transportation cost is involved.
6. There is no major trade with these three countries. Even under the Thailand FTA / Singapore CECA, these products have not given any concessional treatment. But the concern for the association is that, these countries should not be used as the trading bi-pass hubs.
7. Although, anti-dumping duty have been levied on ferro-sillicon products against imports from China and Russia etc., but no such application have been filed against these three countries.
8. There are no non-tariff barriers applicable to the Indian products. The global trend is that in every six-year period,

the trend remains high for three years and the trend remains low for three years. Currently the Indian manufacturers have increased their installed capacity to meet the Indian demand and other export markets. The exports are not significantly done with the three countries under consideration.

9. The FTAs should continue provided that; the domestic industry should get level playing field and import from the partner country should not be given any preferential treatment where actually no manufacturing facilities exist.

INDIAN CHEMICAL COUNCIL

1. The products dealt by the association are as per HS Codes mentioned fully under chapter 28, 29, 38, 39 and partially under chapter 22, 23. Chemical industry is a big area covering different sectors like inorganic chemicals, organic chemicals, petrochemicals and pharmaceuticals etc.
2. The era of globalisation began in India in 1992. Import duty was as high as 300% in the protected regime before that year. Now it has been reduced to 12.50% in the current year.
3. Industry is increasing @15%. Exports are increasing because of opening up of the western markets, specifically the Russian countries. Mega mergers are also happening in these markets led by the Indian investors.
4. High level of import duty is imposed in comparison to the intermediary or finished goods. To avoid such inverted duty structure, all basic raw materials should be included in the FTA, where as the finished goods should be kept out of the preferential/ nil duty structure.
5. Various Organic Treaties are causing barriers in growth of exports.
6. Singapore has high-class infrastructure, low tax rates and low power rates. Labour laws are also flexible there. So, the level playing field should be first created in India.
7. Significant number of new producers have started production in Singapore after the CECA is signed. The Aditya Birla group has made significant investment in Thailand.
8. Since the members of the association are very big industries, they are managing against the injury elements caused by these FTAs.

9. The mis-utilisation of the FTAs is going on by change of country.
10. At least 40% value addition shall be stipulated in the ROOs in case of Singapore and the rules should be strictly implemented to ensure that, the products are actually manufactured in Singapore itself. For example, where as certain products like Pesticides etc. are not manufactured in Singapore, but these are included in the concession list.
11. Along with that, CTH should be a compulsory part of the ROOs.
12. Category of products on which any anti-dumping / anti-subsidy duty is being already levied, should not be given any preferential treatment again under the FTAs.
13. Our entrepreneurs should be allowed to invest in the projects in the partner country, whose products are covered under the FTAs with that country.
14. All trade and taxation laws should be liberalized.
15. Customs clearance procedures should be made transparent and efficient.
16. On an over all basis, the industry is balanced. However, level playing fields should be created before putting the products under preferential duty structure of the FTAs.

ASSOCIATION OF MAN-MADE FIBRE INDUSTRY OF INDIA

1. Mis-utilisation of the ISLFTA is happening. The major threat is coming from the Chinese producers. All the other Asian countries like Srilanka, Nepal etc. are importing from China and exporting back to India after re-packaging.
2. Most of the ASEAN LDCs are rerouting the Chinese goods only. This is bigger threat than direct imports from the ASEAN countries.
3. Thailand is the main competitor in the world in case of Viscose Staple Fibre and Viscose Rayon Based Spun Yarn products. It has 17% cost advantage in comparison to Indian manufacturers.
4. Although Thailand does not manufacture Viscose Filament Yarn, any duty reduction may cause dumping of Chinese products in India via Thailand route.

5. ROOs are to given importance. Value Addition is not verifiable at Srilanka. Along with 40% value addition clause, CTH in place of CTSH should be made compulsory in the ROO clauses. These conditions should be made not negotiable.
6. A VERIFYING MECHANISM should be in place in all the FTAs. Either an independent body or professional accountants should be authorized to carry on the verification jobs instead of government appointed committee members.
7. India is a big market for cheaper textiles.
8. FTAs should be made complimentary and not supplementary. It should be a win-win situation for both the partner countries.
9. Political compulsions should not affect the economic decisions of the Government.
10. These FTAs have neither helped the industry nor affected it.

THE CLOTHING MANUFACTURERS ASSOCIATION OF INDIA

1. All these three FTAs along with the ASEAN & SAARC agreements have problem with ROO issues.
2. Incase of Srilanka, 8 million garments are allowed to be imported out of which 6 million pieces are to be woven from India.
3. In case of Singapore, now 90% of duty is waived.
4. These concessions are of no meaning as concessions are based on the advalerom basis. So reduction of duty in case of Srilanka/ Singapore is not causing significant effects.
5. In case of Thailand, garments are not at all covered under the EHS. No problem therefore arises.
6. The ROOs should be well defined to contain provisions for change in HS Code and minimum value addition of 50%.
7. Exports are increasing because of normal trade growth. Since, the domestic consumption quality is now equivalent to the export quality, the rising domestic consumption is also pushing up the export potentials.
8. The association is targeting job growth of 7.3 million workers at the present level to 23 million workforces by 2010.

9. The changing habits of the fashion oriented middle class families in India are both way pushing up the domestic consumption and exports. The FTAs have no role to play here. The industry is neutralized on an overall basis.

TOOL AND GAUGE MANUFACTURERS ASSOCIATION

1. The products are Dies (HS Code 82073000, 82072000, 84804100, 84804900), Moulds (84807100/3000/6000/7900), Mould Bases (84802000), Jigs & Fixtures (84663000) and other related items (84806000). The potential markets are Automobiles, Auto ancillary, Consumer Durables, Plastics, Electronics, Electrical & General Engineering etc.
2. Although, many of these products have been covered by 100% duty exemption under the Srilankan FTA and Preferential Duty treatment under the Singapore CECA, impact of increased imports has not been much on the industry.
3. Limited impact of the Thai FTA has been felt. Many Japanese automobile makers are routing the trade through Thailand.
4. No shifting of industries has been occurred to these three countries.
5. The industry is not doing significant exports transaction with these three countries and no non-tariff barriers also exist.
6. The western markets have good potential. Even the products are attracting duty exemption in the U.S.A.
7. The members of the industry are fully occupied with orders and the Indian demand itself is big.
8. The FTAs are trade neutral.

APPAREL EXPORT PROMOTION COUNCIL

1. The exports growth in the last two years has been significant.
2. Even though India had been the preferred manufacturing base for the western countries, they had drifted away to the emerging Chinese manufacturing bases. But, China failed in meeting the quality demands of the western countries.

The political situation is also not trade conducive. In India, the production quality is good, finishing of the final textiles are very fine and pricing is competitive. Hence, ultimately the western countries have returned back to India resulting into phenomenal growth of the Indian industry in the last two years.

3. All the exporters have huge orders in hand. So, the Indian exporters are increasing their production capacities.
4. Actual exports are much higher (10-15%) than the official DGCI figures available.
5. Srilanka is not an export market for India as far as textiles is concerned. They import yarns from India and they have already a number of textile mills that produce garments. Infact, the ISLFTA has helped Srilanka in increasing their trade.
6. India is pioneer in making PVPC & 100% Cotton textiles. However, other countries like China are good in CVC products. The markets are different.
7. The FDI in this sector is distributive in the other countries. Where as in India, it is not so. Policies should be made to attract more FDI in this sector. It will create phenomenal growth for the Indian industry.
8. The FTAs with the south Asian countries have not contributed much to the exports kitty. However, these are welcome signs for India where proper infrastructure and skilled labour are available.
9. Government of India is also arranging a lot of trade promotional activities. Participation are made in the majority of the international trade fairs, exhibitions etc. AEPC is actively participating in these programmes and trying to bring all of the Indian exporters into the International Platform.
10. AEPC believes in creating fully transparent systems for growth of international trade. They themselves are issuing 'Certificate of Origins' for the textile products. ***They will welcome foreign accounting professionals to come and verify the certification procedures related to ROO issues, provided similar facilities are also offered to the***

Indian counterparts. AEPC will support such moves, if will be taken by the Government for strengthening the ROO clauses.

AUTOMOTIVE TYRE MANUFACTURERS ASSOCIATION

There is a special **CASE STUDY** on the **Automotive Tyre Industry** mentioned in this dissertation. However, here a brief on overall views of the association is given;

1. There are no Non Tariff Barriers applicable in relation to trade with Srilanka, Thailand and Singapore.
2. No cases of new producers establishing setups in these three countries are reported, in the Post-FTA period. Also there is no significant increase in the production capacities in relation to these FTAs have been made by the members of the association.
3. Indian manufacturers have no plans for shifting their manufacturing bases to Thailand and Singapore.
4. But in Srilanka, CEAT-KELANI TYRES is a joint venture company and two more companies are looking for joint ventures in Srilanka.
5. Both the quantity and value of goods manufactured have been increased because of the tremendous growth happened in the vehicles market in India. The other factors contributing to the growth are adoption of latest technology, change in product mix and improved productivity. The manpower employed by the industry has also gone up because of the rise in the domestic demand for tyres.
6. These FTAs have not been actually benefited the industry.
7. The ROOs have been weakly defined and not perfectly implemented. Some cases of rerouting the imports of tyres (HSC 4011) are happening through Singapore.
8. The clauses for Value Addition, CTSH, Product Specification & TRQs etc. should be well defined in the FTAs.
9. The inverted duty structure is causing harm to the members. Natural rubber is put in the negative list and so; the raw materials are imported paying full duty. However, tyres are imported freely. The association has approached the

authorities for safeguard measures against imports from Srilanka.

10. Even though, Singapore has no manufacturing base, concession on tyres are inconsequential.
11. China and Korea are the major countries from which majority of the cheap imports are coming. These are participants of the Bangkok Agreement. The association has filed suite with the Director General of Anti-Dumping for Anti-Dumping Investigations against these countries. The application is pending for levy of provisional duties.
12. Incase of raw material intensive industry, if the raw material is on the negative list, then the finished products should not be allowed to be imported on preferential basis.
13. The Government should not allow the partner countries to put our export competitive products in their negative lists.

THE SOLVENT EXTRACTORS' ASSOCIATION OF INDIA

1. Oil seed should be excluded from the preferential duties, as it directly affects the farmers.
2. India stands at worldwide position of 3 in palm oil imports, behind China and European Union – 25.
3. No ROOs are followed at Srilanka. Heavy manipulation is going on. The cheap price of imports is the matter of primary concern. Quantity of imports is the secondary concern.
4. The GOI has agreed to put the put the edible oil in the negative list. Interested parties like Malaysia are therefore upset.
5. As on date, no major trade is happening with Thailand. Two years back, production of Thailand was 15 lakh ton and the local demand there was only 7 lakh ton. It implied that, the Thaïs would simply dump their surplus products in the Indian market. The association had made representation with the GOI for blocking Thai imports by not putting the vegetable oils under the EHS. Thailand, Malaysia and Indonesia are lobbying hard for putting these products in the concession list. As on date, these products are in the negative list.
6. There is no production base of palm/ edible oils at Singapore.

7. Imports from Srilanka, Nepal and Bhutan are the major threats.
8. The GOI is now taking friendly steps and considering either to impose higher ROO norms or putting the products under negative list.
9. Since the Indian industry is being already hit by these FTAs, the ground realities should be checked before signing any new FTA.
10. Currently, the TRQs are applicable to the whole country on annual basis. Remedies can be; either the annual quota of imports can be divided over monthly basis or division of the total quota quantity for the 26 states of India individually. The imports can become therefore distributive and unable to cause material injury to the industries based in any particular region.
11. NAFED has been declared as the NODAL AGENCY for importing all vegetable oils. This will act as a non-tariff barrier against the Srilankan exporters.
12. The bilateral trade should increase, but the interests of the industries of the both sides should be considered before signing any FTA.

ORGANIZATION OF PLASTICS PROCESSORS OF INDIA

1. ASEAN is not of much significance.
2. Since, the products of the members are of big size, but light weight, it is not economical either to import or export them.
3. Normally, the raw materials are imported, but the finished products are not.
4. The association has not yet received any information from members towards impact of these 3 FTAs. Hence, it is not in a position to comment about it.

17

AUTOMOTIVE TYRE INDUSTRY- A CASE STUDY

The source of information for this case study have been obtained from the official website of the ATMA (**www.atmaindia.org**) and a publication on **REGIONAL TRADE AGREEMENTS (RTAs)** released by ATMA in May, 2006. **Automotive Tyre Manufacturers' Association (ATMA)** was set up in 1975, registered under The Companies Act, as the representative body of automotive tyre industry in India. 7 large tyre companies representing over 85% of production of tyres in the country are also members of the Association.

INDUSTRY OVERVIEW

The following are the key facts about the Automotive Tyre Industry:

- ✓ 43 tyre companies have 58 tyre plants located all over India.
- ✓ Total tyre production exceeded 60 million numbers in 2004-05.
- ✓ Truck and Bus tyre production exceeded 11 million numbers in 2004-05.
- ✓ 10% growth in total tyre production for 2004-05 over 2003-04.
- ✓ 10 tyre companies account for over 95% of tyre industry turnover.
- ✓ 23% of domestic production of truck and bus tyres is exported.
- ✓ Indian tyres are exported to over 65 countries worldwide.
- ✓ 11% CAGR achieved in export realization value from 1993-94 to 2005-06(estimated).

✓ 54% of total natural rubber consumption in India is made by the tyre industries alone.

GOVERNMENT POLICY

Tyre Industry Delicensed	1987
Export (of tyres and tubes)	Freely allowed
Import (of new tyres and tubes)	Freely allowed Since 2001. No WTO Bound Rates for tyres & tubes.
Import Policy for Used / Retreaded tyres:	Restricted Since April, 2006
Import of all raw materials	Freely allowed (OGL)
Normal rate of basic Customs Duty	12.50%
Central Excise Duty	16%

Total Tyre Production In India

(source:www.atmaindia.org) *(In 000 Nos.)*

CATEGORY	1998-99	1999-00	2000-01	2001-02	2002-03	2003-04	2004-05
Truck & Bus	7913	8969	8612	8474	9863	10821	11092
Passenger Car	4571	6054	6813	7481	8544	9959	11862
Jeep	1247	1283	1155	1247	1384	1440	1462
Light Comml. Veh. (L.C.V.)	1917	1980	2108	2352	2844	3271	3945
Tractor Front	1085	1203	1186	1150	1125	1148	1311
Tractor Rear	839	903	852	785	825	842	1096
Tractor Trailer	223	295	277	320	470	415	408
A.D.V.	593	589	511	488	456	295	197
Scooter	10975	10140	9385	8547	9875	9274	9992
Motor Cycle	7277	9275	11196	12275	15654	16688	18127
Moped	234	516	119	135	185	168	124
Industrial	137	172	219	214	309	295	377
O.T.R.	37	36	38	46	51	74	89
Aero	0	0	0	0	0	0	0
TOTAL	37048	41415	42471	43514	515585	54690	60082

Total Tube Production In India (source: www.atmaindia.org)

(In 000 Nos.)

CATEGORY	1998-99	1999-00	2000-01	2001-02	2002-03	2003-04	2004-05
Truck & Bus	6781	7382	7465	7291	7982	8851	9439
Passenger Car	3563	3949	4322	4277	4762	5331	5947
Jeep	1133	1046	939	972	1038	1056	1040
Light Comm. Veh. (L.C.V.)	1416	1614	1758	1853	2147	2633	3100
Tractor	1221	1259	1108	925	835	907	1053
A.D.V.	295	268	259	216	231	187	140
Scooter	6903	5753	5531	5122	5750	5624	6439
Motor Cycle	6507	7771	9772	11372	13978	15415	18671
Moped	224	564	223	151	176	270	347
Industrial	29	33	48	61	65	50	71
O.T.R.	9	12	9	13	15	19	26
Aero	0	0	0	0	0	0	0
TOTAL	**28081**	**29651**	**31434**	**32235**	**36979**	**40342**	**46273**

Categorywise Tyre Exports

[Nos.]

CATEGORY	1999-00	2000-01	2001- 02	2002-03	2003-04	2004-05
Truck & Bus	1637093	1742264	1805203	2141438	223155	2503956
Passenger Car	28473	86147	287547	364514	591494	1024561
Jeep	0	0	40	20	220	391
Light Commercial Vehicle	362875	423418	610692	700868	962972	1130908
Tractor Front	23217	28747	23431	20698	18990	18202
Tractor Rear	43590	65898	51218	72263	89758	84684
Tractor Trailer	0	0	444	852	1448	3686
Motor Cycle	19760	34511	33019	34088	47333	62710
ADV	0	110	170	20	0	0
Scooter	53877	23319	43391	49966	120725	202656
Implements	15705	13616	15758	9143	6558	2096
Industrial	5834	8994	15570	20716	10702	9885
OTR	14656	16411	21468	29079	21168	23375
Antique	3436	1309	2894	0	0	0
TOTAL	**2208566**	**2444744**	**2910845**	**3443665**	**4102923**	**5067038**

Average Annual Compound growth rate in exports during last one decade is 8%. *(source: www.atmaindia.org)*

Financial Year 2005-2006 (Estimated)
(source: www.atmaindia.org)

Turnover of Indian Tyre Industry	Rs. 14,250 Crores
Tyre Production (Tonnage) (2004-05)	10.36 lakh M.T.
Tyre Production – All Categories (Nos.)	655 Lakh
Tyre Export from India (Value):	Rs. 2000 crores
Number of tyre companies:	43
Industry Concentration	10 Large tyre companies account for over 95% of total tyre production.
Production range except Aircraft and Snow	All categories of tyres tyres.
Radialisation Level Current (as a % of total tyre production)	Passenger Car tyres: 85% Light Commercial Vehicles: 10% Heavy Vehicles (Truck & Bus): 2%

Calendar Year 2005 (Estimated)

Turnover of Indian Tyre Industry	US $ 3.13 Billion
Installed Capacity (Nos.)	60.5 Million
Capacity Utilitsation	85%
Total Tyre Production (Nos.)	65 Million
Total Tyre Import (In 000 Nos.)	868
Taxes & Duties	US $ 900 Million

(source: www.atmaindia.org)

Relevance of these three FTAs with the Automative Tyre Industry

Particular	India-Srilanka FTA	India-Thailand FTA	India-Singapore CECA
New Tyre/ Tubes	• New Tyre/Tubes can be imported at nmil customs duty. • Sri Lanka is a net tyre importing country and local production is limited. However, a little growth in imports of tyre has been observed.	Currently, tyres are not included in the initial list of items under the *Early Harvest Scheme* eligible for concessional / duty free imports.	• Truck and Bus (Bias) and P. Car (Bias) and all other tyres at preferential duty 9.38% (MFN – 12.50%), Aircraft Tyres 2.25% (MFN – 3%). • No practical consequences as there is no production of Bias Truck and Bus & P. Car tyres in Singapore. • Stringent Value Additional and Rules of Origin norms take care of third country exports re-routed through Singapore.
Raw material for Tyre Industry	• Natural Rubber, Reclaimed/ Waste/ Retreaded rubber, Used and Retreaded Tyres are in India's Negative list. • Several other raw materials are eligible for duty concessions of varying magnitude upto 100% also. • No practical implication, since import of Natural Rubber from Sri Lanka can be effected through Bangkok Agreement at concessional tariff and there is hardly any import of other raw materials from Sri Lanka.	Natural Rubber is included in India's Negative list. Not eligible for any preferential duty concession.	• 9 raw materials of tyre industry eligible for concessional import and 10%, 25%, 100% margin of preference over MFN rate. • However, there is either nil/ negligible imports from Singapore. Hence no impact on the industry.
Used Tyres and Retreaded Tyres	• Currently under the Negative List. • No practical implication; No major imports of these items from Sri Lanka. More over, under the Foreign Trade Policy, 2006, import of these items has been placed under Restrictive List which is a more stringent provision.	No Comments	• Used Tyres (solid rubber)/ retreaded tyres 9.38%(MFN – 12.50%) • No practical implication; under the Foreign Trade Policy, 2006, import of these items has been placed under Restrictive List.
Future Duty Structure	No Comments	Listing of items under the Early Harvest Scheme may be expanded in future. In that case; • If tyres are included under EHS, it would adversely impact the domestic tyre industry. ATMA has sought inclusion of tyres (especially Bias Truck / Bus & P. Car radial tyres) under India's Negative List. • Inclusion of Natural Rubber under EHS will help the Indian Industry.	Tariffs to be reduced in five stages leading to 50% of MFN tariffs w.e.f. April, 2009.

HS Classification	*Product / Category*	*Basic Customs Duty*	*India-Srilanka FTA*	*India-Thailand FTA*	*Indo Singapore CECA*
Tyres					
4011	New Tyres (All)	12.5%	Nil Duty	Not covered in EHS	9.38% (T&B/P. Car-Blas Ply only) + All other tyres
4011 30 00	Aero Tyres	3%	Nil Duty	Not covered in EHS	2.25%
4012 20 00	Used Rubber Tyres	12.5%	In Negative List	Not covered in EHS	9.38% (Applicable for Solid Tyres only)
4012 10 00	Retreaded Tyres	12.5%	In Negative List	Not covered in EHS	-do-
4013 10 00	Inner Tubes	12.5%	Not Covered	Not covered in EHS	Not Covered
4008 21 20	Retreaded Rubber	12.5%	Not Covered	Not covered in EHS	-do-
Raw-Material(s)					
4001 21 00	Natural Rubber	20%	In Negative List	Not covered in EHS	Not Covered
4001 10 00	NR Latex	70%	Not Covered	Not covered in EHS	-do-
5402 10 10	Nylon Tyre Yarn	10%	In Negative List	Not covered in EHS	-do-
5902 10 10	NTC Fabric	12.5%	9.37%	Not covered in EHS	-do-
7312 90 10	Steel Tyre Cord	12.5%	Nil Duty	Not covered in EHS	9.38%
5902 20 00	Polyester Tyre Cord	12.5%	9.37%	Not covered in EHS	Not Covered
2803 00 10	Carbon Black	10%	Nil Duty	Not covered in EHS	Not Covered
2802 00 10	Precipitated Silica/Sulphur	10%	Nil Duty	Not covered in EHS	Nil Duty
2817 00 10	Zinc Oxide (Ref. Note 3)	12.5%	Nil Duty	Not covered in EHS	Not Covered
2907 21 00	Resorcinol	12.5%	Nil Duty	Not covered in EHS	9.38%
7217 90 99	Bead Wire	5%	Nil Duty	Not covered in EHS	Not Covered
2823 00 10	Titanium Dioxide	12.5%	Nil Duty	Not covered in EHS	11.25%
3823 11 09	Stearic Acid	20%	Nil Duty	Not covered in EHS	Not Covered
2707 99 00	Process Oil	12.5%	Nil Duty	Not covered in EHS	-do-
2710 00 00	Naptha	5%	Nil Duty	Not covered in EHS	-do-
2912 11 00	Formaldehyde	12.5%	Nil Duty	Not covered in EHS	-do-
2921 41 00	Analiene	12.5%	Nil Duty	Not covered in EHS	11.25%
2933 71 00	Caprolactum	10%	Nil Duty	Not covered in EHS	7.5%
2707 00 00	Carbon Black Feedstock	10%	Nil Duty	Not covered in EHS	Not Covered
3812 10 00	Rubber Chemicals	12.5%	Not Covered	Not covered in EHS	9.38% (Antioxidant 6PPD)
4002 90 00	VP Latex	12.5%	Nil Duty	Not covered in EHS	Not Covered
4002 39 00	Neoprene Rubber	12.5%	Nil Duty	Not covered in EHS	-do-
4003 00	Reclaimed Rubber	12.5%	Negative List	Not covered in EHS	-do-
3910 00 00	Silicone Emulsion	12.5%	Nil Duty	Not covered in EHS	-do-
2503 00 90	Insoluble Sulphur	5%	Nil Duty	Not covered in EHS	Nil Duty
2712 20 10	Paraffin Wax	10%	Nil Duty	Not covered in EHS	Not Covered
4002 70 00	EPDM	12.5%	Nil Duty	Not covered in EHS	11.25%
2711 14 00	Butadiene	10%	Nil Duty	Not covered in EHS	Not Covered
Customs Notification notifying the concessional/ preferential rate of duty			Notification No. 150-Cus dt. 14.10..2003		Notification No(s) 73/74/75-Cus dt. 22.07.05 / Notification No. 38/2006- Cus dt. 28.04..2006

Trend of Impact of these three FTAs on the Automotive Tyre Industry

- In the past, most of these countries did not offer any concessions on exports of tyres from India, no impact was observed in case of exports. Under the India-Srilanka FTA, although the imports of tyres were allowed at duty free rate, because of the negligible/ small volume of imports, the injury caused to the industry was not much significant. Also, since the volume of raw materials being imported by tyre industry from these countries being small, effect of these FTAs was not of practical significances.
- Since the focus has been changed to now signing more and more FTAs instead of PTAs, even marginal concessions in customs tariffs is tilting the scales in favour of the countries with which trade can be carried out on a preferential / duty free basis.
- As the customs duty is already low and further reducing, India is expected to concede more than what it receives. The trend is likely to continue.
- Tyre imports from Srilanka, Thailand and Singapore are likely to increase under the FTAs signed. There is no manufacturing base in Singapore for tyres. At present, although the preferential duty is of no consequence, but in future there may be routing of third country exports via Singapore.
- Political pressure may mount on India from Srilanka and Thailand to keep Natural Rubber (the major raw material for the tyre industry) under the preferential/concessional list, instead of the present position being in the Negative List. A number of other raw materials may also be put in the concessional list.
- Tyre industry has sought for including truck & bus tyres (HSC 401110), passenger car tyres (HSC 401120) and Used Tyres (HSC 4012 – all descriptions) under the negative list under the India-Thailand FTA. The reasons are;
- World's top three tyre manufacturing companies having market share of more than 60% of global production are having plants at Thailand.

- The size of Indian tyre industry is only 0.06% of annual turnover of these 3 global companies.
- Inverted duty structure will affect the industry as the basic raw material natural rubber being in the negative list, concessional duty on import of finish product, i.e., tyres are undesirable.
- Indian industries may shift their manufacturing base to Thailand.
- Already, the industry is facing intense competition from the imports of China made tyres. Additional competition from Thailand because of concessional duty structure is undesirable.
- The competitiveness of the Indian tyre manufacturers in exporting tyres to other countries shall be eroded.
- More than 8,00,000 persons working in the tyre / ancillary industries and growing of natural rubbers shall be displaced, if cheap Thai imports affects the local producers.

SECTION - VI

(Final Conclusion and Recommendations)

Contents

18

FINAL CONCLUSIONS AND RECOMMENDATIONS

CONCLUDING OBSERVATIONS

The final conclusions are based on the overall observations from the data analysis & comparisons, real interviews done with the relevant industry associations and our overall assessment of the economic situations prevailing in the particular regions. The **observations** from Data Analysis follows:

SRILANKA- IMPORTS

- From Rs. 8026.85 lakhs of imports in 1998-99 from Srilanka, the figure has reached upto Rs. 149083.85 lakhs in 2004-05 (18.57 times) against India's world imports rising from Rs. 470811.07 lakhs to Rs. 3,318,220.98 lakhs (7.05 times) for the sampled products.
- It is seen that, the relative fastness of weighted average CAGR in most cases are far higher in case of imports from Srilanka in case of India's world imports for the same products.
- It is observed that the varieties of parameters {like incremental trend of volume & value of imports from Srilanka as well as India's total imports from the world, market share % in volume & value, unit prices, CAGR of the items (volume and value both) of imports from Srilanka and the world and correlation factors of various trend series} of the high value items have shown positive growth rate after the FTA is implemented. The growth under the FTA, have exceeded the growth of world trade of India under different parameters also.
- The surge in imports observed in selected cases have shown that; in a selected cases like products of Copper, Spices & Vanaspati / edible oils etc., there is total trade diversion to Srilanka.

- However the over all growth pattern shows trade creation in imports as value wise India's imports from the world have also been risen a number of times.
- Even imports of some of the products covered under the Negative list also have grown fast. The chapter-wise growth under different concession levels also reflects mostly the same result as visualized in the case of individual products. Interesting to note that; a lot of negative list items are also showing high growth.
- Market share of products of zero duty and phased residual list have been moved decently and since maximum of the sampled products (75 out of total 111) pertains to the phased residual list category, the movement of the all sampled products curve also followed the same pattern.
- Market share of Products of Negative list have moved up and down and later on stabilized at slightly higher level than the base year of 1998-99.
- Out of the top 10% chapters (total chapters are 37) selected showing the *Highest CAGR* and *Highest Value of Imports in 2004-05*, it is observed that;
  a) The highest positive movement has been shown for CHAPTER-74 (Phased Residual List). As the concessional duty level goes on increasing, the trend of imports for the COPPER PRODUCTS kept on increasing and capturing the markets of India's world imports. Trade diversion is clearly established from this fact as far as copper industry is concerned.
  b) Incase of CHAPTER 9 products (Coffee, Tea and Spices), the growth can be said to be decent, as the curve has managed to grow and sustained its trend after falling in 2003-04.
  c) For Chapter 28 (Inorganic Chemicals) & Chapter 85 (Audio Visual goods and electrical machinery), even though there are rising curves, in absence of manufacturing base of such industries in Srilanka, it is to be seen whether the surge has been caused by using the FTA route to avail concessional duty access to Indian Markets by the manufacturers of other countries.

d) The growth of market share for Chapter 73 (Articles of Iron or Steel) and Chapter 84 (Machinery and Appliances) have been modest.

- **The conclusion can therefore be derived that the FTA has caused significant growth in imports and the Injury has been done in the case of selected industries.**

SRILANKA- EXPORTS

- From Rs. 34631.27 lakhs of exports in 1998-99 to Srilanka, the figure has reached upto Rs. 418790.58 lakhs in 2004-05 (12.09 times) against India's world exports rising from Rs. 3091827.93 lakhs to Rs.12364459.51 lakhs (3.99 times) for the sampled products.
- Interesting to note is that products that are neither covered under any concession list offered by Srilanka nor the negative list stipulated have shown tremendous increase in turnover in 2003-04 and 2004-05. Value wise, the products under this category (other items at MFN rate) constitute 23.349% of the total value of exports to Srilanka in 2004-05.
- Where as the weighted average CAGR in cases of Zero Duty, SLR & Negative list are more for exports to Srilanka in comparison to India's world exports, it is less in cases of exports of products covered under F II and Other items at MFN Rate. The results are similar when the products are considered individually or being grouped under chapters.
- The **majority of products sampled pertain to either the Negative list** (23.073% value wise of total exports in 2004-05) **or Other Items at MFN Rate** (23.349% of the total value of exports to Srilanka in 2004-05). From the total sample size of 68.776% of total value of exports in 2004-05, these two category alone accounts for 46.422%.
- There is only one sampled product falling under the zero duty category.
- Products under F II category have shown lower growth rate in comparison to the world exports. The only concessional items showing high growth of exports to Srilanka in comparison to world exports are those falling under the SLR category only.

- In most of the sampled items covered it can be observed that the variety of parameters {like incremental trend of volume & value of exports to Srilanka as well as India's total exports to the world, market share % in volume & value, unit prices and CAGR of the items (volume and value both) of exports to Srilanka and the world} **of the** top 25 high value exported items, top 20% of sampled products covered under each category (sorted on the basis of **value of exports** in 2004-05) & top 10% of sampled products covered under each category (sorted on the basis of **CAGR**-value of exports to srilanka) **have shown moderate growth rate only . A lot of products showing high growth are covered under either the Negative List or Other Items at MFN Rate.**
- The chapter-wise growth under different concession levels also reflecting mostly the similar results as visualized in the case of individual products.
- Out of the two criteria applied for selecting top 10% chapters, it is observed that products under the Negative List and products not covered under any list (MFN Rate) (CHAPTER 87, 85, 40 & 10) have risen more both Value of Exports and CAGR wise.
- Significantly the conclusion is that the FTA has not benefited much to Indian exporters in comparison to their surge in exports to the whole world. **The relatively slow growth in India's preferential exports to Srilanka is due to smaller duty free list, longer phase out and larger negative list**. The rise in exports to Srilanka can be attributed to other factors like competitiveness of the Indian products, general trend in growth in world exports and geographical proximity to Srilanka etc.

THAILAND - IMPORTS

- From Rs. 105668.99 lakhs of imports in 2001-02 from Thailand, the figure has reached upto Rs. 291889.83 lakhs in 2004-05 (2.76 times) against India's world imports rising from Rs. 1961469.89 lakhs to Rs. 5707305.52 lakhs (2.91 times) for the sampled products.
- It is seen that, the relative fastness of weighted average CAGR in all cases are higher in case of imports from

Thailand. Since, a number of items have shown import turnover only in the year 2004-05, the weighted average CAGR in cases of sample products (mostly CHAPTER 85 PRODUCTS) covered under EHS is showing lower growth rate. However, the same EHS products when grouped under chapters, the position becomes better and the relative fastness increased more than 150%. The opposite trend observed in case of sample products not covered under EHS, when grouped under different chapters with relative fastness declining from 2.25 to 1.53.

- In case of most of the top 30 high value imported sampled items, it is observed that the varieties of parameters {like incremental trend of volume & value of imports from Thailand as well as India's total imports from the world, market share % in volume & value, unit prices, CAGR of the items (volume and value both) of imports from Thailand and the world and correlation factors of various trend series} **have shown positive growth rate after the FTA is implemented. The growth patterns of the EHS products are relatively higher (excluding the exceptional case of HSC** 84151010) **with cheaper imports of basically Chapter 85 products.**
- Most of the products when grouped under different chapters covered under EHS have shown positive growth for key parameters {like incremental trend of value of imports from Thailand as well as India's total imports from the world, market share % in value and CAGR of the chapters (value only) } along with the implementation of the EHS of the FTA. The correlations among trend in value of imports from Thailand and World imports have been closely related in positive manner.
- Most of the chapters not covered under EHS have also shown positive growth along with the implementation of the EHS of the FTA. The correlation among trend in value of imports from Thailand and World imports has been closely related in positive manner. This signifies that; people have anticipated enlargement of the EHS list in near future and the trade relation between both of the countries have developed significantly.
- The market share of the products coming under EHS category have rise sharply in the year 2004-05. Where as

for products not covered under EHS, the movement is not significant. The result being the EHS under the FTA has caused surge in imports of the sampled products, where as the non-EHS products move in tandem with general trend of world imports combined with future anticipation of the enlargement of the EHS list.

- ***For EHS products***; products of Chapter 94 (Furniture Items) have shown heavy rise followed by Chapter 76 (Aluminium and Articles thereof) and Chapter 85 (Audio Visual Equipments incl. TV). Moderate growth found in case of Chapter 71 (Natural stones, metals and imitation jewellery) products. Stability observed for Chapter 39 (Plastics and Articles thereof) and slight decline in share observed for Chapter 73 (Articles of Iron or Steel) and Chapter 84(Machinery and Mechanical appliances) products.
- The surges in imports observed in most of the cases of all the 33 sampled products covered under EHS, signifies the diversion of trade to Thailand for products covered under EHS. The market shares of these products have also increased.
- The growth in the imports of the NON EHS items also signifies the fact that there are more opportunities available to the Thailand producers to tap the vast Indian market. It also alerts that, our domestic producers need to produce more competitive products.
- **So, the surges in import have been observed in the Furniture, Aluminium, Audio Visual Equipments and Television products.**
- **The conclusion can therefore that, the FTA has affected small number of particular industries although overall surge in imports are there. Thailand producers have been benefited by surge in imports from them in comparison to India's world imports. The surge might have been caused in anticipation of enlargement of the EHS list at a later stage.**

THAILAND - EXPORTS

- From Rs. 166751.93 lakhs of exports in 2001-02 to Thailand, the figure has reached upto Rs. 309065.65lakhs in 2004-05

(1.85 times) against India's world exports rising from Rs. 5,026,480.20 lakhs to Rs. 10,759,419.76 lakhs (2.14 times) for the sampled products.

- It is seen that; the relative fastness of weighted average CAGR in all cases are higher in case of exports to Thailand. The fastness of weighted average CAGR for sampled products covered under EHS is much higher than the NON EHS products. However, the value wise rise is not much significant in case of EHS products and also lesser number of EHS products are covered under the sample.
- In most of the top 20 high value exported sampled items; it is be observed that the varieties of key parameters { like incremental trend of volume & value of exports to Thailand as well as India's total exports to the world, market share % in volume & value, unit prices and CAGR of the items (volume and value both) of exports to Thailand and the world } have shown positive growth rate after the FTA is implemented. The growth patterns of the EHS products are relatively higher, but only two EHS products have come under the top 20 high value items exported.
- The surge in exports observed in most of cases of the 11 sampled products covered under EHS signifies the diversion of trade of India to Thailand for products covered under EHS. The market shares of these products have also increased.
- The growth in the exports of the top 10 sampled products (CAGR wise) of NON EHS category also signifies the fact that there are more opportunities available to the Indian producers to tap the Thailand market.
- The key parameters { like incremental trend of value of exports to Thailand as well as India's total exports to the world, market share % in value and CAGR of the chapters (value only) } of most of the chapters covered under EHS (total 8 chapters) have shown positive growth along with the implementation of the EHS of the FTA. The highest growths have been observed in the case of CHAPTER 87 products (Vehicles and Accessories) commanding 42.57% market share of India's world exports of same product in 2004-05. However all these sampled EHS products constitute only 3.58% of India's total value of exports with Thailand during 2004-05.

- Most of the chapters not covered under EHS have shown positive growth in market share along with the implementation of the EHS of the FTA.
- The value wise market share of the all the sampled products coming under EHS category have declined during the year 2004-05 than the year 2003-04, although these were on rising trend from 2001-02 to 2004-05. Where as for products not covered under EHS, the movement is not significant, although the declining trend till 2003-04 has reversed in 2004-05.
- *The market share movement of 8 chapters of sample products covered under the EHS:* Products of Chapter 87 (Vehicles and Accessories) have shown heavy rise and products of Chapter 72 (Iron and Steel) have shown heavy fall in market share. Moderate growth found in case of Chapter 73 (Articles of Iron or Steel) products & Chapter 85 (Audio Visual Equipments incl. TV) products. Stability observed for Chapter 28 (Inorganic Chemicals and Metallic Compounds) and Chapter 71 (Natural stones, metals and imitation jewellery) products. Slight decline in share observed for Chapter 76 (Aluminium and articles thereof). Products of Chapter 84(Machinery and Mechanical appliances) stabilized at the 2001-02 level. **So, the surge in exports has been observed in the Vehicles and Accessories products.**
- **The results signify that; where as the NON EHS products are moving in tandem with world exports, there is need to push further the export competitive products into the EHS list to derive maximum benefit under the FTA. It requires for extensive Government consultation with industries before the concession lists are finalized.**

SINGAPORE - IMPORTS

- Based on the criteria taken for deriving ALERT cases {*simultaneous satisfaction of the following criterias*: Incremental Trend in value of imports in comparison to the base year 2003-04 is more than 50%, Incremental Trend in value of imports in comparison to the base year 2004-05 is more than 20% and CAGR of value of imports from

Singapore (over the years 2003-04 to 2005-06) is more than 20%}, summary of products of Chapters for which Indian industry should do further analysis to assess and adopt precautionary measures to protect from the material injury which may cause to them in future is given below:

Chapter	Products	List of Concession
29	Organic Chemicals	EHP
84	Machinery and Mechanical appliances Data Processing Machines Computors	EHP, including PE &
85	Audio Visual Equipments incl. TV	EHP, PR
90	Optical, Photographic, Medical Surgical instruments	EHP, and PR
49	Printed materials	PE

- Apart from above, sampled products grouped under Chapter 29 (Organic Chemicals), 73(Articles of Iron or Steel) & 76(Aluminium and articles) have shown high growth although the respective products were covered under the NEGATIVE LIST.
- It is found that 24 out of 67 sampled products under the *Early Harvest Programme*, 10 out of 35 sampled products under the *Phased Elimination in Duty* and 6 out of 21 sampled products under the *Phased Reduction in Duty* satisfied the criteria for selecting the cases where Indian industry needs to be alerted. Also it is found that; 7 out of 32 sampled products under the *Negative List* satisfy the requirement of qualifying for HIGH GROWTH items. In totality, the year wise total value of imports for these 47 ALERT/ HIGH GROWTH products constitutes 33.25% & 42.74% of total value of imports made during the financial years 2004-05 & 2005-06 respectively from Singapore.
- A majority of the total 24 alerted cases under the *Early Harvest Programme* found to be related to the IT products which are required to be imported at nil duty from the whole world. Out of 36 chapters covering 155 sampled products, it is observed that only 11 chapters (common chapters under different list were counted separately) have shown real growth both trend and CAGR wise.

- Since a lot of products under chapter 84 and 85 are already made duty free because of the WTO Agreement on IT Products (*Import duty on 217 IT Products is already zero under the WTO IT Agreement signed under the Singapore Declaration*), the true impact is minimized.
- <u>*Hence, it can be concluded that;*</u> **the impacts of CECA remain limited to a selected sector of industries only. But threat exists, in case the third countries route their products through Singapore to manipulate the benefits under CECA. The apprehension is to be positively considered as Singapore is a global trading hub and not a base for manufacturing activities.**

FINAL CONCLUSIONS

Exports

It can be broadly observed that; both the geographical and population size of the partner countries are very small compared to India. Other than India, these countries are already doing trade with China and other Asian counties with whom our products have to compete. These other countries supply a variety of products at much cheaper prices. Hence, even under the concessional duty treatment in the partner countries, our export products face tough competition. The bottlenecks in taxation structure and infrastructure problems prevailing in our domestic scenarios add further negative factors in creating competitiveness.

Indian industries have not therefore derived relative benefit on account of growth of exports under these FTAs.

Imports

A. **It is observed that; in the case of FTA with Srilanka and Thailand, surge in imports in some selected industries have injured the Indian manufacturers badly**. Examples are; Copper & Vanaspati / Edible oil in case of FTA with Srilanka and Television Industry in case of FTA with Thailand. The fact of injury have also been revealed by the concerned industries / industry associations while conducting the real interviews with them.

B. **A number of industries are also expecting potential threats from cheap imports from Thailand and Singapore under the respective FTA/ CECA as the**

case may be. Even in our data analysis part, I have pointed out some cases where Indian industries need to remain **alert** because of increased imports from Singapore. The high growth items and chapters have also been reported in case of imports from Srilanka and Thailand.

REMOVING THE INJURIES

Strong implementation of the ROO clauses and adopting the Safeguard measures under the FTAs can help in removal of unwanted injuries caused by surge in cheap imports. The situation can be further improved by holding renegotiations for either expansion of India's Negative List or by shifting of the products to low concessional duty category. A *Causal Influence Diagram* narrating the rectification mechanism is produced below.

Casual Influence Diagram

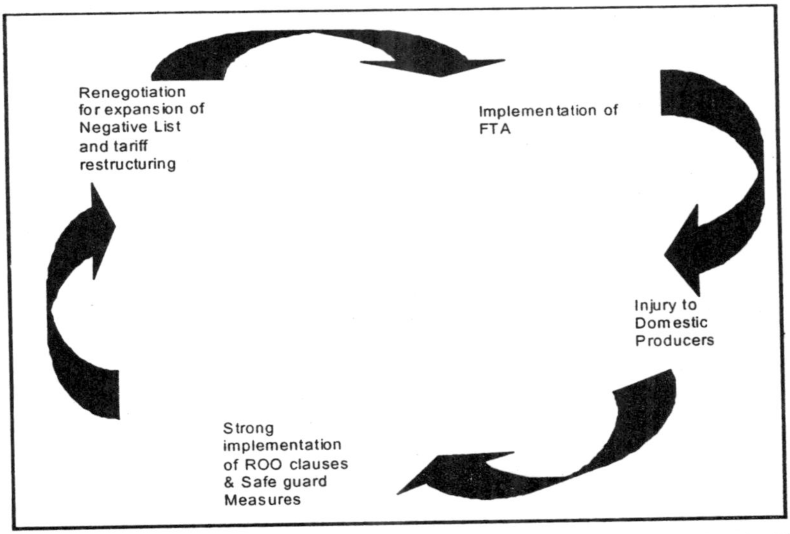

(Diagram 1: Causal Influence links between injury and remedies under the FTA)

FINAL RECOMMENDATIONS

The last objective of the impact study is to suggest recommendations for improving the whole situation. Our recommendations can be summarized as mentioned below:

A. A manufacturer friendly foreign trade policy combined with rational taxation laws and adequate infrastructure facilities can help our producers to derive benefit under the FTAs.

B. Also it is necessary to remove the inherent bottlenecks prevailing in our domestic scenarios to create a level playing field.

C. The inverted duty structure existing in some cases is adding further blows to the domestic producers. Therefore there should be stricter Government mechanism to curb such unwanted imports to come under the FTA veil.

D. Stricter implementation of the Rules of Origin clauses and effective Audit mechanism should be institutionalized.

E. Rules of Origin factors should be brought in the Customs Act of India itself. Enforceability of the ROO clauses in any FTA can come after that only.

F. Where as the safeguard actions are prospective based only, but no remedy exists for past injuries caused on industries because of cheap imports. Steps should be there fore taken to remove these anomalies.

G. Efforts also should be taken to put our export competitive products in the concession schedules of the partner countries.

H. The EHS list under the Thailand FTA should be broad based at the earliest after prior consulting being made with the domestic industries in this regard.

I. It is expected that the Government of India should take proactive steps rather than protective steps in signing of the FTAs.

J. The over all situations should be win-win for every body and trade creation because of the FTAs should become realistic.

K. The last opinion can be that; FTAs are here to stay. Industries need to understand the market dynamics playing in the global free trade regime and the role of FTAs in boosting trade within the specified regions. The deadlocks happening in the multilateral talks at WTO further emphasise the role of increasing FTAs among consenting partner countries. **It is the time for our industries to analyse the impacts and take adequate steps to remain competitive.**

SECTION - VII

(Annexures and Tables Forming Part of Data Analysis)

Contents

ANNEXURE- I

Article XXIV: Territorial Application- Frontier Traffic - Customs Unions and Free-trade Areas

1. The provisions of this Agreement shall apply to the metropolitan customs territories of the contracting parties and to any other customs territories in respect of which this Agreement has been accepted under Article XXVI or is being applied under Article XXXIII or pursuant to the Protocol of Provisional Application. Each such customs territory shall, exclusively for the purposes of the territorial application of this Agreement, be treated as though it were a contracting party; *Provided* that the provisions of this paragraph shall not be construed to create any rights or obligations as between two or more customs territories in respect of which this Agreement has been accepted under Article XXVI or is being applied under Article XXXIII or pursuant to the Protocol of Provisional Application by a single contracting party.
2. For the purposes of this Agreement a customs territory shall be understood to mean any territory with respect to which separate tariffs or other regulations of commerce are maintained for a substantial part of the trade of such territory with other territories.
3. The provisions of this Agreement shall not be construed to prevent:
   a) Advantages accorded by any contracting party to adjacent countries in order to facilitate frontier traffic;
   b) Advantages accorded to the trade with the Free Territory of Trieste by countries contiguous to that territory, provided that such advantages are not in conflict with the Treaties of Peace arising out of the Second World War.
4. The contracting parties recognize the desirability of increasing freedom of trade by the development, through voluntary agreements, of closer integration between the

economies of the countries parties to such agreements. They also recognize that the purpose of a customs union or of a free-trade area should be to facilitate trade between the constituent territories and not to raise barriers to the trade of other contracting parties with such territories.

5. Accordingly, the provisions of this Agreement shall not prevent, as between the territories of contracting parties, the formation of a customs union or of a free-trade area or the adoption of an interim agreement necessary for the formation of a customs union or of a free-trade area; *Provided* that:

   a) With respect to a customs union, or an interim agreement leading to a formation of a customs union, the duties and other regulations of commerce imposed at the institution of any such union or interim agreement in respect of trade with contracting parties not parties to such union or agreement shall not on the whole be higher or more restrictive than the general incidence of the duties and regulations of commerce applicable in the constituent territories prior to the formation of such union or the adoption of such interim agreement, as the case may be;

   b) with respect to a free-trade area, or an interim agreement leading to the formation of a free-trade area, the duties and other regulations of commerce maintained in each of the constituent territories and applicable at the formation of such free–trade area or the adoption of such interim agreement to the trade of contracting parties not included in such area or not parties to such agreement shall not be higher or more restrictive than the corresponding duties and other regulations of commerce existing in the same constituent territories prior to the formation of the free-trade area, or interim agreement as the case may be; and

   (*c*) any interim agreement referred to in subparagraphs (*a*) and (*b*) shall include a plan and schedule for the formation of such a customs union or of such a free-trade area within a reasonable length of time.

6. If, in fulfilling the requirements of subparagraph 5 (*a*), a contracting party proposes to increase any rate of duty inconsistently with the provisions of Article II, the procedure

set forth in Article XXVIII shall apply. In providing for compensatory adjustment, due account shall be taken of the compensation already afforded by the reduction brought about in the corresponding duty of the other constituents of the union.

7. *a*) Any contracting party deciding to enter into a customs union or free-trade area, or an interim agreement leading to the formation of such a union or area, shall promptly notify the CONTRACTING PARTIES and shall make available to them such information regarding the proposed union or area as will enable them to make such reports and recommendations to contracting parties as they may deem appropriate.

b) If, after having studied the plan and schedule included in an interim agreement referred to in paragraph 5 in consultation with the parties to that agreement and taking due account of the information made available in accordance with the provisions of subparagraph (*a*), the CONTRACTING PARTIES find that such agreement is not likely to result in the formation of a customs union or of a free-trade area within the period contemplated by the parties to the agreement or that such period is not a reasonable one, the CONTRACTING PARTIES shall make recommendations to the parties to the agreement. The parties shall not maintain or put into force, as the case may be, such agreement if they are not prepared to modify it in accordance with these recommendations.

c) Any substantial change in the plan or schedule referred to in paragraph 5 (*c*) shall be communicated to the CONTRACTING PARTIES, which may request the contracting parties concerned to consult with them if the change seems likely to jeopardize or delay unduly the formation of the customs union or of the free-trade area.

8. For the purposes of this Agreement:

a) A customs union shall be understood to mean the substitution of a single customs territory for two or more customs territories, so that

(i) duties and other restrictive regulations of commerce (except, where necessary, those permitted under Articles XI, XII, XIII, XIV, XV and XX) are eliminated with respect to substantially all the trade between the constituent territories of the union or at least with respect to substantially all the trade in products originating in such territories, and,

(ii) subject to the provisions of paragraph 9, substantially the same duties and other regulations of commerce are applied by each of the members of the union to the trade of territories not included in the union;

b) A free-trade area shall be understood to mean a group of two or more customs territories in which the duties and other restrictive regulations of commerce (except, where necessary, those permitted under Articles XI, XII, XIII, XIV, XV and XX) are eliminated on substantially all the trade between the constituent territories in products originating in such territories.

9. The preferences referred to in paragraph 2 of Article I shall not be affected by the formation of a customs union or of a free-trade area but may be eliminated or adjusted by means of negotiations with contracting parties affected.* This procedure of negotiations with affected contracting parties shall, in particular, apply to the elimination of preferences required to conform with the provisions of paragraph 8 (*a*)(i) and paragraph 8 (*b*).

10. The CONTRACTING PARTIES may by a two-thirds majority approve proposals which do not fully comply with the requirements of paragraphs 5 to 9 inclusive, provided that such proposals lead to the formation of a customs union or a free-trade area in the sense of this Article.

11. Taking into account the exceptional circumstances arising out of the establishment of India and Pakistan as independent States and recognizing the fact that they have long constituted an economic unit, the contracting parties agree that the provisions of this Agreement shall not prevent the two countries from entering into special arrangements with respect to the trade between them, pending the establishment of their mutual trade relations on a definitive basis.*

12. Each contracting party shall take such reasonable measures as may be available to it to ensure observance of the provisions of this Agreement by the regional and local governments and authorities within its territories.

Ad Article XXIV

Paragraph 9. It is understood that the provisions of Article I would require that, when a product which has been imported into the territory of a member of a customs union or free-trade area at a preferential rate of duty is re-exported to the territory of another member of such union or area, the latter member should collect a duty equal to the difference between the duty already paid and any higher duty that would be payable if the product were being imported directly into its territory.

Paragraph 11. Measures adopted by India and Pakistan in order to carry out definitive trade arrangements between them, once they have been agreed upon, might depart from particular provisions of this Agreement, but these measures would in general be consistent with the objectives of the Agreement.

URUGUAY ROUND AGREEMENT

Understanding on the Interpretation of Article XXIV of the General Agreement on Tariffs and Trade 1994

Members,

Hereby *agree* as follows:

1. Customs unions, free-trade areas, and interim agreements leading to the formation of a customs union or free-trade area, to be consistent with Article XXIV, must satisfy, *inter alia,* the provisions of paragraphs 5, 6, 7 and 8 of that Article.

Article XXIV:5

2. The evaluation under paragraph 5(a) of Article XXIV of the general incidence of the duties and other regulations of commerce applicable before and after the formation of a customs union shall in respect of duties and charges be based upon an overall assessment of weighted average tariff rates and of customs duties collected. This assessment shall be based on import statistics for a previous representative period to be supplied by the customs union, on a tariff-line basis and in values and quantities, broken down by WTO country of origin. The Secretariat shall compute the weighted average tariff rates and customs duties collected in accordance with the methodology used in the assessment of tariff offers in the Uruguay Round of Multilateral Trade Negotiations. For this purpose, the duties and charges to be taken into consideration shall be the applied rates of duty.

It is recognized that for the purpose of the overall assessment of the incidence of other regulations of commerce for which quantification and aggregation are difficult, the examination of individual measures, regulations, products covered and trade flows affected may be required.

3. The "reasonable length of time" referred to in paragraph 5(c) of Article XXIV should exceed 10 years only in exceptional cases. In cases where Members parties to an interim agreement believe that 10 years would be insufficient they shall provide a full explanation to the Council for Trade in Goods of the need for a longer period.

Article XXIV:6

1. Paragraph 6 of Article XXIV establishes the procedure to be followed when a Member forming a customs union proposes to increase a bound rate of duty. In this regard Members reaffirm that the procedure set forth in Article XXVIII, as elaborated in the guidelines adopted on 10 November 1980 (BISD 27S/26-28) and in the Understanding on the Interpretation of Article XXVIII of GATT 1994, must be commenced before tariff concessions are modified or withdrawn upon the formation of a customs union or an interim agreement leading to the formation of a customs union.

5. These negotiations will be entered into in good faith with a view to achieving mutually satisfactory compensatory adjustment. In such negotiations, as required by paragraph 6 of Article XXIV, due account shall be taken of reductions of duties on the same tariff line made by other constituents of the customs union upon its formation. Should such reductions not be sufficient to provide the necessary compensatory adjustment, the customs union would offer compensation, which may take the form of reductions of duties on other tariff lines. Such an offer shall be taken into consideration by the Members having negotiating rights in the binding being modified or withdrawn. Should the compensatory adjustment remain unacceptable, negotiations should be continued. Where, despite such efforts, agreement in negotiations on compensatory adjustment under Article XXVIII as elaborated by the Understanding on the Interpretation of Article XXVIII of GATT 1994 cannot be reached within a reasonable period from the initiation of

negotiations, the customs union shall, nevertheless, be free to modify or withdraw the concessions; affected Members shall then be free to withdraw substantially equivalent concessions in accordance with Article XXVIII.

6. GATT 1994 imposes no obligation on Members benefiting from a reduction of duties consequent upon the formation of a customs union, or an interim agreement leading to the formation of a customs union, to provide compensatory adjustment to its constituents.

Review of Customs Unions and Free-Trade Areas

7. All notifications made under paragraph 7(a) of Article XXIV shall be examined by a working party in the light of the relevant provisions of GATT 1994 and of paragraph 1 of this Understanding. The working party shall submit a report to the Council for Trade in Goods on its findings in this regard. The Council for Trade in Goods may make such recommendations to Members as it deems appropriate.

8. In regard to interim agreements, the working party may in its report make appropriate recommendations on the proposed time-frame and on measures required to complete the formation of the customs union or free-trade area. It may if necessary provide for further review of the agreement.

9. Members parties to an interim agreement shall notify substantial changes in the plan and schedule included in that agreement to the Council for Trade in Goods and, if so requested, the Council shall examine the changes.

10. Should an interim agreement notified under paragraph 7(a) of Article XXIV not include a plan and schedule, contrary to paragraph 5(c) of Article XXIV, the working party shall in its report recommend such a plan and schedule. The parties shall not maintain or put into force, as the case may be, such agreement if they are not prepared to modify it in accordance with these recommendations. Provision shall be made for subsequent review of the implementation of the recommendations.

11. Customs unions and constituents of free-trade areas shall report periodically to the Council for Trade in Goods, as envisaged by the CONTRACTING PARTIES to GATT 1947 in their instruction to the GATT 1947 Council concerning

reports on regional agreements (BISD 18S/38), on the operation of the relevant agreement. Any significant changes and/or developments in the agreements should be reported as they occur.

Dispute Settlement

12. The provisions of Articles XXII and XXIII of GATT 1994 as elaborated and applied by the Dispute Settlement Understanding may be invoked with respect to any matters arising from the application of those provisions of Article XXIV relating to customs unions, free-trade areas or interim agreements leading to the formation of a customs union or free-trade area.

Article XXIV:12

13. Each Member is fully responsible under GATT 1994 for the observance of all provisions of GATT 1994, and shall take such reasonable measures as may be available to it to ensure such observance by regional and local governments and authorities within its territory.
14. The provisions of Articles XXII and XXIII of GATT 1994 as elaborated and applied by the Dispute Settlement Understanding may be invoked in respect of measures affecting its observance taken by regional or local governments or authorities within the territory of a Member. When the Dispute Settlement Body has ruled that a provision of GATT 1994 has not been observed, the responsible Member shall take such reasonable measures as may be available to it to ensure its observance. The provisions relating to compensation and suspension of concessions or other obligations apply in cases where it has not been possible to secure such observance.
15. Each Member undertakes to accord sympathetic consideration to and afford adequate opportunity for consultation regarding any representations made by another Member concerning measures affecting the operation of GATT 1994 taken within the territory of the former.

Article V: Economic Integration

1. This Agreement shall not prevent any of its Members from being a party to or entering into an agreement liberalizing

trade in services between or among the parties to such an agreement, provided that such an agreement:

a) has substantial sectoral coverage(1), and

b) provides for the absence or elimination of substantially all discrimination, in the sense of Article XVII, between or among the parties, in the sectors covered under subparagraph (a), through:

(i) elimination of existing discriminatory measures, and/or

(ii) prohibition of new or more discriminatory measures, either at the entry into force of that agreement or on the basis of a reasonable time-frame, except for measures permitted under Articles XI, XII, XIV and XIV bis.

2. In evaluating whether the conditions under paragraph 1(b) are met, consideration may be given to the relationship of the agreement to a wider process of economic integration or trade liberalization among the countries concerned.

3. a) Where developing countries are parties to an agreement of the type referred to in paragraph 1, flexibility shall be provided for regarding the conditions set out in paragraph 1, particularly with reference to subparagraph (b) thereof, in accordance with the level of development of the countries concerned, both overall and in individual sectors and subsectors.

b) Notwithstanding paragraph 6, in the case of an agreement of the type referred to in paragraph 1 involving only developing countries, more favourable treatment may be granted to juridical persons owned or controlled by natural persons of the parties to such an agreement.

4. Any agreement referred to in paragraph 1 shall be designed to facilitate trade between the parties to the agreement and shall not in respect of any Member outside the agreement raise the overall level of barriers to trade in services within the respective sectors or subsectors compared to the level applicable prior to such an agreement.

5. If, in the conclusion, enlargement or any significant modification of any agreement under paragraph 1, a Member intends to withdraw or modify a specific

commitment inconsistently with the terms and conditions set out in its Schedule, it shall provide at least 90 days advance notice of such modification or withdrawal and the procedure set forth in paragraphs 2, 3 and 4 of Article XXI shall apply.

2. A service supplier of any other Member that is a juridical person constituted under the laws of a party to an agreement referred to in paragraph 1 shall be entitled to treatment granted under such agreement, provided that it engages in substantive business operations in the territory of the parties to such agreement.

7. a) Members which are parties to any agreement referred to in paragraph 1 shall promptly notify any such agreement and any enlargement or any significant modification of that agreement to the Council for Trade in Services. They shall also make available to the Council such relevant information as may be requested by it. The Council may establish a working party to examine such an agreement or enlargement or modification of that agreement and to report to the Council on its consistency with this Article.

   b) Members which are parties to any agreement referred to in paragraph 1 which is implemented on the basis of a time-frame shall report periodically to the Council for Trade in Services on its implementation. The Council may establish a working party to examine such reports if it deems such a working party necessary.

   c) Based on the reports of the working parties referred to in subparagraphs (a) and (b), the Council may make recommendations to the parties as it deems appropriate.

8. A Member which is a party to any agreement referred to in paragraph 1 may not seek compensation for trade benefits that may accrue to any other Member from such agreement.

Article V bis: Labour Markets Integration Agreements

This Agreement shall not prevent any of its Members from being a party to an agreement establishing full integration of the labour markets between or among the parties to such an agreement, provided that such an agreement:

a) exempts citizens of parties to the agreement from requirements concerning residency and work permits;

b) is notified to the Council for Trade in Services.

ANNEXURE- II

DETAILS OF POSITION OF VARIOUS RTAs AT WTO AS ON 15.06.2006

		GATT/WTO notification				Examination process	
Agreement	**Date of entry into force**	**Date**	**Related provisions**	**Type of agreement**	**Document series**	**Status**	**Ref.**
El Salvador - Mexico	15-Mar-01	30-May-06	GATS Art. V	Services agreement	WT/REG212 S/C/N/367	Examination not requested	...
El Salvador - Mexico	15-Mar-01	30-May-06	GATT Art. XXIV	Free trade agreement	WT/REG212	Examination not requested	...
Dominican Republic-Central America-United States (CAFTA-DR)	1-Mar-06	28-Mar-06	GATS Art. V	Services agreement	WT/REG211 S/C/N/365-6	Factual examination not started	...
Dominican Republic-Central America-United States (CAFTA-DR)	1-Mar-06	28-Mar-06	GATT Art. XXIV	Free trade agreement	WT/REG211	Factual examination not started	...
Republic of Korea - Singapore	2-Mar-06	24-Feb-06	GATS Art. V	Services agreement	WT/REG210 S/C/N/363	Factual examination not started	...
Republic of Korea - Singapore	2-Mar-06	24-Feb-06	GATT Art. XXIV	Free trade agreement	WT/REG210	Factual examination not started	...

Turkey – Morocco	1-Jan-06	21-Feb-06	GATT Art. XXIV	Free trade agreement	WT/REG209	Factual examination not started	...
United States - Morocco	1-Jan-06	16-Jan-06	GATS Art. V	Services agreement	WT/REG208 S/C/N/362	Factual examination not started	...
United States - Morocco	1-Jan-06	16-Jan-06	GATT Art. XXIV	Free trade agreement	WT/REG208	Factual examination not started	...
Thailand - New Zealand	1-Jul-05	2-Dec-05	GATS Art. V	Services agreement	WT/REG207 S/C/N/361	Factual examination not started	...
Thailand - New Zealand	1-Jul-05	2-Dec-05	GATT Art. XXIV	Free trade agreement	WT/REG207	Factual examination not started	...
Mexico - Nicaragua	1-Jul-98	2-Nov-05	GATS Art. V	Services agreement	WT/REG206 S/C/N/359	Factual examination not started	...
Mexico - Nicaragua	1-Jul-98	2-Nov-05	GATT Art. XXIV	Free trade agreement	WT/REG206	Factual examination not started	...
EC-Chile	1-Mar-05	1-Nov-05	GATS Art. V	Services agreement	WT/REG164 S/C/N/360	Factual examination not started	...
Croatia - Serbia and Montenegro	1-Jul-04	22-Sep-05	GATT Art. XXIV	Free trade agreement	WT/REG205	Factual examination not started	...
Turkey - Palestinian Authority	1-Jun-05	15-Sep-05	GATT Art. XXIV	Free trade agreement	WT/REG204	Factual examination not started	...

Turkey - Tunisia	1-Jul-05	15-Sep-05	GATT Art. XXIV	Free trade agreement	WT/REG203	Factual examination not started	...
ECOWAS	1993	26-Sep-05	Enabling Clause	Preferential arrangement	WT/COMTD/N/21 WT/COMTD/54	Examination not requested	...
EFTA - Tunisia	1-Jun-05	7-Jun-05	GATT Art. XXIV	Free trade agreement	WT/REG201	Factual examination not started	...
FYROM - Bosnia and Herzegovina	15-Jul-02	11-May-05	GATT Art. XXIV	Free trade agreement	WT/REG200	Factual examination not started	...
Romania - Israel	1-Jul-01	25-Apr-05	GATT Art. XXIV	Free trade agreement	WT/REG199	Factual examination not started	...
Japan - Mexico	1-Apr-05	22-Apr-05	GATT Art. XXIV	Free trade agreement	WT/REG198	Factual examination not started	...
Japan - Mexico	1-Apr-05	22-Apr-05	GATS Art. V	Services agreement	WT/REG198 S/C/N/328	Factual examination not started	...
Panama - El Salvador	11-Apr-03	5-Apr-05	GATS Art. V	Services agreement	WT/REG196 S/C/N/325	Factual examination not started	...
Croatia - FYROM	30-Oct-97	1-Apr-05	GATT Art. XXIV	Free trade agreement	WT/REG197	Factual examination not started	...
Panama - El Salvador	11-Apr-03	18-Mar-05	GATT Art. XXIV	Free trade agreement	WT/REG196	Factual examination not started	...

Bulgaria - Serbia and Montenegro	1-Jun-04	11-Mar-05	GATT Art. XXIV	Free trade agreement	WT/REG195	Factual examination not started	...
Bulgaria - Bosnia and Herzegovina	1-Dec-04	11-Mar-05	GATT Art. XXIV	Free trade agreement	WT/REG194	Factual examination not started	...
Romania - FYROM	1-Jan-04	14-Feb-05	GATT Art. XXIV	Free trade agreement	WT/REG193	Factual examination not started	...
Romania - Serbia and Montenegro	1-Jul-04	14-Feb-05	GATT Art. XXIV	Free trade agreement	WT/REG192	Factual examination not started	...
Romaria - Bosnia and Herzegovina	24-Oct-03	14-Feb-05	GATT Art. XXIV	Free trade agreement	WT/REG191	Factual examination not started	...
Moldova - Serbia and Montenegro	1-Sep-04	28-Jan-05	GATT Art. XXIV	Free trade agreement	WT/REG190	Factual examination not started	...
Moldova - Croatia	1-Oct-04	31-Jan-05	GATT Art. XXIV	Free trade agreement	WT/REG189	Factual examination not started	...
Moldova - FYROM	1-Dec-04	31-Jan-05	GATT Art. XXIV	Free trade agreement	WT/REG188	Factual examination not started	...
Moldova - Bosnia and Herzegovina	1-May-04	28-Jan-05	GATT Art. XXIV	Free trade agreement	WT/REG187	Factual examination not started	...
Moldova - Bulgaria	1-Dec-04	28-Jan-05	GATT Art. XXIV	Free trade agreement	WT/REG186	Factual examination not started	...

Thailand - Australia	1-Jan-05	5-Jan-05	GATT Art. XXIV	Free trade agreement	WT/REG185	Factual examination not started	...
Thailand - Australia	1-Jan-05	5-Jan-05	GATS Art. V	Services agreement	WT/REG185 S/C/N/311	Factual examination not started	...
United States - Australia	1-Jan-05	23-Dec-04	GATT Art. XXIV	Free trade agreement	WT/REG184	Factual examination not started	...
United States - Australia	1-Jan-05	23-Dec-04	GATS Art. V	Services agreement	WT/REG184 S/C/N/310	Factual examination not started	...
ASEAN - China	1-Jul-03	21-Dec-04	Enabling Clause	Preferential arrangement	WT/COMTD/N/20 WT/COMTD/51	Examination not requested	...
Albania - Moldova	1-Nov-04	20-Dec-04	GATT Art. XXIV	Free trade agreement	WT/REG183	Factual examination not started	...
Albania - FYROM	1-Jul-02	14-Dec-04	GATT Art. XXIV	Free trade agreement	WT/REG182	Factual examination not started	...
Albania - Bosnia and Herzegovina	1-Dec-04	14-Dec-04	GATT Art. XXIV	Free trade agreement	WT/REG181	Factual examination not started	...
Albania - Romania	1-Jan-04	14-Dec-04	GATT Art. XXIV	Free trade agreement	WT/REG180	Factual examination not started	...
EFTA - Chile	1-Dec-04	10-Dec-04	GATT Art. XXIV	Free trade agreement	WT/REG179	Factual examination not started	...

EFTA - Chile	1-Dec-04	10-Dec-04	GATS Art. V	Services agreement	WT/REG179 S/C/N/309	Factual examination not started	...
Albania - Serbia Montenegro	1-Sep-04	19-Oct-04	GATT Art. XXIV	Free trade agreement	WT/REG178	Factual examination not started	...
EC - Egypt	1-Jun-04	4-Oct-04	GATT Art. XXIV	Free trade agreement	WT/REG177	Factual examination not started	...
SADC	1-Sep-00	9-Aug-04	GATT Art. XXIV	Free trade agreement	WT/REG176	Factual examination not started	...
Bangkok Agreement - Accession of China	1-Jan-02	29-Jul-04	Enabling Clause	Accession to Preferential arrangement	WT/COMTD/N/19	Examination not requested	...
Armenia - Turkmenistan	7-Jul-96	27-Jul-04	GATT Art. XXIV	Free trade agreement	WT/REG175	Factual examination not started	...
Armenia - Russian Federation	25-Mar-93	27-Jul-04	GATT Art. XXIV	Free trade agreement	WT/REG174	Factual examination not started	...
Armenia - Moldova	21-Dec-95	27-Jul-04	GATT Art. XXIV	Free trade agreement	WT/REG173	Factual examination not started	...
Armenia - Kazakhstan	25-Dec-01	27-Jul-04	GATT Art. XXIV	Free trade agreement	WT/REG172	Factual examination not started	...
Armenia - Ukraine	18-Dec-96	27-Jul-04	GATT Art. XXIV	Free trade agreement	WT/REG171	Factual examination not started	...

EU Enlargement	1-May-04	30-Apr-04	GATT Art. XXIV	Accession to customs union	WT/REG170	Factual examination concluded	...
EU Enlargement	1-May-04	28-Apr-04	GATS Art. V	Accession to services agreement	WT/REG170 S/C/N/303	Factual examination not started	...
Republic of Korea - Chile	1-Apr-04	19-Apr-04	GATT Art. XXIV	Free trade agreement	WT/REG169	Factual examination concluded	...
Republic of Korea - Chile	1-Apr-04	19-Apr-04	GATS Art. V	Services agreement	WT/REG169 S/C/N/302	Factual examination concluded	...
Albania - UNMIK (Kosovo)	1-Oct-03	8-Apr-04	GATT Art. XXIV	Free trade agreement	WT/REG168	Factual examination not started	...
Albania - Bulgaria	1-Sep-03	31-Mar-04	GATT Art. XXIV	Free trade agreement	WT/REG167	Factual examination not started	...
Croatia - Albania	1-Jun-03	31-Mar-04	GATT Art. XXIV	Free trade agreement	WT/REG166	Factual examination not started	...
CEFTA accession of Croatia	1-Mar-03	3-Mar-04	GATT Art. XXIV	Accession to free trade agreement	WT/REG11	Factual examination not started	...
Chile - El Salvador	1-Jun-02	16-Feb-04	GATT Art. XXIV	Free trade agreement	WT/REG165	Factual examination concluded	...

Chile - El Salvador	1-Jun-02	17-Mar-04	GATS Art. V	Services agreement	WT/REG165 S/C/N/299	Factual examination concluded	...
EC - Chile	1-Feb-03	18-Feb-04	GATT Art. XXIV	Free trade agreement	WT/REG164	Under factual examination	...
China - Macao, China	1-Jan-04	12-Jan-04	GATT Art. XXIV	Free trade agreement	WT/REG163	Factual examination concluded	...
China - Macao, China	1-Jan-04	12-Jan-04	GATS Art. V	Services agreement	WT/REG163 S/C/N/265	Factual examination concluded	...
China - Hong Kong, China	1-Jan-04	12-Jan-04	GATT Art. XXIV	Free trade agreement	WT/REG162	Factual examination concluded	...
China - Hong Kong, China	1-Jan-04	12-Jan-04	GATS Art. V	Services agreement	WT/REG162 S/C/N/264	Factual examination concluded	...
United States - Singapore	1-Jan-04	19-Dec-03	GATT Art. XXIV	Free trade agreement	WT/REG161	Factual examination concluded	...
United States - Singapore	1-Jan-04	19-Dec-03	GATS Art. V	Services agreement	WT/REG161 S/C/N/263	Factual examination concluded	...
United States — Chile	1-Jan-04	19-Dec-03	GATT Art. XXIV	Free trade agreement	WT/REG160	Factual examination concluded	...
United States — Chile	1-Jan-04	19-Dec-03	GATS Art. V	Services agreement	WT/REG160 S/C/N/262	Factual examination concluded	...

Croatia - Bosnia and Herzegovina	1-Jan-01	6-Oct-03	GATT Art. XXI V	Free trade agreement	WT/REG159	Factual examination not started	...
Singapore - Australia	28-Jul-03	1-Oct-03	GATS Art. V	Services agreement	WT/REG158 S/C/N/233	Factual examination concluded	...
Singapore - Australia	28-Jul-03	1-Oct-03	GATT Art. XXI V	Free trade agreement	WT/REG158	Factual examination concluded	...
Turkey - Bosnia and Herzegovina	1-Jul-03	8-Sep-03	GATT Art. XXI V	Free trade agreement	WT/REG157	Factual examination not started	...
Turkey - Croatia	1-Jul-03	8-Sep-03	GATT Art. XXI V	Free trade agreement	WT/REG156	Factual examination concluded	...
EC - Lebanon	1-Mar-03	4-Jun-03	GATT Art. XXI V	Free trade agreement	WT/REG153	Factual examination not started	...
Bulgaria - Israel	1-Jan-02	14-Apr-03	GATT Art. XXI V	Free trade agreement	WT/REG150	Factual examination not started	...
CARICOM	1-Jul-97	19-Feb-03	GATS Art. V	Services agreement	WT/REG155 S/C/N/229	Factual examination concluded	...
EFTA - Singapore	1-Jan-03	24-Jan-03	GATS Art. V	Services agreement	WT/REG148 S/C/N/226	Under factual examination	...
EFTA - Singapore	1-Jan-03	24-Jan-03	GATT Art. XXI V	Free trade agreement	WT/REG148	Under factual examination	...

Canada — Costa Rica	1-Nov-02	17-Jan-03	GATT Art. XXIV	Free trade agreement	WT/REG147	Factual examination concluded	...
EC — Croatia	1-Mar-02	20-Dec-02	GATT Art. XXIV	Free trade agreement	WT/REG142	Factual examination concluded	...
EC — Jordan	1-May-02	20-Dec-02	GATT Art. XXIV	Free trade agreement	WT/REG141	Factual examination concluded	...
EFTA	1-Jun-02	3-Dec-02	GATS Art. V	Services agreement	WT/REG154 S/C/N/207	Factual examination concluded	...
Japan - Singapore	30-Nov-02	14-Nov-02	GATS Art. V	Services agreement	WT/REG140 S/C/N/206	Factual examination concluded	...
Japan - Singapore	30-Nov-02	14-Nov-02	GATT Art. XXIV	Free trade agreement	WT/REG140	Factual examination concluded	...
United States — Jordan	17-Dec-01	18-Oct-02	GATS Art. V	Services agreement	WT/REG134 S/C/N/193	Factual examination concluded	...
India — Sri Lanka	15-Dec-01	27-Jun-02	Enabling Clause	Free trade agreement	WT/COMTD/N/16	Examination not requested	...
EC — Mexico	1-Mar-01	21-Jun-02	GATS Art. V	Services agreement	WT/REG109 S/C/N/192	Under factual examination	...
Chile — Costa Rica	15-Feb-02	24-May-02	GATS Art. V	Services agreement	WT/REG136 S/C/N/191	Factual examination concluded	...

Chile — Costa Rica	15-Feb-02	14-May-02	GATT Art. XXIV	Free trade agreement	WT/REG136	Factual examination concluded	...
United States — Jordan	17-Dec-01	5-Mar-02	GATT Art. XXIV	Free trade agreement	WT/REG134	Factual examination concluded	...
EFTA — Jordan	1-Jan-02	22-Jan-02	GATT Art. XXIV	Free trade agreement	WT/REG133	Factual examination concluded	...
EFTA — Croatia	1-Jan-02	22-Jan-02	GATT Art. XXIV	Free trade agreement	WT/REG132	Factual examination concluded	...
EC — FYROM	1-Jun-01	21-Nov-01	GATT Art. XXIV	Free trade agreement	WT/REG129	Factual examination concluded	...
New Zealand - Singapore	1-Jan-01	19-Sep-01	GATT Art. XXIV	Free trade agreement	WT/REG127	Factual examination concluded	...
New Zealand - Singapore	1-Jan-01	19-Sep-01	GATS Art. V	Services agreement	WT/REG127 S/C/N/169	Factual examination concluded	...
EFTA - Mexico	1-Jul-01	22-Aug-01	GATT Art. XXIV	Free trade agreement	WT/REG126	Factual examination concluded	...
EFTA - Mexico	1-Jul-01	22-Aug-01	GATS Art. V	Services agreement	WT/REG126 S/C/N/166	Under factual examination	...
Chile — Mexico	1-Aug-99	14-Mar-01	GATS Art. V	Services agreement	WT/REG125 S/C/N/142	Factual examination concluded	...

Chile — Mexico	1-Aug-99	8-Mar-01	GATT Art. XXIV	Free trade agreement	WT/REG125	Factual examination concluded	...
Israel - Mexico	1-Jul-00	8-Mar-01	GATT Art. XXIV	Free trade agreement	WT/REG124	Factual examination concluded	...
Georgia — Armenia	11-Nov-98	21-Feb-01	GATT Art. XXIV	Free trade agreement	WT/REG119	Under factual examination	...
Georgia — Azerbaijan	10-Jul-96	21-Feb-01	GATT Art. XXIV	Free trade agreement	WT/REG120	Under factual examination	...
Georgia — Kazakhstan	16-Jul-99	21-Feb-01	GATT Art. XXIV	Free trade agreement	WT/REG123	Under factual examination	...
Georgia — Russian Federation	10-May-94	21-Feb-01	GATT Art. XXIV	Free trade agreement	WT/REG118	Under factual examination	...
Georgia — Turkmenistan	1-Jan-00	21-Feb-01	GATT Art. XXIV	Free trade agreement	WT/REG122	Under factual examination	...
Georgia — Ukraine	4-Jun-96	21-Feb-01	GATT Art. XXIV	Free trade agreement	WT/REG121	Under factual examination	...
EFTA — Former Yugoslav Republic of Macedonia	1-Jan-01	31-Jan-01	GATT Art. XXIV	Free trade agreement	WT/REG117	Factual examination concluded	...
Turkey — Former Yugoslav Republic of Macedonia	1-Sep-00	22-Jan-01	GATT Art. XXIV	Free trade agreement	WT/REG115	Factual examination concluded	...

Kyrgyz Republic — Armenia	27-Oct-95	4-Jan-01	GATT Art. XXIV	Free trade agreement	WT/REG114	Under factual examination	...
EC — South Africa	1-Jan-00	21-Nov-00	GATT Art. XXIV	Free trade agreement	WT/REG113	Factual examination not started	...
EC — Morocco	1-Mar-00	8-Nov-00	GATT Art. XXIV	Free trade agreement	WT/REG112	Factual examination concluded	...
EC — Israel	1-Jun-00	7-Nov-00	GATT Art. XXIV	Free trade agreement	WT/REG110	Factual examination concluded	...
EAC	7-Jul-00	11-Oct-00	Enabling Clause	Preferential arrangement	WT/COMTD/N/14 WT/COMTD/25	Examination not requested	...
CEMAC	24-Jun-99	29-Sep-00	Enabling Clause	Preferential arrangement	WT/COMTD/N/13 WT/COMTD/24	Examination not requested	...
EC — Mexico	1-Jul-00	1-Aug-00	GATT Art. XXIV	Free trade agreement	WT/REG109	Factual examination concluded	...
EFTA — Morocco	1-Dec-99	18-Feb-00	GATT Art. XXIV	Free trade agreement	WT/REG91	Factual examination concluded	...
WAEMU/UEMOA	1-Jan-00	3-Feb-00	Enabling Clause	Preferential arrangement	WT/COMTD/N/11 WT/COMTD/23	Examination not requested	...

Bulgaria — Former Yugoslav Republic of Macedonia	1-Jan-00	18-Feb-00	GATT Art. XXIV	Free trade agreement	WT/REG90	Factual examination concluded	...
MSG	22-Jul-93	7-Oct-99	Enabling Clause	Preferential arrangement	WT/COMTD/N/9 WT/COMTD/21	Examination not requested	...
CIS	30-Dec-94	1-Oct-99	GATT Art. XXIV	Free trade agreement	WT/REG82	Under factual examination	...
Kyrgyz Republic — Kazakhstan	11-Nov-95	29-Sep-99	GATT Art. XXIV	Free trade agreement	WT/REG81	Under factual examination	...
EFTA — Palestinian Authority	1-Jul-99	21-Sep-99	GATT Art. XXIV	Free trade agreement	WT/REG79	Factual examination not started	...
Kyrgyz Republic — Moldova	21-Nov-96	15-Jun-99	GATT Art. XXIV	Free trade agreement	WT/REG76	Factual examination concluded	...
Kyrgyz Republic — Russian Federation	24-Apr-93	15-Jun-99	GATT Art. XXIV	Free trade agreement	WT/REG73	Under factual examination	...
Kyrgyz Republic — Ukraine	19-Jan-98	15-Jun-99	GATT Art. XXIV	Free trade agreement	WT/REG74	Under factual examination	...
Kyrgyz Republic — Uzbekistan	20-Mar-98	15-Jun-99	GATT Art. XXIV	Free trade agreement	WT/REG75	Under factual examination	...
Bulgaria — Turkey	1-Jan-99	4-May-99	GATT Art. XXIV	Free trade agreement	WT/REG72	Factual examination concluded	...

EAEC	8-Oct-97	21-Apr-99	GATT Art. XXIV	Customs union	WT/REG71	Under factual examination	...
CEFTA accession of Bulgaria	1-Jan-99	24-Mar-99	GATT Art. XXIV	Accession to free trade agreement	WT/REG11	Consultations on draft report	...
EC — Tunisia	1-Mar-98	23-Mar-99	GATT Art. XXIV	Free trade agreement	WT/REG69	Factual examination concluded	...
Turkey - Israel	1-May-97	18-May-98	GATT Art. XXIV	Free trade agreement	WT/REG60	Factual examination concluded	...
Romania — Turkey	1-Feb-98	18-May-98	GATT Art. XXIV	Free trade agreement	WT/REG59	Factual examination concluded	...
EC — Andorra	1-Jul-91	9-Mar-98	GATT Art. XXIV	Customs union	WT/REG53	Factual examination concluded	...
CEFTA accession of Romania	1-Jul-97	8-Jan-98	GATT Art. XXIV	Accession to free trade agreement	WT/REG11	Consultations on draft report	...
Canada — Chile	5-Jul-97	13-Nov-97	GATS Art. V	Services agreement	WT/REG38 S/C/N/65	Factual examination concluded	...
Romania — Moldova	1-Jan-95	24-Sep-97	GATT Art. XXIV	Free trade agreement	WT/REG44	Factual examination concluded	...

Canada — Chile	5-Jul-97	26-Aug-97	GATT Art. XXIV	Free trade agreement	WT/REG38	Factual examination concluded	...
EC — Palestinian Authority	1-Jul-97	30-Jun-97	GATT Art. XXIV	Free trade agreement	WT/REG43	Factual examination not started	...
EC — Bulgaria	1-Feb-95	25-Apr-97	GATS Art. V	Services agreement	WT/REG1 .S/C/N/55	Under factual examination	...
EC — Faroe Islands	1-Jan-97	19-Feb-97	GATT Art. XXIV	Free trade agreement	WT/REG21	Under factual examination	...
Canada — Israel	1-Jan-97	23-Jan-97	GATT Art. XXIV	Free trade agreement	WT/REG31	Factual examination concluded	...
EEA	1-Jan-94	10-Oct-96	GATS Art. V	Services agreement	WT/REG138 S/C/N/28	Factual examination concluded	...
EC — Romania	1-Feb-95	9-Oct-96	GATS Art. V	Services agreement	WT/REG2 S/C/N/27	Under factual examination	...
Faroe Islands — Norway	1-Jul-93	13-Mar-96	GATT Art. XXIV	Free trade agreement	WT/REG25	Factual examination concluded	...
Faroe Islands — Switzerland	1-Mar-95	8-Mar-96	GATT Art. XXIV	Free trade agreement	WT/REG24	Factual examination concluded	...
Faroe Islands — Iceland	1-Jul-93	23-Jan-96	GATT Art. XXIV	Free trade agreement	WT/REG23	Factual examination concluded	...

EC — Turkey	1-Jan-96	22-Dec-95	GATT Art. XXIV	Customs union	WT/REG22	Under factual examination	...
CER	1-Jan-89	22-Nov-95	GATS Art. V	Services agreement	WT/REG40 S/C/N/7	Consultations on draft report	...
EC (Treaty of Rome)	1-Jan-58	10-Nov-95	GATS Art. V	Services agreement	WT/REG39 S/C/N/6	Under factual examination	...
COMESA	8-Dec-94	29-Jun-95	Enabling Clause	Preferential arrangement	WT/COMTD/N/3	Examination not requested	...
NAFTA	1-Apr-94	1-Mar-95	GATS Art. V	Services agreement	WT/REG4 S/C/N/4	Consultations on draft report	...
EC accession of Austria, Finland and Sweden	1-Jan-95	20-Jan-95	GATT Art. XXIV	Accession to customs union	WT/REG3 L/7614/Add.1	Consultations on draft report	...
EC accession of Austria, Finland and Sweden	1-Jan-95	20-Jan-95	GATS Art. V	Accession to services agreement	WT/REG3 S/C/N/6	Consultations on draft report	...
EC — Bulgaria	31-Dec-93	23-Dec-94	GATT Art. XXIV	Free trade agreement	WT/REG1	Factual examination concluded	...
EC — Romania	1-May-93	23-Dec-94	GATT Art. XXIV	Free trade agreement	WT/REG2	Factual examination concluded	...

SAPTA	7-Dec-95	25-Apr-97	Enabling Clause	Preferential arrangement	WT/COMTD/10	Examination not requested	...
EFTA — Bulgaria	1-Jul-93	7-Jul-93	GATT Art. XXIV	Free trade agreement	WT/REG12	Factual examination concluded	...
EFTA — Romania	1-May-93	24-May-93	GATT Art. XXIV	Free trade agreement	WT/REG16	Factual examination concluded	...
NAFTA	1-Jan-94	1-Feb-93	GATT Art. XXIV	Free trade agreement	WT/REG4	Consultations on draft report	...
EFTA — Israel	1-Jan-93	1-Dec-92	GATT Art. XXIV	Free trade agreement	WT/REG14	Factual examination concluded	...
AFTA	28-Jan-92	30-Oct-92	Enabling Clause	Preferential arrangement	L/4581	Examination not requested	...
CAN	25-May-88	12-Oct-90	Enabling Clause	Preferential arrangement	L/6737	Examination not requested	...
ECO	not available	22-Jul-92	Enabling Clause	Preferential arrangement	L/7047	Examination not requested	...
EFTA — Turkey	1-Apr-92	6-Mar-92	GATT Art. XXIV	Free trade agreement	WT/REG86	Report adopted	40S/48 17.12.93
MERCOSUR	29-Nov-91	5-Mar-92	Enabling Clause	Customs union	WT/COMTD/1	Factual examination concluded	...

Laos — Thailand	20-Jun-91	29-Nov-91	Enabling Clause	Preferential arrangement	L/6947	Examination not requested	
EC accession of Portugal and Spain	1-Jan-86	11-Dec-85	GATT Art. XXIV	Accession to customs union	L/5936	Report adopted	35S/293 19.10.88
United States — Israel	19-Aug-85	13-Sep-85	GATT Art. XXIV	Free trade agreement	L/5862 L/5862/Add.1	Report adopted	34S/58 14.05.87
GCC	not available	11-Oct-84	Enabling Clause	Preferential arrangement	L/5676	Examination not requested	...
CER	1-Jan-83	14-Apr-83	GATT Art. XXIV	Free trade agreement	WT/REG111	Report adopted	31S/170 02.10.84
LAIA	18-Mar-81	1-Jul-82	Enabling Clause	Preferential arrangement	L/5342	Examination not requested	...
SPARTECA	1-Jan-81	20-Feb-81	Enabling Clause	Preferential arrangement	L/5100	Examination not requested	...
EC accession of Greece	1-Jan-81	24-Oct-79	GATT Art. XXIV	Accession to customs union	L4845	Report adopted	30S/168 09.03.83
EC — Syria	1-Jul-77	15-Jul-77	GATT Art. XXIV	Free trade agreement	WT/REG104	Report adopted	25S/123 17.05.78
PATCRA	1-Feb-77	20-Dec-76	GATT Art. XXIV	Free trade agreement	L/4451 L/4451/Add.1	Report adopted	24S/63 11.11.77

Bangkok Agreement	17-Jun-76	2-Nov-76	Enabling Clause	Preferential arrangement	L/4418 L/4418/Corr.1	Report adopted	25S/109 14.03.78
EC — Algeria	1-Jul-76	28-Jul-76	GATT Art. XXIV	Free trade agreement	WT/REG105	Report adopted	24S/80 11.11.77
CARICOM	1-Aug-73	14-Oct-74	GATT Art. XXIV	Customs union	WT/REG92	Report adopted	24S/68 02.03.77
EC — Norway	1-Jul-73	13-Jul-73	GATT Art. XXIV	Free trade agreement	WT/REG137	Report adopted	21S/83 28.03.74
EC — Iceland	1-Apr-73	24-Nov-72	GATT Art. XXIV	Free trade agreement	WT/REG95	Report adopted	20S/158 19.10.73
EC — Switzerland and Liechtenstein	1-Jan-73	27-Oct-72	GATT Art. XXIV	Free trade agreement	WT/REG94	Report adopted	20S/196 19.10.73
EC accession of Denmark, Ireland and United Kingdom	1-Jan-73	7-Mar-72	GATT Art. XXIV	Accession to customs union	L/3677	Report adopted	C/M/107 11.07.75
GSTP	19-Apr-89	25-Sep-89	Enabling Clause	Preferential arrangement	L/6564/Add.1	Examination not requested	...
PTN	11-Feb-73	9-Nov-71	Enabling Clause	Preferential arrangement	L/3598 18S/11	Examination not requested	...
EC — OCTs	1-Jan-71	14-Dec-70	GATT Art. XXIV	Free trade agreement	WT/REG106	Report adopted	18S/143 09.11.71

EFTA accession of Iceland	1-Mar-70	30-Jan-70	GATT Art. XXIV	Accession to free trade agreement	L/3328 L/3328/Add.1	Report adopted	18S/174 29.09.70
TRIPARTITE	1-Apr-68	23-Feb-68	Enabling Clause	Preferential arrangement	L/2980 L/2980/Add.1	Report adopted	16S/83 14.11.68
CACM	12-Oct-61	24-Feb-61	GATT Art. XXIV	Customs union	WT/REG93	Report adopted	10S/98 23.11.61
EFTA (Stockholm Convention)	3-May-60	14-Nov-59	GATT Art. XXIV	Free trade agreement	WT/REG85	Report adopted	9S/70 04.06.60
EC (Treaty of Rome)	1-Jan-58	24-Apr-57	GATT Art. XXIV	Customs union	L/626	Report adopted	6S/70 & 109 29.11.57

ANNEXURE- III

IMPORTANT REGIONAL TRADE AGREEMENTS

AFTA	ASEAN Free Trade Area	Brunei Darussalam Cambodia Indonesia Laos Malaysia Myanmar Philippines Singapore Thailand Vietnam Thailand Vietnam
ASEAN	Association of South East Asian Nations	Brunei Darussalam Cambodia Indonesia Laos Malaysia Myanmar Philippines Singapore Thailand Vietnam
BAFTA	Baltic Free-Trade Area	Estonia Latvia Lithuania
BANGKOK	Bangkok Agreement	Bangladesh China India Republic of Korea Laos Sri Lanka
CAN	Andean Community	Bolivia Colombia Ecuador Peru Venezuela
CARICOM	Caribbean Community and Common Market	Antigua & Barbuda Bahamas Barbados Belize Dominica Grenada Guyana Haiti Jamaica Monserrat Trinidad & Tobago St. Kitts & Nevis St. Lucia St. Vincent & the Grenadines Surinam
CACM	Central American Common Market	Costa Rica El Salvador Guatemala Honduras Nicaragua
CEFTA	Central European Free Trade Agreement	Bulgaria Croatia Romania
CEMAC	Economic and Monetary Community of Central Africa	Cameroon Central African Republic Chad Congo Equatorial Guinea Gabon
CER	Closer Trade Relations Trade Agreement	Australia New Zealand
CIS	Commonwealth Independent States	Azerbaijan Armenia Belarus Georgia Moldova of Kazakhstan Russian Federation Ukraine Uzbekistan Tajikistan Kyrgyz Republic
COMESA	Common Market for Eastern and Southern Africa	Angola Burundi Comoros Democratic Republic of Congo Djibouti Egypt Eritrea Ethiopia Kenya Madagascar Malawi Mauritius Namibia Rwanda Seychelles Sudan Swaziland Uganda Zambia Zimbabwe

EAC	East African Cooperation	Kenya Tanzania Uganda
EAEC	Eurasian Economic Community	Belarus Kazakhstan Kyrgyz Republic Russian Federation Tajikistan
EC	European Communities	Austria Belgium Cyprus Czech Republic Denmark Estonia Finland France Germany Greece Hungary Ireland Italy Latvia Lithuania Luxembourg Malta Netherlands Poland Portugal Slovak Republic Slovenia Spain Sweden United Kingdom
ECO	Economic Cooperation Organization	Afghanistan Azerbaijan Iran Kazakhstan Kyrgyz Republic Pakistan Tajikistan Turkey Turkmenistan Uzbekistan
EEA	European Economic Area	EC Iceland Liechtenstein Norway
EFTA	European Free Trade Association	Iceland Liechtenstein Norway Switzerland
GCC	Gulf Cooperation Council	Bahrain Kuwait Oman Qatar Saudi Arabia United Arab Emirates
GSTP	General System of Trade Preferences among Developing Countries	Algeria Argentina Bangladesh Benin Bolivia Brazil Cameroon Chile Colombia Cuba Democratic People's Republic of Korea Ecuador Egypt Ghana Guinea Guyana India Indonesia Islamic Republic of Iran Iraq Libya Malaysia Mexico Morocco Mozambique Myanmar Nicaragua Nigeria Pakistan Peru Philippines Republic of Korea Romania Singapore Sri Lanka Sudan Thailand Trinidad and Tobago Tunisia United Republic of Tanzania Venezuela Vietnam Yugoslavia Zimbabwe
LAIA	Latin American Integration Association	Argentina Bolivia Brazil Chile Colombia Cuba Ecuador Mexico Paraguay Peru Uruguay Venezuela
MERCOSUR	Southern Common Market	Argentina Brazil Paraguay Uruguay
MSG	Melanesian Spearhead Group	Fiji Papua New Guinea Solomon Islands Vanuatu
NAFTA	North American Free Trade Agreement	Canada Mexico United States
OCT	Overseas Countries and Territories	Greenland New Caledonia French Polynesia French Southern and Antarctic Territories Wallis and Futuna Islands Mayotte Saint Pierre and Miquelon Aruba Netherlands Antilles Anguilla Cayman Islands Falkland Islands South Georgia and South Sandwich Islands Montserrat Pitcairn Saint Helena Ascension Island Tristan da Cunha Turks and Caicos Islands British Antarctic Territory British Indian Ocean Territory British Virgin Islands

PATCRA	Agreement on Trade and Commercial Relations between the Government of Australia and the Government of Papua New Guinea	Australia, Papua New Guinea
PTN	Protocol relating to Trade Negotiations among Developing Countries	Bangladesh Brazil Chile Egypt Israel Mexico Pakistan Paraguay Peru Philippines Republic of Korea Romania Tunisia Turkey Uruguay Yugoslavia
SADC	Southern African Development Community	Angola Botswana Lesotho Malawi Mauritius Mozambique Namibia South Africa Swaziland Tanzania Zambia Zimbabwe
SAPTA	South Asian Preferential Trade Arrangement	Bangladesh Bhutan India Maldives Nepal Pakistan Sri Lanka
SPARTECA	South Pacific Regional Trade and Economic Cooperation Agreement	Australia, Newzealand Cook Islands Fiji Kiribati Marshall Islands Micronesia Nauru Niue Papua New Guinea Solomon Islands Tonga Tuvalu Western Samoa Vanuatu
TRIPARTITE	Tripartite Agreement	Egypt India Yugoslavia
UEMOA WAEMU	West African Economic and Monetary Union	Benin Burkina Faso Côte d'Ivoire Guinea Bissau Mali Niger Senegal Togo

(Source: www.wto.org)

ANNEXURE- IV

Products covered under the early harvest scheme of the india-thailand FTA

Sl. No.	6-digit HS Code	Description
1.	080450	ex. Fresh mangosteens, mangoes
2.	080610	Fresh
3.	080810	Apples
4.	081060	Durians
5.	081090	ex. Fresh rambutans, longans, pomegranates
6.	100110	Durum wheat
7.	100190	Other
8.	160411	Salmon
9.	160413	Sardines, sardinella and brisling or sprats
10.	160415	Mackerel
11.	160510	Crab
12.	250100	Salt (including table salt and denatured salt) and pure sodium chloride, whether or not in aqueous solution or containing added anti-caking or free-flowing agents; sea water.
13.	261000	Chromium ores and concentrates.
14.	281119	Other
15.	281820	Aluminium oxide, other than artificial corundum
16.	281830	Aluminium hydroxide
17.	291739	Other
18.	390690	Other
19.	390710	Polyacetals
20.	390730	Epoxide resins
21.	390740	Polycarbonates
22.	390799	Other
23.	390810	Polyamide-6,-11,-12,-6,6,-6,9,-6,10, or -6,12

24.	390890	Other
25.	390950	Polyurethanes
26.	391990	Other
27.	441219	Other
28.	710310	Unworked or simply sawn or roughly shaped
29.	710490	Other
30.	710510	Of diamonds
31.	711319	Of other precious metal, whether or not plated or clad with precious metal
32.	720150	Alloy pig iron; Spiegeleisen
33.	720711	Of rectangular (including square) cross-section, the width measuring less than twice the thickness
34.	720719	Other
35.	722619	Other
36.	722990	Other
37.	730792	Threaded elbows, bends and sleeves
38.	732020	Helical springs
39.	732690	Other
40.	760110	Aluminium, not alloyed
41.	760120	Aluminium alloys
42.	840490	Parts
43.	840991	Suitable for use solely or principally with spark-ignition internal combustion piston engines
44.	841360	Other rotary positive displacement pumps
45.	841381	Pumps
46.	841451	Table, floor, wall, window, ceiling or roof fans, with a self-contained electric motor of an output not exceeding 125 W
47.	841459	Other
48.	841490	Parts
49.	841510	Window or wall types, self-contained or "split-system"
50.	841821	Compression-type
51.	841990	Parts
52.	842199	Other
53.	842390	Weighing machine weights of all kinds; parts of weighing machinery

54.	842549	Other
55.	843221	Disc harrows
56.	843780	Other machinery
57.	844820	Parts and accessories of machines of heading 84.44 or of their auxiliary machinery
58.	844833	Spindles, spindle flyers, spinning rings and ring travelers
59.	847141	Comprising in the same housing at least a central processing unit and an input and output unit, whether or not combined
60.	847190	Other
61.	847290	Other
62.	847751	For moulding or retreading pneumatic tyres or for moulding or otherwise forming inner tubes
63.	847989	Other
64.	847990	Parts
65.	848079	Other
66.	848180	Other appliances
67.	848210	Ball bearings
68.	848350	Flywheels and pulleys, including pulley blocks
69.	850431	Having a power handling capacity not exceeding 1 kVA
70.	851220	Other lighting or visual signalling equipment
71.	851711	Line telephone sets with cordless handsets
72.	851790	Parts
73.	852390	Other
74.	852812	Colour
75.	852910	Aerials and aerial reflectors of all kinds; parts suitable for use therewith
76.	853400	Printed circuits
77.	854011	Colour
78.	870840	Gear boxes
79.	903289	Other
80.	903290	Parts and accessories
81.	910211	With mechanical display only
82.	940190	Parts

ANNEXURE- V

Product Specific Rules (PSR) under Interim Rules of Origin of the INDIA-THAILAND FTA

Sl.No. item	*Tariff products (HS2002)*	*Description of*	*Applicable Rule*
1604		Prepared or preserved fish; caviar and caviar substitutes prepared from fish eggs.	
1.	160411	Salmon	Local Value Added Content not less than 20%
2.	160413	Sardines, sardinella and brisling or sprats	Local Value Added Content not less than 30%
3.	160415	Mackerel	Local Value Added Content not less than 30%
1605		Crustaceans, molluscs and other aquatic invertebrates, prepared or preserved.	
4.	160510	Crab	Local Value Added Content not less than 30%
7104		Synthetic or reconstructed precious or semi-precious stones, whether or not worked or graded but not strung, mounted or set; ungraded synthetic or reconstructed precious or semi-precious stones, temporarily strung for convenience of transport.	
5.	710490	Other	Change at 4-digit H.S level (Change to subheading 710490 from any other headings), provided that there is a Local Value Added Content not less than 20%
7105		Dust and powder of natural or synthetic precious or semi-precious stones.	
6.	710510	Of diamond	Change at 4-digit H.S level (Change to subheading 710510 from any other headings), provided that there is a Local Value Added Content not less than 20%
	7113	Articles of jewellery and parts thereof, of precious metal or of metal clad with precious metal	
7.	711319	Of other precious	Change at 4-digit H.S level (Change to subheading 711319 metal, whether or from any other headings), not plated or clad provided that there is a Local Value Added with precious metal Content not less than 20%
7307		Tube or pipe fittings (for example, couplings, elbows, sleeves), of iron or steel	
8.	730792	Threaded elbows, bends and sleeves	Change at 4-digit H.S level (Change to subheading 730792 from any other headings), provided that there is a Local Value Added Content not less than 20%
8413		Pumps for liquids, whether or not fitted with a measuring device; liquid elevators.	
9.	841381	Pumps	Change at 6-digit H.S level (Change to subheading 841381 from any other subheadings), provided that there is a Local Value Added Content not less than 40%

8414		Air or vacuum pumps, air or other gas compressors and fans; ventilating or recycling hoods incorporating a fan, whether or not fitted with filters.	
10.	841451	Table, floor, wall, window, ceiling or roof fans, with a self-contained electric motor of an output not exceeding 125 W	Change at 6-digit H.S level (Change to subheading 841451 from any other subheadings), provided that there is a Local Value Added Content not less than 40%
11.	841459	Other	Change at 6-digit H.S level (Change to subheading 841459 from any other subheadings), provided that there is a Local Value Added Content not less than 40%
12.	841490	Parts	Change at 6-digit H.S level (Change to subheading 841490 from any other subheadings), provided that there is a Local Value Added Content not less than 40%
8415		Air conditioning machines, comprising a motor-driven fan and elements for changing the temperature and humidity, including those machines in which the humidity cannot be separately regulated.	
13.	841510	Window or wall types, self-contained or "split-system"	Change at 6-digit H.S level (Change to subheading 841510 from any other subheadings), provided that there is a Local Value Added Content not less than 40%
8418		Refrigerators, freezers and other refrigerating or freezing equipment, electric or other; heat pumps other than air conditioning machines of heading 8415.	
14.	841821	Compression-type	Change at 6-digit H.S level (Change to subheading 841821 from any other subheadings), provided that there is a Local Value Added Content not less than 40%
8437		Machines for cleaning, sorting or grading seed, grain or dried leguminous vegetables; machinery used in the milling industry or for the working of cereals or dried leguminous vegetables, other than farm-type machinery.	
15.	843780	Other machinery	Change at 6-digit H.S level (Change to subheading 843780 from any other subheadings), provided that there is a Local Value Added Content not less than 40%
8479		Machines and mechanical appliances having individual functions, not specified or included elsewhere in this Chapter.	
16.	847989	Other	Change at 6-digit H.S level (Change to subheading 847989 from any other subheadings), provided that there is a Local Value Added Content not less than 40%
8481		Taps, cocks, valves and similar appliances for pipes, boiler shells, tanks, vats or the like, including pressure-reducing valves and thermostatically controlled valves.	
17.	848180	Other appliances	Change at 6-digit H.S level (Change to subheading 848180 from any other subheadings), provided that there is a Local Value Added Content not less than 40%
8482		Ball or roller bearings.	
18.	848210	Ball bearings	Change at 6-digit H.S level (Change to subheading 848210 from any other subheadings), provided that there is a Local Value Added Content not less than 40%
8504		Electrical transformers, static converters (for example, rectifiers) and inductors	

19.	850431	Having a power handling capacity not exceeding 1 kVA	Change at 6-digit H.S level (Change to subheading 850431 from any other subheadings), provided that there is a Local Value Added Content not less than 40%
8512		Electrical lighting or signalling equipment (excluding articles of heading 8539), windscreen wipers, defrosters and demisters, of a kind used for cycles or motor vehicles.	
20.	851220	Other lighting or visual signalling equipment	Change at 6-digit H.S level (Change to subheading 851220 from any other subheadings), provided that there is a Local Value Added Content not less than 40%
8517		Electrical apparatus for line telephony or line telegraphy, including line telephone sets with cordless handsets and telecommunication apparatus for carrier-current line systems or for digital line systems; videophones.	
21.	851711	Line telephone sets with cordless handsets	Change at 6-digit H.S level (Change to subheading 851711 from any other subheadings), provided that there is a Local Value Added Content not less than 40%
22.	851790	Parts	Change at 6-digit H.S level (Change to subheading 851790 from any other subheadings), provided that there is a Local Value Added Content not less than 40%
8528		Reception apparatus for television, whether or not incorporating radio-broadcast receivers or sound or video recording or reproducing apparatus; video monitors and video projectors.	
23.	852812	Colour	Change at 6-digit H.S level (Change to subheading 852812 from any other subheadings), provided that there is a Local Value Added Content not less than 40%
8540		Thermionic, cold cathode or photo-cathode valves and tubes (for example, vacuum or vapour or gas filled valves and tubes, mercury arc rectifying valves and tubes, cathode-ray tubes, television camera tubes).	
24.	854011	Colour	Change at 6-digit H.S level (Change to subheading 854011 from any other subheadings), provided that there is a Local Value Added Content not less than 40%
9032		Automatic regulating or controlling instruments and apparatus.	
25.	903289	Other	Change at 6-digit H.S level (Change to subheading 903289 from any other subheadings), provided that there is a Local Value Added Content not less than 40%

Tables Forming Part of Section - IV

(Data Analysis and Comparison)

Index of Tables and 40 tables containing various analysis figures are attached here after as ANNEXURES.

INDEX OF TABLES

TABLE–1

DETAILS OF SAMPLING (IMPORT PRODUCTS FROM SRILANKA)

(Value in Rs. Lakh)

	2004-05	
Total No. of Products imported during the year from SRILANKA	1102	
Total No. of Producs sampled	111	10.07%
Total No. of Sampled Products covered under ZERO DUTY	18	1.63%
Total No. of Sampled Products covered under PHASED RESIDUAL LIST: IR	75	6.81%
Total No. of Sampled Products covered under PREFERENTIAL DUTY	4	0.36%
Total No. of Sampled Products covered under NEGATIVE LIST	14	1.27%
Total Value of Imports during the year from SRILANKA	163725 65	

ALL INDIA FIGURES	**1998-99**	**1999-00**	**2000-01**	**2001-02**	**2002-03**	**2003-04**	**2004-05**	
Total Value of Imports during the year of Sampled Products	470811.07	653866.82	799979.03	1059558.46	1386315.29	2185467.50	3318220.98	
Total Value of Imports of Sampled Products covered under ZERO DUTY	185128.84	244043.29	301097.33	280717.10	274611.61	450088.49	573274.42	
Total Value of Imports of Sampled Products covered under PHASED RESIDUAL LIST: IR	275347.20	400107.92	487995.53	762834.95	1089600.15	1635084.98	2577245.64	
Total Value of Imports of Sampled Products covered under PREFERENTIAL DUTY	2273.78	484.06	397.50	953.93	2715.89	17604.67	31474.79	
Total Value of Imports of Sampled Products covered under NEGATIVE LIST	8061.25	9231.55	10488.67	15052.48	19387.64	82689.36	136226.13	
ONLY SRILANKA FIGURES	**1998-99**	**1999-00**	**2000-01**	**2001-02**	**2002-03**	**2003-04**	**2004-05**	
Total Value of Imports during the year of Sampled Products	8026.85	9621.56	10391.64	18208.27	25560.63	41846.64	149083.85	91.06%
Total Value of Imports of Sampled Products covered under ZERO DUTY	1087.17	1446.24	1392.20	1743.40	1888.62	6073.42	19440.83	11.87%

Total Value of Imports of Sampled Products covered under PHASED RESIDUAL LIST: IR	6454.35	7219.02	7997.00	15592.25	21756.93	30296.69	119589.92	73.04%
Total Value of Imports of Sam1pled Products covered under PREFERENTIAL DUTY	42.40	1.42	35.63	113.47	59.90	477.05	760.26	0.46%
Total Value of Imports of Sampled Products covered under NEGATIVE LIST	442.93	954.88	966.81	759.15	1855.18	4999.48	9292.84	5.68%

	IMPORTS FROM SRILANKA (A)	INDIA'S WORLD IMPORT (B)	RELATIVE FASTNESS (A/B)
Weighted Average CAGR of all the sampled products	166.04%	61.97%	2.68
Weighted Average CAGR of all the sampled products (covered under ZERO DUTY)	122.28%	30.84%	3.96
Weighted Average CAGR of all the sampled products (covered under PHASED RESIDUAL LIST: IR)	174.27%	68.26%	2.55
Weighted Average CAGR of all the sampled products (covered under PREFERENTIAL DUTY)	224.82%	81.38%	2.76
Weighted Average CAGR of all the sampled products (covered under NEGATIVE LIST)	146.85%	69.42%	2.12
Weighted Average CAGR of all the sampled products (covered under ZERO DUTY)- CHAPTER WISE	179.91%	22.19%	8.11
Weighted Average CAGR of all the sampled products (covered under PHASED RESIDUAL LIST: IR)- CHAPTER WISE	403.11%	57.97%	6.95
Weighted Average CAGR of all the sampled products (covered under PREFERENTIAL DUTY)- CHAPTER WISE	62.18%	78.76%	0.79
Weighted Average CAGR of all the sampled products (covered under NEGATIVE LIST)- CHAPTER WISE	152.34%	86.26%	1.77

TABLE- 2

KEY FACTORS FOR TOP 20 HIGH VALUE IMPORTED ITEMS (based on 2004-05 value of imports) FROM SRILANKA

			2004-05		2004-05	2004-05		2004-05	2004-05	2004-05	2004-05	2004-05	2004-05	
Sl. No.	HS Code	List of Concession	% of Total Value of imports from Srilanka in 2004-05	Base year for next two columns	Incremental Trend of imports from Srilanka (Volume) in % in comparison to base yr.	Incremental Trend of imports from Srilanka(Value) in % in comparison to base yr.	Base year for next two columns	Incremental Trend of World Import (Volume) in % in comparison to base yr.	Incremental Trend of World Import (Value) in % in comparison to base yr.	Market Share of imports from Srilanka in World Imports (Volume) in %	Market Share of imports from Srilanka in World Imports (Value) in %	Per Unit Import Price from Srilanka (in Rs.)	Per Unit World Import Price for India (in Rs.)	Base year for next two columns
1	74031900	Phased Residual List: IR	16.31	2001-02	1318.92	2857.89	1998-99	2482.92	5919.05	98.16	98.20	148.63	148.56	2001-02
2	74031200	Phased Residual List: IR	8.50	2002-03	1378.80	3402.76	1998-99	-38.46	26.70	93.22	93.51	153.89	153.41	2002-03
3	84262000	Zero Duty	5.02	2004-05	0.00	0.00	1998-99	1800.00	230.68	0.00	84.07	#DIV/0!	5146936.84	2004-05
4	72044900	Phased Residual List: IR	3.92	1998-99	102.35	357.47	1998-99	264.66	658.63	2.07	2.02	11.63	11.93	1998-99
5	15162091	Phased Residual List: IR	3.92	2004-05	0.00	0.00	1998-99	281.49	217.96	61.24	67.13	39.94	36.43	2004-05
6	74130000	Phased Residual List: IR	3.33	2004-05	0.00	0.00	1998-99	5861.83	539.87	91.82	88.58	235.73	244.35	2004-05
7	9070020	Phased Residual List: IR	2.65	1998-99	508.46	3122.65	1998-99	-53.26	171.46	60.32	75.35	268.35	214.80	1998-99
8	9070010	Phased Residual List: IR	2.19	1998-99	73.27	750.32	1998-99	-81.58	-5.67	55.00	74.48	260.77	192.56	1998-99
9	76012010	Phased Residual List: IR	2.11	2002-03	629.58	814.55	1998-99	17.22	72.37	16.73	16.77	86.80	86.57	2002-03
10	76051100	Phased Residual List: IR	1.98	2004-05	0.00	0.00	1998-99	3601.00	4337.00	95.78	96.09	130.93	130.51	2004-05
11	47079000	Zero Duty	1.78	1998-99	194.01	270.03	1998-99	97.38	138.21	3.19	2.96	6.68	7.20	1998-99
12	85441920	Phased Residual List: IR	1.74	2003-04	100.91	145.66	1998-99	20344.52	22560.78	63.49	69.78	243.50	221.56	2003-04
13	68022190	Phased Residual List: IR	1.72	2000-01	16599.53	21828.73	1998-99	16671.16	15602.69	32.62	41.49	35.79	28.14	2000-01
14	8011100	Negative list	1.71	2000-01	42811.05	42362.16	2000-01	42873.87	42382.52	99.85	99.95	34.09	34.06	2000-01
15	85441990	Phased Residual List: IR	1.58	2003-04	175.92	328.03	2003-04	85.80	90.56	33.28	27.92	225.52	268.77	2003-04
16	68022110	Phased Residual List: IR	1.51	2000-01	7473.20	6994.45	1998-99	28681.71	11180.27	32.59	36.96	27.46	24.21	2000-01
17	74032100	Phased Residual List: IR	1.28	2001-02	84170.80	1176.05	1998-99	1869.37	2135.48	62.26	61.11	99.22	101.09	2001-02
18	39269069	Negative list	1.11	2003-04	95.63	79.38	2003-04	62.25	52.96	40.56	35.70	165.18	187.65	2003-04
19	28241010	Zero Duty	1.07	2002-03	3263.81	5264.95	1998-99	806.11	1312.27	26.32	25.82	49.44	50.39	2002-03
20	85441110	Phased Residual List: IR	0.92	2000-01	33470.33	15591.74	1998-99	211.33	236.18	11.72	11.31	245.53	254.38	2000-01

TABLE- 2

KEY FACTORS FOR TOP 20 HIGH VALUE IMPORTED ITEMS (based on 2004-05 value of imports) FROM SRILANKA

			SRILANKA	SRILANKA		World	World	SRILANKA	World	SRILANKA & World		
Sl. No.	HS Code	List of Concession	CAGR - VOLUME (in %)	CAGR- VALUE (in %)	Base year for next two columns	CAGR- VOLUME (in %)	CAGR- VALUE (in %)	CORRELATION - TREND OF VOLUME / VALUE	CORRELATION - TREND OF VOLUME / VALUE	CORRELATION - TREND OF VOLUME	CORRELATION - TREND OF VALUE	CORRELATION - UNIT PRICE
1	74031900	Phased Residual List: IR	142.10	209.26	1998-99	71.93	97.96	0.99	0.98	0.99	1.00	#DIV/0!
2	74031200	Phased Residual List: IR	284.55	491.84	1998-99	-7.77	4.02	0.99	0.87	-0.04	0.49	#DIV/0!
3	84262000	Zero Duty	0.00	0.00	1998-99	63.35	22.06	1.00	0.96	1.00	0.96	#DIV/0!
4	72044900	Phased Residual List: IR	12.47	28.84	1998-99	24.06	40.18	0.91	0.89	0.52	0.91	0.96
5	15162091	Phased Residual List: IR	0.00	0.00	2003-04	108.58	111.32	1.00	0.99	-0.07	0.00	#DIV/0!
6	74130000	Phased Residual List: IR	0.00	0.00	1998-99	97.65	90.50	1.00	0.67	0.99	0.54	#DIV/0!
7	9070020	Phased Residual List: IR	35.12	78.39	1998-99	-11.91	18.11	0.91	0.30	-0.03	0.87	0.90
8	9070010	Phased Residual List: IR	9.59	42.87	1998-99	-24.57	-0.97	0.95	0.26	-0.07	0.80	0.60
9	76012010	Phased Residual List: IR	170.11	202.42	1998-99	2.68	9.50	1.00	0.94	0.73	0.91	#DIV/0!
10	76051100	Phased Residual List: IR	0.00	0.00	1998-99	82.55	88.15	1.00	1.00	1.00	1.00	#DIV/0!
11	47079000	Zero Duty	19.69	24.37	1998-99	12.00	15.57	0.99	0.96	0.60	0.71	0.90
12	85441920	Phased Residual List: IR	100.91	145.66	1998-99	142.71	146.91	1.00	1.00	1.00	1.00	#DIV/0!
13	68022190	Phased Residual List: IR	259.48	284.82	1998-99	134.83	132.27	0.99	1.00	0.98	0.99	#DIV/0!
14	8011100	Negative list	355.14	353.94	2000-01	355.30	354.00	1.00	1.00	1.00	1.00	#DIV/0!
15	85441990	Phased Residual List: IR	175.92	328.03	2003-04	85.80	90.56	0.99	1.00	0.99	0.96	#DIV/0!
16	68022110	Phased Residual List: IR	195.00	190.22	1998-99	156.95	119.81	1.00	1.00	0.91	0.88	#DIV/0!
17	74032100	Phased Residual List: IR	844.55	502.46	1998-99	64.33	67.84	0.60	0.99	0.97	0.72	#DIV/0!
18	39269069	Negative list	95.63	79.38	2003-04	62.25	52.96	1.00	1.00	1.00	1.00	#DIV/0!
19	28241010	Zero Duty	479.98	632.46	1998-99	44.39	55.47	0.99	0.95	0.92	0.97	#DIV/0!
20	85441110	Phased Residual List: IR	328.04	253.93	1998-99	20.84	22.39	1.00	0.95	0.79	0.91	#DIV/0!

NOTES

1. Base year have been changed, where CAGR for a particular product shows growth of more than 999%.
2. Base year for Trend Calculation have been changed in some cases, keeping in view the base year for CAGR and the actual trade data.
3. Base year for Trend Calculation have been changed in some cases, where trend exceeds 99999%.
4. Correlation among different DATA SERIES have been calculated by using the CORREL function active in the MS EXCEL spreadsheet.
5. Correlation of +1 denotes perfect positive correlation, -1 denotes perfect negative correlation, 0 denotes least correlation among the data series.
6. Trend is taken as 100% and CAGR as 0% in cases where either the data figures prior to 2004-05 are either zero or negligible.

TABLE-3

KEY FACTORS FOR TOP 20% OF SAMPLED PRODUCTS COVERED UNDER EACH CATEGORY (SORTED ON THE BASIS OF VALUE OF IMPORTS IN 2004-05)

			2004-05		2004-05	2004-05
Sl. No.	HS Code	Particulars	% of Total Value of imports from Srilanka in 2004-05	Base year for next two columns	Incremental Trend of imports from Srilanka (Volume) in % in comparison to base yr.	Incremental Trend of imports from Srilanka(Value) in % in comparison to base yr.
		ZERO DUTY				
1	84262000	TOWER CRANES	5.02	2004-05	0.00	0.00
2	47079000	OTHR INCL UNSORTED WASTE AND SCRAP	1.78	1998-99	194.01	270.03
3	28241010	LITHARGE (28241001)	1.07	2002-03	3263.81	5264.95
4	47071000	WSTE AND SCRP OF UNBLECHD KRAFT PAPR OR PAPRBORD OR CORGTD PAPR/PAPRBORD	0.57	1998-99	241.15	323.01
		PHASED RESIDUAL LIST: IR				
1	74031900	OTHER REFINED COPPER,UNWROUGHT	16.31	2001-02	1318.92	2857.89
2	74031200	WIRE-BARS OF REFINED COPPER	8.50	2002-03	1378.80	3402.76
3	72044900	OTHER WASTE AND SCRAP(72044909)	3.92	1998-99	102.35	357.47
4	15162091	OTHR VEG FATS & OILS & THR FRCTNS OF EDBLEGRADE (15162009)	3.92	2004-05	0.00	0.00
5	74130000	STRANDED WIRE,CABLES,PLAITD BANDS & LIKE OF COPPER,NOT ELECTRICALLY INSULATED	3.33	2004-05	0.00	0.00
6	9070020	CLOVE, NOT EXTRACTED (OTHER THAN STEM) (9070002)	2.65	1998-99	508.46	3122.65
7	9070010	CLOVES EXTRACTED (9070001)	2.19	1998-99	73.27	750.32
8	76012010	ALUMINIUM INGOTS -ALLOYED (76012001)	2.11	2002-03	629.58	814.55
9	76051100	ALUMINIUM WIRE-NOT ALLOYED-OF WHICH THE MAXIMUM CROSS-SCTNL DIMENSION EXCEEDS 7 MM	1.98	2004-05	0.00	0.00
10	85441920	PLASTIC INSULATED WIRE (85441902)	1.74	2003-04	100.91	145.66
11	68022190	OTHERS (68022109)	1.72	2000-01	16599.53	21828.73
12	85441990	OTHER WINDING WIRES OF OTHR METLS/SUBSTNCE	1.58	2003-04	175.92	328.03
13	68022110	MARBLE BLOCKS/TILES,POLISHED (68022101)	1.51	2000-01	7473.20	6994.45
14	74032100	COPPER-ZINC BASE ALLOYS(BRASS)	1.28	2001-02	84170.80	1176.05
15	85441110	WINDING WIRE OF ENAMELLED COPPER (85441101)	0.92	2000-01	33470.33	15591.74
		PREFERENTIAL DUTY				
1	52094200	DENIM	0.13	1998-99	2373.68	619.37
		NEGATIVE LIST				
1	8011100	COCONUT DESICCATED	1.71	2000-01	42811.05	42362.16
2	39269069	OTHER HANGERS	1.11	2003-04	95.63	79.38
3	40012100	NATRL RUBR IN SMKD SHEETS	0.73	1998-99	10814.72	19103.22

TABLE-3

KEY FACTORS FOR TOP 20% OF SAMPLED PRODUCTS COVERED UNDER EACH CATEGORY (SORTED ON THE BASIS OF VALUE OF IMPORTS IN 2004-05)

Sl. No.	HS Code	Particulars	Base year for next two columns	2004-05 Incremental Trend of World Import (Volume) in % in comparison to base yr.	2004-05 Incremental Trend of World Import (Value) in % in comparison to base yr.	2004-05 Market Share of imports from Srilanka in World Imports (Volume) in %
		ZERO DUTY				
1	84262000	TOWER CRANES	1998-99	1800.00	230.68	0.00
2	47079000	OTHR INCL UNSORTED WASTE AND SCRAP	1998-99	97.38	138.21	3.19
3	28241010	LITHARGE (28241001)	1998-99	806.11	1312.27	26.32
4	47071000	WSTE AND SCRP OF UNBLECHD KRAFT PAPR OR PAPRBORD OR CORGTD PAPR/PAPRBORD	1998-99	-40.29	-27.66	45.60
		PHASED RESIDUAL LIST: IR				
1	74031900	OTHER REFINED COPPER,UNWROUGHT	1998-99	2482.92	5919.05	98.16
2	74031200	WIRE-BARS OF REFINED COPPER	1998-99	-38.46	26.70	93.22
3	72044900	OTHER WASTE AND SCRAP(72044909)	1998-99	264.66	658.63	2.07
4	15162091	OTHR VEG FATS & OILS & THR FRCTNS OF EDBLEGRADE (15162009)	1998-99	281.49	217.96	61.24
5	74130000	STRANDED WIRE,CABLES,PLAITD BANDS & LIKE OF COPPER,NOT ELECTRICALLY INSULATED	1998-99	5861.83	539.87	91.82
6	9070020	CLOVE, NOT EXTRACTED (OTHER THAN STEM) (9070002)	1998-99	-53.26	171.46	60.32
7	9070010	CLOVES EXTRACTED (9070001)	1998-99	-81.58	-5.67	55.00
8	76012010	ALUMINIUM INGOTS -ALLOYED (76012001)	1998-99	17.22	72.37	16.73
9	76051100	ALUMINIUM WIRE-NOT ALLOYED-OF WHICH THE MAXIMUM CROSS-SCTNL DIMENSION EXCEEDS 7 MM	1998-99	3601.00	4337.00	95.78
10	85441920	PLASTIC INSULATED WIRE (85441902)	1998-99	20344.52	22560.78	63.49
11	68022190	OTHERS (68022109)	1998-99	16671.16	15602.69	32.62
12	85441990	OTHER WINDING WIRES OF OTHR METLS/SUBSTNCE	2003-04	85.80	90.56	33.28
13	68022110	MARBLE BLOCKS/TILES,POLISHED (68022101)	1998-99	28681.71	11180.27	32.59
14	74032100	COPPER-ZINC BASE ALLOYS(BRASS)	1998-99	1869.37	2135.48	62.26
15	85441110	WINDING WIRE OF ENAMELLED COPPER (85441101)	1998-99	211.33	236.18	11.72
		PREFERENTIAL DUTY				
1	52094200	DENIM	1998-99	2992.03	1601.12	2.11
		NEGATIVE LIST				
1	8011100	COCONUT DESICCATED	2000-01	42873.87	42382.52	99.85
2	39269069	OTHER HANGERS	2003-04	62.25	52.96	40.56
3	40012100	NATRL RUBR IN SMKD SHEETS	1998-99	491.70	1027.71	5.87

TABLE-3

KEY FACTORS FOR TOP 20% OF SAMPLED PRODUCTS COVERED UNDER EACH CATEGORY (SORTED ON THE BASIS OF VALUE OF IMPORTS IN 2004-05)

Sl. No.	HS Code	Particulars	2004-05. Market Share of imports from Srilanka in World Imports (Value) in %	2004-05 Per Unit Import Price from Srilanka (in Rs.)	2004-05 Per Unit World Import Price for India (in Rs.)	Base year for next two columns
		ZERO DUTY				
1	84262000	TOWER CRANES	84.07	#DIV/0!	5146936.84	2004-05
2	47079000	OTHR INCL UNSORTED WASTE AND SCRAP	2.96	6.68	7.20	1998-99
3	28241010	LITHARGE (2824100^1)	25.82	49.44	50.39	2002-03
4	47071000	WSTE AND SCRP OF UNBLECHD KRAFT PAPR OR PAPRBORD OR CORGTD PAPR/PAPRBORD	41.76	6.36	6.94	1998-99
		PHASED RESIDUAL LIST: IR				
1	74031900	OTHER REFINED COPPER,UNWROUGHT	98.20	148.63	148.56	2001-02
2	74031200	WIRE-BARS OF REFINED COPPER	93.51	153.89	153.41	2002-03
3	72044900	OTHER WASTE AND SCRAP(72044909)	2.02	11.63	11.93	1998-99
4	15162091	OTHR VEG FATS & OILS & THR FRCTNS OF EDBLEGRADE (15162009)	67.13	39.94	36.43	2004-05
5	74130000	STRANDED WIRE,CABLES,PLAITD BANDS & LIKE OF COPPER,NOT ELECTRICALLY INSULATED	88.58	235.73	244.35	2004-05
6	9070020	CLOVE, NOT EXTRACTED (OTHER THAN STEM) (9070002)	75.35	268.35	214.80	1998-99
7	9070010	CLOVES EXTRACTED (9070001)	74.48	260.77	192.56	1998-99
8	76012010	ALUMINIUM INGOTS -ALLOYED (76012001)	16.77	86.80	86.57	2002-03
9	76051100	ALUMINIUM WIRE-NOT ALLOYED-OF WHICH THE MAXIMUM CROSS-SCTNL DIMENSION EXCEEDS 7 MM	96.09	130.93	130.51	2004-05
10	85441920	PLASTIC INSULATED WIRE (85441902)	69.78	243.50	221.56	2003-04
11	68022190	OTHERS (68022109)	41.49	35.79	28.14	2000-01
12	85441990	OTHER WINDING WIRES OF OTHR METLS/SUBSTNCE	27.92	225.52	268.77	2003-04
13	68022110	MARBLE BLOCKS/TILES,POLISHED (68022101)	36.96	27.46	24.21	2000-01
14	74032100	COPPER-ZINC BASE ALLOYS(BRASS)	61.11	99.22	101.09	2001-02
15	85441110	WINDING WIRE OF ENAMELLED COPPER (85441101)	11.31	245.53	254.38	2000-01
		PREFERENTIAL DUTY				
1	52094200	DENIM	1.38	94.83	144.99	1998-99
		NEGATIVE LIST				
1	8011100	COCONUT DESICCATED	99.95	34.09	34.06	2000-01
2	39269069	OTHER HANGERS	35.70	165.18	187.65	2003-04
3	40012100	NATRL RUBR IN SMKD SHEETS	6.13	60.80	58.17	1998-99

TABLE-3

KEY FACTORS FOR TOP 20% OF SAMPLED PRODUCTS COVERED UNDER EACH CATEGORY (SORTED ON THE BASIS OF VALUE OF IMPORTS IN 2004-05)

			SRILANKA	SRILANKA		World
Sl. No.	HS Code	Particulars	CAGR - VOLUME (in %)	CAGR- VALUE (in %)	Base year for next two columns	CAGR- VOLUME (in %)
		ZERO DUTY				
1	84262000	TOWER CRANES	0.00	0.00	1998-99	63.35
2	47079000	OTHR INCL UNSORTED WASTE AND SCRAP	19.69	24.37	1998-99	12.00
3	28241010	LITHARGE (28241001)	479.98	632.46	1998-99	44.39
4	47071000	WSTE AND SCRP OF UNBLECHD KRAFT PAPR OR PAPRBORD OR CORGTD PAPR/PAPRBORD	22.69	27.17	1998-99	-8.23
		PHASED RESIDUAL LIST: IR				
1	74031900	OTHER REFINED COPPER,UNWROUGHT	142.10	209.26	1998-99	71.93
2	74031200	WIRE-BARS OF REFINED COPPER	284.55	491.84	1998-99	-7.77
3	72044900	OTHER WASTE AND SCRAP(72044909)	12.47	28.84	1998-99	24.06
4	15162091	OTHR VEG FATS & OILS & THR FRCTNS OF EDBLEGRADE (15162009)	0.00	0.00	2003-04	108.58
5	74130000	STRANDED WIRE,CABLES,PLAITD BANDS & LIKE OF COPPER,NOT ELECTRICALLY INSULATED	0.00	0.00	1998-99	97.65
6	9070020	CLOVE, NOT EXTRACTED (OTHER THAN STEM) (9070002)	35.12	78.39	1998-99	-11.91
7	9070010	CLOVES EXTRACTED (9070001)	9.59	42.87	1998-99	-24.57
8	76012010	ALUMINIUM INGOTS -ALLOYED (76012001)	170.11	202.42	1998-99	2.68
9	76051100	ALUMINIUM WIRE-NOT ALLOYED-OF WHICH THE MAXIMUM CROSS-SCTNL DIMENSION EXCEEDS 7 MM	0.00	0.00	1998-99	82.55
10	85441920	PLASTIC INSULATED WIRE (85441902)	100.91	145.66	1998-99	142.71
11	68022190	OTHERS (68022109)	259.48	284.82	1998-99	134.83
12	85441990	OTHER WINDING WIRES OF OTHR METLS/SUBSTNCE	175.92	328.03	2003-04	85.80
13	68022110	MARBLE BLOCKS/TILES,POLISHED (68022101)	195.00	190.22	1998-99	156.95
14	74032100	COPPER-ZINC BASE ALLOYS(BRASS)	844.55	502.46	1998-99	64.33
15	85441110	WINDING WIRE OF ENAMELLED COPPER (85441101)	328.04	253.93	1998-99	20.84
		PREFERENTIAL DUTY				
1	52094200	DENIM	70.70	38.94	1998-99	77.16
		NEGATIVE LIST				
1	8011100	COCONUT DESICCATED	355.14	353.94	2000-01	355.30
2	39269069	OTHER HANGERS	95.63	79.38	2003-04	62.25
3	40012100	NATRL RUBR IN SMKD SHEETS	118.61	140.19	1998-99	34.49

TABLE-3

KEY FACTORS FOR TOP 20% OF SAMPLED PRODUCTS COVERED UNDER EACH CATEGORY (SORTED ON THE BASIS OF VALUE OF IMPORTS IN 2004-05)

			World	SRILANKA	World
Sl. No.	HS Code	Particulars	CAGR-VALUE (in %)	CORRELATION - TREND OF VOLUME / VALUE	CORRELATION - TREND OF VOLUME / VALUE
		ZERO DUTY			
1	84262000	TOWER CRANES	22.06	1.00	0.96
2	47079000	OTHR INCL UNSORTED WASTE AND SCRAP	15.57	0.99	0.96
3	28241010	LITHARGE (28241001)	55.47	0.99	0.95
4	47071000	WSTE AND SCRP OF UNBLECHD KRAFT PAPR OR PAPRBORD OR CORGTD PAPR/PAPRBORD	-5.25	1.00	0.89
		PHASED RESIDUAL LIST: IR			
1	74031900	OTHER REFINED COPPER,UNWROUGHT	97.96	0.99	0.98
2	74031200	WIRE-BARS OF REFINED COPPER	4.02	0.99	0.87
3	72044900	OTHER WASTE AND SCRAP(72044909)	40.18	0.91	0.89
4	15162091	OTHR VEG FATS & OILS & THR FRCTNS OF EDBLEGRADE (15162009)	111.32	1.00	0.99
5	74130000	STRANDED WIRE,CABLES,PLAITD BANDS & LIKE OF COPPER,NOT ELECTRICALLY INSULATED	90.50	1.00	0.67
6	9070020	CLOVE, NOT EXTRACTED (OTHER THAN STEM) (9070002)	18.11	0.91	0.30
7	9070010	CLOVES EXTRACTED (9070001)	-0.97	0.95	0.26
8	76012010	ALUMINIUM INGOTS -ALLOYED (76012001)	9.50	1.00	0.94
9	76051100	ALUMINIUM WIRE-NOT ALLOYED-OF WHICH THE MAXIMUM CROSS-SCTNL DIMENSION EXCEEDS 7 MM	88.15	1.00	1.00
10	85441920	PLASTIC INSULATED WIRE (85441902)	146.91	1.00	1.00
11	68022190	OTHERS (68022109)	132.27	0.99	1.00
12	85441990	OTHER WINDING WIRES OF OTHR METLS/SUBSTNCE	90.56	0.99	1.00
13	68022110	MARBLE BLOCKS/TILES,POLISHED (68022101)	119.81	1.00	1.00
14	74032100	COPPER-ZINC BASE ALLOYS(BRASS)	67.84	0.60	0.99
15	85441110	WINDING WIRE OF ENAMELLED COPPER (85441101)	22.39	1.00	0.95
		PREFERENTIAL DUTY			
1	52094200	DENIM	60.37	99.25	99.81
		NEGATIVE LIST			
1	8011100	COCONUT DESICCATED	354.00	1.00	1.00
2	39269069	OTHER HANGERS	52.96	1.00	1.00
3	40012100	NATRL RUBR IN SMKD SHEETS	49.75	0.98	0.97

TABLE-3
KEY FACTORS FOR TOP 20% OF SAMPLED PRODUCTS COVERED UNDER EACH CATEGORY (SORTED ON THE BASIS OF VALUE OF IMPORTS IN 2004-05)

			SRILANKA & World		
Sl. No.	HS Code	Particulars	CORRELATION - TREND OF VOLUME	CORRELATION - TREND OF VALUE	CORRELATION - UNIT PRICE
		ZERO DUTY			
1	84262000	TOWER CRANES	1.00	0.96	#DIV/0!
2	47079000	OTHR INCL UNSORTED WASTE AND SCRAP	0.60	0.71	0.90
3	28241010	LITHARGE (28241001)	0.92	0.97	#DIV/0!
4	47071000	WSTE AND SCRP OF UNBLECHD KRAFT PAPR OR PAPRBORD OR CORGTD PAPR/PAPRBORD	0.19	0.18	0.54
		PHASED RESIDUAL LIST: IF			
1	74031900	OTHER REFINED COPPER,UNWROUGHT	0.99	1.00	#DIV/0!
2	74031200	WIRE-BARS OF REFINED COPPER	-0.04	0.49	#DIV/0!
3	72044900	OTHER WASTE AND SCRAP(72044909)	0.52	0.91	0.96
4	15162091	OTHR VEG FATS & OILS & THR FRCTNS OF EDBLEGRADE (15162009)	-0.07	0.00	#DIV/0!
5	74130000	STRANDED WIRE,CABLES,PLAITD BANDS & LIKE OF COPPER, NOT ELECTRICALLY INSULATED	0.99	0.54	#DIV/0!
6	9070020	CLOVE, NOT EXTRACTED (OTHER THAN STEM) (9070002)	-0.03	0.87	0.96
7	9070010	CLOVES EXTRACTED (9070001)	-0.07	0.80	0.60
8	76012010	ALUMINIUM INGOTS -ALLOYED (76012001)	0.73	0.91	#DIV/0!
9	76051100	ALUMINIUM WIRE-NOT ALLOYED-OF WHICH THE MAXIMUM CROSS-SCTNL DIMENSION EXCEEDS 7 MM	1.00	1.00	#DIV/0!
10	85441920	PLASTIC INSULATED WIRE (85441902)	1.00	1.00	#DIV/0!
11	68022190	OTHERS (68022109)	0.98	0.99	#DIV/0!
12	85441990	OTHER WINDING WIRES OF OTHR METLS/SUBSTNCE	0.99	0.96	#DIV/0!
13	68022110	MARBLE BLOCKS/TILES,POLISHED (68022101)	0.91	0.88	#DIV/0!
14	74032100	COPPER-ZINC BASE ALLOYS(BRASS)	0.97	0.72	#DIV/0!
15	85441110	WINDING WIRE OF ENAMELLED COPPER (85441101)	0.79	0.91	#DIV/0!
		PREFERENTIAL DUTY			
1	52094200	DENIM	91.85	84.04	#DIV/0!
		NEGATIVE LIST			
1	8011100	COCONUT DESICCATED	1.00	1.00	#DIV/0!
2	39269069	OTHER HANGERS	1.00	1.00	#DIV/0!
3	40012100	NATRL RUBR IN SMKD SHEETS	0.80	0.93	0.95

TABLE- 4

KEY FACTORS FOR TOP 10% OF SAMPLED PRODUCTS COVERED UNDER EACH CATEGORY (SORTED ON THE BASIS OF CAGR-VALUE OF IMPORTS FROM SRILANKA)

			2004-05		2004-05	2004-05		2004-05	2004-05	2004-05	2004-05	2004-05	2004-05	
Sl. No.	HS Code	Particulars	% of Total Value of imports from Srilanka in 2004-05	Base year for next two columns	Incremental Trend of imports from Srilanka (Volume) in % in comparison to base yr.	Incremental Trend of imports from Srilanka(Value) in % in comparison to base yr.	Base year for next two columns	Incremental Trend of World Import (Volume) in % in comparison to base yr.	Incremental Trend of World Import (Value) in % in comparison to base yr.	Market Share of imports from Srilanka in World Imports (Volume) in %	Market Share of imports from Srilanka in World Imports (Value) in %	Per Unit Import Price from Srilanka (in Rs.)	Per Unit World Import Price for India (in Rs.)	Base year for next two columns
		ZERO DUTY												
1	44111190	OTHER BOARD	0.16	2003-04	217.58	722.61	2003-04	2.48	77.09	23.77	32.02	28.52	21.17	2003-04
2	28241010	LITHARGE (28241001)	1.07	2002-03	3263.81	5264.95	1998-99	806.11	1312.27	26.32	25.82	49.44	50.39	2002-03
		PHASED RESIDUAL LIST: IR												
1	69079090	OTHR THAN OTHR UNGLAZED VITRIFIED TLES PLSHD OR NOT	0.12	2003-04	763.06	863.99	2003-04	180.70	268.26	2.25	3.59	323.64	202.99	2003-04
2	74032290	OTHER COPPER-TIN BASE ALLOYS(BRONZE) (74032209)	0.50	2002-03	2159.79	3691.42	1998-99	4337.49	1725.48	80.25	74.72	149.95	161.04	2002-03
3	74032100	COPPER-ZINC BASE ALLOYS(BRASS)	1.28	2001-02	84170.80	1176.05	1998-99	1869.37	2135.48	62.26	61.11	99.22	101.09	2001-02
4	74031200	WIRE-BARS OF REFINED COPPER	8.50	2002-03	1378.80	3402.76	1998-99	-38.46	26.70	93.22	93.51	153.89	153.41	2002-03
5	23022020	RICE BRAN-RAW (23022002)	0.14	2003-04	261.02	483.72	1998-99	-18.21	69.25	48.26	59.43	4.22	3.43	2003-04
6	32064990	OTHER PREPARATIONS (32064909)	0.11	2001-02	8006.45	10617.47	1998-99	33.43	104.13	7.07	4.16	141.59	240.60	2001-02
7	40119900	OTHR PNMTC TYRES OF RUBBER	0.26	2003-04	398.55	353.04	2003-04	16.37	-34.98	10.95	13.37	6295.20	5154.90	2003-04
8	85441990	OTHER WINDING WIRES OF OTHR METLS/SUBSTNCE	1.58	2003-04	175.92	328.03	2003-04	85.80	90.56	33.28	27.92	225.52	268.77	2003-04
		PREFERENTIAL DUTY-TEXTILES												
1	52082990	OTHERS	0.13	2003-04	919.96	736.47	2003-04	130.80	102.10	1.49	1.45	96.17	99.19	2003-04
		NEGATIVE LIST												
1	8011100	COCONUT DESICCATED	1.71	2000-01	42811.05	42362.16	2000-01	42873.87	42382.52	99.85	99.95	34.09	34.06	2000-01
2	40012100	NATRL RUBR IN SMKD SHEETS	0.73	1998-99	10814.72	19103.22	1998-99	491.70	1027.71	5.87	6.13	60.80	58.17	1998-99

NOTES

1 Base year have been changed, where CAGR for a particular product shows growth of more than 999%.
2 Base year for Trend Calculation have been changed in some cases, keeping in view the base year for CAGR and the actual trade data.
3 Base year for Trend Calculation have been changed in some cases, where trend exceeds 99999%.
4 Correlation among different DATA SERIES have been calculated by using the CORREL function active in the MS EXCEL spreadsheet.
5 Correlation of +1 denotes perfect positive correlation, -1 denotes perfect negative correlation, 0 denotes least correlation among the data series.
6 Trend is taken as 100% and CAGR as 0% in cases where either the data figures prior to 2004-05 are either zero or negligible.

TABLE- 4

KEY FACTORS FOR TOP 10% OF SAMPLED PRODUCTS COVERED UNDER EACH CATEGORY (SORTED ON THE BASIS OF CAGR-VALUE OF IMPORTS FROM SRILANKA)

			SRILANKA	SRILANKA		World	World	SRILANKA	World	SRILANKA & World		
Sl. No.	HS Code	Particulars	CAGR - VOLUME (in %)	CAGR- VALUE (in %)	Base year for next two columns	CAGR- VOLUME (in %)	CAGR- VALUE (in %)	CORRELATI ON - TREND OF VOLUME / VALUE	CORREL ATION - TREND OF VOLUME / VALUE	CORREL ATION - TREND OF VOLUME	CORREL ATION - TREND OF VALUE	CORREL ATION - UNIT PRICE
		ZERO DUTY										
1	44111190	OTHER BOARD	217.58	722.61	2003-04	2.48	77.09	0.98	0.95	0.86	0.91	#DIV/0!
2	28241010	LITHARGE (28241001)	479.98	632.46	1998-99	44.39	55.47	0.99	0.95	0.92	0.97	#DIV/0!
		PHASED RESIDUAL LIST: IR										
1	69079090	OTHR THAN OTHR UNGLAZED VITRIFIED TLES PLSHD OR NOT	763.06	863.99	2003-04	180.70	268.26	1.00	1.00	0.97	0.99	#DIV/0!
2	74032290	OTHER COPPER TIN BASE ALLOYS(BRONZE) (74032209)	375.37	515.75	1998-99	88.16	62.27	1.00	0.99	0.99	0.98	#DIV/0!
3	74032100	COPPER-ZINC BASE ALLOYS(BRASS)	844.55	502.46	1998-99	64.33	67.84	0.60	0.99	0.97	0.72	#DIV/0!
4	74031200	WIRE-BARS OF REFINED COPPER	284.55	491.84	1998-99	-7.77	4.02	0.99	0.87	-0.04	0.49	#DIV/0!
5	23022020	RICE BRAN-RAW (23022002)	261.02	483.72	1998-99	-3.30	9.17	0.99	0.86	0.49	0.86	#DIV/0!
6	32064990	OTHER PREPARATIONS (32064909)	332.79	375.00	1998-99	4.92	12.63	1.00	0.67	0.80	0.89	#DIV/0!
7	40119900	OTHR PNMTC TYRES OF RUBBER	398.55	353.04	2003-04	16.37	-34.98	1.00	0.94	0.84	0.63	#DIV/0!
8	85441990	OTHER WINDING WIRES OF OTHR METLS/SUBSTNCE	175.92	328.03	2003-04	85.80	90.56	0.99	1.00	0.99	0.96	#DIV/0!
		PREFERENTIAL DUTY-TEXTILES										
1	52082990	OTHERS	919.96	736.47	2003-04	130.80	102.10	1.00	1.00	0.94	0.93	#DIV/0!
		NEGATIVE LIST										
1	8011100	COCONUT DESICCATED	355.14	353.94	2000-01	355.30	354.00	1.00	1.00	1.00	1.00	#DIV/0!
2	40012100	NATRL RUBR IN SMKD SHEETS	118.61	140.19	1998-99	34.49	49.75	0.98	0.97	0.80	0.93	0.95

TABLE- 5

KEY FACTORS FOR ALL SAMPLED PRODUCTS COVERED UNDER VARIOUS CATEGORIES- CHAPTEI

Sl. No.	CHAPTER	Main Products	% of Total Value of imports from Srilanka in 2004-05 (2004-05)	Value of Imports from Srilanka (in Rs. Lakhs) (2004-05)	Value of World Imports for India (in Rs. Lakhs) (2004-05)	Market Share of imports from Srilanka in World Imports (Value) in % (2004-05)	Base year for next column	Incremental Trend of imports from Srilanka (Value) in % in comparison to base yr. (2004-05)
		Zero Duty						
1	CHAPTER 26	Ores, Slag and Ash	0.15	240.35	6928.71	3.47	2003-04	457.40
2	CHAPTER 28	Inorganic Chemicals, Organic or inorganic compounds of precious metals	1.07	1746.29	6762.36	25.82	2002-03	5264.95
3	CHAPTER 44	Wood and articles of wood	1.72	2814.34	7005.75	40.17	2003-04	291.41
4	CHAPTER 47	Wood Pulp, scrap paper or paper board	2.35	3844.61	100722.19	3.82	1998-99	281.60
5	CHAPTER 84	Machinery and Appliances	6.59	10795.24	451855.41	2.39	1998-99	13448.24
		Total	**11.87**	**19440.83**	**573274.42**			

Sl. No.	CHAPTER	Main Products	Base year for next column	Incremental Trend of World Import (Value) in % in comparison to base yr. (2004-05)	CORRELATION OF TREND IN VALUE - Srilanka/World Imports (2004-05)	Base year for next column	CAGR-VALUE-Srilanka (in %) (2004-05)	Base year for next column	CAGR-VALUE-World Imports(in %) (2004-05)
		Zero Duty							
1	CHAPTER 26	Ores, Slag and Ash	1998-99	502.21	0.93	2003-04	457.40	1998-99	34.88
2	CHAPTER 28	Inorganic Chemicals, Organic or inorganic compounds of precious metals	1998-99	1312.27	0.97	2002-03	632.46	1998-99	55.47
3	CHAPTER 44	Wood and articles of wood	1998-99	10542.18	0.90	2003-04	291.41	1998-99	117.69
4	CHAPTER 47	Wood Pulp, scrap paper or paper board	1998-99	126.71	0.69	1998-99	25.01	1998-99	14.62
5	CHAPTER 84	Machinery and Appliances	1998-99	225.06	0.89	1998-99	126.63	1998-99	21.71

TABLE- 5

KEY FACTORS FOR ALL SAMPLED PRODUCTS COVERED UNDER VARIOUS CATEGORIES- CHAPTERWISE

		Phased Residual List: IR													
1	CHAPTER 8	Edible fruits and nuts	0.17	275.92	454.97	60.65	2003-04	5396.41	2003-04	7457.64	1.00	2004-05	0.00	2004-05	0.00
2	CHAPTER 9	Coffe, Tea and Spices	7.36	12051.78	21953.10	54.90	1998-99	191.11	1998-99	69.90	0.80	1998-99	19.49	1998-99	9.24
3	CHAPTER 15	Animal or Vegitable fats and oils	6.12	10015.62	572594.53	1.75	1998-99	1250.11	1998-99	5439.25	0.45	1998-99	54.31	1998-99	95.24
4	CHAPTER 23	Residues and waste of Food industry	0.51	839.32	3623.67	23.16	2000-01	90.53	1998-99	1521.40	0.52	2000-01	17.49	1998-99	59.09
5	CHAPTER 32	Tanning or Dyeing extracts. Paints, Varnishes and Inks	0.11	177.91	4277.32	4.16	2001-02	10617.47	1998-99	104.13	0.89	2002-03	375.00	1998-99	12.63
6	CHAPTER 40	Rubber and related articles	1.87	3055.68	15998.67	19.10	1998-99	61259.04	1998-99	463.00	0.95	1998-99	191.51	1998-99	33.38
7	CHAPTER 42	Leather goods	0.43	700.04	1976.80	35.41	2001-02	4283.47	1998-99	4471.69	0.91	2001-02	252.59	1998-99	89.09
8	CHAPTER 48	Paper and paper boards, articles related to paper	0.32	526.81	2754.46	19.13	1998-99	1726.03	1998-99	80.81	0.85	1998-99	62.27	1998-99	10.38
9	CHAPTER 68	Articles of stone, plaster, cement, asbestos etc.	3.22	5277.23	13448.92	39.24	2000-01	10986.62	1998-99	13043.98	0.96	2000-01	224.49	1998-99	125.49
10	CHAPTER 69	Ceramic products	0.24	385.28	6539.98	5.89	2003-04	1371.10	2003-04	205.24	0.97	2004-05	0.00	2003-04	205.24
11	CHAPTER 71	Natural or other stones, pearls	0.37	607.97	1151446.00	0.05	1999-00	472.05	1998-99	1203.66	0.80	1999-00	41.74	1998-99	53.41
12	CHAPTER 72	Iron and Steel	4.64	7596.94	436646.76	1.74	1998-99	393.85	1998-99	790.35	0.94	1998-99	30.50	1998-99	43.97
13	CHAPTER 73	Articles of Iron or Steel	0.21	346.75	8621.63	4.02	1999-00	9558.77	1998-99	536.04	0.99	1998-99	471.04	1998-99	36.12
14	CHAPTER 74	Copper and Copper articles	31.55	51663.33	65038.42	79.44	2001-02	4244.71	1998-99	340.49	0.98	1998-99	679.67	1998-99	28.03
15	CHAPTER 76	Aluminium and articles	5.31	8685.99	58316.02	14.89	2002-03	2204.40	1998-99	43.14	0.70	2002-03	380.04	1998-99	6.16
16	CHAPTER 78	Lead and articles	0.47	761.46	48163.24	1.58	2000-01	1921.93	1998-99	242.81	0.87	2000-01	112.05	1998-99	22.79
17	CHAPTER 79	Zinc and articles	1.03	1684.67	2607.57	64.61	2004-05	0.00	1998-99	2258.30	0.85	2004-05	0.00	1998-99	69.34
18	CHAPTER 80	Tin and articles	0.41	672.83	874.03	76.98	2004-05	0.00	2003-04	499.60	0.99	2004-05	0.00	2003-04	499.60
19	CHAPTER 84	Machinery and Appliances	0.35	566.82	36218.77	1.56	2003-04	1366.93	1998-99	66.77	0.28	2004-05	0.00	1998-99	8.90
20	CHAPTER 85	Audio Visual Equipments incl. TV	7.69	12302.40	115623.14	10.89	2000-01	131515.38	1998-99	689.43	0.99	2000-01	502.32	1998-99	41.11
21	CHAPTER 94	Furniture and furnishing materials	0.68	1115.14	10167.64	10.97	2000-01	2010.02	1998-99	1854.83	0.96	2000-01	114.50	1998-99	64.13
		Total	**73.04**	**119589.92**	**2577245.64**										
		TEXTILE ITEMS FALLING UNDER PREFERENTIAL DUTY OF 25%													
1	CHAPTER 52	Cotton	0.35	577.10	30870.18	1.87	1998-99	1881.80	1998-99	3364.51	1.00	1998-99	64.50	1998-99	80.55
2	CHAPTER 56	Wadding, Special yarns, ropes and cables	0.11	183.16	604.61	30.29	1998-99	1279.22	1998-99	-56.27	-0.04	1998-99	54.86	1998-99	-12.88
		Total	0.46	760.26	31474.79										
		INDIA'S NEGATIVE LIST													
1	CHAPTER 5	Other products of Animal Origin	0.12	202.25	202.42	99.92	2003-04	45.05	2003-04	41.06	1.00	2003-04	45.05	2003-04	41.06
2	CHAPTER 8	Edible fruits and nuts	1.71	2794.01	2795.35	99.95	2000-01	42382.52	2000-01	42362.16	1.00	2000-01	353.94	2000-01	354.00
3	CHAPTER 9	Coffe, Tea and Spices	0.73	1190.35	2618.08	45.47	1998-99	255.97	1998-99	25.27	0.62	1998-99	23.57	1998-99	3.83
4	CHAPTER 13	Lacs, Resins, Vegetable Extracts	0.22	357.22	1187.47	30.08	2003-04	-23.08	2003-04	-40.36	0.99	2003-04	-23.08	2003-04	-40.36
5	CHAPTER 26	Ores, Slag and Ash	0.11	173.53	11434.25	1.52	2003-04	-26.06	2003-04	239.99	0.73	2003-04	-26.06	2003-04	239.99
6	CHAPTER 29	Organic Chemicals	0.21	336.65	34168.75	0.99	2004-05	0.00	2003-04	72.39	0.84	2004-05	0.00	2003-04	72.39
7	CHAPTER 39	Plastics and related articles	1.53	2503.76	56941.03	4.40	1998-99	3342.07	1998-99	3106.97	1.00	1998-99	80.36	1998-99	78.24
8	CHAPTER 40	Rubber and related articles	0.73	1194.44	19479.36	6.13	1998-99	19103.22	1998-99	1027.71	0.93	1998-99	140.19	1998-99	49.75
9	CHAPTER 48	Paper and paper boards, articles related to paper	0.33	540.63	7399.42	0.00	1998-99	1728.31	1998-99	199.76	0.91	1998-99	62.31	1998-99	20.08
		Total	**5.68**	**9292.84**	**136226.13**										
		Grand Total	**91.06**	**149083.85**	**3318220.98**										

NOTES

1 Base year have been changed, where CAGR for a particular product shows growth of more than 999%.
2 Base year for Trend Calculation have been changed in some cases, keeping in view the base year for CAGR and the actual trade data.
3 Base year for Trend Calculation have been changed in some cases, where trend exceeds 99999%.
4 Correlation among different DATA SERIES have been calculated by using the CORREL function active in the MS EXCEL spreadsheet
5 Correlation of +1 denotes perfect positive correlation, -1 denotes perfect negative correlation. 0 denotes least correlation among the data series.
6 Trend is taken as 100% and CAGR as 0% in cases where either the data figures prior to 2004-05 are either zero or negligible.

TABLE- 6

Movement of Sum Factors of all sampled products and sampled products grouped under different categories imported from SRILANKA

(Value: in Rs. Lakhs)

Movement of Sum Factors of All 111 sampled products imported from SRILANKA

	1998-99	1999-00	2000-01	2001-02	2002-03	2003-04	2004-05
Sum of Value of imports from Srilanka (A)	8026.85	9621.56	10391.64	18208.27	25560.63	41846.64	149083.85
Sum of Value of impoorts from World (B)	470811.07	653866.82	799979.03	1059558.46	1386315.29	2185467.50	3318220.98
Sum Factor (A/B)	0.02	0.01	0.01	0.02	0.02	0.02	0.04

Movement of 18 sampled products covered under "ZERO DUTY" category

	1998-99	1999-00	2000-01	2001-02	2002-03	2003-04	2004-05
Sum of Value of imports from Srilanka (A)	1087.17	1446.24	1392.20	1743.40	1888.62	6073.42	19440.83
Sum of Value of impoorts from World (B)	185128.84	244043.29	301097.33	280717.10	274611.61	450088.49	573274.42
Sum Factor (A/B)	0.0059	0.0059	0.0046	0.0062	0.0069	0.0135	0.0339

Movement of 75 sampled products covered under "PHASED RESIDUAL LIST: IR" category

	1998-99	1999-00	2000-01	2001-02	2002-03	2003-04	2004-05
Sum of Value of imports from Srilanka (A)	6454.35	7219.02	7997.00	15592.25	21756.93	30296.69	119589.92
Sum of Value of impoorts from World (B)	275347.20	400107.92	487995.53	762834.95	1089600.15	1635084.98	2577245.64
Sum Factor (A/B)	0.0234	0.0180	0.0164	0.0204	0.0200	0.0185	0.0464

Movement of 4 sampled products covered under "PREFERENTIAL DUTY-TEXTILES" category

	1998-99	1999-00	2000-01	2001-02	2002-03	2003-04	2004-05
Sum of Value of imports from Srilanka (A)	42.40	1.42	35.63	113.47	59.90	477.05	760.26
Sum of Value of impoorts from World (B)	2273.78	484.06	397.50	953.93	2715.89	17604.67	31474.79
Sum Factor (A/B)	0.0186	0.0029	0.0896	0.1190	0.0221	0.0271	0.0242

Movement of 14 sampled products covered under "NEGATIVE LIST" category

	1998-99	1999-00	2000-01	2001-02	2002-03	2003-04	2004-05
Sum of Value of imports from Srilanka (A)	442.93	954.88	966.81	759.15	1855.18	4999.48	9292.84
Sum of Value of impoorts from World (B)	8061.25	9231.55	10488.67	15052.48	19387.64	82689.36	136226.13
Sum Factor (A/B)	0.0549	0.1034	0.0922	0.0504	0.0957	0.0605	0.0682

Summary of Sum Factors for Different Categories- Sample Products only

	1998-99	1999-00	2000-01	2001-02	2002-03	2003-04	2004-05
ALL SAMPLED PRODUCTS	0.0170	0.0147	0.0130	0.0172	0.0184	0.0191	0.0449
ZERO DUTY	0.0059	0.0059	0.0046	0.0062	0.0069	0.0135	0.0339
PHASED RESIDUAL LIST: IR	0.0234	0.0180	0.0164	0.0204	0.0200	0.0185	0.0464
PREFERENTIAL DUTY-TEXTILES	0.0186	0.0029	0.0896	0.1190	0.0221	0.0271	0.0242
NEGATIVE LIST	0.0549	0.1034	0.0922	0.0504	0.0957	0.0605	0.0682

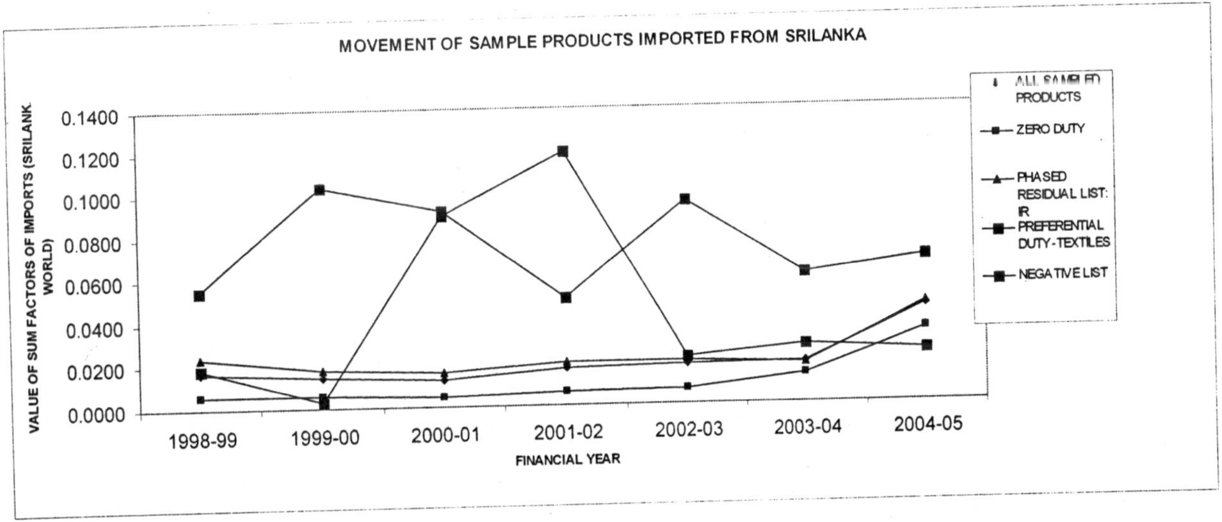

TABLE- 7

MOVEMENT OF SAMPLED PRODUCTS (IMPORTED FROM SRILANKA) COVERED UNDER DIFFERENT CATEGORY- CHAPTERWISE

(Important Chapters selected on the basis of highest CAGR and Value of Imports in 2004-05 basis)

(Value: in Rs. Lakhs)

VALUE WISE TOP 10% OUT OF TOTAL 37 CHAPTERS

CHAPTER NO.	CATEGORY
74	Phased Residual List: IR
85	Phased Residual List: IR
9	Phased Residual List: IR
84	Zero Duty

CAGR WISE TOP 10% OUT OF TOTAL 37 CHAPTERS

CHAPTER NO.	CATEGORY
74	Phased Residual List: IR
28	Zero Duty
85	Phased Residual List: IR
73	Phased Residual List: IR

SUM FACTORS (VALUE OF IMPORTS FROM SRILANKA / INDIA'S WORLD IMPORT) FOR SELECTED CHAPTERS

CHAPTER 74 (Phased Residuai List: IR)

	1998-99	1999-00	2000-01	2001-02	2002-03	2003-04	2004-05
Sum of Value of imports from Srilanka (A)	0.23	0.00	2.50	1189.11	6016.32	7790.57	51663.33
Sum of Value of imports from World (B)	14764.93	17987.30	8877.73	14447.84	12631.69	18804.69	65038.42
Sum Factor (A/B)	0.00002	0.00000	0.00028	0.08230	0.47629	0.41429	0.79435

CHAPTER 85 (Phased Residual List: IR)

	1998-99	1999-00	2000-01	2001-02	2002-03	2003-04	2004-05
Sum of Value of imports from Srilanka (A)	0.22	0.00	9.56	0.81	0.00	4951.60	12582.43
Sum of Value of impoorts from World (B)	14633.83	13676.59	14041.15	19735.53	28982.09	63770.82	115523.14
Sum Factor (A/B)	0.00002	0.00000	0.00068	0.00004	0.00000	0.07765	0.10892

CHAPTER 9 (Phased Residual List: IR)

	1998-99	1999-00	2000-01	2001-02	2002-03	2003-04	2004-05
Sum of Value of imports from Srilanka (A)	4139.92	3942.18	3881.14	11471.89	11723.52	5710.86	12051.78
Sum of Value of impoorts from World (B)	12921.42	7390.67	6850.66	21481.49	23495.97	23065.61	21953.10
Sum Factor (A/B)	0.32039	0.53340	0.56654	0.53404	0.49896	0.24759	0.54898

CHAPTER 84 (Zero Duty)

	1998-99	1999-00	2000-01	2001-02	2002-03	2003-04	2004-05
Sum of Value of imports from Srilanka (A)	79.68	0.38	313.44	352.84	985.50	2142.32	10795.24
Sum of Value of impoorts from World (B)	139006.15	192787.00	242016.75	209588.03	187893.65	339506.67	451855.41
Sum Factor (A/B)	0.00057	0.00000	0.00130	0.00168	0.00524	0.00631	0.02389

CHAPTER 28 (Zero Duty)

	1998-99	1999-00	2000-01	2001-02	2002-03	2003-04	2004-05
Sum of Value of imports from Srilanka (A)	0.00	0.00	0.00	0.00	32.55	1181.90	1746.29
Sum of Value of impoorts from World (B)	478.83	553.65	1299.28	1358.87	2082.80	4242.02	6762.36
Sum Factor (A/B)	0.00000	0.00000	0.00000	0.00000	0.01563	0.27862	0.25824

CHAPTER 73 (Phased Residual List: IR)

	1998-99	1999-00	2000-01	2001-02	2002-03	2003-04	2004-05
Sum of Value of imports from Srilanka (A)	0.01	3.59	7.00	31.06	64.61	188.37	346.75
Sum of Value of impoorts from World (B)	1355.51	1549.01	2057.32	2985.69	2926.48	6343.83	8621.63
Sum Factor (A/B)	0.00001	0.00232	0.00340	0.01040	0.02208	0.02969	0.04022

SUM FACTORS

SL.NO.	CATEGORY OF PRODUCTS	1998-99	1999-00	2000-01	2001-02	2002-03	2003-04	2004-05
1	CHAPTER 74(PRL)	0.00002	0.00000	0.00028	0.08230	0.47629	0.41429	0.79435
2	CHAPTER 85 (PRL)	0.00002	0.00000	0.00068	0.00004	0.00000	0.07765	0.10892
3	CHAPTER 9(PRL)	0.32039	0.53340	0.56654	0.53404	0.49896	0.24759	0.54898
4	CHAPTER 84(Zero Duty)	0.00057	0.00000	0.00130	0.00168	0.00524	0.00631	0.02389
5	CHAPTER 28(Zero Duty)	0.00000	0.00000	0.00000	0.00000	0.01563	0.27862	0.25824
6	CHAPTER 73(PRL)	0.00001	0.00232	0.00340	0.01040	0.02208	0.02969	0.04022

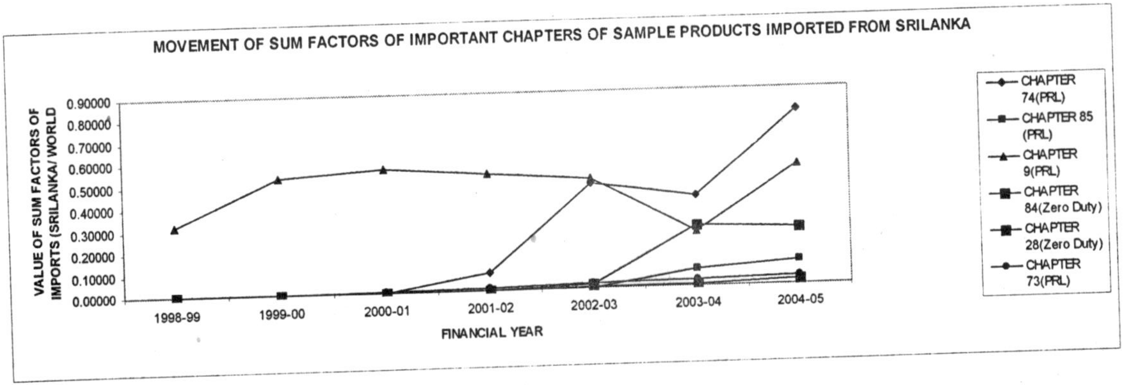

TABLE- 8

MOVEMENT OF MARKET SHARE AND UNIT PRICE OF IMPORTS OF SELECTED 7 SAMPLED PRODUCTS
(High CAGR & Value of Imports from Srilanka in 2004-05 basis)

1 28241010 LITHARGE (28241001)

ZERO DUTY

	1998-99	1999-00	2000-01	2001-02	2002-03	2003-04	2004-05
Market Share (Quantity)	0.00%	0.00%	0.00%	0.00%	1.43%	23.81%	26.32%
Market Share (Value)	0.00%	0.00%	0.00%	0.00%	1.56%	27.86%	25.82%
	1998-99	**1999-00**	**2000-01**	**2001-02**	**2002-03**	**2003-04**	**2004-05**
Price per unit (Imports from Srilanka only)	#DIV/0!	#DIV/0!	#DIV/0!	#DIV/0!	31.00	39.87	49.44
Price per unit (World Import for India)	32.33	28.55	28.11	30.92	28.27	34.07	50.39

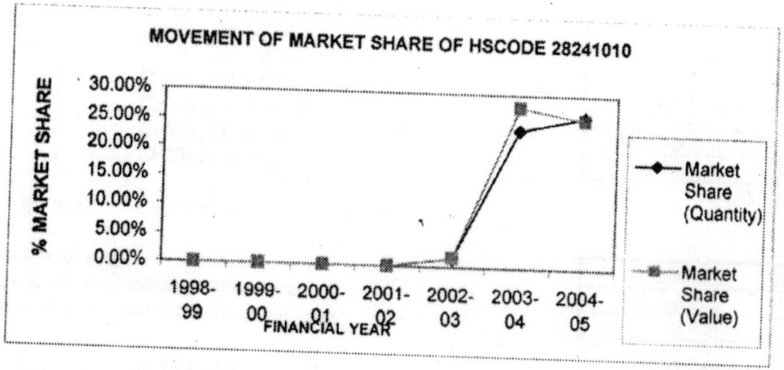

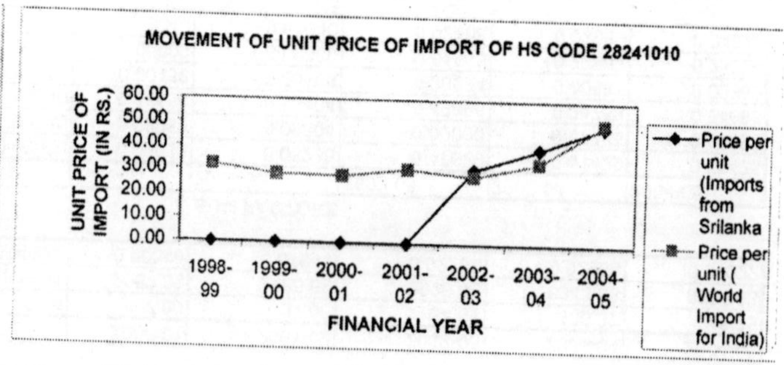

2 15162091 OTHR VEG FATS & OILS & THR FRCTNS OF EDBLEGRADE (15162009 PHASED RESIDUAL LIST: IR

	1998-99	1999-00	2000-01	2001-02	2002-03	2003-04	2004-05
Market Share (Quantity)	0.00%	0.00%	0.00%	0.00%	0.00%	0.00%	61.24%
Market Share (Value)	0.00%	0.00%	0.00%	0.00%	0.00%	0.00%	67.13%
	1998-99	**1999-00**	**2000-01**	**2001-02**	**2002-03**	**2003-04**	**2004-05**
Price per unit (Imports from Srilanka only)	#DIV/0!	#DIV/0!	#DIV/0!	61.00	#DIV/0!	#DIV/0!	39.94
Price per unit (World Import for India)	43.71	30.17	31.25	25.13	33.14	35.96	36.43

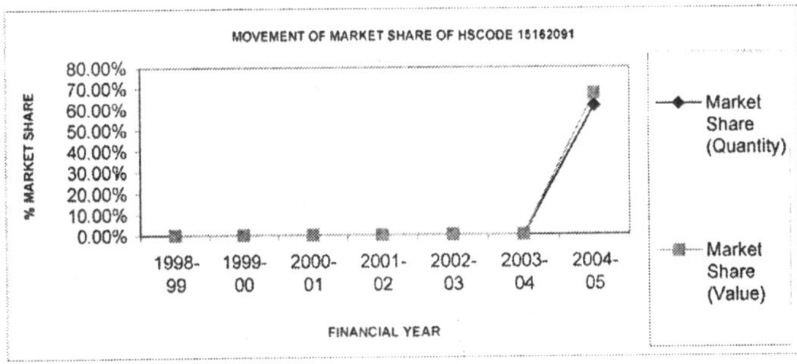

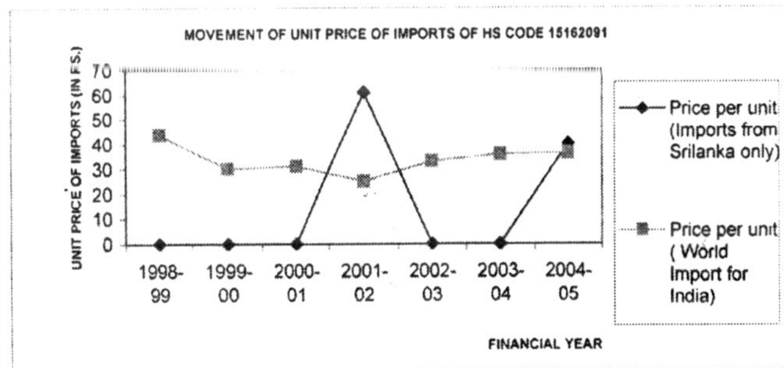

3 74031900 OTHER REFINED COPPER,UNWROUGHT — PHASED RESIDUAL LIST: IR

	1998-99	1999-00	2000-01	2001-02	2002-03	2003-04	2004-05
Market Share (Quantity)	0.00%	0.00%	0.00%	51.39%	89.13%	57.96%	98.16%
Market Share (Value)	0.00%	0.00%	0.00%	43.93%	88.54%	59.60%	98.20%
	1998-99	1999-00	2000-01	2001-02	2002-03	2003-04	2004-05
Price per unit (Imports from Srilanka only)	#DIV/0!	#DIV/0!	#DIV/0!	71.30	66.18	82.98	148.63
Price per unit (World Import for India)	63.75	60.03	107.44	83.42	66.62	80.70	148.56

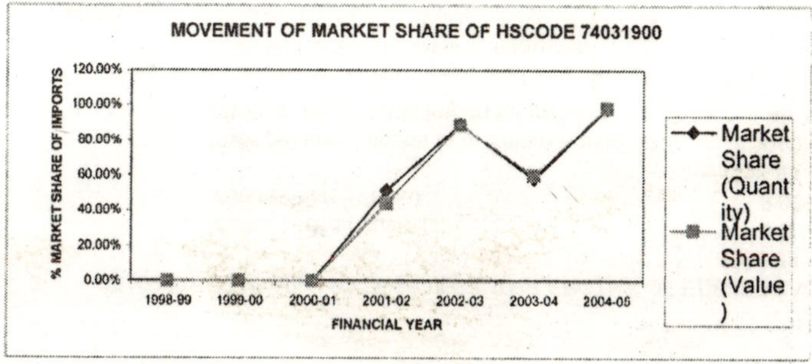

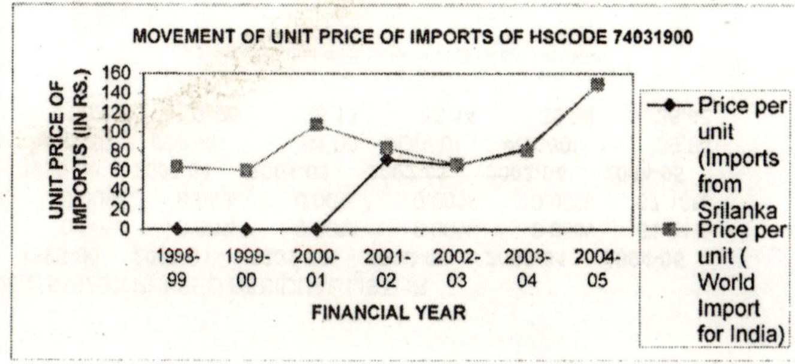

4 9070020 CLOVE, NOT EXTRACTED (OTHER THAN STEM) (9070002) PHASED RESIDUAL LIST: IR

	1998-99	1999-00	2000-01	2001-02	2002-03	2003-04	2004-05
Market Share (Quantity)	4.63%	77.71%	24.54%	55.22%	26.89%	10.37%	60.32%
Market Share (Value)	6.35%	85.94%	28.41%	61.49%	43.70%	18.61%	75.35%
	1998-99	1999-00	2000-01	2001-02	2002-03	2003-04	2004-05
Price per unit (Imports from Srilanka only)	50.67	79.50	143.30	393.68	306.90	163.16	268.35
Price per unit (World Import for India)	36.98	71.89	123.82	353.49	188.86	90.95	214.80

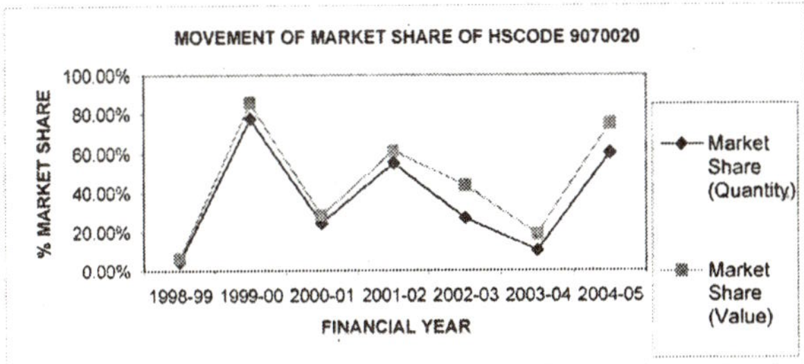

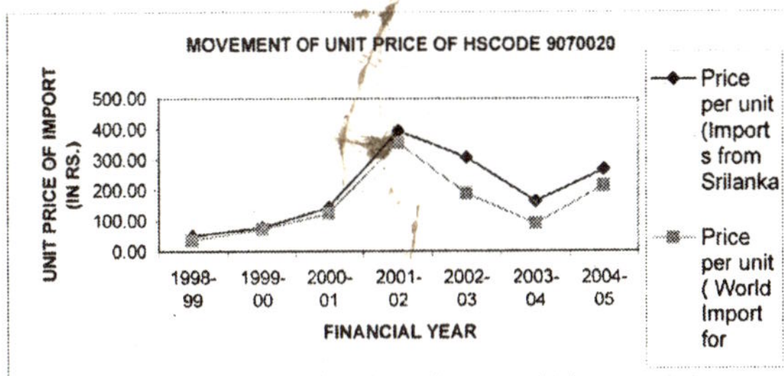

5 74031200 WIRE BARS OF REFINED COPPER PHASED RESIDUAL LIST: IR

	1998-99	1999-00	2000-01	2001-02	2002-03	2003-04	2004-05
Market Share (Quantity)	0.00%	0.00%	0.00%	0.00%	22.11%	66.34%	93.22%
Market Share (Value)	0.00%	0.00%	0.00%	0.00%	16.21%	61.88%	93.51%
	1998-99	1999-00	2000-01	2001-02	2002-03	2003-04	2004-05
Price per unit (Imports from Srilanka only)	#DIV/0!	#DIV/0!	#DIV/0!	#DIV/0!	64.97	86.37	153.89
Price per unit (World Import for India)	74.51	67.49	100.53	80.47	88.58	92.60	153.41

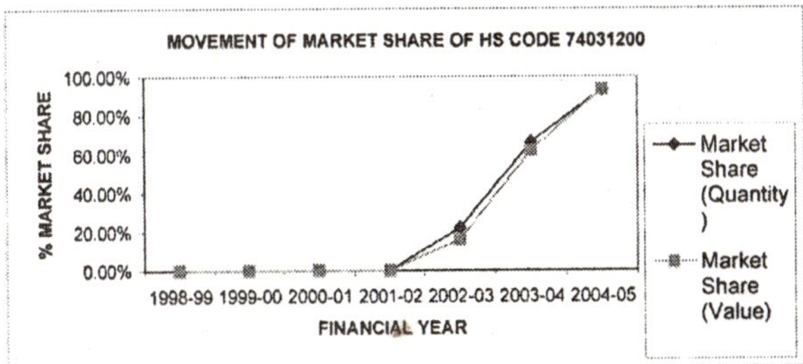

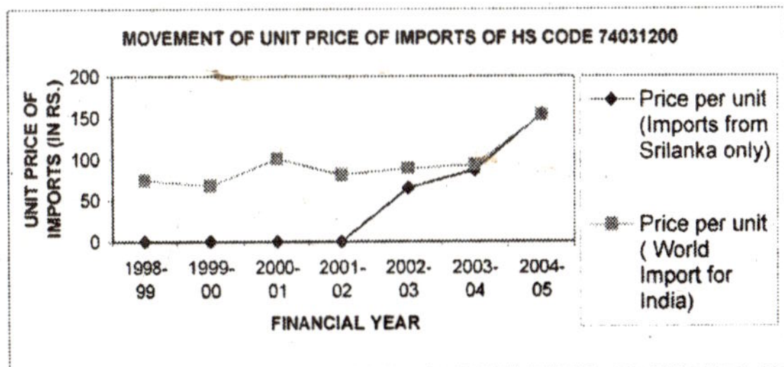

6 52082990 OTHERS

PREFERENTIAL DUTY-TEXTILES

	1998-99	1999-00	2000-01	2001-02	2002-03	2003-04	2004-05
Market Share (Quantity)	#DIV/0!	#DIV/0!	#DIV/0!	#DIV/0!	#DIV/0!	0.34%	1.49%
Market Share (Value)	#DIV/0!	#DIV/0!	#DIV/0!	#DIV/0!	#DIV/0!	0.35%	1.45%
	1998-99	**1999-00**	**2000-01**	**2001-02**	**2002-03**	**2003-04**	**2004-05**
Price per unit (Imports from Srilanka only)	#DIV/0!	#DIV/0!	#DIV/0!	#DIV/0!	#DIV/0!	117.27	96.17
Price per unit (World Import for India)	#DIV/0!	#DIV/0!	#DIV/0!	#DIV/0!	#DIV/0!	113.27	99.19

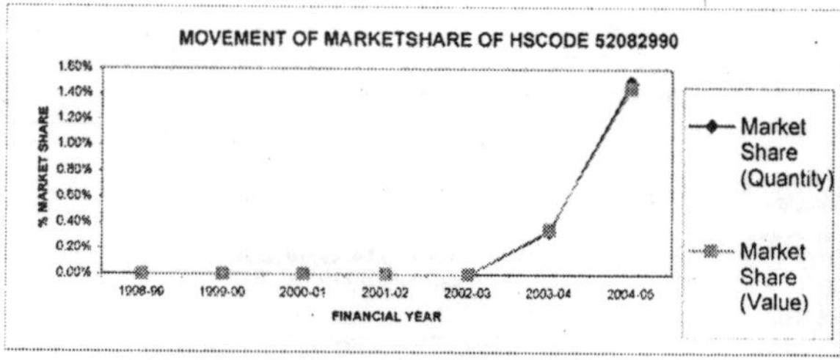

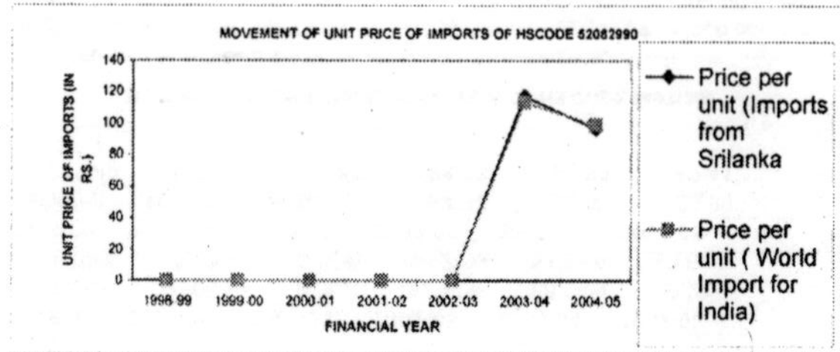

7 8011100 COCONUT DESICCATED

NEGATIVE LIST

	1998-99	1999-00	2000-01	2001-02	2002-03	2003-04	2004-05
Market Share (Quantity)	#DIV/0!	100.00%	100.00%	0.00%	0.00%	98.74%	99.85%
Market Share (Value)	#DIV/0!	100.00%	100.00%	0.00%	0.00%	99.19%	99.95%
	1998-99	**1999-00**	**2000-01**	**2001-02**	**2002-03**	**2003-04**	**2004-05**
Price per unit (Imports from Srilanka only)	#DIV/0!	47.14	34.45	#DIV/0!	#DIV/0!	27.25	34.09
Price per unit (World Import for India)	#DIV/0!	47.14	34.45	8.46	17.71	27.13	34.06

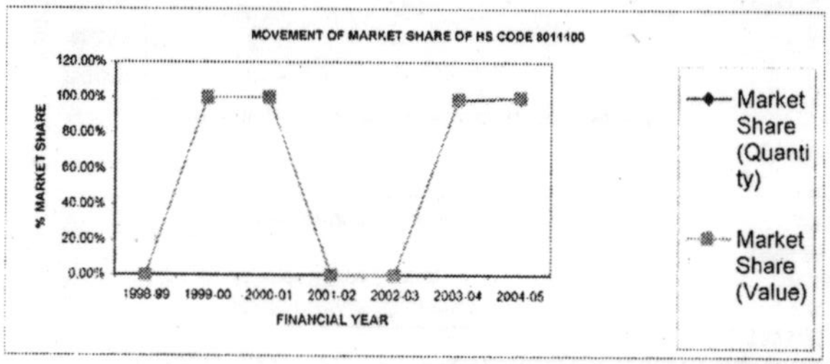

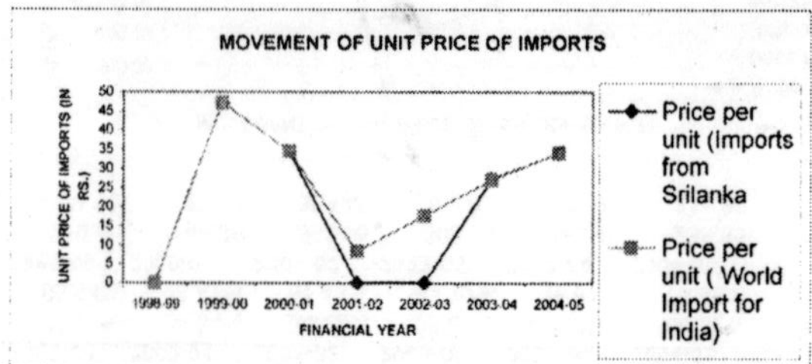

TABLE- 9

DETAILS OF SAMPLING (EXPORT PRODUCTS TO SRILANKA)

(Value: in Rs. Lakhs)

Particulars							2004-05	
Total No. of Products exported during the year to SRILANKA							5203	
Total No. of Producs sampled							130	2.50%
Total No. of Sampled Products covered under F I : ZERO DUTY							1	0.02%
Total No. of Sampled Products covered under F II							12	0.23%
Total No. of Sampled Products covered under SLR							57	1.10%
Total No. of Sampled Products covered under D (ii)							48	0.92%
Total No. of Sampled Products NOTcovered under any category (MFN DUTY)							12	0.23%
Total Value of Exports during the year to SRILANKA							608923.17	
	1998-99	**1999-00**	**2000-01**	**2001-02**	**2002-03**	**2003-04**	**2004-05**	
ALL INDIA FIGURES								
Total Value of Exports during the year of Sampled Products	3091827.93	3776835.99	4200941.95	4341801.12	5711421.37	9641127.68	12364459.51	
Total Value of Exports of Sampled Products covered under F I : ZERO DUTY	0.00	0.00	0.00	0.00	0.00	377219.59	466480.16	
Total Value of Exports of Sampled Products covered under F II	9671.14	11840.13	17388.84	21552.15	68388.78	222029.46	287118.96	
Total Value of Exports of Sampled Products covered under SLR	2437606.99	3386101.87	3684794.89	3683041.35	4671161.01	6344532.35	7150846.86	
Total Value of Exports of Sampled Products covered under D (ii)	644549.80	378893.99	498758.22	637207.62	971871.58	1361252.49	2023962.12	
Total Value of Exports of Sample Products NOTcovered under any category (MFN DUTY)	0.00	0.00	0.00	0.00	0.00	1336093.79	2436051.41	
ONLY SRILANKA FIGURES								
Total Value of Exports during the year of Sampled Products	34631.27	52825.48	60632.45	65283.72	74492.71	339593.2	418790.58	68.78%
Total Value of Exports of Sampled Products covered under F I : ZERO DUTY	0.00	0.00	0.00	0.00	0.00	551.40	1189.80	0.20%
Total Value of Exports of Sampled Products covered under F II	1687.71	2736.59	1395.40	1550.44	5295.17	25674.36	24979.97	4.10%
Total Value of Exports of Sampled Products covered under SLR	15503.85	19008.22	28559.44	26862.15	33238.89	89890.79	109948.16	18.06%
Total Value of Exports of Sampled Products covered under D (ii)	[illegible]	[illegible]	30677.61	36871.13	35958.65	110305.23	140494.11	23.07%
Total Value of Exports of Sample Products NOTcovered under any category (MFN DUTY)	0.00	0.00	0.00	0.00	0.00	113171.42	142178.54	[illegible]

	EXPORTS TO SRILANKA (A)	INDIA'S WORLD EXPORTS (B)	RELATIVE FASTNESS (A/B)
Weighted Average CAGR of all the sampled products	59.39%	44.92%	1.32
Weighted Average CAGR of all the sampled products (covered under F I : ZERO DUTY)	115.78%	23.66%	4.89
Weighted Average CAGR of all the sampled products (covered under F II)	91.66%	109.01%	0.84
Weighted Average CAGR of all the sampled products (covered under SLR)	75.67%	21.46%	3.53
Weighted Average CAGR of all the sampled products (covered under D (ii))	80.36%	42.38%	1.90
Weighted Average CAGR of all the sampled products NOTcovered under any category (MFN DUTY)	19.93%	112.43%	0.18
Weighted Average CAGR of all the sampled products (covered under F I : ZERO DUTY)- CHAPTER WISE	115.78%	23.66%	4.89
Weighted Average CAGR of all the sampled products (covered under F II)- CHAPTER WISE	80.92%	95.41%	0.85
Weighted Average CAGR of all the sampled products (covered under SLR)- CHAPTER WISE	81.85%	34.63%	2.36
Weighted Average CAGR of all the sampled products (covered under D (ii))- CHAPTER WISE	68.15%	44.54%	1.53
Weighted Average CAGR of all the sampled products NOTcovered under any category (MFN DUTY)- CHAPTER WISE	25.78%	82.34%	0.31

TABLE- 10

KEY FACTORS FOR TOP 25 HIGH VALUE EXPORTED ITEMS (based on 2004-05 value of exports) TO SRILANKA

No.	HS Code	List of Concession	2004-05 % of Total Value of exports to Srilanka in 2004-05	Base year for next two columns	2004-05 Incremental Trend of exports to Srilanka (Volume) in % in comparison to base yr.	2004-05 Incremental Trend of exports to Srilanka(Value) in % in comparison to base yr.	Base year for next two columns	2004-05 Incremental Trend of World Export (Volume) in % in comparison to base yr.	2004-05 Incremental Trend of World Export (Value) in % in comparison to base yr.	2004-05 Market Share of exports to Srilanka in World Exports (Volume) in %	2004-05 Market Share of exports to Srilanka in World Exports (Value) in %	2004-05 Per Unit Export Price to Srilanka (in Rs.)	2004-05 Per Unit World Export Price for India (in Rs.)	Base year for next two columns	SRILANKA CAGR - VOLUME (in %)	SRILANKA CAGR-VALUE (in %)	Base year for next two columns	World CAGR-VOLUME (in %)	World CAGR-VALUE (in %)	SRILANKA CORRELATION - TREND OF VOLUME / VALUE	World CORRELATION - TREND OF VOLUME / VALUE	SRILANKA & World CORRELATION - TREND OF VOLUME	SRILANKA & World CORRELATION - TREND OF VALUE	SRILANKA & World CORRELATION - UNIT PRICE
1	27101930	NIL (OTHER ITEMS AT MFN RATE)	16.71	2003-04	-8.62	30.03	2003-04	30.03	83.99	8.31	8.46	16397.65	16102.56	2003-04	-8.62	30.03	2003-04	30.03	83.99	0.98	0.98	0.98	0.98	#DIV/0!
2	10063010	D (ii) : NEGATIVE LIST	3.44	1998-99	1813.46	2309.06	1998-99	19.15	30.24	7.62	8.05	11.49	10.88	1998-99	63.54	69.94	1998-99	2.96	4.50	1.00	0.97	0.56	0.71	0.14
3	87112029	SLR: ZERO DUTY IN 8 YEARS	3.27	2003-04	88.85	72.19	2003-04	49.47	37.71	34.54	33.87	26620.40	27143.93	2003-04	88.85	72.19	2003-04	49.47	37.71	1.00	1.00	0.99	0.99	#DIV/0!
4	87032120	D (ii) : NEGATIVE LIST	1.98	2003-04	89.59	65.95	2003-04	12.08	4.38	60.66	59.25	52175.83	53417.86	2003-04	89.59	65.95	2003-04	12.08	4.38	1.00	1.00	0.96	0.97	#DIV/0!
5	27101920	NIL (OTHER ITEMS AT MFN RATE)	1.96	2003-04	-20.37	-1.98	2003-04	67.84	144.45	3.42	2.84	16132.84	19432.14	2003-04	-20.37	-1.98	2003-04	67.84	144.45	0.99	0.99	0.91	0.89	#DIV/0!
6	30049099	SLR: ZERO DUTY IN 8 YEARS	1.38	1998-99	871.78	651.48	1998-99	1030.88	703.29	3.21	2.97	437.37	472.90	1998-99	46.08	39.95	1998-99	49.82	41.52	0.74	0.98	0.74	0.99	0.39
7	87021019	D (ii) : NEGATIVE LIST	1.20	2003-04	200.00	226.86	2003-04	-81.49	136.59	41.15	37.64	782930.11	855974.34	2003-04	200.00	226.86	2003-04	-81.49	136.59	1.00	0.43	0.35	0.99	#DIV/0!
8	74081190	F II : 50% IMMEDIATE AND UPTO 100% IN 3 YRS by 06 03 03	1.08	1998-99	71253.33	48541.73	1998-99	12084.51	9327.64	9.89	10.05	145.97	143.56	1998-99	198.93	180.44	1998-99	122.66	113.34	0.99	0.98	0.99	1.00	0.28
9	28030010	F II : 50% IMMEDIATE AND UPTO 100% IN 3 YRS by 06.03.03	1.02	2003-04	65.68	66.90	2003-04	146.03	148.53	23.29	23.87	21.85	21.32	2003-04	65.68	66.90	2003-04	146.03	148.53	1.00	1.00	0.98	0.98	#DIV/0!
10	7134000	D (ii) : NEGATIVE LIST	1.00	1998-99	-23.96	-24.14	1998-99	103.56	110.71	21.49	20.40	20.64	21.74	1998-99	-4.46	-4.50	1998-99	12.58	13.23	1.00	1.00	0.67	0.66	0.05
11	39021000	SLR: ZERO DUTY IN 8 YEARS	0.99	1998-99	1249.07	1762.18	1998-99	6024.22	7558.51	3.08	3.11	43.70	43.29	1998-99	54.29	82.81	1998-99	98.54	106.07	0.96	0.93	0.85	0.94	0.93
12	27101910	NIL (OTHER ITEMS AT MFN RATE)	0.97	2004-05	0.00	0.00	2003-04	16.93	37.37	7.92	10.45	20045.27	15188.44	2004-05	0.00	0.00	2003-04	16.93	37.37	1.00	1.00	0.71	0.77	#DIV/0!
13	7031010	D (ii) : NEGATIVE LIST	0.96	1998-99	165.42	115.89	1998-99	303.45	265.88	10.56	9.08	6.36	7.40	1998-99	17.67	13.69	1998-99	26.17	24.13	0.92	0.98	0.76	0.77	0.94
14	25231000	SLR: ZERO DUTY IN 8 YEARS	0.94	1999-00	2632.57	3603.99	1998-99	958.89	1420.72	10.71	10.32	1.27	1.32	1999-00	93.78	105.94	1998-99	48.19	57.40	0.98	0.98	0.92	0.92	#DIV/0!
15	87029099	D (ii) : NEGATIVE LIST	0.91	2003-04	215.00	217.73	2003-04	23.53	53.64	75.00	77.35	879042.86	852303.57	2003-04	215.00	217.73	2003-04	23.53	53.64	1.00	0.99	0.91	0.95	#DIV/0!
16	27101111	NIL (OTHER ITEMS AT MFN RATE)	0.90	2003-04	-61.89	-51.94	2003-04	-37.49	-11.52	1.97	1.94	17970.95	18331.49	2003-04	-61.89	-51.94	2003-04	-37.49	-11.52	1.00	0.98	0.98	0.95	#DIV/0!
17	9042010	D (ii) : NEGATIVE LIST	0.87	1998-99	517.76	334.03	1998-99	236.98	209.65	20.83	18.10	26.78	30.83	1998-99	35.46	27.72	1998-99	22.44	20.73	0.94	0.97	0.58	0.51	0.68
18	27101119	NIL (OTHER ITEMS AT MFN RATE)	0.82	2003-04	8427.66	3553.03	2003-04	340.21	335.76	3.13	2.52	12401.90	15375.32	2004-05	0.00	0.00	2003-04	340.21	335.76	1.00	1.00	0.98	0.98	#DIV/0!
19	87029011	D (ii) : NEGATIVE LIST	0.81	2004-05	0.00	0.00	2003-04	232.26	179.71	54.37	49.52	885092.86	971748.54	2004-05	0.00	0.00	2003-04	232.26	179.71	1.00	1.00	0.95	0.94	#DIV/0!
20	23040010	SLR: ZERO DUTY IN 8 YEARS	0.79	1999-00	16725.12	22654.34	1998-99	11661.03	16249.37	7.42	8.54	11.29	9.81	1999-00	178.74	196.08	1998-99	121.35	133.84	1.00	1.00	0.99	0.99	#DIV/0!
21	10059000	D (ii) : NEGATIVE LIST	0.70	1998-99	37216.98	52934.66	1998-99	43369.12	34300.56	9.41	9.30	6.32	6.39	1998-99	168.32	184.51	1998-99	175.23	164.70	1.00	1.00	0.92	0.94	#DIV/0!
22	87042190	D (ii) : NEGATIVE LIST	0.69	1998-99	13700.00	18911.62	1998-99	158.58	158.62	14.54	12.83	302257.25	342506.95	1998-99	127.32	139.79	1998-99	17.16	17.16	1.00	0.36	-0.12	0.75	#DIV/0!
23	52071000	SLR: ZERO DUTY IN 8 YEARS	0.68	1998-99	55.46	89.67	1998-99	97.66	106.31	3.61	3.10	112.56	131.29	1998-99	7.63	11.26	1998-99	12.03	12.83	0.95	0.99	0.89	0.96	0.57
24	87089900	D (ii) : NEGATIVE LIST	0.67	1998-99	68.98	111.22	1998-99	362.38	352.95	2.27	1.89	129.40	155.46	1998-99	9.14	13.27	1998-99	29.07	28.63	0.95	1.00	0.79	0.86	0.40
25	23040030	SLR: ZERO DUTY IN 8 YEARS	0.87	2003-04	-28.45	-23.69	2003-04	-15.89	-18.28	2.34	2.64	12.09	10.71	2003-04	-28.45	-23.69	2003-04	-15.89	-18.28	1.00	1.00	1.00	1.00	#DIV/0!

NOTES

1 Base year have been changed, where CAGR for a particular product shows growth of more than 999%.
2 Base year for Trend Calculation have been changed in some cases, keeping in view the base year for CAGR and the actual trade data.
3 Base year for Trend Calculation have been changed in some cases, where trend exceeds 99999%.
4 Correlation among different DATA SERIES have been calculated by using the CORREL function active in the MS EXCEL spreadsheet.
5 Correlation of +1 denotes perfect positive correlation, -1 denotes perfect negative correlation, 0 denotes least correlation among the data series.
6 Trend is taken as 100% and CAGR as 0% in cases where either the data figures prior to 2004-05 are either zero or negligible

TABLE-11

KEY FACTORS FOR TOP 20% OF SAMPLED PRODUCTS COVERED UNDER EACH CATEGORY (SORTED ON THE BASIS OF VALUE OF EXPORTS IN 2004-05)

			2004-05		2004-05	2004-05		2004-05	2004-05
Sl. No.	HS Code	Particulars	% of Total Value of exports to Srilanka in 2004-05	Base year for next two columns	Incremental Trend of exports to Srilanka (Volume) in % in comparison to base yr.	Incremental Trend of exports to Srilanka(Value) in % in comparison to base yr.	Base year for next two columns	Incremental Trend of World Export (Volume) in % in comparison to base yr.	Incremental Trend of World Export (Value) in % in comparison to base yr.
		F I : ZERO DUTY IMMEDIATELY							
1	29420090	OTHER DILOXANIDE FUROATE. CIMETIDINE, FAMOTIDINE NES	0.20	2003-04	23.59	115.78	2003-04	22.17	23.66
		F II : 50% IMMEDIATE AND UPTO 100% IN 3 YRS by 05.03.03							
1	74081190	OTHR COPPR WIRE WTH MAX CRS-SEC DIAMTR>6MM (74081109)	1.08	1998-99	71253.33	48541.73	1998-99	12084.51	9327.64
2	28030010	CARBON BLACKS	1.02	2003-04	65.68	66.90	2003-04	146.03	148.53
3	72091590	OTHR FLT RLD PRDCTS IN COILS NT FRTHR WRKD THN COLD RLD OF THCKNS >=3MM (72091500)	0.48	1998-99	1290.16	2637.50	1998-99	179.86	481.57
		SLR: ZERO DUTY IN 8 YEARS							
1	87112029	MOTR CYCLWTH CYLNDR CPCTY >75 BT<=250 CC	3.27	2003-04	88.85	72.19	2003-04	49.47	37.71
2	30049099	OTHER MEDCNE PUT UP FOR RETAIL SALE N.E.S	1.38	1998-99	871.78	651.48	1998-99	1030.88	703.29
3	39021000	POLYPROPYLENE	0.99	1998-99	1249.07	1762.18	1998-99	6024.22	7558.51
4	25231000	CEMENT CLINKERS	0.94	1999-00	2632.57	3603.99	1998-99	958.89	1420.72
5	23040010	OIL-CAKE & OIL-CAKE MEAL OF SOYA BEAN EXPELLER VARIETY (23040001)	0.79	1999-00	16725.12	22654.34	1998-99	11661.03	16249.37
6	52071000	COTON YARN CONTNG COTON>=85% BY WT PUT UP FOR RETAIL SALE	0.68	1998-99	55.46	89.67	1998-99	97.66	106.31
7	23040030	MEAL OF SOYABEAN,SOLVENT EXTRACTED (DEFATTED) VARIETY	0.67	2003-04	-28.45	-23.69	2003-04	-15.89	-18.28
8	54071039	OTHR DYED POLYESTER FABRCS	0.52	1998-99	5485.43	1156.30	1998-99	2739.48	451.68
9	52091190	OTHERS	0.43	2003-04	197.05	178.41	2003-04	51.66	79.47
10	52081190	OTHERS	0.40	2003-04	13.32	27.42	2003-04	-4.66	-0.57
11	76011010	ALUMINIUM INGOTS-NOT ALLOYED (76011001)	0.32	1998-99	962.36	1414.07	1998-99	302.12	503.09
12	87112021	MOTOR CYCL WTH CYLNDR CPCTY >50 BT <= 75 C	0.29	2003-04	49.57	37.06	2003-04	64.67	67.09
		D (ii) : NEGATIVE LIST							
1	10063010	RICE PARBOILED (10063001)	3.44	1998-99	1813.46	2309.06	1998-99	19.15	30.24
2	87032120	THREE-WHEELED VEHICLES WTH CYLNDR CPCTY<=1000 WTH SPRK-IGNTN	1.98	2003-04	89.59	65.95	2003-04	12.08	4.38
3	87021019	OTHR VHCLS(<=13 PERSONS) WTH CMPRSN-IGNTNINTRNL CMBSTN PISTON ENGINE	1.20	2003-04	200.00	226.86	2003-04	-81.49	136.59
4	7134000	LENTILS (MOSUR),DRIED & SHLD	1.00	1998-99	-23.96	-24.14	1998-99	103.56	110.71
5	7031010	ONIONS FRESH OR CHILLED (7031001)	0.96	1998-99	165.42	115.89	1998-99	303.45	265.88
6	87029099	OTHER VHCLS PUB-TRNS TYPE(>13 PERSONS)	0.91	2003-04	215.00	217.73	2003-04	23.53	53.64
7	9042010	CHILLY (9042001)	0.87	1998-99	517.76	334.03	1998-99	236.98	209.65
8	87029011	OTHR INTGRTD MONOCOQUE VHCLS(<=13 PERSONS)	0.8[illegible]	2004-05	0.00	0.00	2003-04	232.26	179.71
9	10059000	OTHER MAIZE (CORN)	0.70	1998-99	37216.98	52934.66	1998-99	43369.12	34300.56
10	87042190	OTHER GOODS VHCLS,WTH CMPRSN IGNTN INTRNL CMBSTN PSTN ENGNWTH G.V.W. <= 5 TON (87042100)	0.69	1998-99	13700.00	18911.62	1998-99	158.58	158.62
		OTHER ITEMS AT MFN RATE							
1	27101930	HIGH SPEED DIESEL (HSD)	16.71	2003-04	-8.62	30.03	2003-04	30.03	83.99
2	27101920	AUIATION TURBINE FUEL (ATF)	1.96	2003-04	-20.37	-1.98	2003-04	67.84	144.45
3	27101910	SUPERIOR KEROSENE OIL (SKO)	0.97	2004-05	0.00	0.00	2003-04	16.93	37.37

NOTES

1 Base year have been changed, where CAGR for a particular product shows growth of more than 999%.
2 Base year for Trend Calculation have been changed in some cases, keeping in view the base year for CAGR and the actual trade data.
3 Base year for Trend Calculation have been changed in some cases, where trend exceeds 99999%.
4 Correlation among different DATA SERIES have been calculated by using the CORREL function active in the MS EXCEL spreadsheet.
5 Correlation of +1 denotes perfect positive correlation, -1 denotes perfect negative correlation, 0 denotes least correlation among the data
6 Trend is taken as 100% and CAGR as 0% in cases where either the data figures prior to 2004-05 are either zero or negligible.

TABLE-11

KEY FACTORS FOR TOP 20% OF SAMPLED PRODUCTS COVERED UNDER EACH CATEGORY (SORTED ON THE BASIS OF VALUE OF EXPORTS IN 2004-05)

			2004-05	2004-05	2004-05	2004-05		SRILANKA	SRILANKA	
Sl. No.	HS Code	Particulars	Market Share of exports to Srilanka in World Exports (Volume) in %	Market Share of exports to Srilanka in World Exports (Value) in %	Per Unit Export Price to Srilanka (in Rs.)	Per Unit World Export Price for India (in Rs.)	Base year for next two columns	CAGR - VOLUME (in %)	CAGR- VALUE (in %)	Base year for next two columns
		F I : ZERO DUTY IMMEDIATELY								
1	29420090	OTHER DILOXANIDE FUROATE, CIMETIDINE, FAMOTIDINE NES	0.87	0.26	554.50	1888.79	2003-04	23.59	115.78	2003-04
		F II : 50% IMMEDIATE AND UPTO 100								
1	74081190	OTHR COPPR WIRE WTH MAX CRS-SEC DIAMTR>6MM (74081109)	9.89	10.05	145.97	143.56	1998-99	198.93	180.44	1998-99
2	28030010	CARBON BLACKS	23.29	23.87	21.85	21.32	2003-04	65.68	66.90	2003-04
3	72091590	OTHR FLT RLD PRDCTS IN COILS NT FRTHR WRKD THN COLD RLD OF THCKNS >=3MM (72091500)	21.75	22.90	27.19	25.82	1998-99	55.06	73.60	1998-99
		SLR: ZERO DUTY IN 8 YEARS								
1	87112029	MOTR CYCLWTH CYLNDR CPCTY >75 BT<=250 CC	34.54	33.87	26620.40	27143.93	2003-04	88.85	72.19	2003-04
2	30049099	OTHER MEDCNE PUT UP FOR RETAIL SALE N.E.S	3.21	2.97	437.37	472.90	1998-99	46.08	39.95	1998-99
3	39021000	POLYPROPYLENE	3.08	3.11	43.70	43.29	1998-99	54.29	62.81	1998-99
4	25231000	CEMENT CLINKERS	10.71	10.32	1.27	1.32	1999-00	93.78	105.94	1998-99
5	23040010	OIL-CAKE & OIL-CAKE MEAL OF SOYA BEAN EXPELLER VARIETY (23040001)	7.42	8.54	11.29	9.81	1999-00	178.74	196.08	1998-99
6	52071000	COTON YARN CONTNG COTON>=85% BY WT PUT UP FOR RETAIL SALE	3.61	3.10	112.56	131.29	1998-99	7.63	11.26	1998-99
7	23040030	MEAL OF SOYABEAN,SOLVENT EXTRACTED (DEFATTED) VARIETY	2.34	2.64	12.09	10.71	2003-04	-28.45	-23.69	2003-04
8	54071039	OTHR DYED POLYESTER FABRCS	2.67	2.57	60.97	63.26	1998-99	95.51	52.47	1998-99
9	52091190	OTHERS	14.46	14.39	61.49	61.80	2003-04	197.05	178.41	2003-04
10	52081190	OTHERS	5.14	5.70	61.29	55.28	2003-04	13.32	27.42	2003-04
11	76011010	ALUMINIUM INGOTS-NOT ALLOYED (76011001)	2.30	2.27	81.68	82.60	1998-99	48.27	57.29	1998-99
12	87112021	MOTOR CYCL WTH CYLNDR CPCTY >50 BT <= 75 C	30.58	27.30	25325.25	28366.70	2003-04	122.86	37.06	2003-04
		D (ii) : NEGATIVE LIST								
1	10063010	RICE PARBOILED (10063001)	7.62	8.05	11.49	10.88	1998-99	63.54	69.94	1998-99
2	87032120	THREE-WHEELED VEHICLES WTH CYLNDR CPCTY<=1000 WTH SPRK-IGNTN	60.66	59.25	52175.83	53417.86	2003-04	89.59	65.95	2003-04
3	87021019	OTHR VHCLS(<=13 PERSONS) WTH CMPRSN-IGNTNINTRNL CMBSTN PISTON ENGINE	41.15	37.64	782930.11	855974.34	2003-04	200.00	226.86	2003-04
4	7134000	LENTILS (MOSUR),DRIED & SHLD	21.49	20.40	20.64	21.74	1998-99	-4.46	-4.50	1998-99
5	7031010	ONIONS FRESH OR CHILLED (7031001)	10.56	9.08	6.36	7.40	1998-99	17.67	13.69	1998-99
6	87029099	OTHER VHCLS PUB-TRNS TYPE(>13 PERSONS)	75.00	77.35	879042.86	852303.57	2003-04	215.00	217.73	2003-04
7	9042010	CHILLY (9042001)	20.83	18.10	26.78	30.83	1998-99	35.46	27.72	1998-99
8	87029011	OTHR INTGRTD MONOCOQUE VHCLS(<=13 PERSONS)	54.37	49.52	885092.86	971748.54	2004-05	0.00	0.00	2003-04
9	10059000	OTHER MAIZE (CORN)	9.41	9.30	6.32	6.39	1998-99	168.32	184.51	1998-99
10	87042190	OTHER GOODS VHCLS,WTH CMPRSN IGNTN INTRNL CMBSTN PSTN ENGNWTH G.V.W. <= 5 TON (87042100)	14.54	12.83	302257.25	342506.95	1998-99	127.32	139.79	1998-99
		OTHER ITEMS AT MFN RATE								
1	27101930	HIGH SPEED DIESEL (HSD)	8.31	8.46	16397.65	16102.56	2003-04	-8.62	30.03	2003-04
2	27101920	AUIATION TURBINE FUEL (ATF)	3.42	2.84	16132.84	19432.14	2003-04	-20.37	-1.98	2003-04
3	27101910	SUPERIOR KEROSENE OIL (SKO)	7.92	10.45	20045.27	15188.44	2004-05	0.00	0.00	2003-04

TABLE-11

KEY FACTORS FOR TOP 20% OF SAMPLED PRODUCTS COVERED UNDER EACH CATEGORY (SORTED ON THE BASIS OF VALUE OF EXPORTS IN 2004-05)

			World	World	SRILANKA	World	SRILANKA & World		
Sl. No.	HS Code	Particulars	CAGR-VOLUME (in %)	CAGR-VALUE (in %)	CORRELATION - TREND OF VOLUME / VALUE	CORRELATION - TREND OF VOLUME / VALUE	CORRELATION - TREND OF VOLUME	CORRELATION - TREND OF VALUE	CORRELATION - UNIT PRICE
		F I : ZERO DUTY IMMEDIATELY							
1	29420090	OTHER DILOXANIDE FUROATE, CIMETIDINE, FAMOTIDINE NES	22.17	23.66	0.96	1.00	1.00	0.96	#DIV/0!
		F II : 50% IMMEDIATE AND UPTO 100							
1	74081190	OTHR COPPR WIRE WTH MAX CRS-SEC DIAMTR>6MM (74081109)	122.66	113.34	0.99	0.98	0.99	1.00	0.28
2	28030010	CARBON BLACKS	146.03	148.53	1.00	1.00	0.98	0.98	#DIV/0!
3	72091590	OTHR FLT RLD PRDCTS IN COILS NT FRTHR WRKD THN COLD RLD OF THCKNS >=3MM (72091500)	18.71	34.10	0.93	0.92	0.60	0.69	0.88
		SLR: ZERO DUTY IN 8 YEARS							
1	87112029	MOTR CYCLWTH CYLNDR CPCTY >75 BT<=250 CC	49.47	37.71	1.00	1.00	0.99	0.99	#DIV/0!
2	30049099	OTHER MEDCNE PUT UP FOR RETAIL SALE N.E.S	49.82	41.52	0.74	0.98	0.74	0.99	0.39
3	39021000	POLYPROPYLENE	98.54	106.07	0.96	0.93	0.85	0.94	0.93
4	25231000	CEMENT CLINKERS	48.19	57.40	0.98	0.98	0.92	0.92	#DIV/0!
5	23040010	OIL-CAKE & OIL-CAKE MEAL OF SOYA BEAN EXPELLER VARIETY (23040001)	121.35	133.84	1.00	1.00	0.99	0.99	#DIV/0!
6	52071000	COTON YARN CONTNG COTON>=85% BY WT PUT UP FOR RETAIL SALE	12.08	12.83	0.95	0.99	0.89	0.96	0.57
7	23040030	MEAL OF SOYABEAN,SOLVENT EXTRACTED (DEFATTED) VARIETY	-15.89	-18.28	1.00	1.00	1.00	1.00	#DIV/0!
8	54071039	OTHR DYED POLYESTER FABRCS	74.67	32.93	0.80	0.76	1.00	0.97	0.99
9	52091190	OTHERS	51.66	79.47	1.00	1.00	0.96	0.98	#DIV/0!
10	52081190	OTHERS	-4.66	-0.57	1.00	1.00	0.99	0.99	#DIV/0!
11	76011010	ALUMINIUM INGOTS-NOT ALLOYED (76011001)	26.70	34.92	1.00	0.96	0.43	0.63	#DIV/0!
12	87112021	MOTOR CYCL WTH CYLNDR CPCTY >50 BT <= 75 C	64.57	67.09	1.00	1.00	1.00	0.99	#DIV/0!
		D (ii) : NEGATIVE LIST							
1	10063010	RICE PARBOILED (10063001)	2.36	4.50	1.00	0.97	0.56	0.71	0.14
2	87032120	THREE-WHEELED VEHICLES WTH CYLNDR CPCTY<=1000 WTH SPRK-IGNTN	12.08	4.38	1.00	1.00	0.96	0.97	#DIV/0!
3	87021019	OTHR VHCLS(<=13 PERSONS) WTH CMPRSN-IGNTNINTRNL CMBSTN PISTON ENGINE	-81.49	136.59	1.00	0.43	0.35	0.99	#DIV/0!
4	7134000	LENTILS (MOSUR),DRIED & SHLD	12.58	13.23	1.00	1.00	0.67	0.66	0.05
5	7031010	ONIONS FRESH OR CHILLED (7031001)	26.17	24.13	0.92	0.98	0.76	0.77	0.94
6	87029099	OTHER VHCLS PUB-TRNS TYPE(>13 PERSONS)	23.53	53.64	1.00	0.99	0.91	0.95	#DIV/0!
7	9042010	CHILLY (9042001)	22.44	20.73	0.94	0.97	0.58	0.51	0.68
8	87029011	OTHR INTGRTD MONOCOQUE VHCLS(<=13 PERSONS)	232.26	179.71	1.00	1.00	0.95	0.94	#DIV/0!
9	10059000	OTHER MAIZE (CORN)	175.23	164.70	1.00	1.00	0.92	0.94	#DIV/0!
10	87042190	OTHER GOODS VHCLS,WTH CMPRSN IGNTN INTRNL CMBSTN PSTN ENGNWTH G.V.W. <= 5 TON (87042100)	17.16	17.16	1.00	0.36	-0.12	0.75	#DIV/0!
		OTHER ITEMS AT MFN RATE							
1	27101930	HIGH SPEED DIESEL (HSD)	30.03	83.99	0.98	0.98	0.98	0.98	#DIV/0!
2	27101920	AUIATION TURBINE FUEL (ATF)	67.84	144.45	0.99	0.99	0.91	0.89	#DIV/0!
3	27101910	SUPERIOR KEROSENE OIL (SKO)	15.93	37.37	1.00	1.00	0.71	0.77	#DIV/0!

TABLE- 12

KEY FACTORS FOR TOP 10% OF SAMPLED PRODUCTS COVERED UNDER EACH CATEGORY (SORTED ON THE BASIS OF CAGR-VALUE OF EXPORTS TO SRILANKA)

			2004-05		2004-05	2004-05		2004-05	2004-05	2004-05	2004-05
Sl. No.	HS Code	Particulars	% of Total Value of exports to Srilanka in 2004-05	Base year for next two columns	Incremental Trend of exports to Srilanka (Volume) in % in comparison to base yr.	Incremental Trend of exports to Srilanka(Value) in % in comparison to base yr.	Base year for next two columns	Incremental Trend of World Export (Volume) in % in comparison to base yr	Incremental Trend of World Export (Value) in % in comparison to base yr.	Market Share of exports to Srilanka in World Exports (Volume) in %	Market Share of exports to Srilanka in World Exports (Value) in %
		F I : ZERO DUTY IMMEDIATELY									
1	29420090	OTHER DILOXANIDE FUROATE, CIMETIDINE, FAMOTIDINE NES	0.20	2003-04	23.59	115.78	2003-04	22.17	23.66	0.87	0.26
		F II : 50% IMMEDIATE AND UPTO 100% IN 3 YRS by 05.03.03									
1	74081190	OTHR COPPR WIRE WTH MAX CRS-SEC DIAMTR>6MM (74081109)	1.08	1998-99	71253.33	48541.73	1998-99	12084.51	9327.64	9.89	10.05
2	74081110	CU WLD WIRE WTH MAX CRS-SEC DIAMTR>6MM (74081101)	0.19	1998-99	15079.78	14849.24	1998-99	17211.11	26394.54	2.93	2.98
		SLR: ZERO DUTY IN 8 YEARS									
1	87113090	OTHR VHCL WTH CYLNDR CPCTY >250 BT<=500 CC	0.23	2003-04	697.22	716.90	2003-04	118.05	82.13	47.52	45.05
2	87019010	OTHER TRACTORS OF ENGN CAPACITY <= 1800CC	0.28	2003-04	406.67	398.82	2003-04	35.29	36.53	36.71	29.98
3	87113020	MOTR CYCLS WTH CYLNDR CPCTY >250 BT<=500CC	0.16	2003-04	385.51	372.94	2003-04	-68.66	147.00	32.65	29.53
4	54071049	PRINTED OTHR POLYESTER FBRCS	0.12	2003-04	552.64	358.90	2003-04	42.61	33.74	12.76	10.84
5	39076090	OTHER POLYETHYLENE TEREPHTHALATE (INCLUDING CLEAN. CLOURLESS GRADES)	0.11	2003-04	209.70	302.11	2003-04	192.10	293.16	0.82	0.79
6	55121990	WOVN FBRCS.OTHR CNTNG POLYETR>=85%	0.13	2003-04	284.91	259.95	2003-04	31.55	17.26	7.15	9.67
		D (ii) : NEGATIVE LIST									
1	85281212	COLOUR TV SET OF SCRN SIZE BETN 36 & 54 CM	0.12	2003-04	760.51	605.06	2003-04	50.60	22.65	6.51	6.97
2	85469090	OTHR ELCTRL INSLTRS OF OTHR MATRLS	0.15	2003-04	201.79	433.97	2003-04	0.61	13.16	16.35	15.54
3	10051000	MAIZE SEED	0.48	2000-01	62122.76	69121.18	1998-99	84542.12	46711.47	13.39	11.87
4	17019910	SUGAR CUBES (17019903)	0.37	2000-01	17067.43	16780.71	1999-00	61857.65	42975.63	39.61	30.14
5	87021019	OTHR VHCLS(<=13 PERSONS) WTH CMPRSN-IGNTNINTRNL CMBSTN PISTON ENGINE	1.20	2003-04	200.00	226.86	2003-04	-81.49	136.59	41.15	37.64
		OTHER ITEMS AT MFN RATE									
1	48101390	OTHER	0.10	2003-04	73.71	122.33	2003-04	45.61	58.35	14.52	13.85
2	48025590	OTHER PAPER	0.10	2003-04	108.73	120.66	2003-04	297.03	300.36	26.36	24.38

NOTES

1 Base year have been changed, where CAGR for a particular product shows growth of more than 999%.
2 Base year for Trend Calculation have been changed in some cases, keeping in view the base year for CAGR and the actual trade data.
3 Base year for Trend Calculation have been changed in some cases, where trend exceeds 99999%.
4 Correlation among different DATA SERIES have been calculated by using the CORREL function active in the MS EXCEL spreadsheet.
5 Correlation of +1 denotes perfect positive correlation, -1 denotes perfect negative correlation, 0 denotes least correlation among the data series.
6 Trend is taken as 100% and CAGR as 0% in cases where either the data figures prior to 2004-05 are either zero or negligible.

Sl. No.	HS Code	Particulars	2004-05 Per Unit Export Price to Srilanka (in Rs.)	2004-05 Per Unit World Export Price for India (in Rs.)	Base year for next two columns	SRILANKA CAGR - VOLUME (in %)	SRILANKA CAGR-VALUE (in %)	Base year for next two columns	World CAGR-VOLUME (in %)	World CAGR-VALUE (in %)	SRILANKA CORRELATION - TREND OF VOLUME / VALUE	World CORRELATION TREND OF VOLUME / VALUE	SRILANKA & World CORRELATION - TREND OF VOLUME	SRILANKA & World CORRELATION - TREND OF VALUE	SRILANKA & World CORRELATION - UNIT PRICE
		F I : ZERO DUTY IMMEDIATELY													
1	29420090	OTHER DILOXANIDE FUROATE, CIMETIDINE, FAMOTIDINE NES	554.50	1888.79	2003-04	23.59	115.78	2003-04	22.17	23.66	0.96	1.00	1.00	0.96	#DIV/0!
		F II : 50% IMMEDIATE AND UPTO 100% IN 3													
1	74081190	OTHR COPPR WIRE WTH MAX CRS-SEC DIAMTR>6MM (74081109)	145.97	143.56	1998-99	198.93	180.44	1998-99	122.66	113.34	0.99	0.98	0.99	1.00	0.28
2	74081110	CU WLD WIRE WTH MAX CRS-SEC DIAMTR>6MM (74081101)	140.43	138.15	1998-99	130.96	130.38	1998-99	136.08	153.43	0.98	0.98	0.97	0.98	#DIV/0!
		SLR: ZERO DUTY IN 8 YEARS													
1	87113090	OTHR VHCL WTH CYLNDR CPCTY >250 BT<=500 CC	49605.92	52321.85	2003-04	697.22	716.90	2003-04	118.05	82.13	1.00	1.00	0.95	0.92	#DIV/0!
2	87019010	OTHER TRACTORS OF ENGN CAPACITY <= 1800CC	[illegible]7371.05	278485.02	2003-04	13.73	398.82	2003-04	35.29	36.53	1.00	1.00	0.88	0.88	#DIV/0!
3	87113020	MOTR CYCLS WTH CYLNDR CPCTY >250 BT<=500CC	29265.97	32362.87	2003-04	385.51	372.94	2003-04	-68.66	147.00	1.00	0.52	0.35	0.98	#DIV/0!
4	54071049	PRINTED OTHR POLYESTER FBRCS	49.02	57.75	2003-04	552.64	358.90	2003-04	42.61	33.74	1.00	1.00	0.87	0.89	#DIV/0!
5	39076090	OTHER POLYETHYLENE TEREPHTHALATE (INCLUDING CLEAN, CLOURLESS GRADES)	47.82	49.23	2003-04	209.70	302.11	2003-04	192.10	293.16	1.00	1.00	1.00	1.00	#DIV/0!
6	55121990	WOVN FBRCS,OTHR CNTNG POLYETR>=85%	79.22	58.55	2003-04	284.91	259.95	2003-04	31.55	17.26	1.00	1.00	0.90	0.88	#DIV/0!
		D (ii) : NEGATIVE LIST													
1	85281212	COLOUR TV SET OF SCRN SIZE BETN 36 & 54 CM	5321.61	4973.62	2003-04	760.51	605.06	2003-04	50.60	22.65	1.00	0.99	0.87	0.82	#DIV/0!
2	85469090	OTHR ELCTRL INSLTRS OF OTHR MATRLS	92.84	97.65	2003-04	201.79	433.97	2003-04	0.61	13.16	0.99	1.00	0.86	0.82	#DIV/0!
3	10051000	MAIZE SEED	6.22	7.02	1999-00	352.24	315.35	1998-99	207.56	178.65	1.00	1.00	0.99	0.99	#DIV/0!
4	17019910	SUGAR CUBES (17019903)	11.30	14.86	2000-01	261.97	260.45	1999-00	261.76	236.39	1.00	1.00	1.00	1.00	#DIV/0!
5	87021019	OTHR VHCLS(<=13 PERSONS) WTH CMPRSN-IGNTNINTRNL CMBSTN PISTON ENGINE	782930.11	855974.34	2003-04	200.00	226.86	2003-04	-81.49	136.59	1.00	0.43	0.35	0.99	#DIV/0!
		OTHER ITEMS AT MFN RATE													
1	48101390	OTHER	34.00	35.63	2003-04	73.71	122.33	2003-04	45.61	58.35	0.99	1.00	1.00	0.99	#DIV/0!
2	48025590	OTHER PAPER	26.03	28.14	2003-04	108.73	120.66	2003-04	297.03	300.36	1.00	1.00	0.98	0.98	#DIV/0!

TABLE- 13

KEY FACTORS FOR ALL SAMPLED PRODUCTS COVERED UNDER VARIOUS CATEGORIES- CHAPTERWISE

			2004-05	2004-05	2004-05	2004-05		2004-05		2004-05	2004-05		2004-05		2004-05
Sl. No.	CHAPTER	Main Products	% of Total Value of exports to Srilanka in 2004-05	Value of exports to Srilanka (in Rs. Lakhs)	Value of World exports for India (in Rs. Lakhs)	Market Share of exports to Srilanka in World exports (Value) in %	Base year for next column	Incremental Trend of exports to Srilanka (Value) in % in comparison to base yr.	Base year for next column	Incremental Trend of World Export (Value) in % in comparison to base yr.	CORRELATION OF TREND IN VALUE - Srilanka/World exports	Base year for next column	CAGR-VALUE-Srilanka (in %)	Base year for next column	CAGR-VALUE-World exports(in %)
		F I : ZERO DUTY IMMEDIATELY													
1	CHAPTER 29	Organic Chemicals	0.20	1189.80	466480.16	0.26	2003-04	115.78	2003-04	23.66	0.96	2003-04	115.78	2003-04	23.66
		F II : 50% IMMEDIATE AND UPTO 100% IN 3 YRS by 05.03.03													
1	CHAPTER 28	Inorganic Chemicals, Organic or inorganic compounds of precious metals	1.02	6169.90	25936.63	23.87	2003-04	66.90	2003-04	148.53	0.98	2003-04	66.90	2003-04	148.53
2	CHAPTER 72	Iron and Steel	1.34	8137.02	130630.26	6.23	1998-99	432.27	1998-99	1524.11	0.92	1998-99	32.14	1998-99	59.14
3	CHAPTER 73	Articles of Iron or Steel	0.34	2088.70	23222.65	8.99	2003-04	11.80	2003-04	121.23	0.94	2003-04	11.80	2003-04	121.23
4	CHAPTER 74	Copper and Copper articles	1.27	7742.76	104873.63	7.38	1998-99	36098.04	1998-99	12356.63	1.00	1998-99	166.96	1998-99	123.48
5	CHAPTER 85	Audio Visual goods and electrical machinery	0.13	821.59	2455.79	33.46	1998-99	497.22	1998-99	212.43	0.73	1998-99	34.70	1998-99	20.91
		SLR: ZERO DUTY IN 8 YEARS													
1	CHAPTER 3	Fish and other aquatic invertebrates	0.11	664.64	1994.16	33.33	1998-99	36.26	1998-99	178.39	0.40	1998-99	5.29	1998-99	18.61
2	CHAPTER 23	Residues and waste of Food industry	1.57	9532.92	218616.07	4.36	1999-00	44866.60	1998-99	63208.26	1.00	1999-00	239.30	1998-99	193.03
3	CHAPTER 25	Salt, mineral products, lime and cement	0.94	5711.92	55330.18	10.32	1999-00	3603.99	1998-99	1420.72	0.92	1999-00	105.94	1998-99	57.40
4	CHAPTER 30	Pharmaceutical products	1.70	10324.81	319960.39	3.23	1998-99	219.44	1998-99	424.90	0.96	1998-99	21.36	1998-99	31.83
5	CHAPTER 39	Plastics and articles	1.11	6740.42	280837.82	2.40	1998-99	1972.25	1998-99	10945.39	0.98	1998-99	65.73	1998-99	119.04
6	CHAPTER 48	Paper and paper boards, articles related to paper	0.34	2056.19	11961.31	17.19	1998-99	16935.54	1998-99	3980.55	0.98	1998-99	135.45	1998-99	85.55
7	CHAPTER 49	Printed materials	0.27	1654.64	28178.30	5.87	1998-99	47.82	1998-99	200.82	0.92	1998-99	6.73	1998-99	20.15
8	CHAPTER 52	Cotton	3.03	18431.99	434910.06	4.24	1998-99	156.36	1998-99	66.61	0.87	1998-99	16.99	1998-99	8.88
9	CHAPTER 54	Man-made filaments	1.22	7401.94	220822.82	3.35	1998-99	2825.21	1998-99	886.13	0.98	1998-99	75.53	1998-99	46.44
10	CHAPTER 55	Man-made staple fibres	0.37	2259.90	48919.35	4.62	2003-04	26.01	2003-04	-2.14	0.99	2003-04	26.01	2003-04	-2.14
11	CHAPTER 60	Knitted and crocheted fabrics	0.11	660.21	5106.13	12.93	1999-00	24443.12	1998-99	328.40	0.69	1999-00	200.60	1998-99	27.44
12	CHAPTER 61	Apparel and clothing accessories(knitted or crocheted)	0.16	948.92	338230.69	0.28	2003-04	-71.45	2003-04	-17.31	0.89	2003-04	-71.45	2003-04	-17.31
13	CHAPTER 62	Apparel and clothing accessories(not knitted or crocheted)	0.32	1956.77	295430.17	0.66	1998-99	15307.64	1998-99	106361.32	0.78	1998-99	131.54	1998-99	219.54
14	CHAPTER 71	Natural or other stones, pearls	0.18	1096.03	4535755.50	0.02	1998-99	243.57	1998-99	127.34	0.62	1998-99	22.84	1998-99	14.67
15	CHAPTER 72	Iron and Steel	0.21	1271.65	18408.10	6.91	1998-99	92.43	1998-99	-19.13	0.46	1998-99	11.53	1998-99	-3.48
16	CHAPTER 73	Articles of Iron or Steel	0.17	1064.91	69040.50	1.54	1998-99	60.14	1998-99	123.40	0.17	1998-99	8.16	1998-99	14.34
17	CHAPTER 76	Aluminium and articles	0.54	3269.34	110826.35	2.95	1998-99	1097.96	1998-99	590.89	0.81	1998-99	51.27	1998-99	38.01
18	CHAPTER 84	Machinery and Appliances	0.34	2065.98	13386.90	15.43	1998-99	277.70	1998-99	189.55	0.92	1998-99	24.79	1998-99	19.39
19	CHAPTER 87	Vehicles and accessories	5.29	32220.88	134254.45	24.00	1998-99	8939.64	1998-99	4222.67	1.00	1998-99	111.85	1998-99	87.34
20	CHAPTER 90	Optical, Photographic, Medical and Surgical instruments	0.10	614.10	8877.61	6.92	1998-99	1122.58	1998-99	291.13	0.70	1998-99	51.78	1998-99	25.52

TABLE- 13

KEY FACTORS FOR ALL SAMPLED PRODUCTS COVERED UNDER VARIOUS CATEGORIES- CHAPTERWISE

			2004-05	2004-05	2004-05	2004-05		2004-05		2004-05	2004-05		2004-05		2004-05
Sl. No.	CHAPTER	Main Products	% of Total Value of exports to Srilanka in 2004-05	Value of exports to Srilanka (in Rs. Lakhs)	Value of World exports for India (in Rs. Lakhs)	Market Share of exports to Srilanka in World exports (Value) in %	Base year for next column	Incremental Trend of exports to Srilanka (Value) in % in comparison to base yr.	Base year for next column	Incremental Trend of World Export (Value) in % in comparison to base yr.	CORRELATION OF TREND IN VALUE - Srilanka/World exports	Base year for next column	CAGR-VALUE-Srilanka (in %)	Base year for next column	CAGR-VALUE-World exports(in %)
		D (ii) : NEGATIVE LIST													
1	CHAPTER 7	Edible vegetables, roots and tubers	2.39	14549.65	117572.21	12.38	1998-99	31.08	1998-99	249.88	0.10	1998-99	4.61	1998-99	23.21
2	CHAPTER 9	Coffe, Tea and Spices	1.28	7807.48	131650.80	5.93	1998-99	327.42	1998-99	53.06	0.57	1998-99	27.39	1998-99	7.35
3	CHAPTER 10	Cereals	5.81	35402.44	574385.19	6.16	1998-99	2154.04	1998-99	32.28	0.69	1998-99	68.07	1998-99	4.77
4	CHAPTER 14	Other vegetable products & plaiting materials	0.17	1043.58	1794.94	58.14	1998-99	126.76	1998-99	35.45	0.99	1998-99	14.62	1998-99	5.19
5	CHAPTER 17	Sugars and confectionery	0.74	4516.31	12003.32	37.63	2000-01	783.75	1998-99	3352.31	0.96	2000-01	72.42	1998-99	80.45
6	CHAPTER 24	Tobacco and substitutes	0.25	1506.66	4527.12	33.28	2004-05	0.00	2003-04	242.97	0.96	2004-05	0.00	2003-04	242.97
7	CHAPTER 25	Salt, mineral products, lime and cement	0.71	4347.40	42411.30	10.25	1999-00	1908.87	1998-99	82994.24	0.84	1999-00	82.22	1998-99	206.62
8	CHAPTER 40	Rubber and related articles	0.80	4876.49	88269.53	5.52	1998-99	55063.91	1998-99	48838.03	1.00	1998-99	186.38	1998-99	180.72
9	CHAPTER 48	Paper and paper boards, articles related to paper	0.18	1109.52	5570.36	19.92	1998-99	6616.22	1998-99	1253.05	0.80	1998-99	101.61	1998-99	54.37
10	CHAPTER 72	Iron and Steel	0.24	1459.17	485612.13	0.30	1998-99	440.73	1998-99	2557.41	0.18	1998-99	32.48	1998-99	72.75
11	CHAPTER 74	Copper and Copper articles	0.11	695.88	33768.65	2.06	1998-99	215.65	1998-99	255.21	0.91	1998-99	21.12	1998-99	23.52
12	CHAPTER 85	Audio Visual goods and electrical machinery	0.38	2326.03	32469.14	7.16	2003-04	173.26	2003-04	-5.28	0.86	2003-04	173.26	2003-04	-5.28
13	CHAPTER 87	Vehicles and accessories	9.99	60853.50	493927.43	12.32	1998-99	2993.71	1998-99	714.66	0.97	1998-99	77.18	1998-99	41.85
		OTHER ITEMS AT MFN RATE													
1	CHAPTER 27	Mineral fuels, oils and side products	22.67	138053.06	2414329.77	5.72	2003-04	24.96	2003-04	82.48	0.98	2003-04	24.96	2003-04	82.48
2	CHAPTER 48	Paper and paper boards, articles related to paper	0.68	4125.48	21721.64	18.99	2003-04	52.96	2003-04	66.32	1.00	2003-04	52.96	2003-04	66.32

NOTES

1 Base year have been changed, where CAGR for a particular product shows growth of more than 999%.
2 Base year for Trend Calculation have been changed in some cases, keeping in view the base year for CAGR and the actual trade data.
3 Base year for Trend Calculation have been changed in some cases, where trend exceeds 99999% in case of srilanka.
4 Correlation among different DATA SERIES have been calculated by using the CORREL function active in the MS EXCEL spreadsheet.
5 Correlation of +1 denotes perfect positive correlation, -1 denotes perfect negative correlation, 0 denotes least correlation among the data series.
6 Trend is taken as 100% and CAGR as 0% in cases where either the data figures prior to 2004-05 are either zero or negligible.

TABLE- 14

MOVEMENT OF SUM FACTORS OF SAMPLED PRODUCTS (EXPORTED TO SRILANKA) COVERED UNDER DIFFERENT CATEGORIES

(Value: in Rs. Lakhs)

Movement of All 130 sampled products EXPORTED TO SRILANKA

	1998-99	1999-00	2000-01	2001-02	2002-03	2003-04	2004-05
Sum of Value of exports to Srilanka (A)	34631.27	52825.48	60632.45	65283.72	74492.71	339593.20	418790.58
Sum of Value of India's exports to World (B)	3091827.93	3776835.99	4200941.95	4341801.12	5711421.37	9641127.68	12364459.51
Sum Factor (A/B)	0.011201	0.013987	0.014433	0.015036	0.013043	0.035223	0.033871

Movement of 1 sampled products covered under " F I : ZERO DUTY IMMEDIATELY" category

	1998-99	1999-00	2000-01	2001-02	2002-03	2003-04	2004-05
Sum of Value of exports to Srilanka (A)	0.00	0.00	0.00	0.00	0.00	551.40	1189.80
Sum of Value of India's exports to World (B)	0.00	0.00	0.00	0.00	0.00	377219.59	466480.16
Sum Factor (A/B)	#DIV/0!	#DIV/0!	#DIV/0!	#DIV/0!	#DIV/0!	0.00146175	0.002550591

Movement of 12 sampled products covered under " F II : 50% IMMEDIATE AND UPTO 100% IN 3 YRS by 05.03.03" category

	1998-99	1999-00	2000-01	2001-02	2002-03	2003-04	2004-05
Sum of Value of exports to Srilanka (A)	1687.71	2736.59	1395.40	1550.44	5295.17	25674.36	24979.97
Sum of Value of India's exports to World (B)	9671.14	11840.13	17388.84	21552.15	68388.78	222029.46	287118.96
Sum Factor (A/B)	0.174510	0.231128	0.080247	0.071939	0.077427	0.115635	0.087002

Movement of 57 sampled producτs covered under " SLR: ZERO DUTY IN 8 YEARS" category

	1998-99	1999-00	2000-01	2001-02	2002-03	2003-04	2004-05
Sum of Value of exports to Srilanka (A)	15503.85	19008.22	28559.44	26862.15	33238.89	89890.79	109948.16
Sum of Value of India's exports to World (B)	2437606.99	3386101.87	3684794.89	3683041.35	4671161.01	6344532.35	7150846.86
Sum Factor (A/B)	0.00636	0.00561	0.00775	0.00729	0.00712	0.01417	0.01538

Movement of 48 sampled products covered under " D (ii) : NEGATIVE LIST" category

	1998-99	1999-00	2000-01	2001-02	2002-03	2003-04	2004-05
Sum of Value of exports to Srilanka (A)	17439.71	31080.67	30677.61	36871.13	35958.65	110305.23	140494.11
Sum of Value of India's exports to World (B)	644549.80	378893.99	498758.22	637207.62	971871.58	1361252.49	2023962.12
Sum Factor (A/B)	0.02706	0.08203	0.06151	0.05786	0.03700	0.08103	0.06942

Movement of 12 sampled products covered under " OTHER ITEMS AT MFN RATE" category

	1998-99	1999-00	2000-01	2001-02	2002-03	2003-04	2004-05
Sum of Value of exports to Srilanka (A)	0.00	0.00	0.00	0.00	0.00	113171.42	142178.54
Sum of Value of India's exports to World (B)	0.00	0.00	0.00	0.00	0.00	1336093.79	2436051.41
Sum Factor (A/B)	#DIV/0!	#DIV/0!	#DIV/0!	#DIV/0!	#DIV/0!	0.0847032	0.058364343

Summary of Sum Factors for Different Categories- Sample Products only

	1998-99	1999-00	2000-01	2001-02	2002-03	2003-04	2004-05
ALL SAMPLED PRODUCTS	0.0112	0.0140	0.0144	0.0150	0.0130	0.0352	0.0339
F I : ZERO DUTY IMMEDIATELY	#DIV/0!	#DIV/0!	#DIV/0!	#DIV/0!	#DIV/0!	0.0015	0.0026
F II : 50% IMMEDIATE AND UPTO 100% IN 3 YRS	0.1745	0.2311	0.0802	0.0719	0.0774	0.1156	0.0870
SLR: ZERO DUTY IN 8 YEARS	0.0064	0.0056	0.0078	0.0073	0.0071	0.0142	0.0154
D (ii) : NEGATIVE LIST	0.0271	0.0820	0.0615	0.0579	0.0370	0.0810	0.0694
OTHER ITEMS AT MFN RATE	#DIV/0!	#DIV/0!	#DIV/C!	#DIV/0!	#DIV/0!	0.0847	0.0584

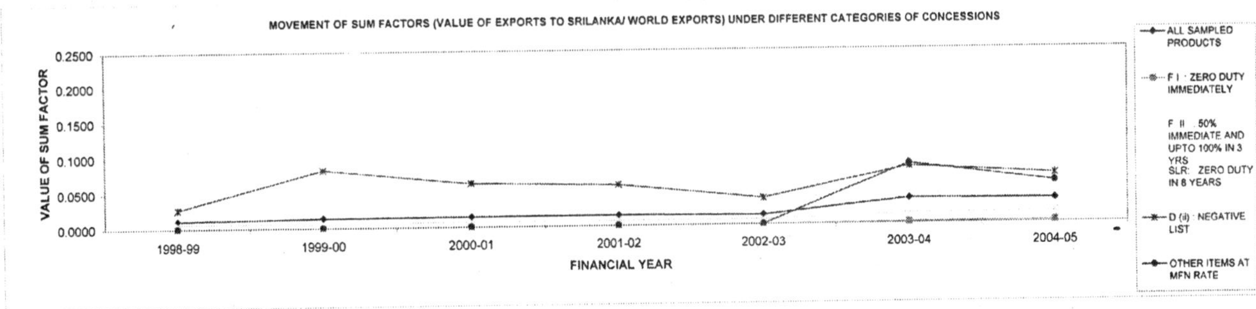

TABLE- 15

MOVEMENT OF SUM FACTORS OF SAMPLED PRODUCTS COVERED UNDER DIFFERENT CATEGORY- CHAPTERWISE

(Important Chapters selected on the basis of highest CAGR and Value of Exports in 2004-05 basis)

(Value: in Rs. Lakhs)

VALUE WISE TOP 10% OUT OF TOTAL 41 CHAPTERS

CHAPTER NO.	CATEGORY
27	OTHER ITEMS AT MFN RATE
87	D (ii) : NEGATIVE LIST
10	D (ii) : NEGATIVE LIST
87	SLR: ZERO DUTY IN 8 YEARS

CAGR WISE TOP 10% OUT OF TOTAL 41 CHAPTERS

CHAPTER NO.	CATEGORY
23	SLR: ZERO DUTY IN 8 YEARS
60	SLR: ZERO DUTY IN 8 YEARS
40	D (ii) : NEGATIVE LIST
85	D (ii) : NEGATIVE LIST

SUM FACTORS (VALUE OF EXPORTS TO SRILANKA / INDIA'S WORLD EXPORTS) FOR SELECTED CHAPTERS

VALUE WISE

CHAPTER 27 (OTHER ITEMS AT MFN RATE)

	1998-99	1999-00	2000-01	2001-02	2002-03	2003-04	2004-05
Sum of Value of exports to Srilanka (A)	0.00	0.00	0.00	0.00	0.00	110474.31	138053.06
Sum of Value of India's exports to World (B)	0.00	0.00	0.00	0.00	0.00	1323033.70	2414329.77
Sum Factor (A/B)	#DIV/0!	#DIV/0!	#DIV/0!	#DIV/0!	#DIV/0!	0.08350075	0.0571807

CHAPTER 87 (D (ii) : NEGATIVE LIST)

	1998-99	1999-00	2000-01	2001-02	2002-03	2003-04	2004-05
Sum of Value of exports to Srilanka (A)	1967.01	2537.68	2863.18	2109.71	2315.24	31611.40	60853.50
Sum of Value of India's exports to World (B)	60629.53	70185.86	111711.82	110678.71	127669.07	389997.02	493927.43
Sum Factor (A/B)	0.032443	0.036157	0.025630	0.019062	0.018135	0.081055	0.123203

CHAPTER 10 (D (ii) : NEGATIVE LIST)

	1998-99	1999-00	2000-01	2001-02	2002-03	2003-04	2004-05
Sum of Value of exports to Srilanka (A)	1570.62	5104.62	418.41	4929.56	12225.25	17147.84	35402.44
Sum of Value of India's exports to World (B)	434207.77	131157.23	120055.00	261445.15	560712.14	428876.73	574385.19
Sum Factor (A/B)	0.00362	0.03892	0.00349	0.01886	0.02180	0.03998	0.06164

CAGR WISE

CHAPTER 23 (SLR: ZERO DUTY IN 8 YEARS)

	1998-99	1999-00	2000-01	2001-02	2002-03	2003-04	2004-05
Sum of Value of exports to Srilanka (A)	0.00	21.20	133.28	29.29	323.22	10781.63	9532.92
Sum of Value of India's exports to World (B)	345.32	3397.77	8242.17	8193.71	12229.40	266375.91	218616.07
Sum Factor (A/B)	0.00000	0.00624	0.01617	0.00357	0.02643	0.04048	0.04361

CHAPTER 60 (SLR: ZERO DUTY IN 8 YEARS)

	1998-99	1999-00	2000-01	2001-02	2002-03	2003-04	2004-05
Sum of Value of exports to Srilanka (A)	0.00	2.69	0.00	157.73	213.31	403.87	660.21
Sum of Value of India's exports to World (B)	1191.90	1145.36	4430.10	3714.98	4884.78	5490.96	5106.13
Sum Factor (A/B)	0.00000	0.00235	0.00000	0.04246	0.04367	0.07355	0.12930

CHAPTER 40 (D (ii) : NEGATIVE LIST)

	1998-99	1999-00	2000-01	2001-02	2002-03	2003-04	2004-05
Sum of Value of exports to Srilanka (A)	8.84	5.87	60.06	142.84	1184.95	4765.81	4876.49
Sum of Value of India's exports to World (B)	180.37	337.46	1222.40	1331.27	12834.45	88375.51	88269.53
Sum Factor (A/B)	0.04901	0.01739	0.04913	0.10730	0.09233	0.05393	0.05525

CHAPTER 87 (SLR: ZERO DUTY IN 8 YEARS)

	1998-99	1999-00	2000-01	2001-02	2002-03	2003-04	2004-05
Sum of Value of exports to Srilanka (A)	356.44	293.17	417.41	573.04	642.33	19030.08	32220.88
Sum of Value of India's exports to World (B)	3105.82	2876.66	6135.51	6008.54	5535.08	91427.13	134254.45
Sum Factor (A/B)	0.11477	0.10191	0.06803	0.09537	0.11605	0.20814	0.24000

SL.NO.	CATEGORY OF PRODUCTS	SUM FACTORS						
		1998-99	1999-00	2000-01	2001-02	2002-03	2003-04	2004-05
1	CHAPTER 27 (OIMR)	#DIV/0!	#DIV/0!	#DIV/0!	#DIV/0!	#DIV/0!	0.08350	0.05718
2	CHAPTER 87 (D (ii))	0.03244	0.03616	0.02563	0.01906	0.01813	0.08106	0.12320
3	CHAPTER 10 (D (ii))	0.00362	0.03892	0.00349	0.01886	0.02180	0.03998	0.06164
4	CHAPTER 87 (SLR)	0.11477	0.10191	0.06803	0.09537	0.11605	0.20814	0.24000

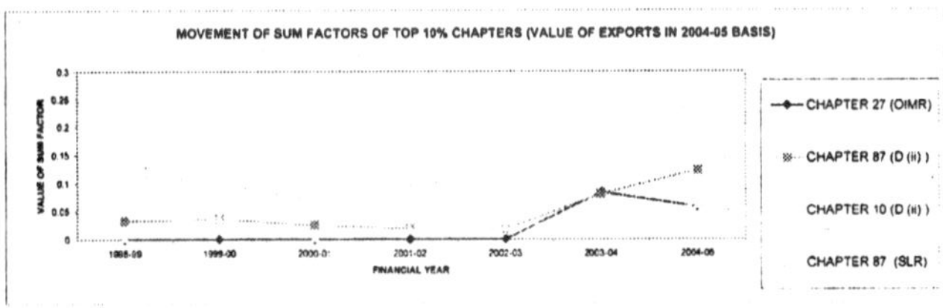

CHAPTER 85 (D (ii) : NEGATIVE LIST)

	1998-99	1999-00	2000-01	2001-02	2002-03	2003-04	2004-05
Sum of Value of exports to Srilanka (A)	0	0	0	0	0	851.21	2326.03
Sum of Value of India's exports to World (B)	0	0	0	0	0	34277.81	32469.14
Sum Factor (A/B)	#DIV/0!	#DIV/0!	#DIV/0!	#DIV/0!	#DIV/0!	0.02483	0.07164

SL.NO.	CATEGORY OF PRODUCTS	SUM FACTORS						
		1998-99	1999-00	2000-01	2001-02	2002-03	2003-04	2004-05
1	CHAPTER 23 (SLR)	0.00000	0.00624	0.01617	0.00357	0.02643	0.04048	0.04361
2	CHAPTER 60 (SLR)	0.00000	0.00235	0.00000	0.04246	0.04367	0.07355	0.12930
3	CHAPTER 40 (D (ii))	0.04901	0.01739	0.04913	0.10730	0.09233	0.05393	0.05525
4	CHAPTER 85 (D (ii))	#DIV/0!	#DIV/0!	#DIV/0!	#DIV/0!	#DIV/0!	0.02483	0.07164

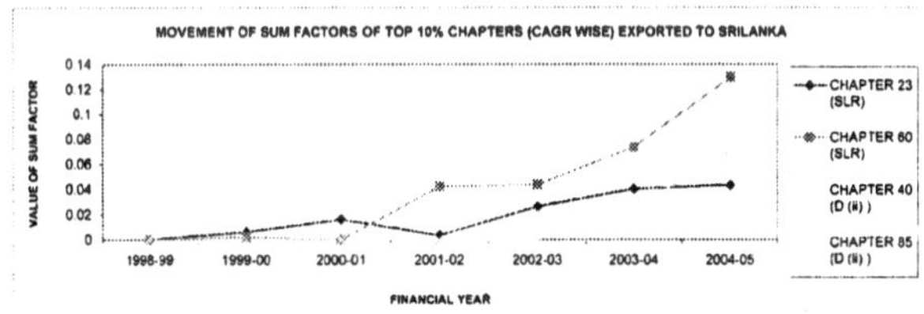

TABLE- 16

MOVEMENT OF SELECTED 8 SAMPLED PRODUCTS (High CAGR & Value of Exports to Srilanka in 2004-05 basis)

1 87113090 OTHR VHCL WTH CYLNDR CPCTY >250 BT<=500 CC

SLR: ZERO DUTY IN 8 YEARS

	1998-99	1999-00	2000-01	2001-02	2002-03	2003-04	2004-05
Market Share (Quantity)	#DIV/0!	#DIV/0!	#DIV/0!	#DIV/0!	#DIV/0!	13.00%	47.52%
Market Share (Value)	#DIV/0!	#DIV/0!	#DIV/0!	#DIV/0!	#DIV/0!	10.04%	45.05%
	1998-99	1999-00	2000-01	2001-02	2002-03	2003-04	2004-05
Price per unit (Exports to Srilanka only)	#DIV/0!	#DIV/0!	#DIV/0!	#DIV/0!	#DIV/0!	48411.1111	49605.92334
Price per unit (World Export for India)	#DIV/0!	#DIV/0!	#DIV/0!	#DIV/0!	#DIV/0!	62642.2383	52321.8543

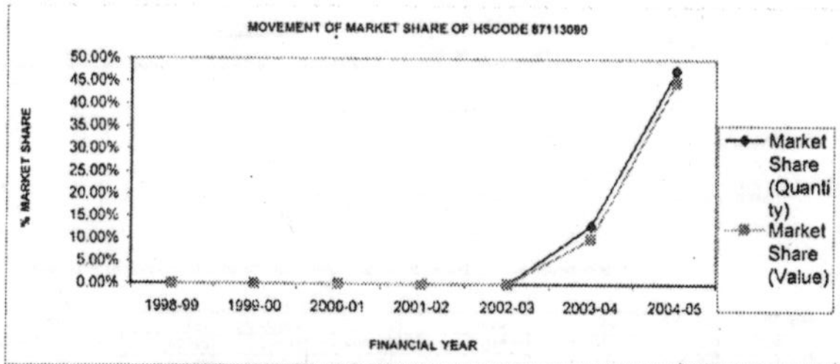

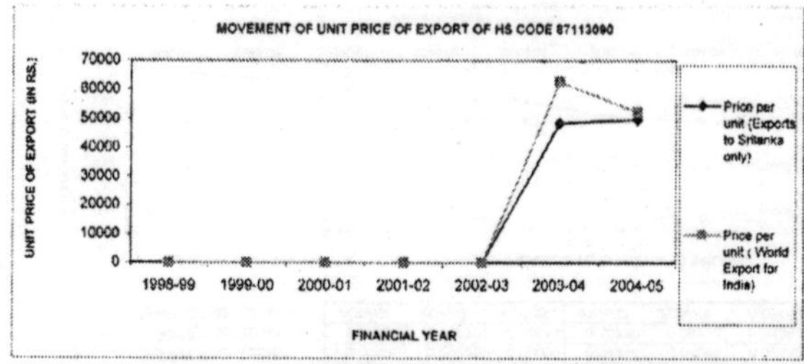

2 85281212 COLOUR TV SET OF SCRN SIZE BETN 36 & 54 CM

D (ii) : NEGATIVE LIST

	1998-99	1999-00	2000-01	2001-02	2002-03	2003-04	2004-05
Market Share (Quantity)	#DIV/0!	#DIV/0!	#DIV/0!	#DIV/0!	#DIV/0!	1.14%	6.51%
Market Share (Value)	#DIV/0!	#DIV/0!	#DIV/0!	#DIV/0!	#DIV/0!	1.21%	6.97%
	1998-99	1999-00	2000-01	2001-02	2002-03	2003-04	2004-05
Price per unit (Exports to Srilanka only)	#DIV/0!	#DIV/0!	#DIV/0!	#DIV/0!	#DIV/0!	6494.90	5321.61
Price per unit (World Export for India)	#DIV/0!	#DIV/0!	#DIV/0!	#DIV/0!	#DIV/0!	6106.91	4973.62

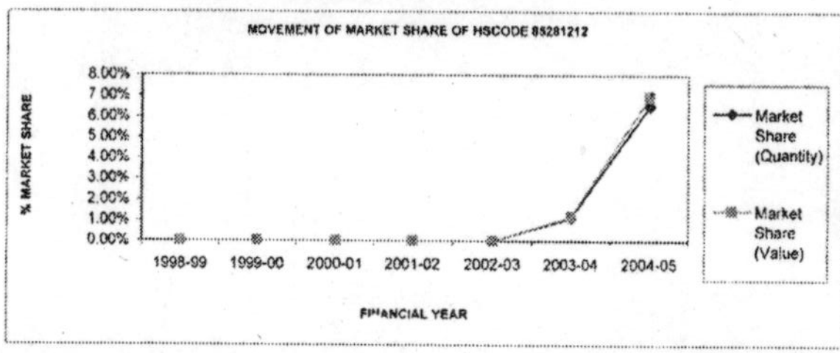

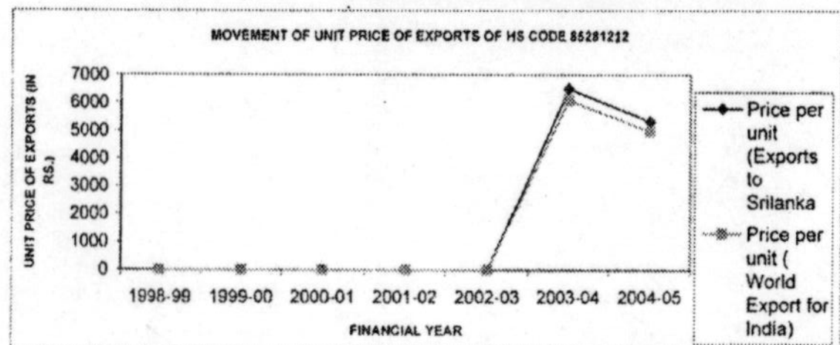

3 85469090 OTHR ELCTRL INSLTRS OF OTHR MATRLS

D (ii) : NEGATIVE LIST

	1998-99	1999-00	2000-01	2001-02	2002-03	2003-04	2004-05
Market Share (Quantity)	#DIV/0!	#DIV/0!	#DIV/0!	#DIV/0!	#DIV/0!	5.45%	16.35%
Market Share (Value)	#DIV/0!	#DIV/0!	#DIV/0!	#DIV/0!	#DIV/0!	3.29%	15.54%
	1998-99	1999-00	2000-01	2001-02	2002-03	2003-04	2004-05
Price per unit (Exports to Srilanka only)	#DIV/0!	#DIV/0!	#DIV/0!	#DIV/0!	#DIV/0!	52.47	92.84
Price per unit (World Export for India)	#DIV/0!	#DIV/0!	#DIV/0!	#DIV/0!	#DIV/0!	86.82	97.65

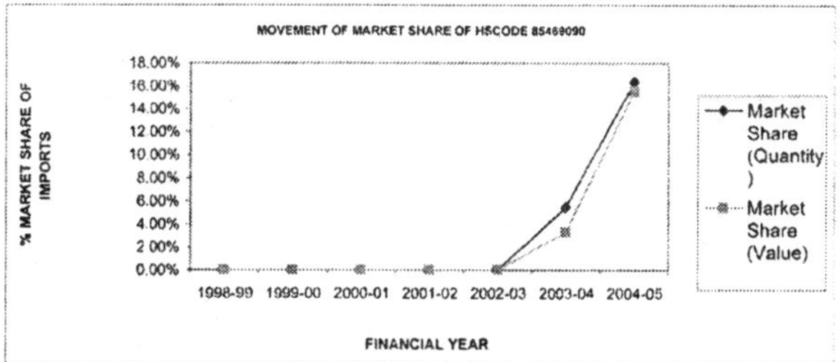

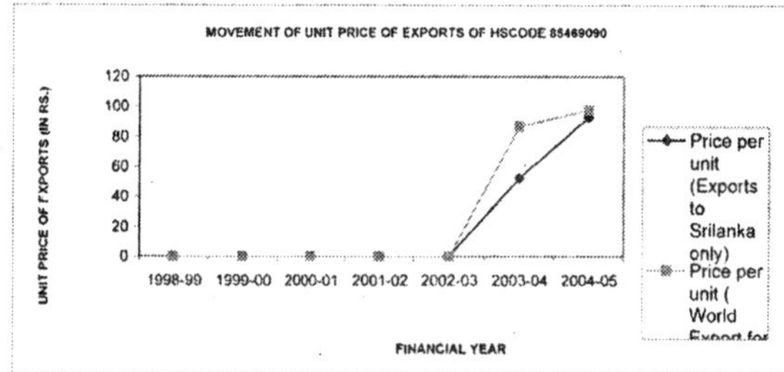

4 87019010 OTHER TRACTORS OF ENGN CAPACITY <= 1800CC

SLR: ZERO DUTY IN 8 YEARS

	1998-99	1999-00	2000-01	2001-02	2002-03	2003-04	2004-05
Market Share (Quantity)	#DIV/0!	#DIV/0!	#DIV/0!	#DIV/0!	#DIV/0!	9.80%	36.71%
Market Share (Value)	#DIV/0!	#DIV/0!	#DIV/0!	#DIV/0!	#DIV/0!	8.20%	29.98%
	1998-99	1999-00	2000-01	2001-02	2002-03	2003-04	2004-05
Price per unit (Exports to Srilanka only)	#DIV/0!	#DIV/0!	#DIV/0!	#DIV/0!	#DIV/0!	230946.67	227371.05
Price per unit (World Export for India)	#DIV/0!	#DIV/0!	#DIV/0!	#DIV/0!	#DIV/0!	275970.59	278485.02

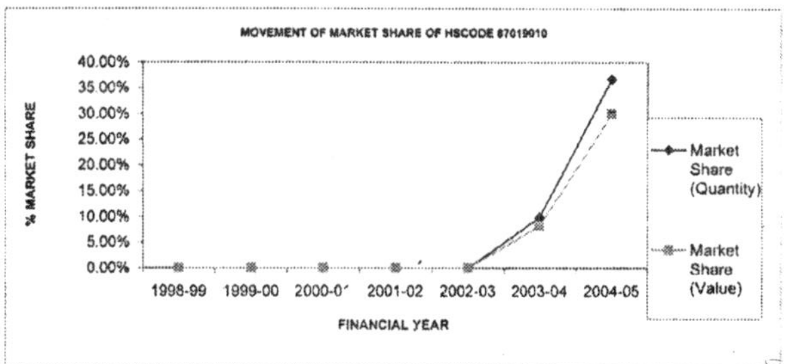

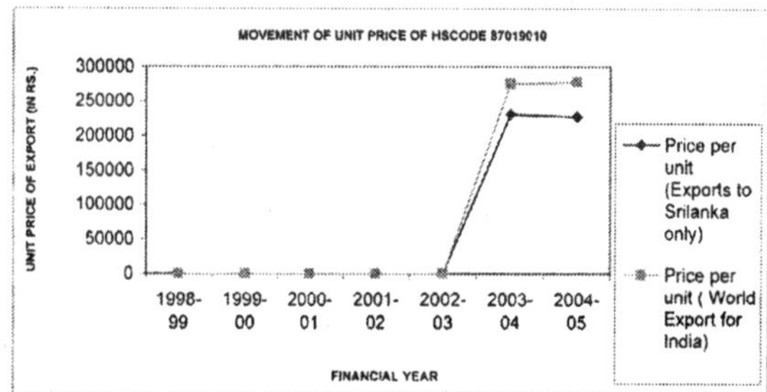

5 27101930 HIGH SPEED DIESEL (HSD)

NIL (OTHER ITEMS AT MFN RATE)

	1998-99	1999-00	2000-01	2001-02	2002-03	2003-04	2004-05
Market Share (Quantity)	#DIV/0!	#DIV/0!	#DIV/0!	#DIV/0!	#DIV/0!	11.83%	8.31%
Market Share (Value)	#DIV/0!	#DIV/0!	#DIV/0!	#DIV/0!	#DIV/0!	11.97%	8.46%
	1998-99	1999-00	2000-01	2001-02	2002-03	2003-04	2004-05
Price per unit (Exports to Srilanka only)	#DIV/0!	#DIV/0!	#DIV/0!	#DIV/0!	#DIV/0!	11522.69	16397.65
Price per unit (World Export for India)	#DIV/0!	#DIV/0!	#DIV/0!	#DIV/0!	#DIV/0!	11379.43	16102.56

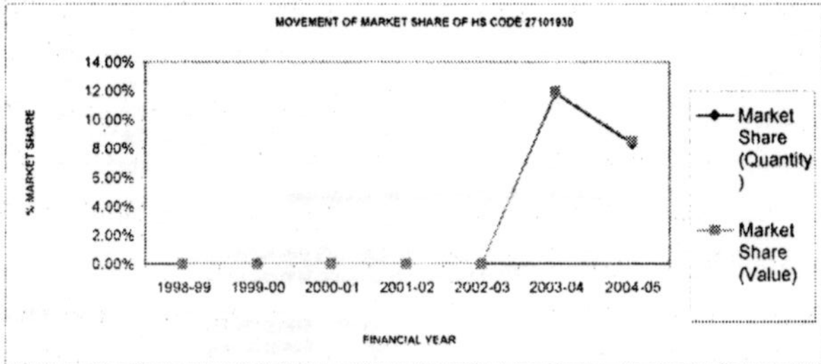

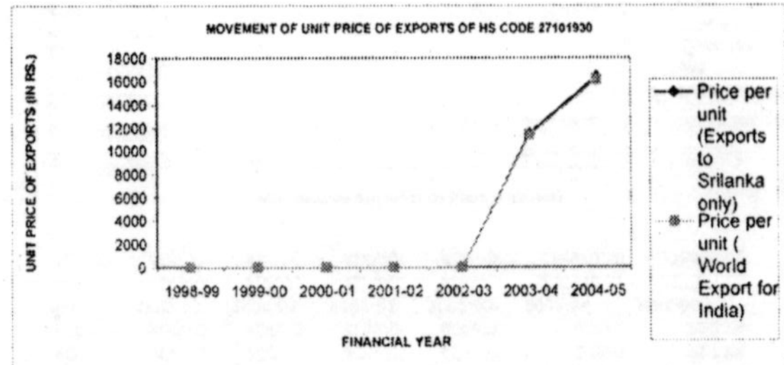

6 10063010 RICE PARBOILED (10063001)

D (ii) : NEGATIVE LIST

	1998-99	1999-00	2000-01	2001-02	2002-03	2003-04	2004-05
Market Share (Quantity)	0.47%	7.21%	0.11%	2.79%	2.44%	0.07%	7.62%
Market Share (Value)	0.44%	5.65%	0.09%	2.54%	2.99%	0.09%	8.05%
	1998-99	1999-00	2000-01	2001-02	2002-03	2003-04	2004-05
Price per unit (Exports to Srilanka only)	9.13	8.26	9.17	7.57	9.09	10.99	11.49
Price per unit (World Export for India)	9.96	10.53	11.31	8.30	7.42	8.10	10.88

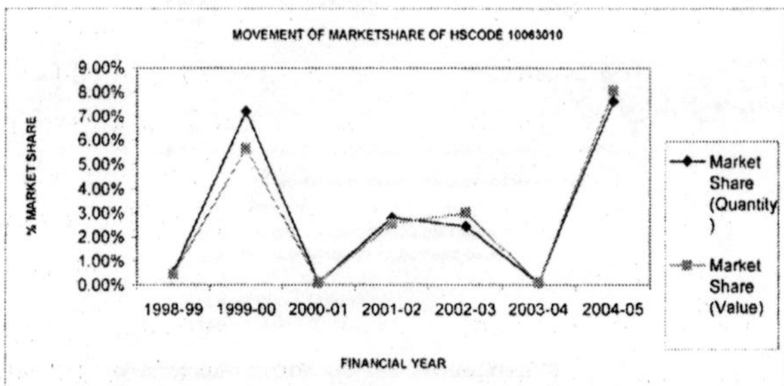

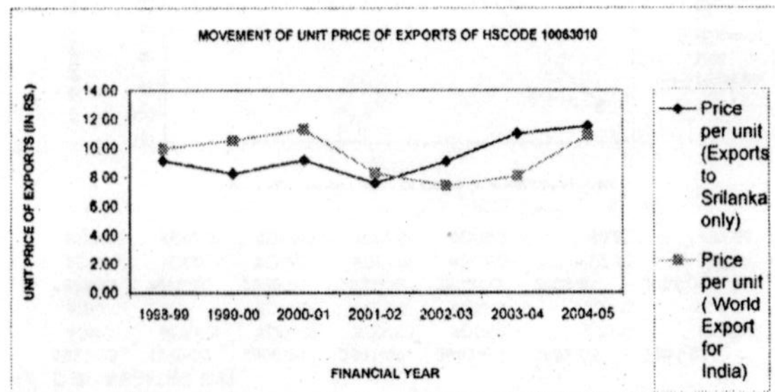

7 87112029 MOTR CYCLWTH CYLNDR CPCTY >75 BT<=250 CC

SLR: ZERO DUTY IN 8 YEARS

	1998-99	1999-00	2000-01	2001-02	2002-03	2003-04	2004-05
Market Share (Quantity)	#DIV/0!	#DIV/0!	#DIV/0!	#DIV/0!	#DIV/0!	27.34%	34.54%
Market Share (Value)	#DIV/0!	#DIV/0!	#DIV/0!	#DIV/0!	#DIV/0!	27.09%	33.87%
	1998-99	**1999-00**	**2000-01**	**2001-02**	**2002-03**	**2003-04**	**2004-05**
Price per unit (Exports to Srilanka only)	#DIV/0!	#DIV/0!	#DIV/0!	#DIV/0!	#DIV/0!	11522.69	16397.65
Price per unit (World Export for India)	#DIV/0!	#DIV/0!	#DIV/0!	#DIV/0!	#DIV/0!	29462.51	27143.93

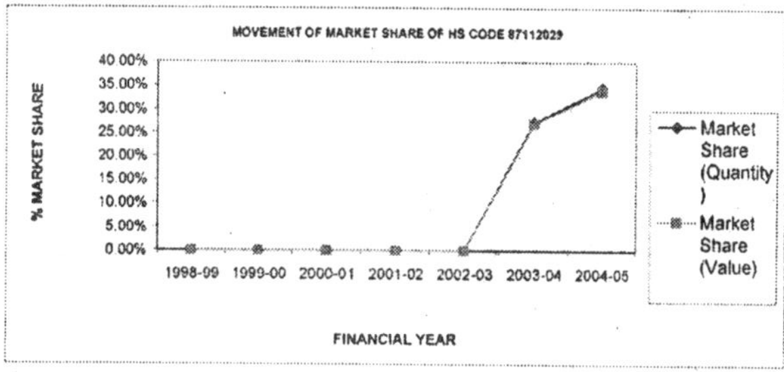

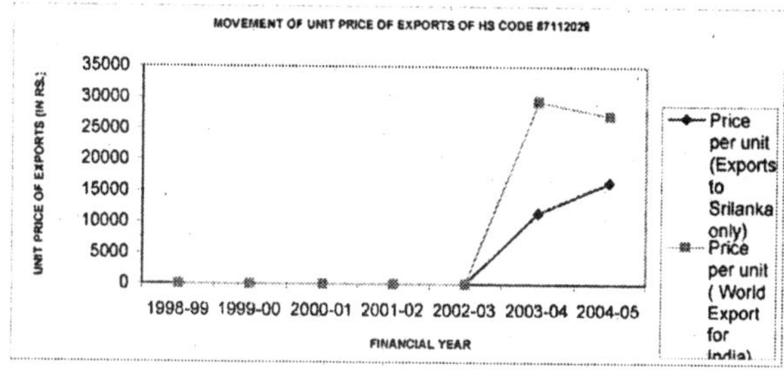

8 87032120 THREE-WHEELED VEHICLES WTH CYLNDR CPCTY<=1000 WTH SPRK-IGNTN D (ii) : NEGATIVE LIST

	1998-99	1999-00	2000-01	2001-02	2002-03	2003-04	2004-05
Market Share (Quantity)	#DIV/0!	#DIV/0!	#DIV/0!	#DIV/0!	#DIV/0!	35.86%	60.66%
Market Share (Value)	#DIV/0!	#DIV/0!	#DIV/0!	#DIV/0!	#DIV/0!	37.27%	59.25%
	1998-99	**1999-00**	**2000-01**	**2001-02**	**2002-03**	**2003-04**	**2004-05**
Price per unit (Exports to Srilanka only)	#DIV/0!	#DIV/0!	#DIV/0!	#DIV/0!	#DIV/0!	59606.89	52175.83
Price per unit (World Export for India)	#DIV/0!	#DIV/0!	#DIV/0!	#DIV/0!	#DIV/0!	57358.73	53417.86

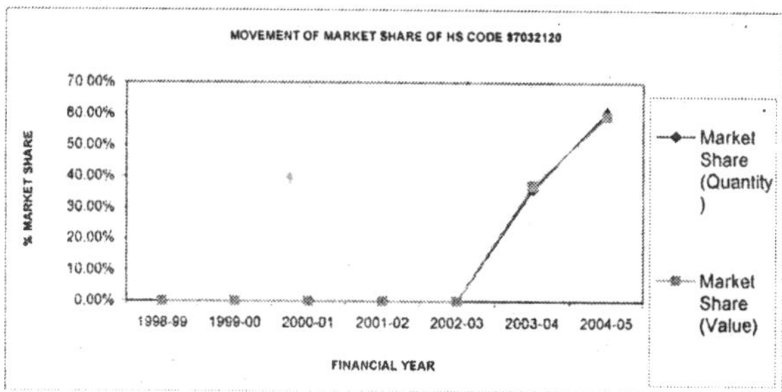

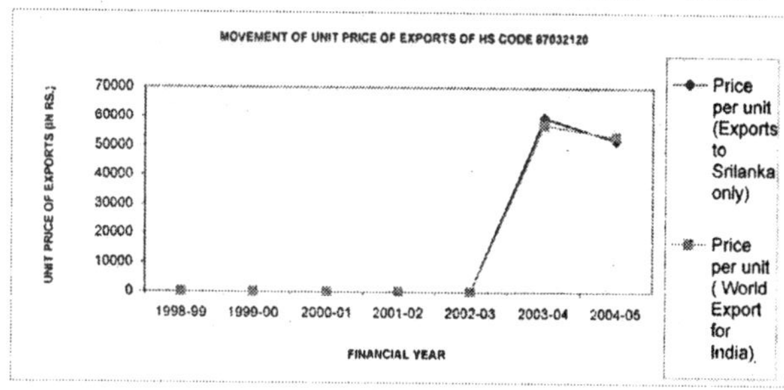

TABLE- 17

DETAILS OF SAMPLING (IMPORT PRODUCTS from THAILAND)

(Value: in Rs. Lakhs)

Particulars				2004-05	
Total No. of Products imported during the year from Thailand				2920	
Total No. of Producs sampled				180	6.16%
Total No. of Sampled Products covered under EHS				33	1.13%
Total No. of Other Products not covered under EHS				147	5.03%
Total Value of Imports during the year from Thailand				374556.8	
ALL INDIA FIGURES	**2001-02**	**2002-03**	**2003-04**	**2004-05**	
Total Value of Imports during the year of Sampled Products	1961469.89	2190449.54	3573041.72	5707306	
Total Value of Imports of Sampled Products covered under EHS	187414.07	265420.06	455293.85	602948.2	
Total Value of Imports of Sampled Products NOT covered under EHS	1774055.82	1925029.48	3117747.87	5104357	
ONLY THAILAND FIGURE					
Total Value of Imports during the year of Sampled Products	105668.99	77741.19	160399.62	291889.8	77.93%
Total Value of Imports of Sampled Products covered under EHS	8868.85	13466.66	30943.24	60216.62	16.08%
Total Value of Imports of Sampled Products NOT covered under EHS	96800.14	64274.53	129456.38	231673.2	61.85%

	IMPORTS FROM THAILAND	INDIA'S WORLD IMPORT	RELATIVE FASTNESS
	(A)	(B)	(A/B)
Weighted Average CAGR of all the sampled products	115.62%	55.32%	2.09
Weighted Average CAGR of all the sampled products (covered under EHS)	90.32%	64.00%	1.41
Weighted Average CAGR of all the sampled products (NOT covered under EHS)	122.20%	54.29%	2.25
Weighted Average CAGR of all the sampled products (covered under EHS)- CHAPTER WISE	200.73%	54.80%	3.66
Weighted Average CAGR of all the sampled products (NOT covered under EHS)- CHAPTER WISE	90.73%	59.39%	1.53

TABLE- 18

KEY FACTORS FOR TOP 30 HIGH VALUE IMPORTED ITEMS (based on 2004-05 value of Imports) FROM THAILAND

			2004-05		2004-05	2004-05		2004-05	2004-05	2004-05	2004-05	2004-05	2004-05
Sl. No.	HS Code	Whether Covered under EARLY HARVEST SCHEME	% of Total Value of imports from Thailand in 2004-05	Base year for next two columns	Incremental Trend of imports from Thailand (Volume) in % in comparison to base yr.	Incremental Trend of imports from Thailand (Value) in % in comparison to base yr.	Base year for next two columns	Incremental Trend of World Import (Volume) in % in comparison to base yr.	Incremental Trend of World Import (Value) in % in comparison to base yr.	Market Share of imports from Thailand in World Imports (Volume) in %	Market Share of imports from Thailand in World Imports (Value) in %	Per Unit Import Price from Thailand (in Rs.)	Per Unit World Import Price for India (in Rs.)
1	87089900	NO	5.82	2001-02	2478.61	3628.85	2001-02	71.06	144.20	7.21	9.32	518.01	401.10
2	84082020	NO	2.53	2002-03	621.77	1199.96	2001-02	2213.68	2831.21	20.36	23.98	105688.60	89717.97
3	59021010	NO	2.47	2001-02	109.74	136.62	2001-02	78.80	89.31	23.02	25.31	158.52	144.17
4	40012100	NO	2.37	2001-02	139.21	385.97	2001-02	88.57	277.38	45.78	45.59	57.93	58.17
5	84733099	NO	2.15	2001-02	-28.97	-84.21	2001-02	4.70	-6.70	8.32	4.84	941.79	1616.86
6	73269099	YES	1.89	2001-02	2539.54	2399.66	2001-02	267.53	309.91	9.64	8.76	298.09	328.10
7	85281212	YES	1.69	2004-05	0.00	0.00	2003-04	2330.71	2331.81	94.91	88.81	6736.47	7198.58
8	33051090	NO	1.67	2001-02	3680.19	9459.91	2001-02	1604.18	2025.37	70.68	79.99	226.64	200.24
9	40012990	NO	1.59	2001-02	188.52	514.33	2001-02	170.53	462.85	36.33	36.25	59.48	59.62
10	39074000	YES	1.52	2001-02	18210.91	14549.08	2001-02	190.10	160.68	17.41	19.89	110.06	96.34
11	72042190	NO	1.49	2001-02	486.12	1395.12	2001-02	136.60	358.53	6.26	7.32	63.02	53.87
12	85281213	YES	1.44	2004-05	0.00	0.00	2003-04	812.90	909.04	93.88	91.14	7955.33	8194.17
13	84717020	NO	1.43	2001-02	6223.59	2838.11	2001-02	218.70	133.12	6.37	5.34	2272.69	2711.55
14	71031029	YES	1.08	2001-02	301.32	317.64	2001-02	394.80	102.76	18.45	21.06	5523.37	4838.41
15	84716027	NO	1.06	2003-04	-21.90	-17.40	2003-04	-10.53	-14.45	41.17	23.94	2010.93	3458.54
16	84159000	NO	1.01	2001-02	115.90	129.03	2001-02	44.78	122.08	10.60	9.53	705.11	783.90
17	85446090	NO	0.95	2001-02	6373.35	6793.04	2001-02	2466.45	1346.80	12.35	22.34	371.69	205.44
18	84143000	NO	0.95	2001-02	55.21	105.26	2001-02	68.17	64.15	5.69	13.81	5171.71	2130.74
19	85281219	YES	0.90	2004-05	0.00	0.00	2003-04	244.80	207.66	56.65	37.62	8210.27	12361.93
20	85072000	NO	0.90	2001-02	1570.32	1919.33	2001-02	56.61	81.95	10.57	26.14	836.11	338.00
21	72091790	NO	0.88	2001-02	12.43	5.67	2001-02	33.29	64.97	8.19	9.70	37.30	31.48
22	29024100	NO	0.86	2004-05	0.00	0.00	2001-02	631.16	1373.38	13.14	11.71	34.70	38.94
23	39013000	NO	0.78	2001-02	71.63	143.16	2001-02	359.06	467.04	12.98	12.63	50.08	51.49
24	40021990	NO	0.74	2001-02	24.37	165.48	2001-02	118.19	246.65	9.51	10.18	69.38	64.80
25	84151010	YES	0.73	2003-04	-18.66	-23.25	2003-04	54.37	16.29	30.34	39.11	10023.82	7775.45
26	85175099	NO	0.69	2003-04	209.20	311.19	2003-04	421.75	141.37	1.07	2.21	95472.86	46444.68
27	39011010	NO	0.69	2001-02	59.87	47.51	2001-02	59.94	122.83	7.50	6.45	40.27	46.81
28	85281214	YES	0.65	2004-05	0.00	0.00	2003-04	4526.25	2666.02	61.20	71.73	10751.30	9172.49
29	87032391	NO	0.64	2003-04	43.75	27.22	2003-04	16.85	29.21	21.82	9.77	208526.96	465943.07
30	74111000	NO	0.64	2001-02	181.44	259.09	2001-02	72.57	102.57	45.78	44.61	196.23	201.39

			THAILAND	THAILAND		World	World	THAILAND	World	THAILAND & World		
Sl. No.	HS Code	Base year for next two columns	CAGR - VOLUME (in %)	CAGR- VALUE (in %)	Base year for next two columns	CAGR- VOLUME (in %)	CAGR- VALUE (in %)	CORRELATION - TREND OF VOLUME / VALUE	CORRELATION - TREND OF VOLUME / VALUE	CORRELATION - TREND OF VOLUME	CORRELATION - TREND OF VALUE	CORRELATION - UNIT PRICE
1	87089900	2001-02	195.43	234.09	2001-02	19.60	34.66	1.00	0.96	0.91	0.99	0.51
2	84082020	2002-03	168.66	260.55	2001-02	184.95	208.33	0.96	0.27	0.89	0.86	#DIV/0!
3	59021010	2001-02	28.00	33.26	2001-02	21.37	23.71	0.89	0.95	0.94	0.99	0.97
4	40012100	2001-02	33.74	69.38	2001-02	23.54	55.69	0.98	0.96	0.95	0.99	1.00
5	84733099	2001-02	-10.78	-45.96	2001-02	1.54	-2.28	0.79	0.52	-0.08	0.81	0.84
6	73269099	2001-02	197.74	192.39	2001-02	54.32	60.04	1.00	1.00	0.95	0.97	-0.63
7	85281212	2004-05	0.00	0.00	2004-05	0.00	0.00	1.00	1.00	1.00	1.00	#DIV/0!
8	33051090	2001-02	235.61	357.25	2001-02	157.34	177.00	0.98	1.00	0.99	1.00	0.99
9	40012990	2001-02	42.36	83.15	2001-02	39.34	77.88	1.00	0.98	0.84	0.92	1.00
10	39074000	2001-02	467.85	427.15	2001-02	42.62	37.63	0.96	0.97	0.97	0.97	0.99
11	72042190	2001-02	80.30	146.35	2001-02	33.25	66.13	0.99	0.97	0.96	0.96	0.99
12	85281213	2004-05	0.00	0.00	2003-04	812.90	909.04	1.00	1.00	0.99	1.00	#DIV/0!
13	84717020	2001-02	298.40	208.57	2001-02	47.16	32.59	1.00	1.00	0.91	0.91	0.90
14	71031029	2001-02	58.91	61.04	2001-02	70.40	26.57	0.99	0.40	0.16	0.98	0.67
15	84716027	2003-04	-21.90	-17.40	2003-04	-10.53	-14.45	1.00	1.00	1.00	1.00	#DIV/0!
16	84159000	2001-02	29.25	31.82	2001-02	13.13	30.47	0.96	0.91	1.00	0.99	0.46
17	85446090	2001-02	301.52	310.02	2001-02	194.97	143.67	0.99	1.00	1.00	0.99	0.55
18	84143000	2001-02	15.78	27.09	2001-02	18.92	17.96	0.75	0.99	0.14	0.81	-0.83
19	85281219	2004-05	0.00	0.00	2003-04	244.80	207.66	1.00	1.00	0.96	0.95	#DIV/0!
20	85072000	2001-02	155.62	172.31	2001-02	16.13	22.08	1.00	0.99	0.84	0.92	0.88

			THAILAND	THAILAND		World	World	THAILAND	World	THAILAND & World		
Sl. No.	HS Code	Base year for next two columns	CAGR - VOLUME (in %)	CAGR-VALUE (in %)	Base year for next two columns	CAGR-VOLUME (in %)	CAGR-VALUE (in %)	CORRELATION - TREND OF VOLUME / VALUE	CORRELATION - TREND OF VOLUME / VALUE	CORRELATION - TREND OF VOLUME	CORRELATION - TREND OF VALUE	CORRELATION - UNIT PRICE
21	72091790	2001-02	3.98	1.86	2001-02	10.05	18.16	0.98	0.99	0.46	0.54	-0.39
22	29024100	2004-05	0.00	0.00	2001-02	94.09	145.15	1.00	1.00	0.99	1.00	#DIV/0!
23	39013000	2001-02	19.73	34.47	2001-02	66.20	78.32	0.97	0.99	0.62	0.88	0.37
24	40021990	2001-02	7.54	38.47	2001-02	29.70	51.34	0.89	0.97	0.52	0.93	1.00
25	84151010	2003-04	-18.66	-23.25	2003-04	54.37	16.29	1.00	0.98	0.91	0.96	#DIV/0!
26	85175099	2003-04	209.20	311.19	2003-04	421.75	141.37	1.00	0.97	0.99	0.98	#DIV/0!
27	39011010	2001-02	16.93	13.83	2001-02	16.94	30.62	0.90	0.87	1.00	0.95	0.29
28	85281214	2004-05	0.00	0.00	2004-05	0.00	0.00	1.00	1.00	1.00	1.00	#DIV/0!
29	87032391	2003-04	43.75	27.22	2003-04	16.85	29.21	1.00	1.00	0.99	1.00	#DIV/0!
30	74111000	2001-02	41.19	53.13	2001-02	19.95	26.53	0.97	0.97	0.95	0.97	0.97

NOTES

1. Base year have been changed, where CAGR for a particular product shows growth of more than 999%.
2. Base year for Trend Calculation have been changed in some cases, keeping in view the base year for CAGR and the actual trade data.
3. Base year for Trend Calculation have been changed in some cases, where trend exceeds 99999%.
4. Correlation among different DATA SERIES have been calculated by using the CORREL function active in the MS EXCEL spreadsheet.
5. Correlation of +1 denotes perfect positive correlation, -1 denotes perfect negative correlation, 0 denotes least correlation among the data series.
6. Trend is taken as 100% and CAGR as 0% in cases where either the data figures prior to 2004-05 are either zero or negligible.

TABLE-19

KEY FACTORS FOR ALL SAMPLED PRODUCTS COVERED UNDER EARLY HARVEST SCHEME

Sl. No.	HS Code	Particulars	2004-05 % of Total Value of imports from Thailand in 2004-05	Base year for next two columns	2004-05 Incremental Trend of imports from Thailand (Volume) in % in comparison to base yr.	2004-05 Incremental Trend of imports from Thailand (Value) in % in comparison to base yr.	Base year for next two columns	2004-05 Incremental Trend of World Import (Volume) in % in comparison to base yr.
1	73269099	ALL OTHER ARTICLES OF IRON/STEEL NES OTHER STEERING OR RUDDER EQUIPMENT FOR SHIPS AND BOATS, N.E.S. (73269019)	1.89	2001-02	2539.54	2399.66	2001-02	267.53
2	85281212	COLOUR TV SET OF SCRN SIZE BETN 36 & 54 CM	1.69	2004-05	0.00	0.00	2003-04	2330.71
3	39074000	POLYCARBONATES	1.52	2001-02	18210.91	14549.08	2001-02	190.10
4	85281213	COLOUR TV SET OF SCRN SIZE BETN 54 & 68 CM	1.44	2004-05	0.00	0.00	2003-04	812.90
5	71031029	OTHER SEMI PRECIOUS STONE UNCUT (71031009)	1.08	2001-02	301.32	317.64	2001-02	394.80
6	85281219	OTHER LCD TV SET	0.90	2004-05	0.00	0.00	2003-04	244.80
7	84151010	SPLIT SYSTEM AIR CONDITIONING MACHINES	0.73	2003-04	-18.66	-23.25	2003-04	54.37
8	85281214	COLOUR TV SET OF SCRN SIZE BETN 68 & 74 CM	0.65	2004-05	0.00	0.00	2003-04	4526.25
9	76012010	ALUMINIUM INGOTS -ALLOYED (76012001)	0.54	2002-03	982.61	1084.86	2001-02	150.49
10	39073010	EPOXY RESINS (39073001)	0.50	2001-02	180.98	212.07	2001-02	111.33
11	84151090	OTHR WINDOW/WALL TYPES SELF-CONTAINED AIR CONDITIONING MACHINES (84151000)	0.48	2001-02	-41.42	42.63	2001-02	33.62
12	85281211	COLOUR TV SET OF SCREEN SIZE UPTO 36 CM	0.47	2004-05	0.00	0.00	2003-04	1304.91
13	71031019	OTHR PRCS STONE(E.G.AQUAMARINE CHRISOBARYLE-TOPAZ ETC) UNCUT	0.47	2001-02	-59.11	-32.01	2001-02	-68.04
14	85291029	OTHR ANTENNA FR OTHR USE	0.38	2003-04	-41.09	-7.45	2003-04	86.93
15	85401110	CTV PCTR TUB 20/21 EXCEPT 21 F& FST	0.36	2004-05	0.00	0.00	2003-04	6.61
16	85401190	OTHERS	0.26	2004-05	0.00	0.00	2003-04	33.14
17	94019000	OTHER SEATS OF HEADING 9401	0.26	2001-02	14943.69	9633.88	2001-02	43.61
18	84378020	RICE MILL MACHINERY (84378002)	0.25	2001-02	1100.00	841.49	2001-02	1400.00
19	39071000	POLYACETALS	0.21	2001-02	436.64	474.16	2001-02	54.99
20	39079990	OTHER POLYESTERS (SATURATED) NES (39079900)	0.19	2001-02	215.90	168.16	2001-02	122.56
21	71031012	RUBY AND SAPPHIRE,UNCUT (71031002)	0.18	2001-02	219.76	63.52	2001-02	183.06
22	85043100	OTHR TRNSFRMRS HVNG A PWR HNDLNG CAPACITY NOT EXCDNG 1 KVA	0.18	2003-04	338.74	-28.40	2003-04	34.14
23	84798999	OTHERS (84798919)	0.17	2001-02	-60.00	2103.44	2001-02	79.99
24	85122010	HEAD LAMPS,TAIL LAMP,STOP LAMP, SIDE LAMP,BLINKERS (85122001)	0.16	2001-02	223.74	2008.95	2001-02	217.29
25	84182100	COMPRESSION-TYPE REFRIGERATORS,HOUSEHOLD	0.15	2001-02	-60.47	-42.26	2001-02	-18.39
26	84219900	OTHR PARTS OF FLTRNG/PURFYNG MCHNRY	0.15	2001-02	182.43	5.09	2001-02	57.20
27	71031011	EMERALS,UNCUT (71031001)	0.14	2001-02	452.94	126.36	2001-02	43.29
28	71049000	OTHR SYN/RECNCTRCTD PRCS/SEMI PRCS STONES	0.13	2001-02	-18.80	928.87	2001-02	-98.03
29	85179010	POPLTD. LOADED OR STUFFD PRNTD CRCUIT BRDS	0.12	2003-04	393.37	1287.56	2003-04	111.17
30	85179090	OTHR PARTS OF TELEPHONC/TELEGRPHC APPARTS (85179000)	0.11	2001-02	-48.02	44.19	2001-02	34.30
31	39073090	OTHERS (RESINS)(39073009)	0.11	2001-02	736.24	734.08	2001-02	206.00
32	85281215	COLOUR TV SET OF SCRN SIZE BETN 74 & 87 CM	0.11	2003-04	7866.67	4721.22	2003-04	2028.57
33	39081090	OTHERS (POLYAMIDE)	0.11	2003-04	29.95	76.75	2003-04	31.52

NOTES

1. Base year have been changed. where CAGR for a particular product shows growth of more than 999%.
2. Base year for Trend Calculation have been changed in some cases, keeping in view the base year for CAGR and the actual trade data.
3. Base year for Trend Calculation have been changed in some cases, where trend exceeds 99999%.
4. Correlation among different DATA SERIES have been calculated by using the CORREL function active in the MS EXCEL spreadsheet.
5. Correlation of +1 denotes perfect positive correlation, -1 denotes perfect negative correlation, 0 denotes least correlation among the data series.
6. For Trend of imports-Thailand-Volume and CAGR-Thailand-Volume in case of HS Code 84378020, the base year is taken as 2002-03.
7. For CAGR-Thailand-Volume in case of HS Code 85179010, the base year is taken as 2003-04.
8. For CAGR-World imports-Volume in case of HS Codes 85281211 & 85281215, the base year is taken as 2004-05.
9. Trend is taken as 100% and CAGR as 0% in cases where either the data figures prior to 2004-05 are either zero or negligible.

TABLE- 19

KEY FACTORS FOR ALL SAMPLED PRODUCTS COVERED UNDER EARLY HARVEST SCHEME

			2004-05	2004-05	2004-05	2004-05	2004-05
Sl. No.	HS Code	Particulars	Incremental Trend of World Import (Value) in % in comparison to base yr.	Market Share of imports from Thailand in World Imports (Volume) in %	Market Share of imports from Thailand in World Imports (Value) in %	Per Unit Import Price from Thailand (in Rs.)	Per Unit World Import Price for India (in Rs.)
1	73269099	ALL OTHER ARTICLES OF IRON/STEEL NES OTHER STEERING OR RUDDER EQUIPMENT FOR SHIPS AND BOATS, N.E.S. (73269019)	309.91	9.64	8.76	298.09	328.10
2	85281212	COLOUR TV SET OF SCRN SIZE BETN 36 & 54 CM	2331.81	94.91	88.81	6736.47	7198.58
3	39074000	POLYCARBONATES	160.68	17.41	19.89	110.06	96.34
4	85281213	COLOUR TV SET OF SCRN SIZE BETN 54 & 68 CM	909.04	93.88	91.14	7955.33	8194.17
5	71031029	OTHER SEMI PRECIOUS STONE UNCUT (71031009)	102.76	18.45	21.06	5523.37	4838.41
6	85281219	OTHER LCD TV SET	207.66	56.65	37.62	8210.27	12361.93
7	84151010	SPLIT SYSTEM AIR CONDITIONING MACHINES	16.29	30.34	39.11	10023.82	7775.45
8	85281214	COLOUR TV SET OF SCRN SIZE BETN 68 & 74 CM	2666.02	61.20	71.73	10751.30	9172.49
9	76012010	ALUMINIUM INGOTS -ALLOYED (76012001)	204.07	10.40	9.79	81.49	86.57
10	39073010	EPOXY RESINS (39073001)	102.69	22.75	20.08	106.90	121.14
11	84151090	OTHR WINDOW/WALL TYPES SELF-CONTAINED AIR CONDITIONING MACHINES (84151000)	39.59	20.64	27.20	13215.08	10028.21
12	85281211	COLOUR TV SET OF SCREEN SIZE UPTO 36 CM	489.70	21.71	26.33	7088.60	5845.58
13	71031019	OTHR PRCS STONE(E.G.AQUAMARINE CHRISOBARYLE-TOPAZ ETC) UNCUT	-30.46	17.44	13.86	10817.29	13608.50
14	85291029	OTHR ANTENNA FR OTHR USE	94.84	8.70	8.88	928.16	909.95
15	85401110	CTV PCTR TUB 20/21 EXCEPT 21 F& FST	-6.05	7.20	5.73	2035.18	2559.65
16	85401190	OTHERS	13.04	4.20	3.86	2052.23	2230.93
17	94019000	OTHER SEATS OF HEADING 9401	89.00	19.12	29.51	617.52	400.19
18	84378020	RICE MILL MACHINERY (84378002)	745.13	26.67	43.46	768333.33	471433.33
19	39071000	POLYACETALS	91.10	12.94	15.94	67.53	54.81
20	39079990	OTHER POLYESTERS (SATURATED) NES (39079900)	96.64	4.95	4.22	68.95	80.91
21	71031012	RUBY AND SAPPHIRE,UNCUT (71031002)	-21.53	50.48	46.36	8681.21	9451.75
22	85043100	OTHR TRNSFRMRS HVNG A PWR HNDLNG CAPACITY NOT EXCDNG 1 KVA	-0.04	19.42	6.38	16.85	51.31
23	84798999	OTHERS (84798919)	221.67	0.15	0.72	1584825.00	325849.02
24	85122010	HEAD LAMPS,TAIL LAMP,STOP LAMP, SIDE LAMP,BLINKERS (85122001)	109.25	3.40	17.38	136.23	26.67
25	84182100	COMPRESSION-TYPE REFRIGERATORS,HOUSEHOLD	-14.43	8.03	9.34	11186.07	9615.52
26	84219900	OTHR PARTS OF FLTRNG/PURFYNG MCHNRY	94.14	3.35	2.06	589.83	957.47
27	71031011	EMERALS,UNCUT (71031001)	86.72	12.71	6.91	7839.67	14413.85
28	71049000	OTHR SYN/RECNCTRCTD PRCS/SEMI PRCS STONES	385.81	9.00	16.38	3750.75	2060.62
29	85179010	POPLTD, LOADED OR STUFFD PRNTD CRCUIT BRDS	172.36	0.70	0.83	5435.04	4538.81
30	85179090	OTHR PARTS OF TELEPHONC/TELEGRPHC APPARTS (85179000)	89.95	0.57	0.54	2837.36	2971.95
31	39073090	OTHERS (RESINS)(39073009)	271.79	9.90	7.72	116.28	149.11
32	85281215	COLOUR TV SET OF SCRN SIZE BETN 74 & 87 CM	800.88	80.20	63.09	8795.19	11180.87
33	39081090	OTHERS (POLYAMIDE)	75.65	7.21	4.69	80.31	123.45

TABLE- 19

KEY FACTORS FOR ALL SAMPLED PRODUCTS COVERED UNDER EARLY HARVEST SCHEME

				THAILANI	THAILAND		World	World
Sl. No.	HS Code	Particulars	Base year for next two columns	CAGR - VOLUME (in %)	CAGR- VALUE (in %)	Base year for next two columns	CAGR- VOLUME (in %)	CAGR- VALUE (in %)
1	73269099	ALL OTHER ARTICLES OF IRON/STEEL NES OTHER STEERING OR RUDDER EQUIPMENT FOR SHIPS AND BOATS. N.E.S. (73269019)	2001-02	197.74	192.39	2001-02	54.32	60.04
2	85281212	COLOUR TV SET OF SCRN SIZE BETN 36 & 54 CM	2004-05	0.00	0.00	2004-05	0.00	0.00
3	39074000	POLYCARBONATES	2001-02	467.85	427.15	2001-02	42.62	37.63
4	85281213	COLOUR TV SET OF SCRN SIZE BETN 54 & 68 CM	2004-05	0.00	0.00	2003-04	812.90	909.04
5	71031029	OTHER SEMI PRECIOUS STONE UNCUT (71031009)	2001-02	58.91	61.04	2001-02	70.40	26.57
6	85281219	OTHER LCD TV SET	2004-05	0.00	0.00	2003-04	244.80	207.66
7	84151010	SPLIT SYSTEM AIR CONDITIONING MACHINES	2003-04	-18.66	-23.25	2003-04	54.37	16.29
8	85281214	COLOUR TV SET OF SCRN SIZE BETN 68 & 74 CM	2004-05	0.00	0.00	2004-05	0.00	0.00
9	76012010	ALUMINIUM INGOTS -ALLOYED (76012001)	2002-03	229.03	244.22	2001-02	35.81	44.87
10	39073010	EPOXY RESINS (39073001)	2001-02	41.11	46.13	2001-02	28.33	26.55
11	84151090	OTHR WINDOW/WALL TYPES SELF-CONTAINED AIR CONDITIONING MACHINES (84151000)	2001-02	-16.33	12.57	2001-02	10.14	11.76
12	85281211	COLOUR TV SET OF SCREEN SIZE UPTO 36 CM	2004-05	0.00	0.00	2003-04	0.00	489.70
13	71031019	OTHR PRCS STONE(E.G.AQUAMARINE CHRISOBARYLE-TOPAZ ETC) UNCUT	2001-02	-25.78	-12.07	2001-02	-31.63	-11.40
14	85291029	OTHR ANTENNA FR OTHR USE	2003-04	-41.09	-7.45	2003-04	86.93	94.84
15	85401110	CTV PCTR TUB 20/21 EXCEPT 21 F& FST	2004-05	0.00	0.00	2003-04	6.61	-6.05
16	85401190	OTHERS	2004-05	0.00	0.00	2003-04	33.14	13.04
17	94019000	OTHER SEATS OF HEADING 9401	2001-02	431.84	360.00	2001-02	12.82	23.64
18	84378020	RICE MILL MACHINERY (84378002)	2001-02	246.41	111.16	2001-02	146.62	103.69
19	39071000	POLYACETALS	2001-02	75.08	79.07	2001-02	15.73	24.09
20	39079990	OTHER POLYESTERS (SATURATED) NES (39079900)	2001-02	46.73	38.93	2001-02	30.56	25.28
21	71031012	RUBY AND SAPPHIRE,UNCUT (71031002)	2001-02	47.32	17.81	2001-02	41.46	-7.76
22	85043100	OTHR TRNSFRMRS HVNG A PWR HNDLNG CAPACITY NOT EXCDNG 1 KVA	2003-04	338.74	-28.40	2003-04	34.14	-0.04
23	84798999	OTHERS (84798919)	2001-02	-26.32	180.35	2001-02	21.64	47.62
24	85122010	HEAD LAMPS,TAIL LAMP,STOP LAMP, SIDE LAMP,BLINKERS (85122001)	2001-02	47.93	176.28	2001-02	46.94	27.91
25	84182100	COMPRESSION-TYPE REFRIGERATORS,HOUSEHOLD	2001-02	-26.61	-16.73	2001-02	-6.55	-5.06
26	84219900	OTHR PARTS OF FLTRNG/PURFYNG MCHNRY	2001-02	41.35	1.67	2001-02	16.28	24.75
27	71031011	EMERALS,UNCUT (71031001)	2001-02	76.83	31.30	2001-02	12.74	23.14
28	71049000	OTHR SYN/RECNCTRCTD PRCS/SEMI PRCS STONES	2001-02	-6.71	117.50	2001-02	-72.99	69.36
29	85179010	POPLTD, LOADED OR STUFFD PRNTD CRCUIT BRDS	2004-05	393.37	0.00	2003-04	111.17	172.36
30	85179090	OTHR PARTS OF TELEPHONC/TELEGRPHC APPARTS (85179000)	2001-02	-19.59	12.97	2001-02	10.33	23.85
31	39073090	OTHERS (RESINS)(39073009)	2001-02	102.98	102.80	2001-02	45.18	54.92
32	85281215	COLOUR TV SET OF SCRN SIZE BETN 74 & 87 CM	2004-05	0.00	0.00	2003-04	0.00	800.88
33	39081090	OTHERS (POLYAMIDE)	2003-04	29.95	76.75	2003-04	31.52	75.65

TABLE- 19

KEY FACTORS FOR ALL SAMPLED PRODUCTS COVERED UNDER EARLY HARVEST SCHEME

			THAILAND	World	THAILAND & World		
Sl. No.	HS Code	Particulars	CORRELATION - TREND OF VOLUME / VALUE	CORRELATION - TREND OF VOLUME / VALUE	CORRELATION - TREND OF VOLUME	CORRELATION - TREND OF VALUE	CORRELATION - UNIT PRICE
1	73269099	ALL OTHER ARTICLES OF IRON/STEEL NES OTHER STEERING OR RUDDER EQUIPMENT FOR SHIPS AND BOATS, N.E.S. (73269019)	1.00	1.00	0.95	0.97	-0.63
2	85281212	COLOUR TV SET OF SCRN SIZE BETN 36 & 54 CM	1.00	1.00	1.00	1.00	#DIV/0!
3	39074000	POLYCARBONATES	0.96	0.97	0.97	0.97	0.99
4	85281213	COLOUR TV SET OF SCRN SIZE BETN 54 & 68 CM	1.00	1.00	0.99	1.00	#DIV/0!
5	71031029	OTHER SEMI PRECIOUS STONE UNCUT (71031009)	0.99	0.40	0.16	0.98	0.67
6	85281219	OTHER LCD TV SET	1.00	1.00	0.96	0.95	#DIV/0!
7	84151010	SPLIT SYSTEM AIR CONDITIONING MACHINES	1.00	0.98	0.91	0.96	#DIV/0!
8	85281214	COLOUR TV SET OF SCRN SIZE BETN 68 & 74 CM	1.00	1.00	1.00	1.00	#DIV/0!
9	76012010	ALUMINIUM INGOTS -ALLOYED (76012001)	1.00	1.00	0.97	0.98	#DIV/0!
10	39073010	EPOXY RESINS (39073001)	0.98	0.96	0.86	0.88	0.80
11	84151090	OTHR WINDOW/WALL TYPES SELF-CONTAINED AIR CONDITIONING MACHINES (84151000)	0.12	-0.55	-0.48	0.70	0.70
12	85281211	COLOUR TV SET OF SCREEN SIZE UPTO 36 CM	1.00	1.00	1.00	0.99	#DIV/0!
13	71031019	OTHR PRCS STONE(E.G.AQUAMARINE CHRISOBARYLE-TOPAZ ETC) UNCUT	0.82	-0.78	-0.47	1.00	0.59
14	85291029	OTHR ANTENNA FR OTHR USE	0.96	1.00	0.73	0.89	#DIV/0!
15	85401110	CTV PCTR TUB 20/21 EXCEPT 21 F& FST	1.00	1.00	0.61	0.54	#DIV/0!
16	85401190	OTHERS	1.00	0.99	0.73	0.65	#DIV/0!
17	94019000	OTHER SEATS OF HEADING 9401	1.00	0.80	0.82	0.94	-0.99
18	84378020	RICE MILL MACHINERY (84378002)	0.99	0.98	0.99	0.99	#DIV/0!
19	39071000	POLYACETALS	1.00	0.93	0.74	0.94	-0.42
20	39079990	OTHER POLYESTERS (SATURATED) NES (39079900)	0.96	0.98	0.79	0.82	0.99
21	71031012	RUBY AND SAPPHIRE UNCUT (71031002)	0.89	0.51	0.46	0.44	0.99
22	85043100	OTHR TRNSFRMRS HVNG A PWR HNDLNG CAPACITY NOT EXCDNG 1 KVA	0.58	0.98	0.87	0.97	#DIV/0!
23	84798999	OTHERS (84798919)	-0.17	0.00	-0.01	0.87	0.70
24	85122010	HEAD LAMPS,TAIL LAMP,STOP LAMP, SIDE LAMP,BLINKERS (85122001)	0.92	0.89	0.63	1.00	-0.90
25	84182100	COMPRESSION-TYPE REFRIGERATORS,HOUSEHOLD	1.00	0.99	0.93	0.89	0.97
26	84219900	OTHR PARTS OF FLTRNG/PURFYNG MCHNRY	0.51	0.96	0.95	0.43	-0.81
27	71031011	EMERALS,UNCUT (71031001)	0.87	0.75	0.38	0.65	-0.69
28	71049000	OTHR SYN/RECNCTRCTD PRCS/SEMI PRCS STONES	0.14	-0.48	0.71	0.99	0.93
29	85179010	POPLTD, LOADED OR STUFFD PRNTD CRCUIT BRDS	0.99	0.99	0.96	0.95	#DIV/0!
30	85179090	OTHR PARTS OF TELEPHONC/TELEGRPHC APPARTS (85179000)	0.97	0.78	0.87	0.57	0.72
31	39073090	OTHERS (RESINS)(39073009)	0.97	1.00	1.00	0.98	-0.06
32	85281215	COLOUR TV SET OF SCRN SIZE BETN 74 & 87 CM	1.00	1.00	1.00	1.00	#DIV/0!
33	39081090	OTHERS (POLYAMIDE)	0.98	0.98	1.00	1.00	#DIV/0!

TABLE- 20

KEY FACTORS FOR TOP 20 SAMPLED PRODUCTS (CAGR WISE - value of imports in 2004-05) NOT COVERED UNDER EARLY HARVEST SCHEME

			2004-05		2004-05	2004-05		2004-05	2004-05	2004-05	2004-05	2004-05	2004-05		THAILAND	THAILAND
Sl. No	HS Code	Particulars	% of Total Value of imports from Thailand in 2004-05	Base year for next two columns	Incremental Trend of imports from Thailand (Volume) in % in comparison to base yr.	Incremental Trend of imports from Thailand (Value) in % in comparison to base yr.	Base year for next two columns	Incremental Trend of World Import (Volume) in % in comparison to base yr.	Incremental Trend of World Import (Value) in % in comparison to base yr.	Market Share of imports from Thailand in World Imports (Volume) in %	Market Share of imports from Thailand in World Imports (Value) in %	Per Unit Import Price from Thailand (in Rs.)	Per Unit World Import Price for India (in Rs.)	Base year for next two columns	CAGR - VOLUME (in %)	CAGR-VALUE (in %)
1	72279010	BARS & RODS OF VALVE SPRNG STL QULTY (72279001)	0.22	2003-04	695.23	939.22	2001-02	298.17	284.87	20.95	18.85	33.72	37.48	2003-04	695.23	939.22
2	85441190	OTHER WINDING WIRE OF COPPER	0.22	2003-04	301.73	927.45	2003-04	49.25	63.96	6.28	9.60	469.50	306.92	2003-04	301.73	927.45
3	72044900	OTHER WASTE AND SCRAP (72044909)	0.10	2001-02	84388.54	91700.00	2001-02	32.23	163.24	0.13	0.12	10.87	11.93	2001-02	845.36	871.88
4	25210090	LIMESTONE OTHR THN LIMESTONE FLUX (25210009)	0.38	2002-03	3259.53	472.59	2001-02	-17.36	25.39	22.33	22.90	1.38	1.34	2001-02	479.61	750.96
5	85443000	IGNTN WIRING SETS & OTHR WIRING SETS OF A KIND USED IN VEHICLES AIRCRAFT/SHIPS	0.16	2001-02	62212.50	51967.80	2001-02	207.97	255.75	39.00	34.86	410.83	459.59	2001-02	754.13	704.49
6	60012200	LOOPED PILE FBRCS OF MAN-MADE FIBRES	0.11	2001-02	37467.05	44208.42	2001-02	1315.55	1692.92	13.30	11.84	127.33	143.03	2001-02	621.55	662.36
7	85173000	TELEPHONIC/TELEGRPHC SWTCHING APPRTS	0.10	2003-04	463.64	584.70	2003-04	-28.76	39.81	2.68	0.52	63014.52	326628.52	2003-04	463.64	584.70
8	42022190	OTHER LEATHER HAND BAGS. (42022109)	0.11	2001-02	2009.35	27938.82	2001-02	1157.95	2871.63	11.23	61.85	1888.30	342.81	2001-02	176.30	554.52
9	85044029	OTHER RECTIFIERS (85044003)	0.17	2001-02	7076.07	21116.78	2001-02	3975.77	3844.21	6.45	4.20	753.05	1156.87	2001-02	315.56	496.43
10	39219099	OTHR PLTS,SHTS,FILM FOIL,STRIP ETC NES OTHER	0.27	2003-04	661.96	489.02	2003-04	48.44	34.42	10.89	11.26	209.41	202.47	2003-04	661.96	489.02
11	87081090	BUMPERS ETC FOR OTHR VHCLS	0.19	2003-04	236.75	475.35	2003-04	-45.89	-18.97	2.65	11.22	2275.52	538.54	2003-04	236.75	475.35
12	85271300	OTHER APARATUS COMBIND WTH SOUND RECORDNG OR REPRODUCNG APARATUS	0.11	2002-03	852.46	2817.93	2001-02	1690.50	1306.58	5.23	29.60	6835.28	1206.58	2002-03	208.62	440.18
13	85445990	OTHR ELCTRC CNDCTRS FOR 80V<="1000V" WTH FITTED CONNECTRS NT>	0.10	2003-04	333.17	434.74	2003-04	9.27	17.61	2.85	2.77	478.28	492.70	2003-04	333.17	434.74
14	44111990	OTHER BOARD	0.13	2003-04	412.67	422.98	2003-04	20.74	35.80	30.25	30.55	13.82	13.68	2003-04	412.67	422.98
15	72089000	OTHR FLAT ROLLED PRODUCTS. N.E.S	0.62	2001-02	18009.47	13530.75	2001-02	81.09	148.42	1.27	1.29	26.95	26.55	2001-02	465.76	414.64
16	33051090	HAIR SHAMPOOS (NON-SPIRITUOUS) (33051002)	1.67	2001-02	3680.19	9459.91	2001-02	1604.18	2025.37	70.68	79.99	226.64	200.24	2001-02	235.61	357.25
17	85175099	OTHR APARTUS,FR CARRIER/DIGITAL LINE SYSTM	0.69	2003-04	209.20	311.19	2003-04	421.75	141.37	1.07	2.21	95472.86	46444.68	2003-04	209.20	311.19
18	85446090	OTHR ELCTRC CNDCTRS FR A VLTG EXCDG 1000 V (85446000)	0.95	2001-02	6373.35	6793.04	2001-02	2466.45	1346.80	12.35	22.34	371.69	205.44	2001-02	301.52	310.02
19	83023090	OTHERS (83023009)	0.17	2002-03	845.44	1460.33	2001-02	2685.19	1151.52	24.86	17.97	191.39	264.80	2002-03	207.48	295.01
20	85413010	THYRISTORS (85413001)	0.18	2001-02	1255.87	5792.21	2001-02	274.95	-49.41	11.43	12.52	25.12	22.93	2001-02	138.45	289.13

NOTES

1 Base year have been changed, where CAGR for a particular product shows growth of more than 999%.
2 Base year for Trend Calculation have been changed in some cases, keeping in view the base year for CAGR and the actual trade data.
3 Base year for Trend Calculation have been changed in some cases, where trend exceeds 99999%.
4 Correlation among different DATA SERIES have been calculated by using the CORREL function active in the MS EXCEL spreadsheet.
5 Correlation of +1 denotes perfect positive correlation, -1 denotes perfect negative correlation. 0 denotes least correlation among the data series.
6 Base year for CAGR-Thailand-Volume in case of HS Code 25210090 is taken as 2002-03
7 Trend is taken as 100% and CAGR as 0% in cases where either the data figures prior to 2004-05 are either zero or negligible.

Sl. No.	HS Code	Particulars	Base year for next two columns	World	World	THAILAND	World	THAILAND & World		
				CAGR-VOLUME (in %)	CAGR-VALUE (in %)	CORRELATION - TREND OF VOLUME / VALUE	CORRELATION TREND OF VOLUME / VALUE	CORRELATION - TREND OF VOLUME	CORRELATION - TREND OF VALUE	CORRELATION - UNIT PRICE
1	72279010	BARS & RODS OF VALVE SPRNG STL QULTY (72279001)	2001-02	58.50	56.71	1.00	0.98	0.71	0.59	#DIV/0!
2	85441190	OTHER WINDING WIRE OF COPPER	2003-04	49.25	63.96	0.99	1.00	0.91	0.86	#DIV/0!
3	72044900	OTHER WASTE AND SCRAP (72044909)	2001-02	9.76	38.08	0.91	0.98	0.91	0.89	-0.47
4	25210090	LIMESTONE OTHR THN LIMESTONE FLUX (25210009)	2001-02	-6.16	7.83	0.98	0.51	0.05	0.80	-0.45
5	85443000	IGNTN WIRING SETS & OTHR WIRING SETS OF A KIND USED IN VEHICLES AIRCRAFT/SHIPS	2001-02	45.49	52.66	1.00	0.99	0.96	0.94	0.12
6	60012200	LOOPED PILE FBRCS OF MAN-MADE FIBRES	2001-02	141.90	161.73	1.00	1.00	0.97	0.97	0.20
7	85173000	TELEPHONIC/TELEGRPHC SWTCHING APPRTS	2003-04	-28.76	39.81	1.00	0.89	0.53	0.84	#DIV/0!
8	42022190	OTHER LEATHER HAND BAGS. (42022109)	2001-02	132.57	209.74	0.99	0.93	0.87	0.99	0.99
9	85044029	OTHER RECTIFIERS (85044003)	2001-02	244.14	240.40	0.98	0.93	0.99	0.96	#DIV/0!
10	39219099	OTHR PLTS.SHTS,FILM FOIL STRIP ETC NES OTHER	2003-04	48.44	34.42	1.00	1.00	0.85	0.84	#DIV/0!
11	87081090	BUMPERS ETC FOR OTHR VHCLS	2003-04	-45.89	-18.97	0.99	0.97	0.50	0.60	#DIV/0!
12	85271300	OTHER APARATUS COMBIND WTH SOUND RECORDNG OR REPRODUCNG APARATUS	2001-02	161.61	141.39	0.99	0.93	0.87	0.96	#DIV/0!
13	85445990	OTHR ELCTRC CNDCTRS FOR 80V<="1000V" WTH FITTED CONNECTRS NT>	2003-04	9.27	17.61	1.00	1.00	0.79	0.79	#DIV/0!
14	44111990	OTHER BOARD	2003-04	20.74	35.80	1.00	1.00	0.81	0.85	#DIV/0!
15	72089000	OTHR FLAT ROLLED PRODUCTS, N.E.S.	2001-02	21.89	35.43	1.00	0.76	0.58	0.95	0.20
16	33051090	HAIR SHAMPOOS (NON-SPIRITUOUS) (33051002)	2001-02	157.34	177.00	0.98	1.00	0.99	1.00	0.99
17	85175099	OTHR APARTUS,FR CARRIER/DIGITAL LINE SYSTM	2003-04	421.75	141.37	1.00	0.97	0.99	0.98	#DIV/0!
18	85446090	OTHR ELCTRC CNDCTRS FR A VLTG EXCDG 1000 V (85446000)	2001-02	194.97	143.67	0.99	1.00	1.00	0.99	0.55
19	83023090	OTHERS (83023009)	2001-02	203.12	132.17	0.97	0.99	0.98	1.00	#DIV/0!
20	85413010	THYRISTORS (85413001)	2001-02	55.35	-20.32	0.99	-0.30	0.93	-0.37	-0.96

TABLE- 21

KEY FACTORS FOR ALL SAMPLED PRODUCTS (IMPORTED FROM THAILAND) COVERED UNDER EARLY HARVEST SCHEME- CHAPTERWISE

			2004-05	2004-05	2004-05	2004-05		2004-05
Sl. No.	CHAPTER	Main Products	% of Total Value of imports from Thailand in 2004-05	Value of Imports from THAILAND (in Rs. Lakhs)	Value of World Imports for India (in Rs. Lakhs)	Market Share of imports from Thailand in World Imports (Value) in %	Base year for next column	Incremental Trend of imports from Thailand (Value) in % in comparison to base yr.
1	CHAPTER 39	Plastics and Articles thereof	2.65	9923.26	74246.25	13.37	2001-02	802.82
2	CHAPTER 71	Natural stones, metals and imitation jewellery	1.99	7459.63	43597.07	17.11	2001-02	76.38
3	CHAPTER 73	Articles of Iron or Steel	1.89	7064.04	80645.18	8.76	2001-02	2399.66
4	CHAPTER 76	Aluminium and Articles thereof	0.54	2011.41	20553.46	9.79	2002-03	1084.86
5	CHAPTER 84	Machinery and Mechaniacal appliances	1.93	7234.26	136873.45	5.29	2001-02	147.42
6	CHAPTER 85	Audio Visual Equipments incl. TV	6.83	25567.18	243790.07	10.49	2001-02	7787.70
7	CHAPTER 94	Furniture Items	0.26	956.84	3242.71	29.51	2001-02	9633.88
		TOTAL	**16.08**	**60216.62**	**602948.19**			

NOTES

1 Base year have been changed, where CAGR for a particular product shows growth of more than 999%.
2 Base year for Trend Calculation have been changed in some cases, keeping in view the base year for CAGR and the actual trade data.
3 Base year for Trend Calculation have been changed in some cases, where trend exceeds 99999%.
4 Correlation among different DATA SERIES have been calculated by using the CORREL function active in the MS EXCEL spreadsheet.
5 Correlation of +1 denotes perfect positive correlation, -1 denotes perfect negative correlation, 0 denotes least correlation among the data series.
6 Trend is taken as 100% and CAGR as 0% in cases where either the data figures prior to 2004-05 are either zero or negligible.

				2004-05	2004-05		2004-05		2004-05
Sl. No.	CHAPTER	Main Products	Base year for next column	Incremental Trend of World Import (Value) in % in comparison to base yr.	CORRELATION OF TREND IN VALUE - THAILAND/World Imports	Base year for next column	CAGR-VALUE-THAILAND	Base year for next column	CAGR-VALUE-World Imports
1	CHAPTER 39	Plastics and Articles thereof	2001-02	160.65	1.00	2001-02	108.23	2001-02	37.62
2	CHAPTER 71	Natural stones, metals and imitation jewellery	2001-02	28.05	0.99	2001-02	20.82	2001-02	8.59
3	CHAPTER 73	Articles of Iron or Steel	2001-02	309.91	0.97	2001-02	192.39	2001-02	60.04
4	CHAPTER 76	Aluminium and Articles thereof	2001-02	204.07	0.98	2002-03	244.22	2001-02	44.87
5	CHAPTER 84	Machinery and Mechaniacal appliances	2001-02	156.16	0.98	2001-02	35.25	2001-02	36.83
6	CHAPTER 85	Audio Visual Equipments incl. TV	2001-02	463.02	0.88	2001-02	328.86	2001-02	77.90
7	CHAPTER 94	Furniture Items	2001-02	89.00	0.94	2001-02	360.00	2001-02	23.64

TABLE- 22

KEY FACTORS FOR ALL SAMPLED PRODUCTS NOT COVERED UNDER EARLY HARVEST SCHEME- CHAPTERWISE

		2004-05	2004-05	2004-05	2004-05		2004-05		2004-05	2004-05		2004-05		2004-05
Sl. No.	CHAPTER	% of Total Value of imports from Thailand in 2004-05	Value of Imports from THAILAND (in Rs. Lakhs)	Value of World Imports for India (in Rs. Lakhs)	Market Share of imports from Thailand in World Imports (Value) in %	Base year for next column	Incremental Trend of imports from Thailand (Value) in % in comparison to base yr.	Base year for next column	Incremental Trend of World Import (Value) in % in comparison to base yr.	CORRELATION OF TREND IN VALUE - THAILAND/World Imports	Base year for next column	CAGR-VALUE-THAILAND	Base year for next column	CAGR-VALUE-World Imports
1	CHAPTER 05	0.11	410.29	909.71	45.10	2003-04	-29.84	2003-04	-42.50	0.99	2003-04	-29.84	2003-04	-42.50
2	CHAPTER 12	0.43	1616.97	5308.03	30.46	2001-02	373.32	2001-02	145.61	0.88	2001-02	67.90	2001-02	34.92
3	CHAPTER 13	0.16	590.26	1753.71	33.66	2003-04	116.70	2001-02	5897.64	1.00	2003-04	116.70	2001-02	291.44
4	CHAPTER 15	0.29	1067.88	259953.25	0.41	2001-02	336.60	2001-02	38.95	0.79	2001-02	63.44	2001-02	11.59
5	CHAPTER 17	0.57	2147.82	22181.78	9.68	2004-05	0.00	2001-02	12908.32	1.00	2004-05	0.00	2001-02	406.69
6	CHAPTER 22	0.21	792.56	1460.87	54.25	2004-05	0.00	2003-04	20562.94	1.00	2001-05	0.00	2004-05	0.00
7	CHAPTER 23	0.34	1291.27	20886.08	6.18	2001-02	175.14	2001-02	122.68	0.84	2001-02	40.13	2001-02	30.59
8	CHAPTER 25	0.38	1435.77	6269.70	22.90	2001-02	61521.03	2001-02	25.39	0.80	2001-02	750.96	2001-02	7.83
9	CHAPTER 29	3.05	11433.50	404261.90	2.83	2001-02	620.21	2001-02	474.17	0.93	2001-02	93.12	2001-02	79.07
10	CHAPTER 32	0.54	2035.37	12463.21	16.33	2001-02	431.43	2001-02	4.33	0.25	2001-02	74.51	2001-02	1.42
11	CHAPTER 33	1.67	6255.05	7819.44	79.99	2001-02	9459.91	2001-02	2025.37	1.00	2001-02	357.25	2001-02	177.00
12	CHAPTER 35	0.23	849.59	2564.96	33.12	2001-02	2263.91	2001-02	57.65	0.71	2001-02	187.00	2001-02	16.39
13	CHAPTER 39	4.70	17595.44	243965.77	7.21	2001-02	241.11	2001-02	238.26	0.97	2001-02	50.53	2001-02	50.11
14	CHAPTER 40	6.40	23953.27	123168.69	19.45	2001-02	242.65	2001-02	157.75	0.99	2001-02	50.76	2001-02	37.11
15	CHAPTER 42	0.11	426.19	689.12	61.85	2001-02	27938.82	2001-02	2871.63	0.99	2001-02	554.52	2001-02	209.74
16	CHAPTER 44	0.36	1339.23	105870.86	1.26	2003-04	26704.40	2001-02	66.34	0.96	2004-05	0.00	2001-02	18.49
17	CHAPTER 47	0.39	1465.47	45174.61	3.24	2001-02	163.03	2001-02	72.42	0.89	2001-02	38.04	2001-02	19.91
18	CHAPTER 54	0.96	3577.94	69489.10	5.15	2001-02	-36.52	2001-02	36.95	-0.57	2001-02	-14.06	2001-02	11.05
19	CHAPTER 55	1.57	5868.32	17109.21	34.30	2001-02	59.06	2001-02	18.24	0.96	2001-02	16.73	2001-02	5.75
20	CHAPTER 56	0.16	596.69	1070.78	55.72	2001-02	619.60	2001-02	201.42	0.98	2001-02	93.06	2001-02	44.45
21	CHAPTER 57	0.11	405.95	1411.54	28.76	2003-04	109.80	2003-04	102.57	1.00	2003-04	109.80	2003-04	102.57
22	CHAPTER 58	0.10	372.48	3624.99	10.28	2001-02	891.69	2001-02	59.81	0.37	2001-02	114.85	2001-02	16.91

NOTES

1. Base year have been changed, where CAGR for a particular product shows growth of more than 999%.
2. Base year for Trend Calculation have been changed in some cases, keeping in view the base year for CAGR and the actual trade data.
3. Base year for Trend Calculation have been changed in some cases, where trend exceeds 99999%.
4. Correlation among different DATA SERIES have been calculated by using the CORREL function active in the MS EXCEL spreadsheet.
5. Correlation of +1 denotes perfect positive correlation, -1 denotes perfect negative correlation, 0 denotes least correlation among the data series.
6. Trend is taken as 100% and CAGR as 0% in cases where either the data figures prior to 2004-05 are either zero or negligible.

TABLE- 22

KEY FACTORS FOR ALL SAMPLED PRODUCTS NOT COVERED UNDER EARLY HARVEST SCHEME- CHAPTERWISE

		2004-05	2004-05	2004-05	2004-05		2004-05		2004-05	2004-05		2004-05		2004-05
Sl. No.	CHAPTER	% of Total Value of imports from Thailand in 2004-05	Value of Imports from THAILAND (in Rs. Lakhs)	Value of World Imports for India (in Rs. Lakhs)	Market Share of imports from Thailand in World Imports (Value) in %	Base year for next column	Incremental Trend of imports from Thailand (Value) in % in comparison to base yr.	Base year for next column	Incremental Trend of World Import (Value) in % in comparison to base yr.	CORRELATION OF TREND IN VALUE - THAILAND/World Imports	Base year for next column	CAGR-VALUE-THAILAND	Base year for next column	CAGR-VALUE-World Imports
23	CHAPTER 59	3.04	11399.54	62126.10	18.35	2001-02	191.12	2001-02	220.96	0.96	2001-02	42.79	2001-02	47.51
24	CHAPTER 60	0.11	420.93	3553.92	11.84	2001-02	44208.42	2001-02	1692.92	0.97	2001-02	662.36	2001-02	161.73
25	CHAPTER 69	0.10	368.32	1330.97	27.67	2001-02	307.93	2001-02	346.92	0.91	2001-02	59.78	2001-02	64.72
26	CHAPTER 70	0.46	1718.48	5293.61	32.46	2001-02	1457.30	2001-02	410.76	0.96	2001-02	149.72	2001-02	72.22
27	CHAPTER 71	1.70	6362.72	1341905.20	0.47	2001-02	715.45	2001-02	341.84	0.99	2001-02	101.28	2001-02	64.09
28	CHAPTER 72	4.53	16977.71	629938.01	2.70	2001-02	235.96	2001-02	161.70	0.99	2001-02	49.77	2001-02	37.81
29	CHAPTER 73	0.13	468.65	20450.40	2.29	2001-02	4227.33	2001-02	122.59	0.82	2001-02	251.08	2001-02	30.57
30	CHAPTER 74	1.13	4234.28	16992.02	24.92	2001-02	156.24	2001-02	224.31	0.99	2001-02	36.84	2001-02	48.02
31	CHAPTER 76	0.72	2687.92	6604.90	40.70	2001-02	706.58	2001-02	108.54	0.97	2001-02	100.55	2001-02	27.76
32	CHAPTER 82	0.15	566.16	12450.29	4.55	2001-02	19.05	2001-02	238.15	0.66	2001-02	5.98	2001-02	50.10
33	CHAPTER 83	0.17	632.40	3520.14	17.97	2002-03	1460.33	2001-02	1151.52	1.00	2002-03	295.01	2001-02	132.17
34	CHAPTER 84	12.24	45830.89	525412.94	8.72	2001-02	-17.55	2001-02	92.00	0.31	2001-02	-6.23	2001-02	24.29
35	CHAPTER 85	7.01	26258.78	621992.49	4.22	2001-02	1515.53	2001-02	1293.80	0.97	2001-02	152.80	2001-02	140.66
36	CHAPTER 87	6.75	25266.14	272708.39	9.26	2001-02	4223.43	2001-02	179.67	0.98	2001-02	250.98	2001-02	40.89
37	CHAPTER 90	0.33	1231.16	9044.56	13.61	2001-02	371.76	2001-02	130.74	0.97	2001-02	67.72	2001-02	32.14
38	CHAPTER 94	0.10	374.19	5533.45	6.76	2001-02	142.30	2001-02	180.42	0.93	2001-02	34.31	2001-02	41.02
39	CHAPTER 98	0.11	403.59	65913.91	0.61	2001-02	-5.28	2001-02	-60.31	0.02	2001-02	-1.79	2001-02	-26.51
40	CHAPTER 99	0.25	944.04	142178.72	0.66	2001-02	107.67	2001-02	322.44	0.90	2001-02	27.58	2001-02	61.66

NOTES

1 Base year have been changed, where CAGR for a particular product shows growth of more than 999%.
2 Base year for Trend Calculation have been changed in some cases, keeping in view the base year for CAGR and the actual trade data.
3 Base year for Trend Calculation have been changed in some cases, where trend exceeds 99999%.
4 Correlation among different DATA SERIES have been calculated by using the CORREL function active in the MS EXCEL spreadsheet.
5 Correlation of +1 denotes perfect positive correlation, -1 denotes perfect negative correlation, 0 denotes least correlation among the data series.
6 Trend is taken as 100% and CAGR as 0% in cases where either the data figures prior to 2004-05 are either zero or negligible.

TABLE- 23

KEY FACTORS FOR TOP 10 CHAPTERS (SORTED ON CAGR-VALUE-IMPORTS FROM THAILAND basis) (Containing Sampled Products of NON EHS category only)

		2004-05	2004-05	2004-05	2004-05		2004-05		2004-05
Sl. No.	CHAPTER	% of Total Value of imports from Thailand in 2004-05	Value of Imports from THAILAND (in Rs. Lakhs)	Value of World Imports for India (in Rs. Lakhs)	Market Share of imports from Thailand in World Imports (Value) in %	Base year for next column	Incremental Trend of imports from Thailand (Value) in % in comparison to base yr.	Base year for next column	Incremental Trend of World Import (Value) in % in comparison to base yr.
1	CHAPTER 25	0.38	1435.77	6269.70	22.90	2001-02	61521.03	2001-02	25.39
2	CHAPTER 60	0.11	420.93	3553.92	11.84	2001-02	44208.42	2001-02	1692.92
3	CHAPTER 42	0.11	426.19	689.12	61.85	2001-02	27938.82	2001-02	2871.63
4	CHAPTER 33	1.67	6255.05	7819.44	79.99	2001-02	9459.91	2001-02	2025.37
5	CHAPTER 83	0.17	632.40	3520.14	17.97	2002-03	1460.33	2001-02	1151.52
6	CHAPTER 73	0.13	468.65	20450.40	2.29	2001-02	4227.33	2001-02	122.59
7	CHAPTER 87	6.75	25266.14	272708.39	9.26	2001-02	4223.43	2001-02	179.67
8	CHAPTER 35	0.23	849.59	2564.96	33.12	2001-02	2263.91	2001-02	57.65
9	CHAPTER 85	7.01	26258.78	621992.49	4.22	2001-02	1515.53	2001-02	1293.80
10	CHAPTER 70	0.46	1718.48	5293.61	32.46	2001-02	1457.30	2001-02	410.76

NOTES

1. Base year have been changed, where CAGR for a particular product shows growth of more than 999%.
2. Base year for Trend Calculation have been changed in some cases, keeping in view the base year for CAGR and the actual trade data.
3. Base year for Trend Calculation have been changed in some cases, where trend exceeds 99999%.
4. Correlation among different DATA SERIES have been calculated by using the CORREL function active in the MS EXCEL spreadsheet.
5. Correlation of +1 denotes perfect positive correlation, -1 denotes perfect negative correlation, 0 denotes least correlation among the data series.
6. Trend is taken as 100% and CAGR as 0% in cases where either the data figures prior to 2004-05 are either zero or negligible.

TABLE- 23

KEY FACTORS FOR TOP 10 CHAPTERS (SORTED ON CAGR-VALUE-IMPORTS FROM THAILAND basis) (Containing Sampled Products of NON EHS category only)

		2004-05		2004-05		2004-05
Sl. No.	CHAPTER	CORRELATION OF TREND IN VALUE - THAILAND/World Imports	Base year for next column	CAGR-VALUE-THAILAND	Base year for next column	CAGR-VALUE-World Imports
1	CHAPTER 25	0.80	2001-02	750.96	2001-02	7.83
2	CHAPTER 60	0.97	2001-02	662.36	2001-02	161.73
3	CHAPTER 42	0.99	2001-02	554.52	2001-02	209.74
4	CHAPTER 33	1.00	2001-02	357.25	2001-02	177.00
5	CHAPTER 83	1.00	2002-03	295.01	2001-02	132.17
6	CHAPTER 73	0.82	2001-02	251.08	2001-02	30.57
7	CHAPTER 87	0.98	2001-02	250.98	2001-02	40.89
8	CHAPTER 35	0.71	2001-02	187.00	2001-02	16.39
9	CHAPTER 85	0.97	2001-02	152.80	2001-02	140.66
10	CHAPTER 70	0.96	2001-02	149.72	2001-02	72.22

TABLE- 24

KEY FACTORS FOR TOP 10 CHAPTERS (SORTED ON VALUE OF IMPORTS FROM THAILAND IN 2004-05 basis) (Containing Sampled Products of NON EHS category only)

		2004-05	2004-05	2004-05	2004-05		2004-05		2004-05
Sl. No.	CHAPTER	% of Total Value of imports from Thailand in 2004-05	Value of Imports from THAILAND (in Rs. Lakhs)	Value of World Imports for India (in Rs. Lakhs)	Market Share of imports from Thailand in World Imports (Value) in %	Base year for next column	Incremental Trend of imports from Thailand (Value) in % in comparison to base yr.	Base year for next column	Incremental Trend of World Import (Value) in % in comparison to base yr.
1	CHAPTER 84	12.24	45830.89	525412.94	8.72	2001-02	-17.55	2001-02	92.00
2	CHAPTER 85	7.01	26258.78	621992.49	4.22	2001-02	1515.53	2001-02	1293.80
3	CHAPTER 87	6.75	25266.14	272708.39	9.26	2001-02	4223.43	2001-02	179.67
4	CHAPTER 40	6.40	23953.27	123168.69	19.45	2001-02	242.65	2001-02	157.75
5	CHAPTER 39	4.70	17595.44	243965.77	7.21	2001-02	241.11	2001-02	238.26
6	CHAPTER 72	4.53	16977.71	629938.01	2.70	2001-02	235.96	2001-02	161.70
7	CHAPTER 29	3.05	11433.50	404261.90	2.83	2001-02	620.21	2001-02	474.17
8	CHAPTER 59	3.04	11399.54	62126.10	18.35	2001-02	191.12	2001-02	220.96
9	CHAPTER 71	1.70	6362.72	1341905.20	0.47	2001-02	715.45	2001-02	341.84
10	CHAPTER 33	1.67	6255.05	7819.44	79.99	2001-02	9459.91	2001-02	2025.37

NOTES

1 Base year have been changed, where CAGR for a particular product shows growth of more than 999%.
2 Base year for Trend Calculation have been changed in some cases, keeping in view the base year for CAGR and the actual trade data.
3 Base year for Trend Calculation have been changed in some cases, where trend exceeds 99999%.
4 Correlation among different DATA SERIES have been calculated by using the CORREL function active in the MS EXCEL spreadsheet.
5 Correlation of +1 denotes perfect positive correlation, -1 denotes perfect negative correlation, 0 denotes least correlation among the data series.
6 Trend is taken as 100% and CAGR as 0% in cases where either the data figures prior to 2004-05 are either zero or negligible.

TABLE- 24

KEY FACTORS FOR TOP 10 CHAPTERS (SORTED ON VALUE OF IMPORTS FROM THAILAND IN 2004-05 basis) (Containing Sampled Products of NON EHS category only)

		2004-05		2004-05		2004-05
Sl. No.	CHAPTER	CORRELATION OF TREND IN VALUE - THAILAND/World Imports	Base year for next column	CAGR-VALUE-THAILAND	Base year for next column	CAGR-VALUE-World Imports
1	CHAPTER 84	0.31	2001-02	-6.23	2001-02	24.29
2	CHAPTER 85	0.97	2001-02	152.80	2001-02	140.66
3	CHAPTER 87	0.98	2001-02	250.98	2001-02	40.89
4	CHAPTER 40	0.99	2001-02	50.76	2001-02	37.11
5	CHAPTER 39	0.97	2001-02	50.53	2001-02	50.11
6	CHAPTER 72	0.99	2001-02	49.77	2001-02	37.81
7	CHAPTER 29	0.93	2001-02	93.12	2001-02	79.07
8	CHAPTER 59	0.96	2001-02	42.79	2001-02	47.51
9	CHAPTER 71	0.99	2001-02	101.28	2001-02	64.09
10	CHAPTER 33	1.00	2001-02	357.25	2001-02	177.00

TABLE- 25

MOVEMENT OF SUM FACTORS OF SAMPLED PRODUCTS IMPORTED FROM THAILAND

(Value: in Rs. Lakhs)

MOVEMENT OF SAMPLED 33 PRODUCTS COVERED UNDER EHS

	2001-02	2002-03	2003-04	2004-05
Sum of Value of imports from Thailand (A)	8868.85	13466.66	30943.24	60216.62
Sum of Value of impoorts from World (B)	187414.1	265420.1	455293.9	602948.2
Sum Factor (A/B)	0.04732	0.05074	0.06796	0.09987

MOVEMENT OF SAMPLED 147 PRODUCTS NOT COVERED UNDER EHS

	2001-02	2002-03	2003-04	2004-05
Sum of Value of imports from Thailand (A)	96800.14	64274.53	129456.4	231673.2
Sum of Value of impoorts from World (B)	1774056	1925029	3117748	5104357
Sum Factor (A/B)	0.05456	0.03339	0.04152	0.04539

MOVEMENT OF SUM FACTORS OF ALL EHS PRODUCTS / ALL NON EHS PRODUCTS

	2001-02	2002-03	2003-04	2004-05
Sum Factor (EHS PRODUCTS)	0.047322	0.050737	0.067963	0.09987
Sum Factor (non EHS PRODUCTS)	0.054564	0.033389	0.041522	0.045387

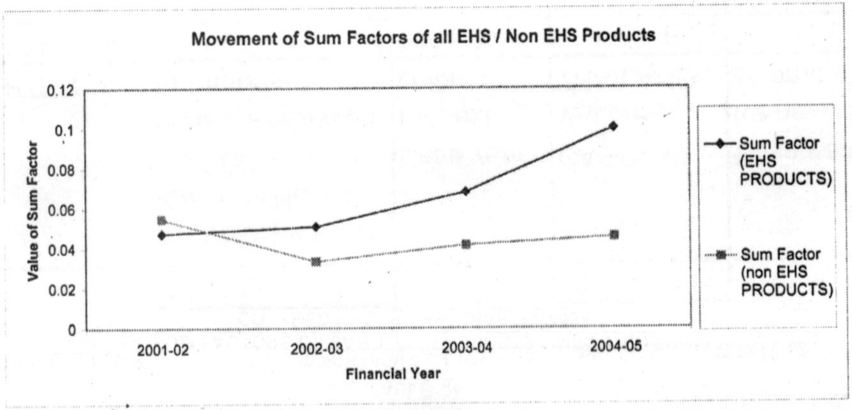

TABLE- 26

MOVEMENT OF SUM FACTORS OF SAMPLED PRODUCTS (IMPORTED FROM THAILAND) COVERED UNDER EHS- CHAPTERWISE

(Value: in Rs. Lakhs)

CHAPTER 39	2001-02	2002-03	2003-04	2004-05
Sum of Value of imports from Thailand (A)	1099.14	2820.31	8450.98	9923.26
Sum of Value of impoorts from World (B)	28485.06	38420.76	66829.39	74246.25
Sum Factor (A/B)	0.03859	0.07341	0.12646	0.13365

CHAPTER 71	2001-02	2002-03	2003-04	2004-05
Sum of Value of imports from Thailand (A)	4229.21	3370.47	5182.48	7459.63
Sum of Value of impoorts from World (B)	34046.44	31976.41	38298.34	43597.07
Sum Factor (A/B)	0.12422	0.10540	0.13532	0.17110

CHAPTER 73	2001-02	2002-03	2003-04	2004-05
Sum of Value of imports from Thailand (A)	282.6	1289.31	6648.15	7064.04
Sum of Value of impoorts from World (B)	19673.78	28081.77	59809.09	80645.18
Sum Factor (A/B)	0.01436	0.04591	0.11116	0.08759

CHAPTER 76	2001-02	2002-03	2003-04	2004-05
Sum of Value of imports from Thailand (A)	0	169.76	2.17	2011.41
Sum of Value of impoorts from World (B)	6759.48	10554.62	9371.16	20553.46
Sum Factor (A/B)	0.00000	0.01608	0.00023	0.09786

CHAPTER 84	2001-02	2002-03	2003-04	2004-05
Sum of Value of imports from Thailand (A)	2923.93	3970.48	6774.9	7234.26
Sum of Value of impoorts from World (B)	53433.17	70645.72	112043.54	136873.45
Sum Factor (A/B)	0.05472	0.05620	0.06047	0.05285

CHAPTER 85	2001-02	2002-03	2003-04	2004-05
Sum of Value of imports from Thailand (A)	324.14	1841.76	3675.13	25567.18
Sum of Value of impoorts from World (B)	43300.44	83752.27	166407.8	243790.07
Sum Factor (A/B)	0.00749	0.02199	0.02209	0.10487

CHAPTER 94	2001-02	2002-03	2003-04	2004-05
Sum of Value of imports from Thailand (A)	9.83	4.57	209.43	956.84
Sum of Value of impoorts from World (B)	1715.7	1988.51	2534.53	3242.71
Sum Factor (A/B)	0.00573	0.00230	0.08263	0.29507

CATEGORY OF PRODUCTS	SUM FACTORS			
	2001-02	2002-03	2003-04	2004-05
CHAPTER 39	0.03859	0.07341	0.12646	0.13365
CHAPTER 71	0.12422	0.10540	0.13532	0.17110
CHAPTER 73	0.01436	0.04591	0.11116	0.08759
CHAPTER 76	0.00000	0.01608	0.00023	0.09786
CHAPTER 84	0.05472	0.05620	0.06047	0.05285
CHAPTER 85	0.00749	0.02199	0.02209	0.10487
CHAPTER 94	0.00573	0.00230	0.08263	0.29507

MOVEMENT OF ALL SAMPLE PRODUCTS COVERED UNDER EHS - CHAPTERWISE

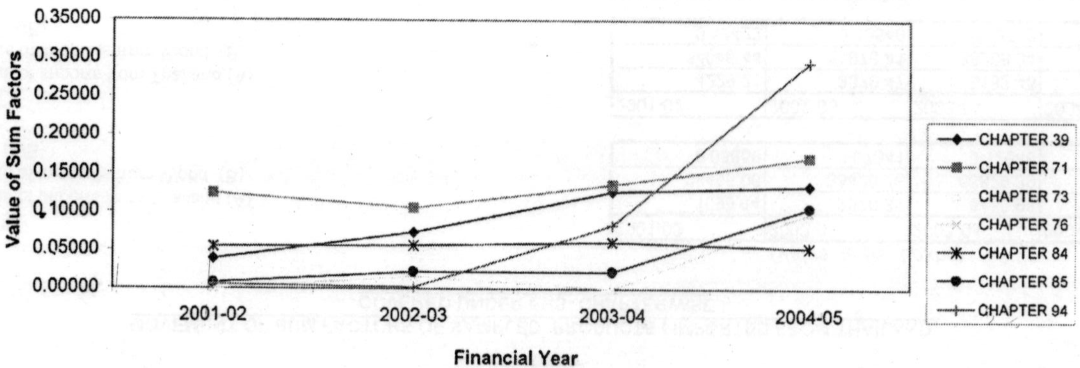

TABLE- 27

MOVEMENT OF MARKET SHARE & UNIT PRICE OF IMPORTS TOP 3 SAMPLED PRODUCTS IMPORTED FROM THAILAND COVERED UNDER EHS (Value of Imports from Thailand in 2004-05 basis)

1 73269099 ALL OTHER ARTICLES OF IRON/STEEL NES OTHER STEERING OR RUDDER EQUIPMENT FOR SHIPS AND BOATS, N.E.S. (73269019)

	2001-02	2002-03	2003-04	2004-05
Market Share (Quantity)	1.34%	3.93%	13.05%	9.64%
Market Share (Value)	1.44%	4.59%	11.12%	8.76%
	2001-02	**2002-03**	**2003-04**	**2004-05**
Price per unit (Imports from Thailand only)	314.7694	321.9653	265.2216	298.0884
Price per unit (World Import for India)	294.1759	275.2564	311.2949	328.0957

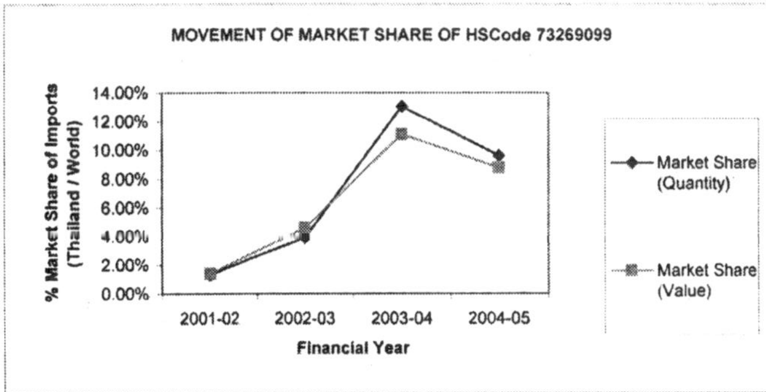

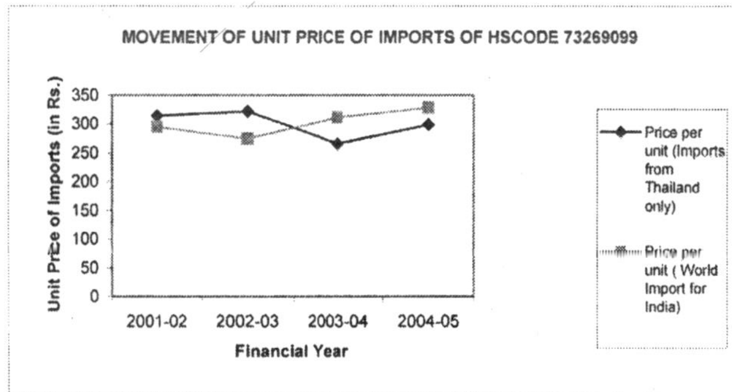

2 85281212 COLOUR TV SET OF SCRN SIZE BETN 36 & 54 CM

	2001-02	2002-03	2003-04	2004-05
Market Share (Quantity)	#DIV/0!	#DIV/0!	0.00%	94.91%
Market Share (Value)	#DIV/0!	#DIV/0!	0.10%	88.81%
	2001-02	**2002-03**	**2003-04**	**2004-05**
Price per unit (Imports from Thailand only)	#DIV/0!	#DIV/0!	#DIV/0!	6736.468
Price per unit (World Import for India)	#DIV/0!	#DIV/0!	7195.332	7198.585

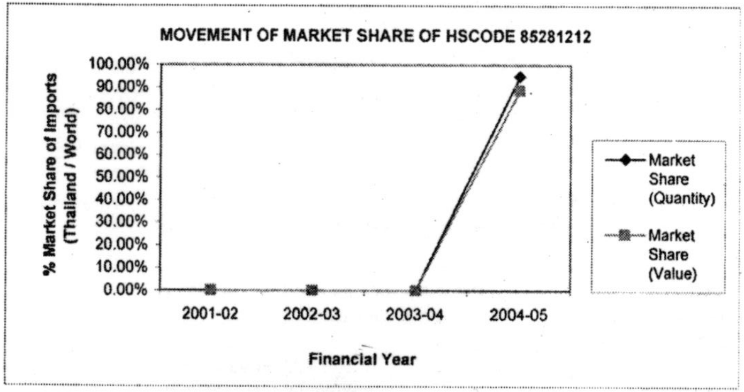

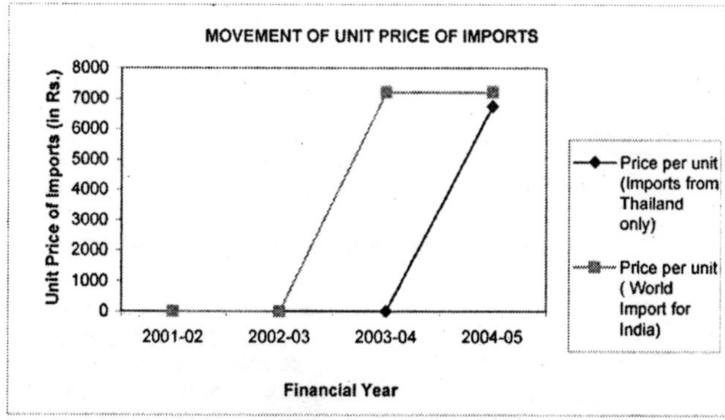

3 39074000 POLYCARBONATES

	2001-02	2002-03	2003-04	2004-05
Market Share (Quantity)	0.002758	0.067374	0.169076	0.174087
Market Share (Value)	0.003539	0.071991	0.167602	0.198873
	2001-02	**2002-03**	**2003-04**	**2004-05**
Price per unit (Imports from Thailand only)	137.5706	87.73026	75.5461	110.0591
Price per unit (World Import for India)	107.2119	82.10345	76.21039	96.34215

(GRAPH IS PRODUCED NEXT PAGE OF THIS TABLE

MOVEMENT OF MARKET SHARE & UNIT PRICE OF IMPORTS TOP 3 SAMPLED PRODUCTS COVERED UNDER EHS (CAGR-VALUE- Imports from Thailand basis)

1 39074000 POLYCARBONATES

	2001-02	2002-03	2003-04	2004-05
Market Share (Quantity)	0.28%	6.74%	16.91%	17.41%
Market Share (Value)	0.35%	7.20%	16.76%	19.89%
	2001-02	**2002-03**	**2003-04**	**2004-05**
Price per unit (Imports from Thailand only)	137.5706	87.73026	75.5461	110.0591
Price per unit (World Import for India)	107.2119	82.10345	76.21039	96.34215

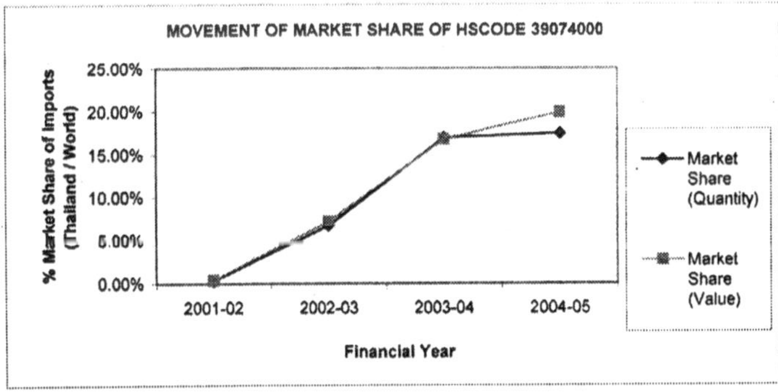

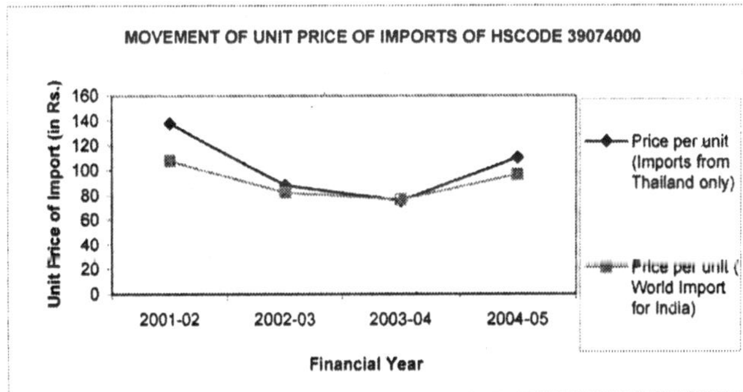

2 94019000 OTHER SEATS OF HEADING 9401

	2001-02	2002-03	2003-04	2004-05
Market Share (Quantity)	0.18%	0.79%	4.13%	19.12%
Market Share (Value)	0.57%	0.23%	8.26%	29.51%
	2001-02	**2002-03**	**2003-04**	**2004-05**
Price per unit (Imports from Thailand only)	954.3689	164.3885	780.2906	617.5153
Price per unit (World Import for India)	304.0835	565.4156	390.0237	400.1864

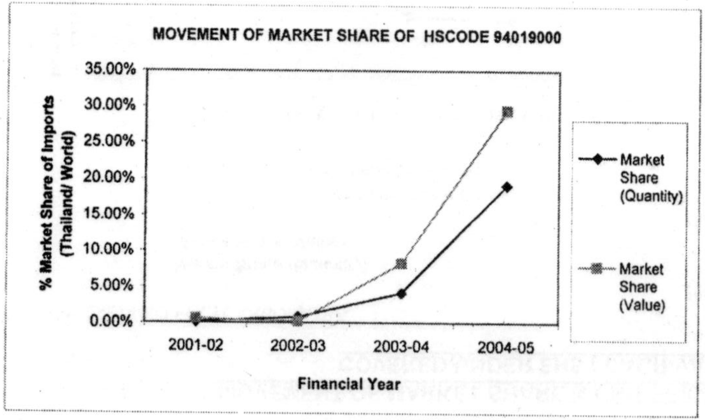

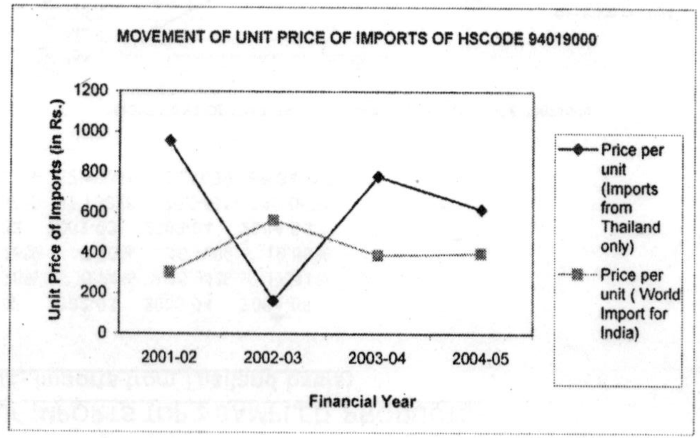

3 76012010 ALUMINIUM INGOTS -ALLOYED (76012001)

	2001-02	2002-03	2003-04	2004-05
Market Share (Quantity)	0.00%	1.57%	0.02%	10.40%
Market Share (Value)	0.00%	1.61%	0.02%	9.79%
	2001-02	**2002-03**	**2003-04**	**2004-05**
Price per unit (Imports from Thailand only)	#DIV/0!	74.45614	72.33333	81.48804
Price per unit (World Import for India)	71.31163	72.8875	77.62917	86.56618

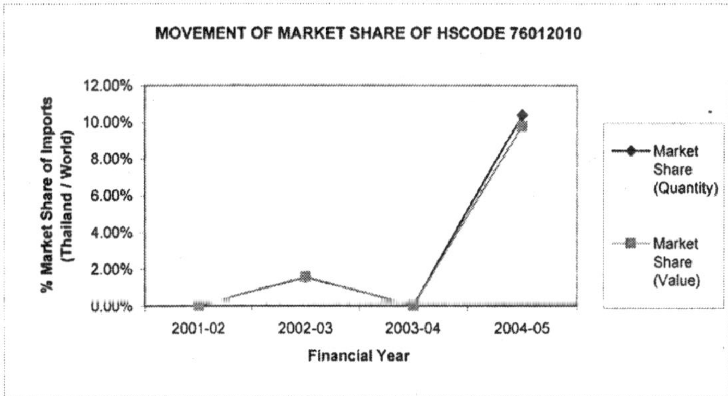

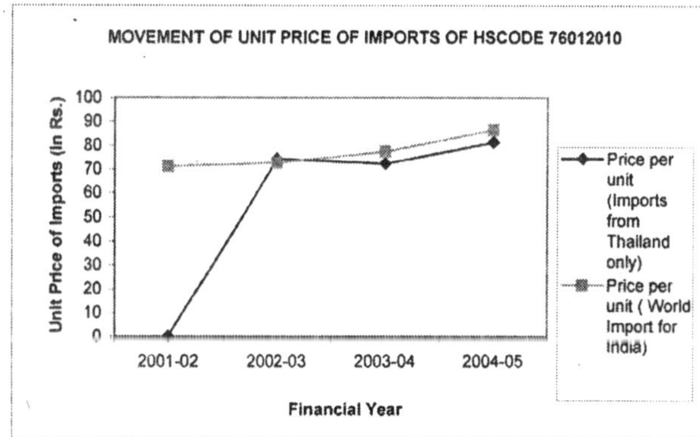

TABLE- 28

DETAILS OF SAMPLING OF EXPORT PRODUCTS TO THAILAND

(Value: in Rs. Lakhs)

Particulars				**2004-05**	
Total No. of Products exported during the year				3106	
Total No. of Producs sampled				103	3.32%
Total No. of Sampled Products covered under EHS				11	0.35%
Total No. of Other Products not covered under EHS				92	2.96%
Total Value of Exports during the year to Thailand				395199.59	
	2001-02	**2002-03**	**2003-04**	**2004-05**	
ALL INDIA FIGURES					
Total Value of Exports during the year of Sampled Products	5026480.20	6450481.75	8336017.33	10759419.76	
Total Value of Exports of Sampled Products covered under EHS	549949.75	763711.27	1056403.58	1521154.16	
Total Value of Exports of Sampled Products NOT covered under EHS	4476530.45	5686770.48	7279613.75	9238265.60	
ONLY THAILAND FIGURES					
Total Value of Exports during the year of Sampled Products	166751.93	187806.00	238407.54	309065.65	78.20%
Total Value of Exports of Sampled Products covered under EHS	2635.60	7360.96	21264.74	14138.77	3.58%
Total Value of Exports of Sampled Products NOT covered under EHS	164116.33	180445.04	217142.80	294926.88	74.63%

	EXPORTS TO THAILAND	INDIA'S WORLD EXPORT	RELATIVE FASTNESS
	(A)	(B)	(A/B)
Weighted Average CAGR of all the sampled products	82.05%	45.70%	1.80
Weighted Average CAGR of all the sampled products (covered under EHS)	261.46%	42.94%	6.09
Weighted Average CAGR of all the sampled products (NOT covered under EHS)	73.45%	46.15%	1.59
Weighted Average CAGR of all the sampled products (covered under EHS)- CHAPTER WISE	260.50%	41.21%	6.32
Weighted Average CAGR of all the sampled products (NOT covered under EHS)- CHAPTER WISE	51.77%	37.99%	1.36

TABLE- 29

KEY FACTORS FOR TOP 20 HIGH VALUE EXPORTED ITEMS (based on 2004-05 value of exports) TO THAILAND

			2004-05		2004-05	2004-05		2004-05	2004-05	2004-05	2004-05	2004-05	2004-05
Sl. No.	HS Code	Whether Covered under EARLY HARVEST SCHEME	% of Total Value of exports to Thailand in 2004-05	Base year for next two columns	Incremental Trend of exports to Thailand (Volume) in % in comparison to base yr.	Incremental Trend of exports to Thailand (Value) in % in comparison to base yr.	Base year for next two columns	Incremental Trend of World export (Volume) in % in comparison to base yr.	Incremental Trend of World export (Value) in % in comparison to base yr.	Market Share of exports to Thailand in World exports (Volume) in %	Market Share of exports to Thailand in World exports (Value) in %	Per Unit Export Price from Thailand (in Rs.)	Per Unit World Export Price for India (in Rs.)
1	71023910	NO	28.67	2001-02	-8.10	16.18	2001-02	27.55	64.30	3.18	2.50	11653.58	14816.91
2	74031100	NO	10.83	2001-02	428.11	856.93	2001-02	162.78	371.74	23.64	24.04	138.41	136.06
3	23040030	NO	2.55	2001-02	-64.80	-55.55	2001-02	-10.32	10.34	6.51	6.47	10.64	10.71
4	71039990	NO	2.43	2001-02	33.35	42.17	2001-02	197.25	-3.99	4.73	15.10	494.53	154.88
5	29420090	NO	1.92	2003-04	30.79	31.33	2003-04	22.17	23.66	1.40	1.62	2185.16	1888.79
6	72139190	NO	1.64	2002-03	641.34	1230.33	2001-02	-9.81	116.77	57.28	55.56	23.59	24.32
7	23064900	NO	1.34	2003-04	1320.15	1359.55	2003-04	404.63	427.28	10.98	12.73	6.56	5.66
8	38170011	NO	1.22	2003-04	135.52	206.73	2003-04	43.27	81.68	20.59	20.57	39.86	39.90
9	72083990	NO	1.18	2002-03	9779.38	8384.09	2001-02	2316.30	4550.43	4.55	4.52	27.15	27.34
10	72139990	NO	1.18	2002-03	317.37	653.48	2001-02	4822.72	7576.34	25.59	24.38	27.63	29.00
11	72011000	NO	1.16	2001-02	26.92	223.08	2001-02	26.25	180.47	10.24	10.55	13.66	13.25
12	72012000	NO	1.11	2003-04	215.00	437.92	2001-02	10132.20	7164.66	49.36	48.82	13.97	14.12
13	87084000	YES	0.99	2001-02	60222.67	66213.54	2001-02	325.54	482.55	32.82	42.57	377.73	291.19
14	71039100	NO	0.97	2003-04	70.40	81.07	2003-04	41.68	43.01	13.94	12.69	553.83	608.58
15	23040010	NO	0.93	2001-02	737.69	845.74	2001-02	493.78	589.04	6.91	6.49	9.21	9.81
16	76011010	YES	0.74	2001-02	824.84	854.07	2001-02	60.59	90.49	3.57	3.44	79.56	82.60
17	87089900	NO	0.69	2001-02	104.67	258.98	2001-02	92.74	123.86	0.73	1.26	267.33	155.46
18	84733010	NO	0.62	2003-04	-65.24	-73.91	2003-04	4.76	1.76	4.98	5.31	7711.14	7220.72
19	38081035	NO	0.58	2003-04	118.31	124.54	2003-04	5.80	5.80	8.84	10.73	380.88	313.70
20	29012400	NO	0.56	2004-05	0.00	0.00	2004-05	0.00	0.00	9.75	9.97	47.00	45.95

NOTES

1. Base year have been changed, where CAGR for a particular product shows growth of more than 999%.
2. Base year for Trend Calculation have been changed in some cases, keeping in view the base year for CAGR and the actual trade data.
3. Base year for Trend Calculation have been changed in some cases, where trend exceeds 99999%.
4. Correlation among different DATA SERIES have been calculated by using the CORREL function active in the MS EXCEL spreadsheet.
5. Correlation of +1 denotes perfect positive correlation, -1 denotes perfect negative correlation, 0 denotes least correlation among the data series.
6. Trend is taken as 100% and CAGR as 0% in cases where either the data figures prior to 2004-05 are either zero or negligible.

TABLE- 29

KEY FACTORS FOR TOP 20 HIGH VALUE EXPORTED ITEMS (based on 2004-05 value of exports) TO THAILAND

				THAILAND	THAILAND		World	World	THAILAND	World	THAILAND & World		
Sl. No.	HS Code	Whether Covered under EARLY HARVEST SCHEME	Base year for next two columns	CAGR - VOLUME (in %)	CAGR- VALUE (in %)	Base year for next two columns	CAGR- VOLUME (in %)	CAGR- VALUE (in %)	CORRELATION - TREND OF VOLUME / VALUE	CORRELATION - TREND OF VOLUME / VALUE	CORRELATION - TREND OF VOLUME	CORRELATION - TREND OF VALUE	CORRELATION - UNIT PRICE
1	71023910	NO	2001-02	-2.78	5.13	2001-02	8.45	18.00	0.65	0.94	-0.62	0.41	0.94
2	74031100	NO	2001-02	74.14	112.31	2001-02	38.00	67.71	0.90	0.92	0.90	0.94	1.00
3	23040030	NO	2001-02	-29.39	-23.68	2001-02	-3.57	3.34	0.98	0.91	0.82	0.66	0.97
4	71039990	NO	2001-02	10.07	12.44	2001-02	43.78	-1.35	1.00	-0.61	0.86	-0.08	-0.57
5	29420090	NO	2003-04	30.79	31.33	2003-04	22.17	23.66	1.00	1.00	1.00	1.00	#DIV/0!
6	72139190	NO	2002-03	172.28	264.74	2001-02	-3.38	29.42	0.99	-0.05	-0.66	0.82	#DIV/0!
7	23064900	NO	2004-05	0.00	0.00	2003-04	404.63	427.28	1.00	1.00	0.99	0.99	#DIV/0!
8	38170011	NO	2003-04	135.52	206.73	2003-04	43.27	81.68	0.99	0.99	0.96	0.97	#DIV/0!
9	72083990	NO	2002-03	893.95	821.09	2001-02	189.10	259.61	1.00	0.98	0.92	0.98	#DIV/0!
10	72139990	NO	2002-03	104.30	174.50	2001-02	266.50	325.00	0.99	1.00	0.99	1.00	#DIV/0!
11	72011000	NO	2001-02	8.27	47.83	2001-02	8.08	41.02	0.93	0.34	0.83	0.53	0.98
12	72012000	NO	2003-04	215.00	437.92	2001-02	367.72	317.26	0.99	0.95	0.88	0.95	#DIV/0!
13	87084000	YES	2001-02	744.94	772.04	2001-02	62.05	79.93	1.00	0.99	0.97	0.99	0.68
14	71039100	NO	2003-04	70.40	81.07	2003-04	41.68	43.01	1.00	1.00	0.99	0.99	#DIV/0!
15	23040010	NO	2001-02	103.09	111.47	2001-02	81.08	90.29	0.98	1.00	0.98	0.97	-0.11
16	76011010	YES	2001-02	109.90	112.09	2001-02	17.10	23.96	0.99	0.96	0.70	0.65	0.59
17	87089900	NO	2001-02	26.97	53.12	2001-02	24.45	30.82	0.90	1.00	0.93	0.96	0.69
18	84733010	NO	2003-04	-65.24	-73.91	2003-04	4.75	-0.33	1.00	1.00	0.81	0.75	#DIV/0!
19	38081035	NO	2003-04	118.31	124.54	2003-04	5.80	-7.90	1.00	1.00	0.90	0.90	#DIV/0!
20	29012400	NO	2004-05	0.00	0.00	2004-05	0.00	0.00	1.00	1.00	1.00	1.00	#DIV/0!

TABLE- 30

KEY FACTORS FOR ALL SAMPLED PRODUCTS (EXPORTED TO THAILAND) COVERED UNDER EARLY HARVEST SCHEME

			2004-05		2004-05	2004-05		2004-05	2004-05	2004-05	2004-05	2004-05	2004-05
Sl. No.	HS Code	Particulars	% of Total Value of exports to Thailand in 2004-05	Base year for next two columns	Incremental Trend of exports to Thailand (Volume) in % in comparison to base yr.	Incremental Trend of exports to Thailand (Value) in % in comparison to base yr.	Base year for next two columns	Incremental Trend of World export (Volume) in % in comparison to base yr.	Incremental Trend of World export (Value) in % in comparison to base yr.	Market Share of exports to Thailand in World exports (Volume) in %	Market Share of exports to Thailand in World exports (Value) in %	Per Unit Export Price from Thailand (in Rs.)	Per Unit World Export Price for India (in Rs.)
1	87084000	GEAR BOXES	0.99	2001-02	60222.67	66213.54	2001-02	325.54	482.55	32.82	42.57	377.73	291.19
2	76011010	ALUMINIUM INGOTS-NOT ALLOYED	0.74	2001-02	824.84	854.07	2001-02	60.59	90.49	3.57	3.44	79.56	82.60
3	28182010	ALUMINA CALCINED	0.41	2001-02	311.08	430.68	2001-02	239.62	474.89	0.89	1.31	20.29	13.90
4	73269099	ALL OTHER ARTICLES OF IRON/STEEL NES OTHER STEERING OR RUDDER EQUIPMENT FOR SHIPS AND BOATS, N.E.S.	0.27	2001-02	654.91	682.23	2001-02	64.58	74.52	3.07	3.83	104.16	83.67
5	85401110	CTV PCTR TUB 20/21 EXCEPT 21 F& FST	0.23	2004-05	0.00	0.00	2003-04	31.98	41.40	3.04	2.74	1633.43	1807.00
6	84322100	DISC HARROWS	0.22	2001-02	21.12	35.80	2001-02	13.84	45.75	39.79	41.95	375.64	356.29
7	72071920	MILD STEEL (M.S.) BILLETS	0.19	2001-02	513.46	22.65	2001-02	425.40	437.24	6.56	5.59	15.78	18.50
8	71131910	JEWELLERY OF GOLD UNSET	0.17	2001-02	233.33	266.29	2001-02	5.09	80.64	0.17	0.20	654930.00	556069.30
9	71131930	JEWELLERY OF GOLD SET WITH DIAMOND	0.14	2001-02	2300.00	148.31	2001-02	343.79	223.39	0.15	0.07	232170.83	523743.97
10	84775100	MCHNRY FR MOULDNG/RETREADNG PNEUMTC TYPES OR FR MOULDNG/OTHERWSE FORMNG INNR TUBES	0.12	2001-02	400.00	256.78	2001-02	64.29	318.09	21.74	10.21	942480.00	2006526.09
11	84818030	INDUSTRIAL VALVES(EXCL PRESSURE-REDUCING VALVES.& THRMSTCLY CONTRLLD VALVES)	0.11	2001-02	314.24	280.06	2001-02	110.94	140.83	0.63	0.85	346.07	253.76

NOTES

1 Base year have been changed, where CAGR for a particular product shows growth of more than 999%.
2 Base year for Trend Calculation have been changed in some cases. keeping in view the base year for CAGR and the actual trade data.
3 Base year for Trend Calculation have been changed in some cases, where trend exceeds 99999%.
4 Correlation among different DATA SERIES have been calculated by using the CORREL function active in the MS EXCEL spreadsheet.
5 Correlation of +1 denotes perfect positive correlation, -1 denotes perfect negative correlation, 0 denotes least correlation among the data series.
6 Trend is taken as 100% and CAGR as 0% in cases where either the data figures prior to 2004-05 are either zero or negligible.

TABLE- 30

KEY FACTORS FOR ALL SAMPLED PRODUCTS (EXPORTED TO THAILAND) COVERED UNDER EARLY HARVEST SCHEME

				THAILAND	THAILAND		World	World	THAILAND	World	THAILAND & World		
Sl. No.	HS Code	Particulars	Base year for next two columns	CAGR - VOLUME (in %)	CAGR- VALUE (in %)	Base year for next two columns	CAGR- VOLUME (in %)	CAGR- VALUE (in %)	CORRELATION - TREND OF VOLUME / VALUE	CORRELATION - TREND OF VOLUME / VALUE	CORRELATION - TREND OF VOLUME	CORRELATION - TREND OF VALUE	CORRELATION - UNIT PRICE
1	87084000	GEAR BOXES	2001-02	744.94	772.04	2001-02	62.05	79.93	1.00	0.99	0.97	0.99	0.68
2	76011010	ALUMINIUM INGOTS-NOT ALLOYED	2001-02	109.90	112.09	2001-02	17.10	23.96	0.99	0.96	0.70	0.65	0.59
3	28182010	ALUMINA CALCINED	2001-02	60.19	74.43	2001-02	50.31	79.14	0.97	0.85	0.77	0.92	0.93
4	73269099	ALL OTHER ARTICLES OF IRON/STEEL NES OTHER STEERING OR RUDDER EQUIPMENT FOR SHIPS AND BOATS, N.E.S.	2001-02	96.17	98.51	2001-02	18.07	20.40	1.00	0.98	0.75	0.72	-0.54
5	85401110	CTV PCTR TUB 20/21 EXCEPT 21 F& FST	2004-05	0.00	0.00	2003-04	31.98	41.40	1.00	1.00	0.72	0.75	#DIV/0!
6	84322100	DISC HARROWS	2001-02	6.60	10.74	2001-02	4.41	13.38	0.96	0.94	0.62	0.88	0.42
7	72071920	MILD STEEL (M.S.) BILLETS	2001-02	83.06	7.04	2001-02	73.85	75.14	0.99	0.98	0.98	0.97	0.55
8	71131910	JEWELLERY OF GOLD UNSET	2001-02	49.38	54.15	2001-02	1.67	21.79	1.00	0.75	-0.15	0.12	0.58
9	71131930	JEWELLERY OF GOLD SET WITH DIAMOND	2001-02	188.45	35.41	2001-02	64.33	47.88	0.96	-0.32	-0.27	0.96	0.26
10	84775100	MCHNRY FR MOULDNG/RETREADNG PNEUMTC TYPES OR FR MOULDNG/OTHERWSE FORMNG INNR TUBES	2001-02	71.00	52.80	2001-02	18.00	61.10	0.93	0.20	0.30	0.14	-0.18
11	84818030	INDUSTRIAL VALVES(EXCL PRESSURE-REDUCING VALVES,& THRMSTCLY CONTRLLD VALVES)	2001-02	60.60	56.06	2001-02	28.25	34.04	0.92	1.00	0.93	1.00	-0.25

TABLE-31

KEY FACTORS FOR TOP 10 SAMPLED PRODUCTS (CAGR WISE - value of exports in 2004-05) NOT COVERED UNDER EARLY HARVEST SCHEME

			2004-05		2004-05	2004-05		2004-05	2004-05	2004-05	2004-05	2004-05
Sl. No.	HS Code	Particulars	% of Total Value of exports to Thailand in 2004-05	Base year for next two columns	Incremental Trend of exports to Thailand (Volume) in % in comparison to base yr.	Incremental Trend of exports to Thailand (Value) in % in comparison to base yr.	Base year for next two columns	Incremental Trend of World export (Volume) in % in comparison to base yr.	Incremental Trend of World export (Value) in % in comparison to base yr.	Market Share of exports to Thailand in World exports (Volume) in %	Market Share of exports to Thailand in World exports (Value) in %	Per Unit Export Price from Thailand (in Rs.)
1	85251090	OTHERS	0.25	2001-02	0.00	96488.46	2001-02	1063.04	1396.31	40.65	30.22	23092.41
2	72083990	OTHR FLAT-ROLD PRDCTS IN COILS OF A THCKNS< 3 MM HOT-RLD,EXCL.PICKL	1.18	2002-03	9779.38	8384.09	2001-02	2316.30	4550.43	4.55	4.52	27.15
3	72224010	ANGLES ETC.OF 80 MM OR MORE	0.16	2001-02	3762.94	7426.25	2001-02	575.02	1351.29	2.03	1.93	89.08
4	27101920	AUIATION TURBINE FUEL (ATF)	0.38	2003-04	606.80	740.51	2003-04	67.84	144.45	0.34	0.36	20595.88
5	72023000	FERRO-SILICO-MANGANESE	0.14	2002-03	3132.56	6944.11	2001-02	175.57	472.06	1.89	1.91	39.98
6	72012000	NON-ALLOY PIG IRON CONTNG> 0.5% PHOSPHRS	1.11	2003-04	215.00	437.92	2001-02	10132.20	7164.66	49.36	48.82	13.97
7	29053100	ETHYLENE GLYCOL (ETHANEDIOL)	0.23	2001-02	11948.33	13384.26	2001-02	985.96	1650.80	1.52	1.81	42.28
8	52114200	DENIM OF YARNS OF DIFFERENT COLOUR OF MXD COTN FABRICS WEIGHING>200 GSM	0.11	2002-03	21649.72	12180.00	2001-02	709.21	512.33	1.05	1.13	107.24
9	32041761	PIGMENT GREEN 7 (PATHALOVYANINE GREEN)	0.13	2002-03	1305.67	1419.37	2001-02	3889.07	3632.54	4.68	4.94	258.29
10	72139190	OTHERS	1.64	2002-03	641.34	1230.33	2001-02	-9.81	116.77	57.28	55.56	23.59

NOTES

1. Base year have been changed, where CAGR for a particular product shows growth of more than 999%.
2. Base year for Trend Calculation have been changed in some cases, keeping in view the base year for CAGR and the actual trade data.
3. Base year for Trend Calculation have been changed in some cases, where trend exceeds 99999%.
4. Correlation among different DATA SERIES have been calculated by using the CORREL function active in the MS EXCEL spreadsheet.
5. Correlation of +1 denotes perfect positive correlation, -1 denotes perfect negative correlation, 0 denotes least correlation among the data series.
6. Base year incase of TREND-THAILAND-VOLUME & CAGR-THAILAND-VOLUME is taken as 2004-05 for HS Code 85251090.
7. Trend is taken as 100% and CAGR as 0% in cases where either the data figures prior to 2004-05 are either zero or negligible.

TABLE-31

KEY FACTORS FOR TOP 10 SAMPLED PRODUCTS (CAGR WISE - value of exports in 2004-05) NOT COVERED UNDER EARLY HARVEST SCHEME

			2004-05		THAILAND	THAILAND		World	World	THAILAND	World	THAILAND & World		
Sl. No.	HS Code	Particulars	Per Unit World Export Price for India (in Rs.)	Base year for next two columns	CAGR - VOLUME (in %)	CAGR-VALUE (in %)	Base year for next two columns	CAGR-VOLUME (in %)	CAGR-VALUE (in %)	CORRELATION - TREND OF VOLUME / VALUE	CORRELATION - TREND OF VOLUME / VALUE	CORRELATION - TREND OF VOLUME	CORRELATION - TREND OF VALUE	CORRELATION - UNIT PRICE
1	85251090	OTHERS	31064.58	2001-02	0.00	888.50	2001-02	126.57	146.42	1.00	0.98	0.67	0.75	#DIV/0!
2	72083990	OTHR FLAT-ROLD PRDCTS IN COILS OF A THCKNS< 3 MM HOT-RLD,EXCL.PICKL	27.34	2002-03	893.95	821.09	2001-02	189.10	259.61	1.00	0.98	0.92	0.98	#DIV/0!
3	72224010	ANGLES ETC.OF 80 MM OR MORE	93.86	2002-03	521.53	767.54	2001-02	88.99	143.92	0.99	0.99	0.77	0.85	#DIV/0!
4	27101920	AUIATION TURBINE FUEL (ATF)	19432.14	2003-04	606.80	740.51	2003-04	67.84	144.45	1.00	0.98	0.89	0.95	#DIV/0!
5	72023000	FERRO-SILICO-MANGANESE	39.58	2002-03	468.56	739.29	2001-02	40.20	78.85	1.00	0.98	0.95	0.97	#DIV/0!
6	72012000	NON-ALLOY PIG IRON CONTNG> 0.5% PHOSPHRS	14.12	2003-04	215.00	437.92	2001-02	367.72	317.26	0.99	0.95	0.88	0.95	#DIV/0!
7	29053100	ETHYLENE GLYCOL (ETHANEDIOL)	35.64	2001-02	393.90	412.79	2001-02	121.45	159.66	1.00	1.00	0.99	0.99	0.85
8	52114200	DENIM OF YARNS OF DIFFERENT COLOUR OF MXD COTN FABRICS WEIGHING>200 GSM	99.11	2003-04	320.70	357.86	2001-02	100.76	82.95	1.00	0.96	0.95	0.97	#DIV/0!
9	32041761	PIGMENT GREEN 7 (PATHALOVYANINE GREEN)	244.89	2002-03	274.92	289.79	2001-02	241.68	234.20	1.00	1.00	0.96	0.96	#DIV/0!
10	72139190	OTHERS	24.32	2002-03	172.28	264.74	2001-02	-3.38	29.42	0.99	-0.05	-0.66	0.82	#DIV/0!

TABLE- 32

KEY FACTORS FOR ALL SAMPLED PRODUCTS COVERED UNDER EARLY HARVEST SCHEME- CHAPTERWISE

			2004-05	2004-05	2004-05	2004-05		2004-05	
Sl. No.	CHAPTER	Main Products	% of Total Value of exports to Thailand in 2004-05	Value of Exports to THAILAND (in Rs. Lakhs)	Value of World Exports for India (in Rs. Lakhs)	Market Share of exports to Thailand in World Exports (Value) in %	Base year for next column	Incremental Trend of Exports to Thailand (Value) in % in comparison to base yr.	Base year for next column
1	CHAPTER 28	Inorganic Chemicals and Metallic Compounds	0.41	1621.43	124117.81	1.31	2001-02	430.68	2001-02
2	CHAPTER 71	Natural stones, metals and imitation jewellery	0.31	1212.14	1173262.12	0.10	2001-02	200.63	2001-02
3	CHAPTER 72	Iron and Steel	0.19	740.78	13240.83	5.59	2001-02	22.65	2001-02
4	CHAPTER 73	Articles of Iron or Steel	0.27	1059.45	27678.14	3.83	2001-02	682.23	2001-02
5	CHAPTER 76	Aluminium and articles thereof	0.74	2926.99	85035.77	3.44	2001-02	854.07	2001-02
6	CHAPTER 84	Machinery and Mechaniacal appliances	0.44	1747.56	55413.97	3.15	2001-02	99.79	2001-02
7	CHAPTER 85	Audio Visual Equipments incl. TV	0.23	911.29	33199.94	2.74	2004-05	0.00	2003-04
8	CHAPTER 87	Vehicles and Accessories	0.99	3919.13	9205.58	42.57	2001-02	66213.54	2001-02
		TOTAL	**3.58**	**14138.77**	**1521154.16**				

NOTES

1 Base year have been changed, where CAGR for a particular product shows growth of more than 999%.
2 Base year for Trend Calculation have been changed in some cases, keeping in view the base year for CAGR and the actual trade data.
3 Base year for Trend Calculation have been changed in some cases, where trend exceeds 99999%.
4 Correlation among different DATA SERIES have been calculated by using the CORREL function active in the MS EXCEL spreadsheet.
5 Correlation of +1 denotes perfect positive correlation, -1 denotes perfect negative correlation, 0 denotes least correlation among the data series.
6 Trend is taken as 100% and CAGR as 0% in cases where either the data figures prior to 2004-05 are either zero or negligible.

TABLE- 32

KEY FACTORS FOR ALL SAMPLED PRODUCTS COVERED UNDER EARLY HARVEST SCHEME- CHAPTERWISE

			2004-05	2004-05		2004-05		2004-05
Sl. No.	CHAPTER	Main Products	Incremental Trend of World Export (Value) in % in comparison to base yr.	CORRELATION OF TREND IN VALUE - THAILAND/World Exports	Base year for next column	CAGR-VALUE-THAILAND (in %)	Base year for next column	CAGR-VALUE-World Exports(in %)
1	CHAPTER 28	Inorganic Chemicals and Metallic Compounds	474.89	0.92	2001-02	74.43	2001-02	79.14
2	CHAPTER 71	Natural stones, metals and imitation jewellery	166.01	0.39	2001-02	44.33	2001-02	38.56
3	CHAPTER 72	Iron and Steel	437.24	0.97	2001-02	7.04	2001-02	75.14
4	CHAPTER 73	Articles of Iron or Steel	74.52	0.72	2001-02	98.51	2001-02	20.40
5	CHAPTER 76	Aluminium and articles thereof	90.49	0.65	2001-02	112.09	2001-02	23.96
6	CHAPTER 84	Machinery and Mechaniacal appliances	143.55	0.79	2001-02	25.95	2001-02	34.54
7	CHAPTER 85	Audio Visual Equipments incl. TV	41.40	0.75	2004-05	0.00	2003-04	41.40
8	CHAPTER 87	Vehicles and Accessories	482.55	0.99	2001-02	772.04	2001-02	79.93

TABLE- 33

KEY FACTORS FOR ALL SAMPLED PRODUCTS NOT COVERED UNDER EARLY HARVEST SCHEME- CHAPTERWISE

		2004-05	2004-05	2004-05	2004-05		2004-05		2004-05	2004-05		2004-05		2004-05
Sl. No.	CHAPTER	% of Total Value of exports to Thailand in 2004-05	Value of Exports to THAILAND (in Rs. Lakhs)	Value of World Exports for India (in Rs. Lakhs)	Market Share of exports to Thailand in World Exports (Value) in %	Base year for next column	Incremental Trend of Exports to Thailand (Value) in % in comparison to base yr.	Base year for next column	Incremental Trend of World Export (Value) in % in comparison to base yr.	CORRELATION OF TREND IN VALUE - THAILAND/World Exports	Base year for next column	CAGR-VALUE-THAILAND (in %)	Base year for next column	CAGR-VALUE-World Exports(in %)
1	CHAPTER 03	1.32	5208.87	364841.68	1.43	2001-02	-40.96	2001-02	40.83	-0.31	2001-02	-16.11	2001-02	12.09
2	CHAPTER 08	0.15	591.42	210834.88	0.28	2003-04	43.84	2001-02	46.93	0.61	2003-04	43.84	2001-02	13.68
3	CHAPTER 15	1.20	4740.40	96006.21	4.94	2003-04	39.71	2003-04	59.83	1.00	2003-04	39.71	2003-04	59.83
4	CHAPTER 19	0.12	486.03	1724.34	28.19	2001-02	3148.86	2001-02	317.59	0.95	2001-02	219.09	2001-02	61.03
5	CHAPTER 23	5.36	21179.11	272461.54	7.77	2001-02	-15.99	2001-02	77.53	0.69	2001-02	-5.64	2001-02	21.09
6	CHAPTER 25	0.22	863.49	105427.04	0.82	2001-02	23.92	2001-02	47.52	0.85	2001-02	7.41	2001-02	13.84
7	CHAPTER 27	0.38	1499.38	420208.28	0.36	2003-04	740.51	2003-04	144.45	0.95	2003-04	740.51	2003-04	144.45
8	CHAPTER 28	0.44	1755.60	21546.34	8.15	2001-02	533.77	2001-02	367.51	0.32	2001-02	85.06	2001-02	67.21
9	CHAPTER 29	4.70	18566.46	638201.51	2.91	2001-02	216.11	2001-02	925.13	0.98	2001-02	46.76	2001-02	117.23
10	CHAPTER 30	0.63	2490.22	350332.83	0.71	2001-02	144.21	2001-02	126.09	0.99	2001-02	34.66	2001-02	31.25
11	CHAPTER 32	0.69	2723.36	53421.42	5.10	2001-02	62.57	2001-02	20.34	0.79	2001-02	17.58	2001-02	6.36
12	CHAPTER 38	2.57	10161.65	144230.56	7.05	2001-02	290.60	2001-02	416.56	0.91	2001-02	57.49	2001-02	72.86
13	CHAPTER 39	0.50	1994.80	409027.37	0.49	2001-02	524.74	2001-02	305.75	0.99	2001-02	84.18	2001-02	59.50
14	CHAPTER 41	1.04	4095.01	115727.65	3.54	2003-04	-33.38	2003-04	20.69	0.92	2003-04	-33.38	2003-04	20.69
15	CHAPTER 52	0.99	3924.31	245214.74	1.60	2001-02	437.17	2001-02	15.72	0.48	2001-02	75.13	2001-02	4.99
16	CHAPTER 54	0.10	395.61	8077.67	4.90	2001-02	3828.60	2001-02	23.89	0.34	2001-02	239.95	2001-02	7.40
17	CHAPTER 71	32.64	129001.20	4749296.03	2.72	2001-02	18.79	2001-02	64.52	0.47	2001-02	5.91	2001-02	18.05
18	CHAPTER 72	7.19	28430.22	408935.34	6.95	2001-02	1244.41	2001-02	498.30	0.93	2001-02	137.78	2001-02	81.54
19	CHAPTER 73	0.14	553.87	69040.50	0.80	2001-02	158.12	2001-02	-10.78	0.18	2001-02	37.17	2001-02	-3.73
20	CHAPTER 74	11.21	44293.49	197066.68	22.48	2001-02	868.21	2001-02	372.81	0.94	2001-02	113.14	2001-02	67.84
21	CHAPTER 76	0.44	1725.48	44981.52	3.84	2001-02	819.37	2001-02	286.87	0.81	2001-02	109.49	2001-02	56.98
22	CHAPTER 84	1.42	5600.90	83400.05	6.72	2001-02	1475.37	2001-02	72.55	0.72	2001-02	150.68	2001-02	19.94
23	CHAPTER 85	0.25	1004.52	3323.91	30.22	2001-02	96488.46	2001-02	1396.31	0.75	2001-02	888.50	2001-02	146.42
24	CHAPTER 87	0.82	3227.65	220060.29	1.47	2001-02	322.41	2001-02	123.52	0.99	2001-02	61.65	2001-02	30.75
25	CHAPTER 91	0.10	413.83	4877.22	8.48	2001-02	707.95	2001-02	101.70	0.66	2001-02	100.66	2001-02	26.35

NOTES

1. Base year have been changed, where CAGR for a particular product shows growth of more than 999%.
2. Base year for Trend Calculation have been changed in some cases, keeping in view the base year for CAGR and the actual trade data.
3. Base year for Trend Calculation have been changed in some cases, where trend exceeds 99999%.
4. Correlation among different DATA SERIES have been calculated by using the CORREL function active in the MS EXCEL spreadsheet.
5. Correlation of +1 denotes perfect positive correlation, -1 denotes perfect negative correlation, 0 denotes least correlation among the data series.
6. Trend is taken as 100% and CAGR as 0% in cases where either the data figures prior to 2004-05 are either zero or negligible.

TABLE- 34

KEY FACTORS FOR TOP 10 CHAPTERS (SORTED ON CAGR-VALUE-EXPORTS TO THAILAND basis) (Containing Sampled Products of NON EHS category only)

		2004-05	2004-05	2004-05	2004-05		2004-05		2004-05	2004-05		2004-05		2004-05
Sl. No.	CHAPTER	% of Total Value of exports to Thailand in 2004-05	Value of Exports to THAILAND (in Rs. Lakhs)	Value of World Exports for India (in Rs. Lakhs)	Market Share of exports to Thailand in World Exports (Value) in %	Base year for next column	Incremental Trend of exports to Thailand (Value) in % in comparison to base yr.	Base year for next column	Incremental Trend of World Export (Value) in % in comparison to base yr.	CORRELATION OF TREND IN VALUE - THAILAND/ World Exports	Base year for next column	CAGR-VALUE-THAILAND (in %)	Base year for next column	CAGR-VALUE-World Exports(in %)
1	CHAPTER 85	0.25	1004.52	3323.91	30.22	2001-02	96488.46	2001-02	1396.31	0.75	2001-02	888.50	2001-02	146.42
2	CHAPTER 27	0.33	1499.38	420208.28	0.36	2003-04	740.51	2003-04	144.45	0.95	2003-04	740.51	2003-04	144.45
3	CHAPTER 54	0.10	395.61	8077.67	4.90	2001-02	3828.60	2001-02	23.89	0.34	2001-02	239.95	2001-02	7.40
4	CHAPTER 19	0.12	486.03	1724.34	28.19	2001-02	3148.86	2001-02	317.59	0.95	2001-02	219.09	2001-02	61.03
5	CHAPTER 84	1.42	5600.90	83400.05	6.72	2001-02	1475.37	2001-02	72.55	0.72	2001-02	150.68	2001-02	19.94
6	CHAPTER 72	7.19	28430.22	408935.34	6.95	2001-02	1244.41	2001-02	498.30	0.93	2001-02	137.78	2001-02	81.54
7	CHAPTER 74	11.21	44293.49	197066.68	22.48	2001-02	868.21	2001-02	372.81	0.94	2001-02	113.14	2001-02	67.84
8	CHAPTER 76	0.44	1725.48	44981.52	3.84	2001-02	819.37	2001-02	286.87	0.81	2001-02	109.49	2001-02	56.98
9	CHAPTER 91	0.10	413.83	4877.22	8.48	2001-02	707.95	2001-02	101.70	0.66	2001-02	100.66	2001-02	26.35
10	CHAPTER 28	0.44	1755.60	21546.34	8.15	2001-02	533.77	2001-02	367.51	0.32	2001-02	85.06	2001-02	67.21

NOTES

1 Base year have been changed, where CAGR for a particular product shows growth of more than 999%.
2 Base year for Trend Calculation have been changed in some cases, keeping in view the base year for CAGR and the actual trade data.
3 Base year for Trend Calculation have been changed in some cases, where trend exceeds 99999%.
4 Correlation among different DATA SERIES have been calculated by using the CORREL function active in the MS EXCEL spreadsheet.
5 Correlation of +1 denotes perfect positive correlation, -1 denotes perfect negative correlation, 0 denotes least correlation among the data series.
6 Trend is taken as 100% and CAGR as 0% in cases where either the data figures prior to 2004-05 are either zero or negligible.

TABLE- 35

KEY FACTORS FOR TOP 10 CHAPTERS (SORTED ON VALUE OF EXPORTS TO THAILAND IN 2004-05 basis) (Containing Sampled Products of NON EHS category only)

		2004-05	2004-05	2004-05	2004-05		2004-05		2004-05	2004-05		2004-05		2004-05
Sl. No.	CHAPTER	% of Total Value of exports to Thailand in 2004-05	Value of Exports to THAILAND (in Rs. Lakhs)	Value of World Exports for India (in Rs. Lakhs)	Merket Share of exports to Thailand in World Exports (Value) in %	Base year for next column	Incremental Trend of exports to Thailand (Value) in % in comparison to base yr.	Base year for next column	Incremental Trend of World Export (Value) in % in comparison to base yr.	CORRELATION OF TREND IN VALUE - THAILAND/ World Exports	Base year for next column	CAGR-VALUE-THAILAND (in %)	Base year for next column	CAGR-VALUE-World Exports(in %)
1	CHAPTER 71	32.64	129001.20	4749296.03	2.72	2001-02	18.79	2001-02	64.52	0.47	2001-02	5.91	2001-02	18.05
2	CHAPTER 74	11.21	44293.49	197066.68	22.48	2001-02	868.21	2001-02	372.81	0.94	2001-02	113.14	2001-02	67.84
3	CHAPTER 72	7.19	28430.22	408935.34	6.95	2001-02	1244.41	2001-02	498.30	0.93	2001-02	137.78	2001-02	81.54
4	CHAPTER 23	5.36	21179.11	272461.54	7.77	2001-02	-15.99	2001-02	77.53	0.69	2001-02	-5.64	2001-02	21.09
5	CHAPTER 29	4.70	18566.46	638201.51	2.91	2001-02	216.11	2001-02	925.13	0.98	2001-02	46.76	2001-02	117.23
6	CHAPTER 38	2.57	10161.65	144230.56	7.05	2001-02	290.60	2001-02	416.56	0.91	2001-02	57.49	2001-02	72.86
7	CHAPTER 84	1.42	5600.90	83400.05	6.72	2001-02	1475.37	2001-02	72.55	0.72	2001-02	150.68	2001-02	19.94
8	CHAPTER 03	1.32	5208.87	364841.68	1.43	2001-02	-40.96	2001-02	40.83	-0.31	2001-02	-16.11	2001-02	12.09
9	CHAPTER 15	1.20	4740.40	96006.21	4.94	2003-04	39.71	2003-04	59.83	1.00	2003-04	39.71	2003-04	59.83
10	CHAPTER 41	1.04	4095.01	115727.65	3.54	2003-04	-33.38	2003-04	20.69	0.92	2003-04	-33.38	2003-04	20.69

NOTES

1 Base year have been changed, where CAGR for a particular product shows growth of more than 999%.
2 Base year for Trend Calculation have been changed in some cases, keeping in view the base year for CAGR and the actual trade data.
3 Base year for Trend Calculation have been changed in some cases, where trend exceeds 99999%.
4 Correlation among different DATA SERIES have been calculated by using the CORREL function active in the MS EXCEL spreadsheet.
5 Correlation of +1 denotes perfect positive correlation, -1 denotes perfect negative correlation, 0 denotes least correlation among the data series.
6 Trend is taken as 100% and CAGR as 0% in cases where either the data figures prior to 2004-05 are either zero or negligible.

TABLE- 36

MOVEMENT OF SUM FACTORS OF SAMPLED PRODUCTS EXPORTED TO THAILAND

(Value: in Rs. Lakhs)

MOVEMENT OF SAMPLED 11 PRODUCTS COVERED UNDER EHS

	2001-02	2002-03	2003-04	2004-05
Sum of Value of exports to Thailand (A)	2635.60	7360.96	21264.74	14138.77
Sum of Value of exports to World (B)	549949.75	763711.27	1056403.58	1521154.16
Sum Factor (A/B)	0.00479	0.00964	0.02013	0.00929

MOVEMENT OF SAMPLED 92 PRODUCTS NOT COVERED UNDER EHS

	2001-02	2002-03	2003-04	2004-05
Sum of Value of exports to Thailand (A)	164116.33	180445.04	217142.80	294926.88
Sum of Value of exports to World (B)	4476530.45	5686770.48	7279613.75	9238265.60
Sum Factor (A/B)	0.03666	0.03173	0.02983	0.03192

MOVEMENT OF ALL EHS PRODUCTS / ALL NON EHS PRODUCTS

	2001-02	2002-03	2003-04	2004-05
Sum Factor (EHS PRODUCTS)	0.00479	0.00964	0.02013	0.00929
Sum Factor (non EHS PRODUCTS)	0.03666	0.03173	0.02983	0.03192

MOVEMENT OF SUM FACTORS OF ALL EHS PRODUCTS / ALL NON EHS PRODUCTS

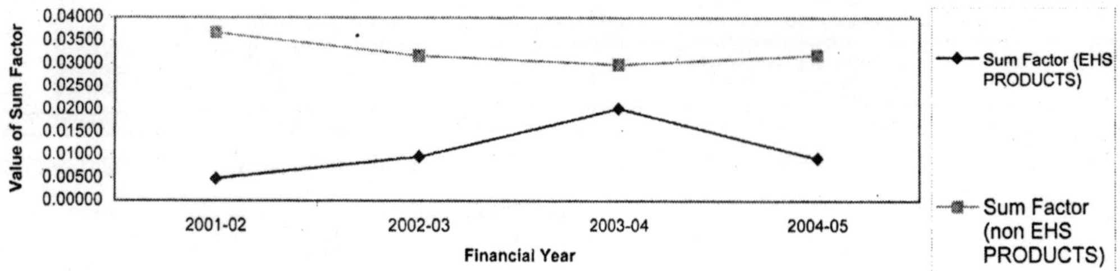

TABLE- 37

MOVEMENT OF SUM FACTORS OF SAMPLED PRODUCTS (EXPORTED TO THAILAND) COVERED UNDER EHS- CHAPTERWISE

(Value: in Rs. Lakhs)

CHAPTER 28	2001-02	2002-03	2003-04	2004-05
Sum of Value of exports to Thailand (A)	305.54	724.25	694.29	1621.43
Sum of Value of exports to World (B)	21589.72	86896.87	78572.91	124117.81
Sum Factor (A/B)	0.01415	0.00833	0.00884	0.01306

CHAPTER 71	2001-02	2002-03	2003-04	2004-05
Sum of Value of exports to Thailand (A)	403.20	1510.02	822.90	1212.14
Sum of Value of exports to World (B)	441063.39	573448.72	774197.59	1173262.12
Sum Factor (A/B)	0.00091	0.00263	0.00106	0.00103

CHAPTER 72	2001-02	2002-03	2003-04	2004-05
Sum of Value of exports to Thailand (A)	604.00	1993.93	14004.56	740.78
Sum of Value of exports to World (B)	2464.59	18102.19	48694.09	13240.83
Sum Factor (A/B)	0.24507	0.11015	0.28760	0.05595

CHAPTER 73	2001-02	2002-03	2003-04	2004-05
Sum of Value of exports to Thailand (A)	135.44	27.97	89.84	1059.45
Sum of Value of exports to World (B)	15859.86	17054.15	24847.94	27678.14
Sum Factor (A/B)	0.00854	0.00164	0.00362	0.03828

CHAPTER 76	2001-02	2002-03	2003-04	2004-05
Sum of Value of exports to Thailand (A)	306.79	1415.23	4405.90	2926.99
Sum of Value of exports to World (B)	44639.76	35799.80	64334.91	85035.77
Sum Factor (A/B)	0.00687	0.03953	0.06848	0.03442

CHAPTER 84	2001-02	2002-03	2003-04	2004-05
Sum of Value of exports to Thailand (A)	874.72	1428.98	1093.53	1747.56
Sum of Value of exports to World (B)	22752.22	29658.03	39466.00	55413.97
Sum Factor (A/B)	0.03845	0.04818	0.02771	0.03154

CHAPTER 85	2001-02	2002-03	2003-04	2004-05
Sum of Value of exports to Thailand (A)	0.00	0.00	0.12	911.29
Sum of Value of exports to World (B)	0.00	0.00	23479.91	33199.94
Sum Factor (A/B)	#DIV/0!	#DIV/0!	0.00001	0.02745

CHAPTER 87	2001-02	2002-03	2003-04	2004-05
Sum of Value of exports to Thailand (A)	5.91	260.58	153.60	3919.13
Sum of Value of exports to World (B)	1580.21	2751.51	2810.23	9205.58
Sum Factor (A/B)	0.00374	0.09470	0.05466	0.42573

CATEGORY OF PRODUCTS	SUM FACTORS			
	2001-02	2002-03	2003-04	2004-05
CHAPTER 28	0.01415	0.00833	0.00884	0.01306
CHAPTER 71	0.00091	0.00263	0.00106	0.00103
CHAPTER 72	0.24507	0.11015	0.28760	0.05595
CHAPTER 73	0.00854	0.00164	0.00362	0.03828
CHAPTER 76	0.00687	0.03953	0.06848	0.03442
CHAPTER 84	0.03845	0.04818	0.02771	0.03154
CHAPTER 85	#DIV/0!	#DIV/0!	0.00001	0.02745
CHAPTER 87	0.00374	0.09470	0.05466	0.42573

MOVEMENT OF SUM FACTORS OF SAMPLE PRODUCTS COVERED UNDER EHS- CHAPTERWISE

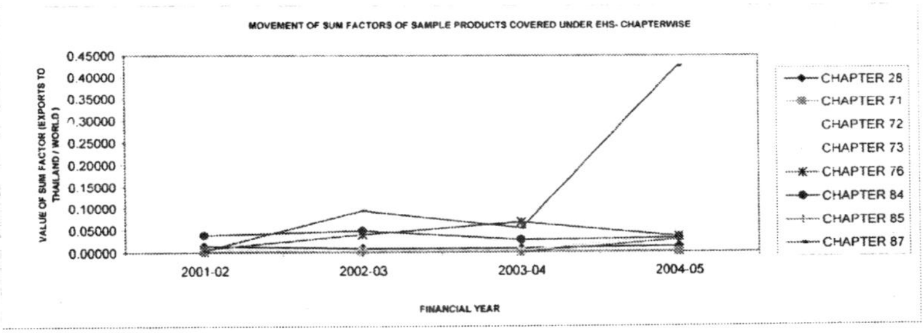

TABLE- 38

MOVEMENT OF SUM FACTORS OF TOP 3 SAMPLED PRODUCTS COVERED UNDER EHS (Value of Exports to Thailand in 2004-05 basi:

1 87084000 GEAR BOXES

	2001-02	2002-03	2003-04	2004-05
Market Share (Quantity)	0.23%	8.83%	3.59%	32.82%
Market Share (Value)	0.37%	9.47%	5.47%	42.57%
	2001-02	**2002-03**	**2003-04**	**2004-05**
Price per unit (Exports to Thailand only)	343.60	223.16	292.35	377.73
Price per unit (World Export for India)	212.70	208.03	191.96	291.19

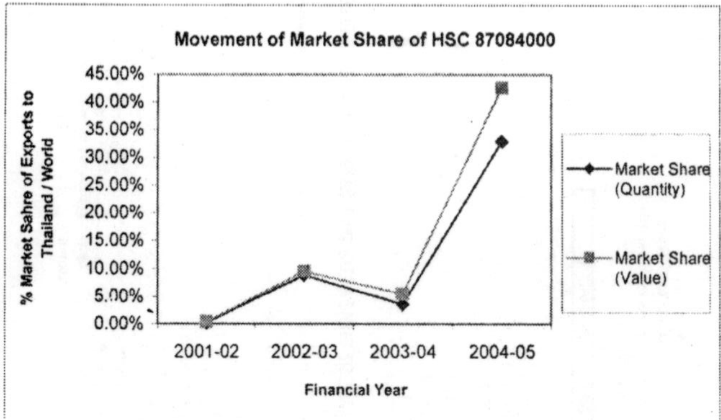

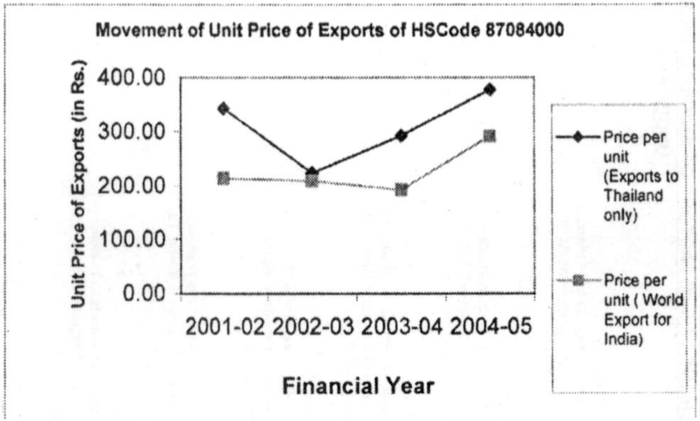

2 76011010 ALUMINIUM INGOTS-NOT ALLOYED

	2001-02	2002-03	2003-04	2004-05
Market Share (Quantity)	0.62%	4.30%	6.82%	3.57%
Market Share (Value)	0.69%	3.95%	6.85%	3.44%
	2001-02	**2002-03**	**2003-04**	**2004-05**
Price per unit (Exports to Thailand only)	77.13	67.74	68.01	79.56
Price per unit (World Export for India)	69.63	73.65	67.77	82.60

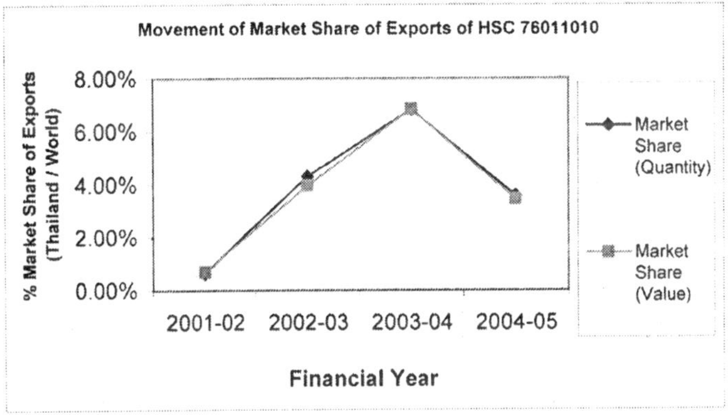

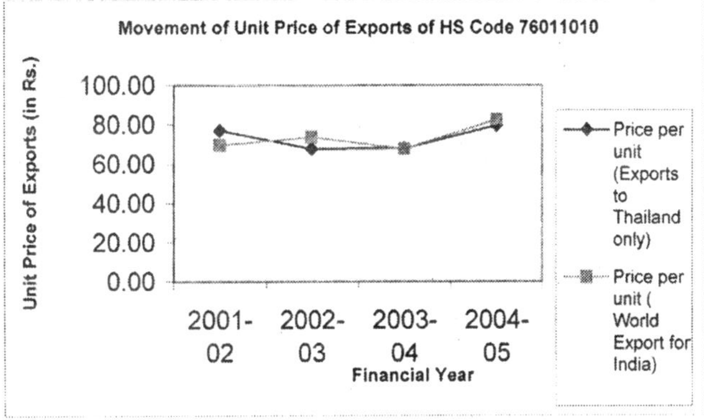

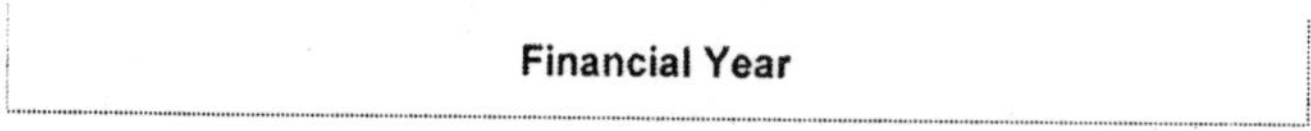

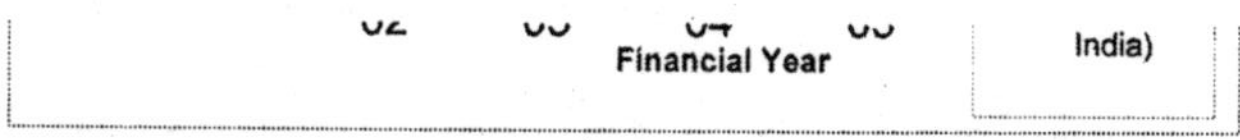

3 28182010 ALUMINA CALCINED

	2001-02	2002-03	2003-04	2004-05
Market Share (Quantity)	0.74%	0.50%	0.58%	0.89%
Market Share (Value)	1.42%	0.83%	0.88%	1.31%
	2001-02	**2002-03**	**2003-04**	**2004-05**
Price per unit (Exports to Thailand only)	15.72	13.97	15.00	20.29
Price per unit (World Export for India)	8.21	8.33	9.77	13.90

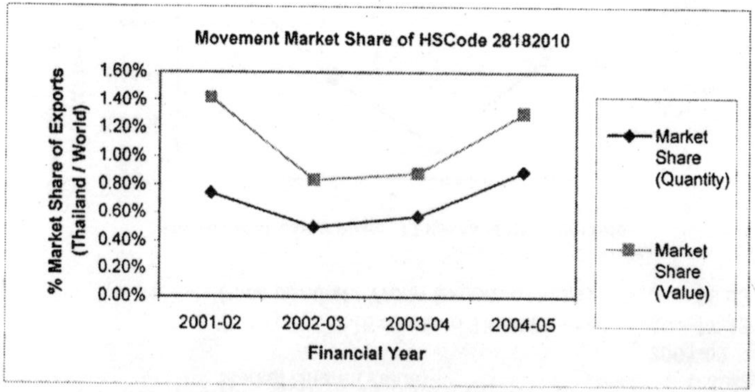

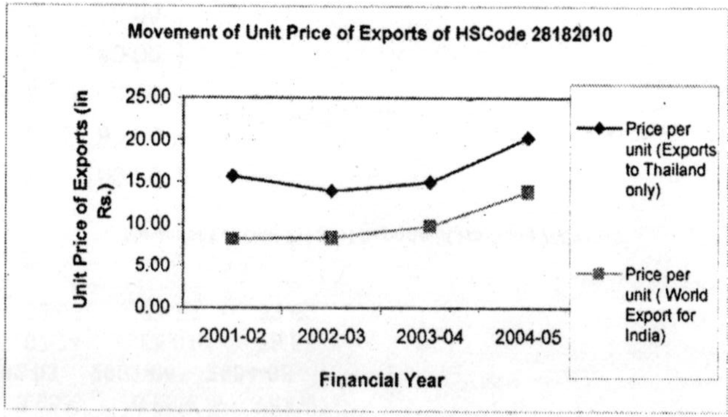

MOVEMENT OF SUM FACTORS OF TOP 3 SAMPLED PRODUCTS COVERED UNDER EHS (CAGR-VALUE- Exports to Thailand basis)

SAME PRODUCTS AS ABOVE, HENCE NOT REPEATED

TABLE-39

KEY FACTORS FOR CHAPTERS UNDER DIFFERENT CATEGORIES (IMPORTS FROM SINGAPORE) & SCRUTINY OF CASES WHERE INDIAN INDUSTRY NEEDS TO BE ALERTED

(Value: in Rs. Lakhs)

			2004-05	2005-06	2004-05	2005-06	2005-06	2005-06	2005-06	
Sl. No.	CHAPTER	Main Products	Value of Imports from Singapore (in Rs. Lakhs)	Value of Imports from Singapore (in Rs. Lakhs)	% of Total Value of imports from Singapore in 2004-05	% of Total Value of imports from Singapore in 2005-06	Incremental Trend of imports from Singapore (Value) in % in comparison to 2003-04	Incremental Trend of imports from Singapore(Value) in % in comparison to 2004-05	CAGR-VALUE-Singapore (in %)	STATUS
		Early Harvest Programme								
1	CHAPTER 29	Organic Chemicals	57198.43	74440.98	4.93	5.01	186.43	30.15	69.24	ALERT
2	CHAPTER 39	Plastics and Articles thereof	3735.38	3834.67	0.32	0.26	-3.71	2.66	-1.87	
3	CHAPTER 84	Computors	251300.39	354749.39	21.64	23.89	72.26	41.17	31.25	ALERT
4	CHAPTER 85	Audio Visual Equipments incl. TV	147400.25	183289.85	12.69	12.34	53.34	24.35	23.83	ALERT
5	CHAPTER 88	Aircrafts, Space crafts and parts	16748.04	19272.71	1.44	1.30	16.18	15.07	7.79	
6	CHAPTER 90	Optical, Photographic, Medical and Surgical instruments	11069.47	16499.70	0.95	1.11	62.26	49.06	27.38	ALERT
		Total	487451.96	652087.30	41.97	43.92				
		Phased Elimination in Duty								
1	CHAPTER 29	Organic Chemicals	54641.13	40518.20	4.71	2.73	50.36	-25.85	22.62	
2	CHAPTER 38	Miscellaneous Chemical Products	5894.98	6624.70	0.51	0.45	2.23	12.38	1.11	
3	CHAPTER 49	Printed materials	71160.10	106341.71	6.13	7.16	355.11	49.44	113.33	ALERT
4	CHAPTER 71	Natural or other stones, pearls	8824.77	5854.04	0.76	0.39	-32.05	-33.68	-17.57	
5	CHAPTER 73	Articles of Iron or Steel	4766.79	3604.31	0.41	0.24	129.62	-24.39	51.53	
6	CHAPTER 75	Nickel and Articles	1342.96	85.13	0.12	0.01	-92.31	-93.66	-72.27	
7	CHAPTER 84	Computors	16678.64	24384.04	1.44	1.64	111.56	46.20	45.45	ALERT
8	CHAPTER 85	Audio Visual Equipments incl. TV	1492.26	409.92	0.13	0.03	-93.25	-72.53	-74.01	
9	CHAPTER 89	Ships, Boats and Floating Structures	76754.25	45471.91	6.61	3.06	-52.53	-40.76	-31.10	
10	CHAPTER 90	Optical, Photographic, Medical and Surgical instruments	13696.86	13088.13	1.18	0.88	112.88	-4.44	45.90	
		Total	255252.74	246382.09	21.98	16.59				

NOTE

1 ALERT cases under Concessional Duties and HIGH GROWTH chapters under Negative List were selected on the basis of simultaneous satisfaction of the following criterias:

(a) Incremental Trend in value of imports in comparison to the base year 2003-04 is more than 50%

(b) Incremental Trend in value of imports in comparison to the base year 2004-05 is more than 20%

(c) CAGR of value of imports from Singapore (over the years 2003-04 to 2005-06) is more than 20%

TABLE-39

KEY FACTORS FOR CHAPTERS UNDER DIFFERENT CATEGORIES (IMPORTS FROM SINGAPORE) & SCRUTINY OF CASES WHERE INDIAN INDUSTRY NEEDS TO BE ALERTED

(Value: in Rs. Lakhs)

			2004-05	2005-06	2004-05	2005-06	2005-06	2005-06	2005-06	
Sl. No.	CHAPTER	Main Products	Value of Imports from Singapore (in Rs. Lakhs)	Value of Imports from Singapore (in Rs. Lakhs)	% of Total Value of imports from Singapore in 2004-05	% of Total Value of imports from Singapore in 2005-06	Incremental Trend of imports from Singapore (Value) in % in comparison to 2003-04	Incremental Trend of imports from Singapore(Value) in % in comparison to 2004-05	CAGR-VALUE-Singapore (in %)	STATUS
		Phased Reduction in Duty								
1	CHAPTER 29	Organic Chemicals	10087.11	3666.20	0.87	0.25	254.16	-63.65	88.19	
2	CHAPTER 39	Plastics and Articles thereof	4578.28	4464.46	0.39	0.30	17.49	-2.49	8.39	
3	CHAPTER 71	Natural or other stones, pearls	6578.42	17.43	0.57	0.00	-96.98	-99.74	-89.89	
4	CHAPTER 84	Computors	16150.15	11688.40	1.39	0.79	-4.93	-27.63	-2.50	
5	CHAPTER 85	Audio Visual Equipments incl. TV	18343.83	25857.93	1.58	1.74	223.61	40.96	79.89	ALERT
6	CHAPTER 90	Optical, Photographic, Medical and Surgical instruments	2120.36	3385.84	0.18	0.23	80.12	59.68	34.21	ALERT
		Total	**57858.15**	**49080.26**	**4.98**	**3.31**				
		Negative List								
1	CHAPTER 27	Mineral fuels, oils and side products	4011.69	1984.91	0.35	0.13	0.96	-50.52	0.48	
2	CHAPTER 29	Organic Chemicals	21396.93	32567.47	1.84	2.19	184.43	52.21	68.65	HIGH GROWTH
3	CHAPTER 32	Tanning or Dyeing extracts, Paints, Varnishes and Inks	3386.98	2754.25	0.29	0.19	759.84	-18.68	193.23	
4	CHAPTER 39	Plastics and Articles thereof	26013.70	26627.57	2.24	1.79	36.51	2.36	16.84	
5	CHAPTER 48	Paper and paper boards, articles related to paper	1422.22	489.11	0.12	0.03	-34.74	-65.61	-19.22	
6	CHAPTER 49	Printed materials	3388.99	2098.12	0.29	0.14	#DIV/0!	#DIV/0!	#DIV/0!	
7	CHAPTER 72	Iron and Steel	23066.56	15670.61	1.99	1.06	9.95	-32.06	4.86	
8	CHAPTER 73	Articles of Iron or Steel	1172.75	4300.41	0.10	0.29	1469.72	266.69	296.20	HIGH GROWTH
9	CHAPTER 74	Copper and Copper articles	4341.04	4614.10	0.37	0.31	267.99	6.29	91.83	
10	CHAPTER 76	Aluminium and articles	3356.50	6034.40	0.29	0.41	187.18	79.78	69.46	HIGH GROWTH
11	CHAPTER 84	Machinery and Mechaniacal appliances including Data Processing Machines &	4741.18	4502.56	0.41	0.30	38.58	-5.03	17.72	
12	CHAPTER 85	Audio Visual Equipments incl TV	1103.90	141.60	0.10	0.01	-52.70	-87.17	-31.23	
13	CHAPTER 87	Vehicles and accessories	3229.40	1652.05	0.28	0.11	16.54	-48.84	7.95	
14	CHAPTER 98	Project Imports, Passengers' baggage, personal importation , ship stores	4185.48	583.59	0.36	0.04	39.95	-86.06	18.30	
		Total	**104817.32**	**104020.75**	**9.03**	**7.01**				

NOTE

1 ALERT cases under Concessional Duties and HIGH GROWTH chapters under Negative List were selected on the basis of simultaneous satisfaction of the following criterias:

(a) Incremental Trend in value of imports in comparison to the base year 2003-04 is more than 50%

(b) Incremental Trend in value of imports in comparison to the base year 2004-05 is more than 20%

(c) CAGR of value of imports from Singapore (over the years 2003-04 to 2005-06) is more than 20%

TABLE-40

KEY FACTORS FOR PRODUCTS UNDER DIFFERENT CATEGORIES (IMPORTS FROM SINGAPORE) FOR WHICH INDIAN INDUSTRY NEEDS TO BE ALERTED

(Value in Rs. Lakhs)

			2004-05	2005-06	2004-05	2005-06	2005-06	2005-06	2005-06	
SL. No.	HS CODE	PRODUCT	Value of Imports from Singapore (in Rs. Lakhs)	Value of Imports from Singapore (in Rs. Lakhs)	% of Total Value of imports from Singapore in 2004-05	% of Total Value of imports from Singapore in 2005-06	Incremental Trend of imports from Singapore (Value) in % in comparison to 2003-04	Incremental Trend of imports from Singapore(Value) in % in comparison to 2004-05	CAGR-VALUE-Singapore (in %)	STATUS
		Early Harvest Programme								
1	29025000	STYRENE	50039.66	60647.18	4.31	4.08	183.55	21.20	68.39	ALERT
2	84733099	OTHER	31773.05	47335.78	2.74	3.19	163.90	48.98	62.45	ALERT
3	84715000	DIGITL PROCESNG UNITS EXCL OF SUB HDNGS 847141 & 847149,WH/NOT CONT ONE/TWO TYPS OF UNI,LIKE STORG/INPUT/OUTPUT UNITS	26790.12	35079.64	2.31	2.36	126.04	30.94	50.35	ALERT
4	85422990	OTHR MONOLITHIC INTEGRATED CIRCUITS	20906.09	25473.58	1.80	1.72	95.02	21.85	39.65	ALERT
5	84733030	PRTS & ACCSSRS OTHR MNTD PRNTD CRCIT BRDS	20493.89	29512.79	1.76	1.99	75.19	44.01	32.36	ALERT
6	84716026	LASER ZET PRINTER	19682.04	58100.70	1.69	3.91	218.42	195.20	78.44	ALERT
7	84733050	INK CARTRIDGES WITH PRINT HEAD ASSEMBLY	14812.37	27085.54	1.28	1.82	64.36	82.86	28.20	ALERT
8	85252017	CELLULAR TELEPHONE	13573.84	22795.43	1.17	1.54	355.18	67.94	113.35	ALERT
9	85175099	OTHR APARTUS FR CARRIER/DIGITAL LINE SYSTM	12388.10	34656.66	1.07	2.33	725.04	179.76	187.23	ALERT
10	85179090	OTHR PARTS OF TELEPHONC/TELEGRPHC APPARTS	8076.11	10595.54	0.70	0.71	117.94	31.20	47.63	ALERT
11	84714900	OTHR DIGITL AUTOMATC DATAPROCESNG MACHINE PRESENTED IN THE FORM OF SYSTEM	7667.98	12731.19	0.66	0.86	87.28	66.03	36.85	ALERT
12	84713090	OTHR DGTL AUTOMATC DATA-PROCESNG MACHINE WEGHNG <=10KG WTH A KEYBOARD & DISPLAY CONSISTNG OF A CENTRAL PROCESNG MACHINE	6245.17	9036.36	0.54	0.61	204.63	44.69	74.54	ALERT
13	84717090	OTHERS	5543.26	6815.09	0.48	0.46	149.82	22.94	58.06	ALERT
14	85412900	OTHER TRANSISTOR,OTHER THAN PHOTOSENSITIVE TRANSISTORS	5353.24	7433.69	0.46	0.50	59.04	38.86	26.11	ALERT
15	84713010	PERSONAL COMPUTER (LAPTOP,PALMTOP,ETC)	4645.53	10840.85	0.40	0.73	178.96	133.36	67.02	ALERT
16	90272000	CHROMATOGRAPHS & ELECTROPHORESIS INSTRMNT	3617.08	6899.71	0.31	0.46	68.15	90.75	29.67	ALERT
17	29161210	BUTYL ACRYLATE	3420.10	9103.18	0.29	0.61	219.16	166.17	78.65	ALERT
18	85299090	OTHE PARTS FR OTHR USE	3082.58	5050.20	0.27	0.34	99.41	63.83	41.21	ALERT
19	90318000	OTHR MSRNG&CHCKNG INSTRMNTS,APPLNCS&MCHNS	2026.40	3205.89	0.17	0.22	81.46	58.21	34.71	ALERT
20	85173000	TELEPHONIC/TELEGRPHC SWTCHING APPRTS	1989.67	3253.78	0.17	0.22	249.79	63.53	87.03	ALERT
21	84733091	NETWORK ACCESS CONTROLLERS	1975.85	3300.00	0.17	0.22	75.09	67.02	32.32	ALERT
22	29011000	SATURATED ACYCLIC HYDROCARBONS	1849.52	3899.30	0.16	0.26	480.94	110.83	141.03	ALERT
23	84716090	OTHERS	1619.00	3257.47	0.14	0.22	90.58	101.20	38.05	ALERT
24	84717050	CARTRIDGE TAPE DRIVE	1560.70	2354.51	0.13	0.16	244.87	50.86	85.71	ALERT

TABLE-40

KEY FACTORS FOR PRODUCTS UNDER DIFFERENT CATEGORIES (IMPORTS FROM SINGAPORE) FOR WHICH INDIAN INDUSTRY NEEDS TO BE ALERTED

(Value: in Rs. Lakhs)

SL. No.	HS CODE	PRODUCT	2004-05 Value of imports from Singapore (in Rs. Lakhs)	2005-06 Value of imports from Singapore (in Rs. Lakhs)	2004-05 % of Total Value of imports from Singapore in 2004-05	2005-06 % of Total Value of imports from Singapore in 2005-06	2005-06 Incremental Trend of imports from Singapore (Value) in % in comparison to 2003-04	2005-06 Incremental Trend of imports from Singapore(Value) in % in comparison to 2004-05	2005-06 CAGR-VALUE-Singapore (in %)	STATUS
		Phased Elimination in Duty								
1	49070030	DOCUMENTS OF TITLE CONVEYING THE RIGHT TO USE INFORMATION TECHNOLOGY SOFTWARE	52995.84	80872.54	4.56	5.45	3642.66	52.60	511.77	ALERT
2	84522900	OTHER SEWING MACHINES	8548.35	14677.46	0.74	0.99	206.73	71.70	75.14	ALERT
3	90329000	PARTS AND ACCESSORIES OF INSTRMNTS OF 9032	3536.65	4521.08	0.30	0.30	122.59	27.84	49.19	ALERT
4	89011040	BARGES	2951.09	5152.17	0.25	0.35	174.59	74.59	74.59	ALERT
5	84314990	PRTS OF OTHR MACNRY OF HD 8426,8429,8430	2843.86	5744.01	0.24	0.39	63.87	101.98	28.01	ALERT
6	38112100	ADDTVS FR LBRCTNG OILS CONTNG OILS OBTND FROM PETROLEUM & BITUMINOUS MINERALS	1924.48	2416.17	0.17	0.16	54.95	25.55	24.48	ALERT
7	90181990	OTHR ELCTRO-DIAGNOSTC APPRTS	1752.66	2403.78	0.15	0.16	310.83	37.15	102.69	ALERT
8	49011010	PRINTED BOOKS	1547.84	2900.19	0.13	0.20	151.86	87.37	58.70	ALERT
9	29420090	OTHER DILOXANIDE FUROATE, CIMETIDINE, FAMOTIDINE NES	1420.32	4398.37	0.12	0.30	204.47	209.67	74.49	ALERT
10	84799090	PRTS OF OTHR MCHNRY & MCHNCL APPLNCS,HVNG INDVDL FUNCTNS	1154.62	1762.03	0.10	0.12	164.68	52.61	62.69	ALERT
		Phased Reduction in Duty								
1	85243111	DISCS WITH INFORMATION TECHNOLOGY SOFTWARE	6874.00	13285.55	0.59	0.89	722.20	93.27	186.74	ALERT
2	90330000	PRTS & ACCESSORIES FR MACHINES,APPLIANCES,INSTRUMENTS/APPARATUS OF CHAPTER 90,NES	2120.36	3385.84	0.18	0.23	80.12	59.68	34.21	ALERT
3	85438999	OTHERS	2064.22	3515.89	0.18	0.24	174.45	70.33	65.67	ALERT
4	85389000	OTHER PARTS OF HDG 8538	1820.64	3338.60	0.16	0.22	127.54	83.38	50.84	ALERT
5	85044090	OTHERS	1811.08	2732.57	0.16	0.18	100.05	50.88	41.44	ALERT
6	85439000	PARTS OF ARTICLES OF HEADING 8543	1386.64	1998.04	0.12	0.13	111.22	44.09	45.34	ALERT
		Negative List								
1	29153200	VINYL ACETATE	8685.76	12835.47	0.75	0.86	115.84	47.78	46.92	HIGH GROWTH
2	29152100	ACETIC ACID	4715.94	9289.57	0.41	0.63	410.10	96.98	125.85	HIGH GROWTH
3	74040012	COPPER SCRAP COVERED BY ISRI CODE BARLEY, BERRY ,BIRCH,CANDY,CLIFF,CLOBE,CUBRA,COCOADREAM AND PALMS	2355.63	2867.63	0.20	0.19	246.25	21.74	86.08	HIGH GROWTH
4	39013000	ETHYLENE-VINYL ACETATE COPOLYMERS	1924.01	5224.41	0.17	0.35	569.62	171.54	158.77	HIGH GROWTH
5	29141100	ACETONE	1769.33	3396.16	0.15	0.23	831.96	91.95	205.28	HIGH GROWTH
6	76020010	ALUMINIUM SCRAP COVERD BY ISRI CODE TABLETTABLOID,TABOO,TAINT/TABOR,TAKE,TALAP, TALCRED,TALDACK,TALDON,TALDORK,TALENT ETC	1682.32	5130.66	0.14	0.35	313.57	204.98	103.36	HIGH GROWTH
7	73062090	OTHER CASING&TUBING USED IN DRILING FOR OIL OR GAS MADE UP OF OTHER	1172.75	4300.41	0.10	0.29	1469.72	266.69	296.20	HIGH GROWTH
			386189.74	**634612.66**						
			33.25%	**42.74%**						

NOTE

1 ALERT cases under Concessional Duties and HIGH GROWTH chapters under Negative List were selected on the basis of simultaneous satisfaction of the following criterias:

(a) Incremental Trend in value of imports in comparison to the base year 2003-04 is more than 50%

(b) Incremental Trend in value of imports in comparison to the base year 2004-05 is more than 20%

(c) CAGR of value of imports from Singapore (over the years 2003-04 to 2005-06) is more than 20%